MEDIA

A Citizen's Guide

POLITICS

Shanto Iyengar
Stanford University

Jennifer McGrady
Stanford University

W · W · Norton & Company
New York London

W. W. Norton & Company has been independent since its founding in 1923, when William Warder Norton and Mary D. Herter Norton first published lectures delivered at the People's Institute, the adult education division of New York City's Cooper Union. The Nortons soon expanded their program beyond the Institute, publishing books by celebrated academics from America and abroad. By mid-century, the two major pillars of Norton's publishing program—trade books and college texts—were firmly established. In the 1950s, the Norton family transferred control of the company to its employees, and today—with a staff of four hundred and a comparable number of trade, college, and professional titles published each year—W. W. Norton & Company stands as the largest and oldest publishing house owned wholly by its employees.

The text of this book is composed in Fairfield LH Light
with the display set in Scala.
Book design by Margaret M. Wagner
Composition by MidAtlantic Books & Journals, Inc.
Manufacturing by Victor Graphics
Production manager: Benjamin Reynolds

PHOTO CREDITS
Clinton, p. 1: Corbis/Sygma
Bush, p. 1: AP Images
Mike McCurry, p. 175: Time & Life Pictures/Getty Images

ISBN 10: 0-393-92819-5
ISBN 13: 978-0-393-92819-8

W. W. Norton & Company, Inc.,
500 Fifth Avenue, New York, N.Y. 10110-0017
www.wwnorton.com

W. W. Norton & Company Ltd.,
Castle House, 75/76 Wells Street, London W1T 3QT

1 2 3 4 5 6 7 8 9 0

Contents

Video Features on the *Media Politics* DVD

THE *MEDIA POLITICS* DVD includes Video Features on the topics listed below. Each Video Feature presents clips that illustrate the discussion in the text. An icon in the margins of the text indicates when a corresponding clip is available.

Acknowledgments

A substantial part of this book derives from a series of collaborative research projects conducted over the past twenty-five years. The senior author has had the good fortune to cross paths with several distinguised scholars, including Stephen Ansolabehere, Roy Behr, James Fishkin, Franklin Gilliam Jr., Simon Jackman, Donald Kinder, Jon Krosnick, Daniel Lowenstein, Robert Luskin, William McGuire, Helmut Norpoth, John Petrocik, Markus Prior, Adam Simon, and Nicholas Valentino. We thank them all for their ongoing contributions to the study of media politics.

No less important was the continuous support provided by graduate and undergraduate research assistants at Yale University, the State University of New York–Stony Brook, UCLA, and Stanford. Most recently, Kyu Hahn (currently a postdoctoral fellow at Stanford) deserves special mention for his untiring assistance with data collection and statistical analysis.

We are further indebted to several individuals for making possible the accompanying compilation of broadcast news footage and other video examples. Ann Fotiades (CBS) and Nancy Cole (NBC) went well beyond the call of duty in searching their video archives for relevant footage. Tony Brackett at ABC helped us navigate the permissions process. Unfortunately, CNN and Fox News refused permission to reproduce their news reports. John Walker, technical director of the Political Communication Lab at Stanford, compiled the multimedia content no matter what the format of the source material. John was also largely responsible for preparing the graphs and other figures that appear in the text.

Scott Althaus, Matthew Baum, Jamie Druckman, Steven Livingston, Robert Sahr, James Endersby, and Russell Neuman contributed insightful commentary on individual chapters; the end result was a significantly strengthened manuscript. Daniel Lowenstein not only reviewed but also revised our account of campaign finance reform. John Zaller made available his data on election forecasts. Finally, we thank Ann Shin, our editor at Norton, for helping make this book more reader-friendly, and Stephanie Hiebert for her fine copy editing.

Shanto Iyengar
Jennifer McGrady

MEDIA
POLITICS

A Citizen's Guide

CHAPTER 1

INTRODUCTION

Image Is Everything

January 26, 1998—President Clinton declares that he did not have a sexual relationship with Monica Lewinsky.

May 1, 2003—On the deck of the USS *Abraham Lincoln*, President Bush claims victory in the war against Iraq.

THESE TWO INCIDENTS ILLUSTRATE a basic maxim of American politics: *image is everything*. Politicians feel no compunction about making exaggerated claims before national television audiences; they expect their messages to be taken at face value. This is hardly surprising, given that, for most Americans, the media are their only contact with the world of public affairs. On the flip side, from the perspective of the public, events *not* covered by the news media make no greater impression than the proverbial tree falling in the forest. For the public, what's covered on the news is all there is to know.

Media-Based Politics in the United States

The power of media imagery reverberates throughout political life. The incidents illustrated in Video Feature 1.1 reflect extreme situations, at opposite ends of the politician's comfort gradient. President Bush's declaration of victory on board the USS *Abraham Lincoln* in May 2003 was carefully staged to reinforce his own contributions to the successful invasion of Iraq, at a time when the possibility of actual victory seemed plausible. President Clinton's emphatic (and false) denial of a sexual relationship with Monica Lewinsky was an attempt to stem the rising tide of doubts about his fitness for office. Even though most officials usually find themselves between these two extremes, dealing with the media is their major day-to-day focus and preoccupation.

No longer confined to elections and campaigns, media appeals have become standard fare in the day-to-day conduct of government and are used by private interests as well as by candidates. During legislative debates, spokespersons for both sides appear regularly on television news programs and talk shows to cast their individual "spin" on the policy or problem in question. Rather than relying solely on "old-fashioned" lobbying methods, private parties now sponsor television ads intended to cue officials about issues such as health care, immigration, or Social Security reform.

The habit of playing to the public has even spread to policy arenas not typically associated with partisan politics. The bipartisan Warren Commission established to investigate the assassination of President Kennedy conducted its business behind closed doors. In contrast, the Kean Commission appointed by President Bush to investigate the 9/11 terrorist attacks conducted its business in televised hearings (except for the testimonies of President Bush, Vice President Cheney, and some high-level intelligence officials). The substantive jurisdiction of both commissions involved sensitive matters of state, but our expectations about how an inquiry of this type should properly be conducted have changed greatly. Moreover, the media coverage of the Kean Commission's work was not limited to the actual hearings; several members of the commission appeared as regular guests on news programs and talk shows where they were prepared to and did discuss the developing findings in partisan terms. Indeed, their daily media appearances were utterly predictable; Republican members denied that the Bush administration shared culpability at any level, and Democrats seized upon the intelligence breakdowns as symptomatic of the general unpreparedness of the administration.

More recently, media coverage of Hurricane Katrina was inevitably politicized. The federal government's inexplicably slow response to the disaster generated a wave of negative publicity for the Bush administration. In an attempt to stem the tide of bad news, officials resorted to a standard script; the president ended his summer vacation early, dispatched high-profile spokespersons (such as Secretary of State Condoleezza Rice) to the affected areas, and replaced the head of FEMA (the Federal Emergency Management Agency). In addition, the government announced that news organizations would be prevented from covering the recovery of the dead. It was only the threat of a lawsuit by CNN that caused the government to abandon the effort to censor the news.

In sum, the use—even the manipulation—of the mass media for political purposes has transformed the practice of leadership and governance. Policy makers resort to the very same tactics that are used by candidates running for election. Television advertising, credit taking, blame avoidance, finger-pointing, and other forms of campaign rhetoric air long after the election is over. Campaigns are continuous.

The effect that the unceasing use of the media to further partisan and self-serving objectives has on the collective welfare is problematic. The flood of attacks and counterattacks has bred cynicism toward elections and the act of voting. The role of the voter has shrunk from foot soldier and occasional activist to disgruntled spectator. Electoral victors are those who excel at projecting powerful imagery and symbolism, but not necessarily those who offer substantive expertise, political experience, or pragmatism. The role of policy maker has devolved from decision making based on bargaining and accommodation to attempts to intimidate and coerce opponents through media exposure. On more than one occasion, the result has been gridlock and paralysis in government, as rival elites are unable to reach negotiated solutions. Thus the practice of media politics amounts to a tragedy of the commons: individual participants may be able to manipulate the media to their advantage, but in the long run both the body politic and the politician are weakened.

Outline of the Book

In this book we have the following goals:

- To explain the rise of media-based politics in the United States
- To describe the media strategies used to contest elections and win over policy opponents

- To document the "payoffs" associated with these strategies: increases in the candidate's share of the vote on election day, higher approval ratings while in office, and assured reelection

- To assess the liabilities of media-based politics, offer some modest proposals for making news coverage of campaigns and governance more issue-oriented, and speculate on the emergence of a new, technology-based system of campaigning featuring direct communication between candidates and voters

We begin, in Chapter 2, by providing a theoretical perspective. In democratic societies the news media are expected to contribute three important public services. First, they provide an electoral forum in which all candidates can solicit support from voters. In the United States, the forum is a combination of paid and free media appearances, but primarily the former. In most European democracies, on the other hand, the mix favors the latter: free television time is awarded to all the major parties before the election. Second, the news media are expected to erect a "public sphere" where voters can sample from a variety of perspectives on the issues that concern them. In effect, news and other forms of public affairs programming are expected to facilitate the expression of informed opinion. Third, the press is expected to act as an agent of the public by policing the behavior of government officials. Citizens lack the resources to monitor the actions of their leaders on a daily basis; they delegate this "watchdog" task to the media. In short, democratic theory casts news organizations as multitasking, public utilities.

Against the standards of democratic theory, most contemporary media systems fall short of meeting their civic responsibilities, but the American media appear especially inadequate. A distinctive feature of the American media system is that virtually all news outlets are privately owned. Private ownership creates an inherent tension between the profit motive and civic responsibility. The need to survive forces owners to value audience size over news content; they deliver content that sells rather than content that informs. Inevitably, "infotainment" takes precedence over serious coverage of national and international issues.

Most democratic societies deal with the dilemma of civic shirking by providing public subsidies to news organizations. The BBC in the United Kingdom, CBC in Canada, ARD in Germany, and NHK in Japan are major television networks, watched by millions of viewers and financed by taxpayers. Freed from market forces, these organizations deliver more news, documentaries, and other forms of public-spirited programming than their privately owned competitors do.

The American approach to encouraging the free flow of public affairs information has evolved from early regulations requiring "public service" programming to a more laissez-faire reliance on the market. Supporters of regulation assume that the existence of multiple media organizations does not necessarily create a flourishing marketplace. In the early years of broadcasting, for instance, the FCC (Federal Communications Commission) required all national networks to provide a minimal amount of daily news programming in exchange for their free use of the airwaves. The antiregulation argument, on the other hand, rests on the assumption that the sheer number of news outlets—daily newspapers, national television networks, local television stations, cable networks, Internet blogs—provides Americans with ample opportunity to encounter the proverbial "marketplace of ideas."

On a more practical level, "media politics"—as exemplified by the American system—requires two conditions. The first is universal access to the media. No matter how independent or civic-minded the press is, societies with low levels of literacy or with relatively few television sets will be characterized by alternative forms of political communication, simply because mass media will not be the most efficient means for politicians to reach voters. When the news media's reach is restricted, those who seek votes through media strategies are disadvantaged. The case of Howard Dean's Internet-based 2004 presidential campaign is revealing. Although he succeeded in raising vast sums of money over the Web, and in so doing established himself as the early front-runner for the Democratic nomination, Dean's use of technology did not translate into even one primary victory. In 2004, most primary voters (unlike donors) remained on the wrong side of the digital divide.

The second necessary condition for the flourishing of media politics is the diminished role of political parties in selecting candidates. In most democratic societies, political parties recruit and sponsor candidates. Parties offer competing policy bundles, voters choose among parties, and, depending on the party's share of the popular vote, some number of the individual candidates running under the party banner are declared elected. When party organizations lose control over the selection of candidates, "free agent" candidates turn to the media as the most efficient form of communicating with voters. Media politics becomes a substitute for party politics.

In fact, the rise of media politics in the United States coincides with the increased reach of the broadcast media and the weakening influence of party elites over the selection of candidates. Beginning in the 1960s, candidates became less dependent on their party organizations and migrated to the mass media as the principal means of reaching voters. Because candidates for elective office represent a significant revenue stream during political campaigns (in the form of paid television advertising), media owners have been only too happy to encourage this form of "cash on the barrelhead" electioneering.

BEHAVIOR AND PERFORMANCE OF THE PRESS

In Chapter 3 we examine the performance of the American media in two stages. First we trace programming decisions to the pull of market forces, and to the professional values and aspirations of journalists. Market forces compromise the public sphere, as we have noted already. Somewhat paradoxically, the independence that is so valued by modern journalism has also exacted a toll on press performance. As professionals, journalists seek autonomy and control over their work product. They are unwilling to act as stenographers for campaigns and actively resist candidates' efforts to use them as mouthpieces. Instead, they prefer to provide their own professional analysis of the candidates' actions. Presidential candidates still tour the country making as many public appearances as possible, but their voices are rarely encountered in news presentations. Instead of the candidates, whose speeches represent "bias," journalists have turned to a coterie of expert commentators for "objective" analysis of the campaign. Interpretive or analytic journalism has largely supplanted old-fashioned, descriptive reporting.

Professional norms are but one element of a broader "organizational process" model of journalism. In this view, the news is determined by the culture of the newsroom and the routines of the workplace. The importance of authoritative sources makes journalists especially reliant on government officials. The Pentagon, State Department, and White House together account for the great majority of news reports on a daily basis. And the pecking order within journalism creates a strong copycat mentality: what is reported in this morning's *New York Times* and *Washington Post* is inevitably repeated in the evening network newscasts.

The second stage of our analysis extends the analysis of press performance to the question of adversarial journalism. In Chapter 4 we show that the stylized account of a watchdog press does not fit well with the facts, particularly reporters' heavy reliance on government officials as news sources. Every day, the Washington press corps converges on the White House press office for the official briefing from the presidential press secretary. In the aftermath of the American invasion of Iraq, a similar daily ritual was played out at the Pentagon and, although only briefly, at the Iraqi Ministry of Information in Baghdad.

The dependence on government sources does not necessarily inject partisan bias into the news; after all, Democratic sources can easily be neutralized by Republicans, and vice versa. But the preoccupation of the press with official sources means that incumbents have a sizable advantage over their challengers in gaining access to the press. Some official sources are more newsworthy than others. The president is the prime official source; any presidential event—no matter how trivial or stage-managed—elicits considerable news coverage.

Even though coverage of government policy can be "indexed" to reflect the degree of diversity among the opinions of elites, sometimes elite disagreement is quashed and one particular perspective achieves dominance. The prototypical case of elite consensus occurs during times of military tension or imminent conflict, when opponents of the incumbent administration tend to fall silent as the nation prepares for war. During these periods, the news becomes dominated by official accounts of events, and the press is generally in no position to scrutinize, discount, or otherwise cast doubts on these accounts.

In the aftermath of the "shock and awe" military campaign in Iraq, news reports from American journalists embedded with the American invading force were overwhelmingly celebratory in tone and devoid of references to the pain and suffering inflicted on Iraqi civilians. Given the one-sided presentation, it was inevitable that a significant number of Americans would come to believe that Iraq did in fact possess weapons of mass destruction and that the Hussein regime was implicated in the September 11 attacks on the United States. As late as August 2004, nearly 30 percent of the public believed that the United States had *found* weapons of mass destruction. When opposition sources fall silent, the news becomes a conduit for the official version of events. This is a far cry from watchdog journalism.

In a third and final look at the behavior of the press, Chapter 5 addresses whether the civic capacity of the media has been strengthened or weakened by the revolution in information technology. Paradoxically, public affairs information may flow even *less* freely in the aftermath of the technology-induced transformation of the media marketplace. In 1968, most Americans got their news from one of the three national network newscasts because they had no other choice; today, the same newscasts compete with cable and satellite networks, local news programming, a variety of "soft news" programs, and millions of Web sites the world over. This bewildering array of media choices makes it almost certain that exposure to the news will be more selective; like consumers of goods and services, people will seek out "preferred" providers or programs and tune out others. Because people typically prefer to be entertained than to be informed, the enhanced media environment has substantially reduced the audience for public affairs programs. In 1960, some 60 million Americans tuned in to the presidential debates between Richard Nixon and John Kennedy. In 2000, the audience for George W. Bush and Al Gore was a third less.

The increased fragmentation of media audiences raises important questions about the nature of consumer behavior. Some have suggested that the explosion of online news sites encourages consumers to seek out news that reinforces their own opinions and reduces chance encounters with unknown or disagreeable voices. The increased availability of news sources with a distinct slant on the news (Fox News, for instance) makes it possible for consumers to choose news programs on the basis of whether they expect to agree with the message being presented. No longer will all Americans be subject to the same media messages; instead, they will encounter their preferred candidates or point of view.

Others have suggested that the increasing popularity of the Internet will inevitably curtail social interaction; instead of conversing with friends and neighbors, people will engage in the solitary act of surfing their favorite Web sites, in many cases taking the opportunity to consume pornography and other antisocial messages. By this account, the increased use of information technology weakens "social capital" and individuals' sense of belonging to a community.

Academic investigations into the effects of new-media use (which we summarize in Chapter 5) suggest that pessimistic reports about the increasing isolation and fragmentation of new-media users are exaggerated. The fact that Americans can choose from multiple news outlets does not necessarily mean that they tune in only to sources that share their own values. Rather than constructing "gated communities" to nurture their partisan preferences, consumers resort to a more utilitarian form of screening by seeking out information on issues that are the most important to them. For elderly voters, paying more attention to the issue of health care or Social Security is hardly an impediment to deliberation. Similarly, there is considerable evidence that the availability of the Internet has not significantly diminished Americans' participation in more conventional forms of mass or interpersonal communication. Regular users of the Internet are not misanthropes who prefer to be closeted with a computer rather than interacting with their friends and neighbors.

SHAPING THE NEWS: CANDIDATES, ADVOCACY GROUPS, AND ELECTED OFFICIALS

Having dealt with the theory and practice of press performance, we turn next to the second set of players in media politics: the candidate and advocacy groups that seek to shape the news. A candidate's overriding goal is to attract more votes than the opponent. For their part, interest groups seek to promote or prevent the passage of particular policies. Ever since the onset of media politics in the 1960s, political campaigns have become increasingly professionalized with cadres of media consultants, campaign managers, and strategists, all of whom are well aware of the norms and values of journalists, and who hope to capitalize on this expertise to achieve the most favorable media treatment of their clients.

From the perspective of the candidate, there are two sets of media opportunities. *Free media* refers to news coverage, even though it is hardly cost-free. In fact, campaigns invest extensively in hiring well-known media consultants and public relations firms to maximize their client's visibility in the news. Candidates also rely heavily on *paid media*, typically in the form of televised political advertisements. The content of the ads, their timing, and even their appearance during specific television programs are all a matter of careful calibration and analysis.

Facing a hostile press corps, how do campaign managers inject their spin into the news? Among other things, they take advantage of competition among news sources to identify outlets that are likely to provide the most sympathetic treatment for their candidates. When the national press was hounding presidential candidate Bill Clinton over various allegations of marital infidelity and womanizing, his campaign turned to local news stations and other unconventional outlets, such as MTV, to get out their message.

In addition, campaigns adapt to the more aggressive behavior of journalists. Once reporters decided to take off the gloves and publish hard-hitting "ad watch" reports challenging the veracity of campaign advertisements, consultants responded by producing ads with a veneer of objectivity (by citing newspaper reports in the ads, for instance). More interesting, they began to produce ads that were designed as "bait" to elicit ad-watch coverage, with the aim of generating more free media coverage for their candidates. Because they take a strategic approach to adapting their "game" to the prevailing actions of the press, campaign consultants generally succeed in getting coverage that is beneficial to their clients.

The continuing struggle between journalists and campaign operatives to control the news provides a classic instance of a collective-action dilemma. Society benefits when journalists and campaigners cooperate: the news focuses on what the candidates say, the candidates focus on the issues, and voters learn about matters of substance rather than strategy. Because presidential campaigns typically feature two evenly matched sides, old-fashioned descriptive reporting guaranteed that the electorate would be exposed to equal amounts of opposing (and offsetting) "spin." Today, in contrast, journalists prefer to inject their voices into the news to tear away the façade of the campaign and reveal the candidates' vote-seeking strategies. The end result is that voters come away with a cynical sense of the process.

Dealing with the press is but one element of campaign strategy. Candidates also have access to the paid element of media—namely, advertisements. In the most general terms, all advertising campaigns are idiosyncratic. Advertising strategy varies depending on the stage of the campaign, the persona and reputation of the sponsoring candidate, and the overall state of the political race. Even allowing for these contextual variations, however, there are several tried-and-true tactics in paid-media strategy, including the use of advertising to set the campaign agenda, to focus attention on the candidate's strengths, and to attack the opponent relentlessly. We outline these strategies in Chapter 6 using a series of illustrations from recent presidential and statewide campaigns.

Advertising is the largest expenditure incurred by candidates. No account of advertising strategy is complete without reference to the rules governing campaign finance. We close Chapter 6 with a brief survey of federal legislation on the subject—from the 1974 amendments, to the Federal Election Campaign Act of 1971 that established the system of public financing of presidential campaigns (and associated expenditures and contributions limits), to the Bipartisan Campaign Reform Act of 2002, which eliminated so-called *soft money* (money raised by political parties rather than by specific candidate organizations) and which also banned the airing of *issue ads* (ads advocating the passage or defeat of particular legislation) in the weeks preceding the election.

The same media revolution that swept through the arena of campaigns has similarly transformed the nature of executive leadership. In the pre-media era, the campaign ended on election day. The president-elect (or governor-elect) would assemble a broad-based coalition consisting of legislative allies and supportive interest groups, who would work together to implement the administration's policy initiatives. The process typically involved bargaining and accommodation between rival camps.

As described in Chapter 7, bargaining with the opposition has fallen out of fashion in Washington and state capitals. Elected officials now prefer to "go public." They resort to public relations tactics designed to cultivate the appearance of responsive leadership—through rhetorical posturing, credit claiming, and avoidance of blame. Their key advisors are no longer party or interest group leaders, but the legions of pundits, spokespersons, and media consultants who make their daily rounds on television news programs and the editorial pages of our newspapers.

The acceleration of "going public" can be traced to the gradual encroachment of election campaigns on the policy process. Elected officials and interest groups have accumulated considerable expertise in the use of public relations strategies while attempting to win elections, and it is only to be expected that they seek to capitalize on this expertise when formulating and debating legislation. Campaign techniques such as television advertising are now used long after election day. The "Harry and Louise" ad campaign mounted by the health insurance industry proved instrumental in swaying moderate Democrats and Republicans in Congress against the Clinton health reform package in 1994. More recently, the pharmaceutical industry launched a significant ad campaign in opposition to congressional attempts to extend prescription drug benefits to Medicare recipients.

Going public is designed to maintain elected officials' popularity. A president who attracts high marks from the American public can use personal popularity as leverage to get policy agendas passed. The premium on popularity has led chief executives to avoid putting themselves on the media "firing line." They avoid press conferences, where they may be asked tough questions, in favor of the more scripted opportunity of the presidential speech. During the Clinton presidency, the ratio of speeches to press conferences was more than 20 to 1. And George W. Bush has so far maintained a similar ratio during his time in office. Naturally, presidential speeches coincide with the color of the electoral map; the great majority of a president's domestic trips are to states that are in play in the next election.

In theory, popular leaders are more able to persuade their opponents. State legislators may defer to a popular governor's legislative proposals, fearing that opposition could jeopardize their reelection. Conversely, when the president's opponents sense that majority opinion is on their side, they seize the opportunity to push their own policy agenda. In the aftermath of the Monica Lewinsky scandal, for instance, congressional Republicans mistakenly assumed that the public would approve of their efforts to remove President Clinton from office. In fact, the scandal did little to weaken public approval of Clinton's performance as president, the impeachment effort failed, and the Republican Party suffered unprecedented losses in the 1998 midterm elections.[1]

MEDIA EFFECTS

Having outlined how candidates and elected officials use the media, we turn next to assessing the consequences of their actions. How do the content and form of news coverage influence public opinion, and do candidates and elected officials who wage more sophisticated media campaigns secure more votes and influence as a result?

We present the evidence in three separate chapters, beginning in Chapter 8, where we take a panoramic view of the entire field of "media effects" research. Following an initial preoccupation with political propaganda campaigns, the field gradually adopted a more encompassing definition of *media effects* that ranged from influencing what Americans see as the important problems facing the country (*agenda setting*), to shifting citizens' take on public issues (*framing*), to altering the criteria by which voters make their choices (*priming*). And when conditions were ripe—namely, during periods of one-sided news coverage favoring a particular candidate or policy position—the evidence demonstrated considerable change in public sentiment (*persuasion*). Thus, the initial expectation of wholesale changes in public sentiment was replaced by a more cautious definition of the effects of political communication. Against this more realistic baseline, study after study demonstrated that the news media exercise considerable leverage over public opinion. We summarize this evidence in Chapter 8.

In Chapter 9 we take up the parallel question of campaign effects. Despite the enormous investments in advertising and the scrupulously choreographed nature of every campaign event and utterance, there remains considerable doubt over the capacity of campaigns to sway voters. Political scientists can forecast presidential election outcomes quite precisely (with the notable exception of the 2000 election) using indicators that seem to have little bearing on the candidates' media strategies. The state of the economy and the approval level of the incumbent administration, for instance, are among the factors used to forecast the vote. If the annual rate of growth in per capita GDP (gross domestic product) in 1999 yields an accurate prediction of the vote count in 2000, surely the time and effort committed to changing voters' opinions is of secondary importance!

In fact, we show that the forecasting models are consistent with the arguments that campaigns matter. The so-called fundamental forces used by fore-

casters—the state of the economy, the level of presidential popularity, or public concern over the continued involvement of the United States in a foreign
war—are precisely the issues on which the candidates campaign. "It's the
economy, stupid!" became the slogan for the 1992 Clinton campaign because
voters expressed pessimism over the national economy. *Multilateral*, used
instead of *unilateral* to describe intervention, was a buzzword of the Kerry–
Edwards ticket because of widespread concern over continued American military involvement in Iraq. In short, presidential campaigns are debates about
the fundamentals; over time, as more voters encounter the candidates' messages, their opinions on the fundamentals become more closely aligned with
their candidate preference.

Campaigns do more than activate voters' positions on the state of the economy or the performance of the incumbent. Voters acquire considerable information about the candidates' personal qualities, as well as their positions on
the issues. Campaigns also shift the salience of particular issues in the minds
of voters. Finally, campaigns can also affect the level of election turnout. On
the positive side, get-out-the-vote efforts can mobilize large numbers of voters.
Simultaneously, negative campaigning can be used to "demobilize" voters
whose partisan attachments are weak and who might find the spectacle of
attacks and counterattacks sufficiently distasteful to drop out.

The final collection of evidence that we present on media effects concerns
the impact of going public on incumbents' level of public approval (Chapter
10). We evaluate two competing theories. One theory proposes that political
leaders are prisoners of events and relatively powerless to shape public opinion on their own. In this view, Ronald Reagan's popularity had less to do with
his communication skills and more to do with the fact that he presided over
events that reflected well on his leadership. Popularity is simply a matter of
good fortune for those who hold office during peace and prosperity.

The opposing argument is that leaders can use the media to insulate
themselves from any rising tide of public discontent or to even improve their
standing in the aftermath of policy failures. In this view, events do not speak
for themselves. In many instances, political events are ambiguous (representing neither a major success nor a debacle) and how the public views an
event and the actions of a president or governor very much depends on
media presentations of that event and those actions. In 1983, President Reagan was able to justify the American invasion of the tiny island of Grenada
as a response to a communist threat. Ten years later, President Clinton convinced Congress and the American people that there were several compelling
reasons to send American troops to Somalia. In both cases, the president's
ability to command media attention, coupled with the willingness of admin-

istration critics to remain silent, created a one-sided flow of news in favor of the administration.

We consider both of these arguments—history versus media management—in the context of recent presidencies. Using polling data extending back to the 1940s, we trace the ebbs and flows of presidential popularity. We show that, over time, popularity has become less tied to the state of the national economy and more sensitive to news coverage concerning national security. In the case of President George W. Bush, economic indicators such as the unemployment rate or the performance of the stock market have had little impact on changes in his public approval. The frequency of news reports on terrorism, on the other hand, have served to boost the president's popularity. In the aftermath of 9/11, the president's performance as commander in chief appears to be the major ingredient of his public image. Thus, media management is a significant resource for presidents; all else being equal, the ability to direct and shape news coverage makes a difference to a president's political fortunes.

On the surface at least, the increased importance of public approval to the exercise of leadership suggests a more popularly influenced form of government. On issues where clear majorities exist—as in the case of law and order—policy makers must converge on the majority position if they are to remain in office. This is why there is bipartisan consensus on the merits of "three-strikes" legislation. However, the fact that media politics has made policy makers more sensitive to public opinion does not necessarily mean that opinion drives policy.

Media politics might encourage officials to resort to polling in order to identify the issues on which they have more or less leeway. On issues where the public has strong opinions, such as crime, officials may go to great lengths to avoid the wrath of the electorate, even if that means proposing or endorsing bad public policy. No doubt many elected officials were moved to support three-strikes laws on the grounds that the public demanded nothing less. But, as we point out in the case of the defeat of Proposition 66 (a measure that would have weakened the provisions of the California three-strikes law), public support for harsh treatment of violent criminals is driven more by hysteria spawned by advertising and sound-bite news than by any well-considered judgment about the pros and cons of punishment versus rehabilitation as elements of criminal justice policy.

The annual cost of incarcerating a prisoner in New York State in 2001 was $36,835 (US Dept. of Justice, 2004)—approximately the same as the cost of sending a student to Harvard—yet 61.7 percent of those committed to prison in the state in 2000 were nonviolent offenders (Correctional Association of New York, 2004). Why, then, should they be kept in prison at enormous expense to taxpayers? Elected officials do not raise the question, for fear of providing sound bites that label them "soft on crime." Thus, one of the effects of media politics is to weaken the ability of public officials to lead—that is, to enact policies on the merits and then persuade voters to concur.

In sum, media politics encourages public officials to engage in cosmetic rather than genuine problem-solving behavior. American society faces any number of deep-seated, structural problems: the working poor, the urban underclass, racial disparities in the criminal justice process, and health care based on economic status, to name but a few. A political officeholder cannot take action to treat these festering problems without incurring short-term political costs (such as increased taxes) or arousing the wrath of entrenched interests (such as the pharmaceutical industry). In this era of media politics, elected officials generally cannot afford to bear these costs.

To close the discussion, in Chapter 11 we consider how society might short-circuit the escalating use of media appeals in public life. Asking public officials to moderate their rhetoric, scale back on attack advertising, and advocate policies that are unpopular with voters is hardly plausible. One possible pathway to reform is to restore political parties to their rightful place as the principal link between voters and policy makers. A campaign featuring extensive televised advertising from the two political parties on behalf of their entire team of candidates would free individual candidates from the burden of anticipating and avoiding attacks on their record, making it more likely that they would tackle rather than sidestep pressing political issues. As in Europe, party advertising would necessarily be less personalized because the message would be an appeal on behalf of hundreds of candidates. By running on their platforms, parties would encourage substantive rather than image-based voting.

No resurgence of parties in American politics appears imminent. The leaders of the campaign reform movement have worked hard to undermine the voice of the party in election campaigns. Just as the national party committees were poised to regain a semblance of influence in presidential campaigns—through their use of soft money—Congress enacted the Bipartisan Campaign Reform Act of 2002 banning soft money. With "reforms" such as these, the prospects for media-based politics remain excellent.

A more realistic design for reform would reimpose significant public service requirements on the media. Since the 1970s, Congress and the FCC have stripped away the obligations of the broadcast media to contribute to serious, substantive discussions about the issues of the day. In return for unrestricted use of the publicly owned airwaves, broadcasters owe society a minimal level of public affairs programming. Yet, while media revenues from campaign advertising have soared, news coverage of issues has shrunk to negligible proportions. Clearly the media cannot be counted on to voluntarily live up to their civic obligations. Hence, it is time for legislation that would require the broadcast media to provide significant amounts of free airtime for all candidates and in a manner that maximizes public exposure. In the case of the presidential election, for example, requiring all major networks to simultaneously air free-media presentations would increase the "captive" audience.

The revolution in information technology provides the seeds of a more radical solution to the problem of superficial and issueless politics. As the personal computer begins to rival the television as the center of Americans' information universe, politicians and interest groups are regaining the ability to communicate directly with voters. Candidates, political parties, political action committees, and nonprofit civic groups have all turned to the Internet to publicize their causes, raise money, and recruit activists. Given the distractions offered by the Internet, however, we do not see Web-based campaigns as capturing a large audience in the near term. A potentially more promising approach is candidates' use of digital campaign "handbooks" that can be mass-produced at trivial cost but that provide the same breadth of information, interactivity, and appealing, easy-to-browse multimedia presentations.

Research conducted during the 2000 and 2002 elections shows that access to multimedia campaign CDs featuring the public speeches, debates, and televised advertisements of the major candidates empowered voters; use of the campaign CDs resulted in greater interest in the campaign, a greater sense that one's opinions mattered, and most importantly, higher levels of voter turnout. Extrapolating from these preliminary studies, we suggest that the increased use of direct candidate-to-voter communication will make voter autonomy a more viable reality, and will increase the breadth and depth of the policy debate, as well as candidates' control over their messages. These gains, significant in themselves, may ultimately be overshadowed by the collective benefit of having a more enthusiastic, informed, and engaged citizenry.

NOTE

1. The Republicans lost only a handful of House seats. However, it is quite remarkable for the party of the incumbent president to pick up House seats in a midterm election—a circumstance that has, in fact, arisen only once since the Civil War.

CHAPTER 2

THE PRESS AND THE DEMOCRATIC PROCESS

The American System in Comparative Perspective

THE NEWS MEDIA CAN, and arguably should, contribute to the democratic process in several important ways. First, the media can provide a forum for candidates and political parties to debate their qualifications for office before a national audience. Second, even when there is no forthcoming election, news programs can contribute to informed citizenship by providing a variety of perspectives on the important issues of the day. Third, acting as agents of citizens, the media can monitor the acts of public officials, thus helping to deter them from violating the public trust.

In modern industrialized democracies, the broadcast media reach virtually all adults and provide a national forum for candidates and political parties. From country to country, however, the candidates' practical ability to access this forum varies significantly. In the United States, entry costs are significant barriers; there is no guaranteed minimum level of free access. In most European democracies, access is provided at no cost, and television stations typically provide an equal (or proportionate) amount of free airtime to major political parties shortly before the election.

In the delivery of the electoral forum, the extent to which candidates' messages are unmediated or mediated also varies across cultures. American parties and candidates must reach voters though news media that interpret and scrutinize the candidates' rhetoric and actions. In performing this function, the news media have become increasingly hostile and unwilling to permit candidates to speak for themselves. In European countries, by contrast, in part because of free access, party spokespersons have greater ability to solicit votes without going through the filter of news organizations; their messages are delivered without accompanying analysis or commentary.

A closely related civic responsibility of the media is to keep the citizenry abreast of public affairs. The news media are expected—again, to a greater or lesser extent, depending on the country—to supply programming that encompasses a broad range of political perspectives, and to provide citizens with opportunities for expressing their own viewpoints. This dialogue is viewed as necessary if citizens are to make informed decisions about public issues. As eloquently stated by Peter Goldmark (2001),

> News is for the citizen. The citizen is that dimension of each one of us that is responsible for, contributes to, and benefits from the cooperative endeavor of self-government. The citizen is the basic constituent element of the public dimension of human activity. Without the citizen, there is no self-government, no individual basis for responsibility, choice and values; there is only the state in all its fearful, unchecked power and unaccountability. And without the independent news function, the citizen is starved, paralyzed, neutered, rendered insensate, ineffective, and robotic. (p. 9)

Of course, the democratic ideal of fully informed citizens is rarely realized. Ordinary people are preoccupied with their personal affairs and have little time for keeping abreast of public issues. Indeed, citizens prefer to watch sitcoms or sports. Naturally, the ability of the media to perform the function of keeping the public informed is compromised when citizens are uninterested. As we show in Chapter 3, the news media cannot be expected to deliver a steady stream of in-depth public affairs programming that no one will watch.

Accordingly, over time, the old-fashioned ideal of attentive citizens who scour the media for political information has given way to the notion that democracy can function through "efficient" citizens who either pay attention only to issues of personal importance or rely on a variety of psychological cues, such as a candidate's party affiliation, to compensate for a lack of factual information. A related alternative to the classic ideal of informed citizenship is that citizens do pay attention, but only when the media sound an alarm alerting them to issues that threaten the well-being of society or the nation.

Even if judged by weaker standards, however, the performance of the American media can be questioned. Widespread famine in Ethiopia in the early 1980s went unnoticed until a BBC television report caught the attention of an NBC News producer based in London. The collapse of the American savings and loan industry in the late 1980s was similarly ignored and ultimately cost taxpayers $175 billion in the form of a government bailout.

No matter how low one sets the bar for the delivery of public affairs information, the American media do not rate a high grade.

A third important function of the media is to serve as a "watchdog" on behalf of citizens, scrutinizing the actions of government officials and blowing the whistle when those officials cross the bounds of political propriety. Individual citizens do not have the means to keep abreast of their numerous elected representatives; they delegate this task to the media. Maintaining an adversarial posture toward government is one of the basic principles of modern journalism.

In Focus: Three Important Functions of Media in Democratic Societies

- To provide a forum for candidates and political parties to debate their qualifications for office before a national audience

- To contribute to informed citizenship by providing a variety of perspectives on the important issues of the day

- To serve as a "watchdog" scrutinizing the actions of government officials on behalf of citizens, most of whom do not have the opportunity to closely follow the actions of politicians and the government

---

The ability of the news media to deliver on the electoral forum, public sphere, and watchdog functions (or more broadly, civic performance) varies considerably across societies and media systems. Two key factors affect media performance: regulatory policy and market forces. Regulatory policy comes from the applicable regulatory framework. In the United States, the agency charged with regulating the media (the Federal Communications Commission, or FCC) has taken an increasingly laissez-faire approach, arguing that free-market competition is sufficient to ensure the delivery of diverse perspectives on public affairs issues. Most other advanced industrialized democracies, on the other hand—while also moving in the direction of deregulation—have maintained much tighter control over media programming, with the aim of ensuring the delivery of necessary public goods.

Market forces have a significant effect on levels of civic performance. In societies where the broadcast media are predominantly privately owned (as is the case in the United States), competitive market pressures compel media owners to shirk their civic responsibilities. To be profitable, the media must deliver more entertainment than news; and when they do deliver news, they must use formats that are designed to be entertaining rather than to provide information on substantive issues. The alternative to exclusively private own-ership is a mixed model consisting of both privately owned and publicly sub-sidized media. In most European democracies, at least one television network is financed from government revenues. Public subsidies offer broadcasters significant protection from market forces, enhancing their ability to deliver serious (rather than entertaining) news programming. Thus, societies in which media ownership is mixed rather than entirely private are more likely to sup-port informed citizenship.

Both regulatory policy and market forces influence the production of news. The political significance of media programming, however, ultimately depends on the strength of political parties. Countries with strong political parties are less dependent on the news media to provide an electoral forum and guide voters' choices. Parties control the selection of their candidates and can rely on their supporters to cast "informed" (party-line) votes. In these systems, accordingly, what the media might offer by way of public affairs pre-sentations is likely to be of little consequence to the outcome of elections.

Compared to most other democracies, the United States is characterized by weak political parties. Most notably, party leaders have little say over the selection of candidates. For American voters, candidate and issue consider-ations compete with party affiliation as important voting cues. Many Amer-icans lack strong ties to a party. In this world of "floating voters," electoral outcomes are especially dependent on what the media offer by way of news programming.

We'll outline the effects of news coverage on voter attitudes and behavior in later chapters; in the rest of this chapter we'll put the American system in perspective by comparing the role of political parties and the media in the United States and Europe. Regarding political parties, we'll focus on American reforms that have undermined the influence of party organization and contrast these with the strong party systems that predominate in Europe. Regarding media systems, we'll compare the American and European models in terms of the extent of government regulation and the structure of media ownership.

Media Politics as the Successor to Party Politics

How and why did the mass media become so central to political life in the United States? Certainly the sheer size of the country contributed to the sit-uation. It would be difficult for any presidential candidate to traverse all fifty states to meet and greet each eligible voter in person. Congressional candidates, too, would have a hard time connecting with all their constituents in person; most US senators represent many millions of citizens (over thirty-five million in California, for example), and the average population of a US House of Representatives district is 647,000 (the US Constitution originally suggested one representative for every thirty thousand citizens).

However, the reliance on the mass media is not simply a result of population growth. In the 1896 presidential campaign, for instance, the Democratic candidate alone "criss-crossed the country delivering more than 600 public speeches to a total audience estimated to exceed five million people" (Iyengar, 1997, p. 143). Certainly the population at that time was smaller and the media options were fewer, but even as late as the 1960s, campaigns relied heavily on teams of volunteers who organized local appearances for the candidate, canvassed neighborhoods, knocked on doors, distributed campaign flyers, and transported people to the polls on election day. What was it, then, that precipitated the switch to media-based campaigns?

The explanation is rooted in the candidate nomination process. As documented by Nelson Polsby (1983), rule changes adopted in the late 1960s weakened the influence of party elites on the selection of candidates and created a void that was filled by the news media. Prior to 1968, the selection of delegates to the national party conventions, and therefore the nomination of the party's presidential candidate, was controlled by state and local party organizations. Although some states did hold primary elections, the great majority of the convention delegates were selected by the party leadership.

The turmoil that engulfed the 1968 presidential campaign—the unexpected withdrawal of President Johnson as a candidate for nomination, the assassination of Robert Kennedy, the ensuing clashes between supporters of Eugene McCarthy and Hubert Humphrey, and the climactic suppression of the protests outside the convention hall—led the Democratic Party to establish a commission to reform the delegate selection process (for a detailed account, see Polsby, 1983). This commission recommended primary elections as the means of selecting candidates. The widespread adoption of primaries, along with changes in campaign finance regulations following the 1972 Watergate scandal, fundamentally altered the incentives of presidential hopefuls in such a way as to diminish the role of party organizations and increase the importance of the media. By 1972, as Figure 2.1 shows, a majority of the delegates to both party conventions were selected on the basis of primary elections.

The adoption of primaries meant that, instead of cultivating party activists and leaders, candidates had to appeal directly to the public. At the same time,

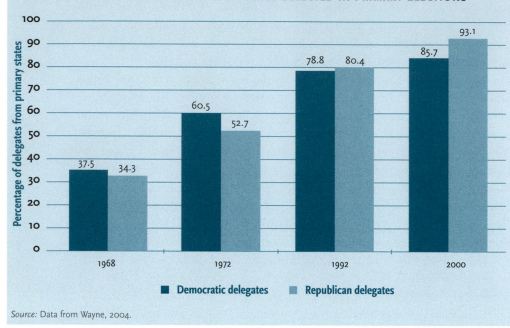

FIGURE 2.1 NATIONAL CONVENTION DELEGATES SELECTED IN PRIMARY ELECTIONS

Source: Data from Wayne, 2004.

technological developments—in particular, the widespread proliferation of television—made it possible for candidates to reach statewide and national audiences. By 1963, 91 percent of American households had at least one television set, up from only 45 percent just ten years earlier (see Figure 2.2).

Although radio had been almost as widespread (more than 80 percent of American households had a radio set in 1940) and had also commanded huge audiences, it was no match for television's visual imagery. By enabling the audience to experience major events (such as the Army-McCarthy hearings and the aftermath of the assassination of President Kennedy, including the on-air shooting of his assassin) in real time, almost as though they were at the scene, television soon supplanted radio and newspapers as the public's principal source of information. Politicians could not ignore this new mass medium even if they were inclined to do so, particularly in light of the weakening of political parties and the fact that other social institutions (clubs, newspapers, etc.) that had been important in grassroots-type politics were declining at the same time.

The end result of party reform and the rapid spread of television was a shift from party-based campaigns to candidate-based campaigns waged on television. Those who seek elective office covet exposure to large audiences;

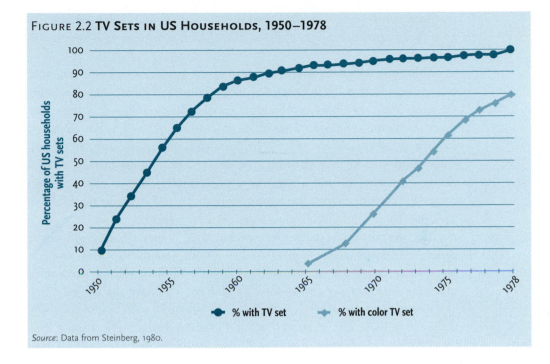

FIGURE 2.2 **TV SETS IN US HOUSEHOLDS, 1950–1978**

Source: Data from Steinberg, 1980.

increasingly it was television that delivered the goods. As the public became entirely dependent on television for political information, candidates altered their campaign strategies to maximize their television exposure.

The most fundamental consequence of party reform was a transformed relationship between candidates and party leaders. Today, after meeting only the most perfunctory requirements, any American citizen can seek a party's nomination for president, senator, or other public office. To qualify for the primary ballot in California, for example, a would-be Republican candidate for president must gather signatures from only 1 percent of the state's registered Republicans (for the Democratic Party, the California signature requirement is 1 percent of registered Democrats, or five hundred—whichever is fewer—in each of the state's congressional districts). In Vermont, a prospective nominee needs the signatures of only a thousand voters of *any* partisan affiliation. In the primary election system, moreover, any voter who has simply checked a box on a registration form to claim affiliation with a party has a say in selecting the party nominee. In states that have *open* primaries—in which any registered voter can vote in the primary for any party—voters don't even have to be registered with the party to participate in candidate selection. In addition, some states hold *modified open* primaries, in which registered partisans can vote only in their own party's primary, but independents can vote in any primary (in all of these systems, each voter may vote in only one party's primary).

Although candidates who are not established party figures (and who may lack support from party leaders) may be at some disadvantage when seeking the presidency, they have proven quite capable of winning—or at least seriously competing—for statewide office. Movie star Arnold Schwarzenegger easily won the special election for governor of California by using his *Terminator* image to win over California voters. And by dipping heavily into his personal fortune to fund a massive television advertising campaign, newcomer Jon Corzine defeated veteran congressman and governor Jim Florio in the 2000 Democratic US Senate primary in New Jersey.

Moreover, because parties now realize that, if they want to win in the general election, they are well advised to embrace candidates who are capable of funding and operating an effective media campaign, some party elites may choose to support and endorse candidates who have not played much of a role in the party, or whose ideology is inconsistent with that of the party, if they have more resources with which to fight a media battle against their general-election opponent. This was the case with Corzine, who was endorsed by Al Gore in the 2000 primary, and also with Arnold Schwarzenegger—the ultimate media campaigner—who was supported by President George W. Bush in the 2003 California recall election, despite his relatively "liberal" stances on many policy issues.

In contrast with the American model, party organizations in most other industrialized democracies exercise decisive control over candidate selection. As a result, campaigns are run primarily on the level of the party rather than on the level of the individual candidate. In many cases, candidates are prohibited from making individual appeals separate from the party message and can be sanctioned (or expelled from the party) for doing so.

To maintain rigid control over candidate selection, parties in other democracies impose strict eligibility requirements. In general, only "party members" can be potential candidates. In most countries party membership represents a much greater political commitment than in the United States. At a minimum, members are required to pay monthly dues to the party organization, but expectations are typically more comprehensive, including representing the party in internal and external organizations and in the community, and campaigning for the party.[1] Often there are additional requirements for candidate eligibility; Hazan (2002) cites the case of the Belgian Socialist Party, which, in addition to requiring party membership for at least five years, specifies that potential candidates must, among other things, have been regular subscribers to the party newspaper and have sent their children to state schools.

Merely meeting the eligibility requirements in no way guarantees selection by the party; would-be candidates still have to survive the selection process. In most democracies, the procedure for selecting candidates is adopted at the discretion of political parties, and the *selectorate* (the group that actually selects the candidate) is much more restrictive than in the United States. In their most inclusive form, selectorates include all registered members of a party (defined, again, in the strict sense, and not in the loose American sense); a slight variation on this model of the selectorate is those parties that require an additional condition to be met by members—such as a minimum length of membership—before they become eligible to participate in the selection of party candidates. However, cases of even more exclusive selectorates—consisting of small party committees—are common, as are *multistage* systems, in which a small body either preselects a group of candidates (from which a broader selectorate, consisting of all party members, selects one) or selects from candidates nominated by a broader selectorate. In many countries (including Australia, Canada, France, Germany, Italy, Japan, and the United Kingdom), some political parties give their national leaders the power to veto or otherwise alter the roster of candidates selected by a broader selectorate.

The degree of party control over candidate selection also depends on the electoral system. Whereas the United States employs a single-member district plurality voting system[2] (in which whoever wins the most votes in a district wins the office), many other countries use multimember-district and proportional representation systems in which parties compete for multiple seats within a single district and the number of seats each party wins is allocated in proportion to their share of the vote. In the common *closed party list* version of proportional representation, parties determine the order in which the candidates are listed on the ballot, and the voter simply casts a vote for the party. For most major parties, candidates appearing at the top of the list are assured election, and those at the bottom have little chance of winning. Candidates who lose favor with the party leadership may find themselves consigned to the bottom of the candidate list.

Thus, in countries with strong parties, it is important for candidates to defer to party leaders. Accordingly, political campaigns in European and other democracies—and media coverage thereof—are more party-oriented than are campaigns in the United States. It is true that the media are becoming increasingly important in campaigns around the world, that there is a growing global cadre of political professionals, and that political parties in more and more countries are adopting American-style campaign techniques. Indeed, there is mounting concern in many European countries about the "mediatization" or "Americanization" of political campaigns—the increasing emphasis on party leaders rather than party policies, for example. Nonetheless, traditional methods of campaigning—such as door-to-door canvassing by candidates and party activists—still play a significant role in other industrialized democracies.[3] And perhaps more important, party-centered campaigns are more likely to generate issue-focused news coverage by the media, because campaign events are themselves more issue-oriented (the release of a party manifesto in Ireland, for example, as opposed to the release of a new attack ad in the United States).

Although weak political parties and universal access to media were both necessary to the development of media-based politics in the United States, they do not alone explain the civic performance of American news organizations. In Chapters 3 and 4 we'll describe how a combination of professional norms and economic pressures have severely limited candidates' access to media audiences, constrained both the sheer amount and the range of perspectives represented in news programs, and contributed to the weakening of watchdog journalism. But before we examine the supply and content of news programming, let's take a moment to put the American media system in some comparative perspective.

Patterns of Media Ownership and Regulation

American media differ from most other media systems in two fundamental respects: autonomy from government regulation and the scope of private ownership. In relation to the media in most other democracies, US media are much less subject to government regulation and are almost entirely privately owned. These differences hold the key to explaining why American media are less likely to make good on their civic obligations.

In Focus: What's Different About American Media?

- **More private ownership.** Media entities in the United States, including broadcast media, are almost entirely privately owned and operated; most other democracies have at least one government-funded broadcast network.

- **Less regulation.** The regulatory structure governing the behavior of American media is considerably more lax than that in most other democracies.

The structure of the media industry—in particular, whether media are owned and operated by government organizations or by private enterprises—has a major impact on the supply of news because government-subsidized media outlets are typically required (by statute) to provide minimal levels of public affairs content, whereas privately owned outlets are generally free to do as they please. Although the issue of public versus private ownership generally applies only to broadcast media, other regulations governing aspects of ownership apply to all forms of media. In the case of election coverage, for example, explicit regulations may directly spell out the subject matter to be covered, as well as when and where the coverage is to occur.

PUBLIC VERSUS COMMERCIAL OWNERSHIP OF BROADCAST MEDIA

There are three models of ownership of broadcast media: purely public, mixed, and purely commercial. The rationale for publicly owned television (and radio) is that the electromagnetic spectrum, as a scarce public resource, must be utilized for the public good.[4] The concept of public service broadcasting was first put into practice in the United Kingdom with the establishment of the British Broadcasting Corporation (BBC) in 1927, and was soon emulated in some form by most democracies in western Europe and beyond. In most cases, this entailed the creation of a state-owned broadcasting system that functioned either as a monopoly or as a dominant broadcaster. Typically, the public broadcasting network was financed from radio or television license fees or taxes.

Although these publicly owned media entities are generally free from political interference, they are expected to follow certain principles (the exact details of which vary by country), such as providing universal service and informative, educational, and diverse programming.

In 1979, all but three countries in Europe had monopolistic public television channels; and two of the three that did not (Great Britain and Italy) had mixed systems, with both publicly owned and commercial television channels. By 1997, however, as a result of significant deregulation across Europe, only three countries had exclusively public-sector television markets. Still, even in the now dominant mixed model, public television channels enjoy large audience shares. In fifteen of the seventeen European Union countries with mixed-ownership television markets, the public television channels hold the number one market spot and capture larger audience shares than would be expected from the number of commercial channels with which they compete. The audience share enjoyed by public television in Europe ranges from a low of about 25 percent for the Italian-speaking cantons of Switzerland, to a high of about 69 percent in Denmark (see Figure 2.3).

In return for government financing, public broadcasters are required to provide sustained levels of public affairs programming, and to represent a diversity of regions, cultures, and viewpoints. Sweden's STV (Sveriges Television), for example, is "obliged to carry cultural and quality programming,

---

In Focus: Public Broadcasting and the BBC

Public broadcasting refers to systems in which television and radio receive funding from the public. Such funding can come directly from the public in the form of fees ("license" fees) or indirectly through state subsidies financed by taxes. Some public broadcasters (for example, Radio Telefís Éireann, or RTÉ, the national broadcaster in Ireland) also run commercial advertising to supplement their revenues.

The BBC (British Broadcasting Corporation), based in the United Kingdom, was the model upon which many public broadcasting systems around the world were based. The principal funding source for the BBC, which does not carry commercial advertising, is the television license. Any person who wishes to operate a television in the United Kingdom is required to purchase a TV license[5] (government-subsidized licenses are available for some groups of people, such as the elderly). The license fee is set by Parliament (in 2005, it was 126 British pounds per year).

FIGURE 2.3 **PUBLIC BROADCASTERS' AUDIENCE SHARE BY COUNTRY**

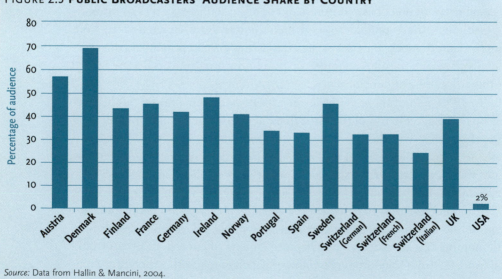

Source: Data from Hallin & Mancini, 2004.

and 55% of its programming must be produced regionally outside Stockholm" (Williams, 2003, p. 39). Thus, public broadcasters in Europe tend to produce higher quantities of public affairs programs (which, as we'll discuss, are of higher "quality" than most programs found on commercial television). These programs reach large audiences; the early localized evening newscast on BBC ONE in the United Kingdom, for instance, attracts approximately 30 percent of the television audience. European audiences are not disinclined to watch serious news.

Unlike the European model, the American television market is dominated by commercial broadcasters. Instead of adopting public ownership, US telecommunications policy has followed a "trusteeship" approach, by which access to the public resource of the spectrum was granted to those who pledged to act in the "public interest, convenience, and necessity."[6] The Federal Communications Commission (FCC) is the agency responsible for setting and enforcing the requirements that broadcasters must follow to meet that public interest standard.

Initially the FCC set fairly high standards for broadcasters' public interest obligations, requiring them, for example, to "promote the discussion of public issues, serve minority interests, and eliminate superfluous advertising" (Zechowski, n.d.). These standards were quickly abandoned, however, because broadcasters considered them an undue economic burden. The regulations that followed were less stringent and not strictly enforced, and most have since been abandoned.

Contrary to appearances, the United States does not fit a purely commercial model. Congress established the Public Broadcasting Service (PBS) in 1967. However, most PBS funding comes from private corporations and individual donors, and even the small portion of its funding that does come from the government is frequently under threat for political reasons (most often from Republicans in Congress who accuse PBS of displaying a "liberal bias"). In stark contrast to European public broadcasters, as Figure 2.3 reveals, PBS reaches only 2 percent of the American television audience.

The effects of public ownership on programming decisions are clear. In Germany, Finland, Belgium, and the Netherlands, public television stations deliver higher levels of politically related content than commercial outlets do. BBC ONE, the flagship public station in the United Kingdom, devoted 22.1 percent of its 2002 peak-hour broadcasts to news and current affairs, compared to only 9.9 percent by the newest commercial British channel, Five. Comparing one recent week (selected at random) of BBC ONE programming with that of the commercial American networks yields similar results (see Figure 2.4). Whereas BBC ONE aired an average of 2.2 hours of news and public affairs programming during prime time on weekdays, NBC, CBS, and ABC averaged only one hour each. Although PBS performed better than the commercial networks (2.5 hours of weekday prime-time public affairs programming), its audience share is so small that almost no one benefits. Note that the commercial British networks were more similar to their American counterparts than to the BBC.

Not only do public broadcasting systems supply a greater quantity of news programming, but they also produce more substantive, issue-oriented programming than commercial stations do. For example, Krüger (1996) found that 37 percent of the news reports broadcast on the three commercial television channels in Germany could be categorized as *infotainment* (what he called "boulevard" news) compared to just 7 percent on the two public channels. Similarly, a study by Canninga (1994, as cited in Brants, 1998) found that news items on commercial television news in the Netherlands and Belgium were shorter than those on public channels.

Another difference between news programming on public and commercial television concerns the more limited geographic reach of the latter. In

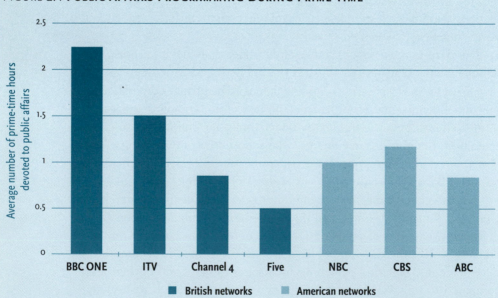

FIGURE 2.4 **PUBLIC AFFAIRS PROGRAMMING DURING PRIME TIME**

Average number of prime-time hours devoted to public affairs

British networks   American networks

BBC ONE   ITV   Channel 4   Five   NBC   CBS   ABC

Note: These data are based on weekday programming during the week of September 6 to 12, 2004. Prime time is defined as 6:00 PM to 11:00 PM. Local news programming was included in these averages, based on a London location in the case of the UK channels, and a San Francisco location in the case of the US channels.

his analysis of the proportion of national versus international news in the news broadcasts of sixteen channels across eight countries, Heinderyckx (1993) focused mainly on public television channels. However, the two commercial channels that he examined (French TF1 and Belgian VTM) had slightly lower proportions of international news (39 and 44 percent, respectively) than the average (47 percent) for the public channels.

The restricted reach of international news in the offerings of commercial networks is also evident in a recent study by Zuckerman (2003), which analyzed the frequency of references to various countries on the Web sites of major television news outlets (working on the reasonable premise that Web site stories were an adequate indication of the attention given to those countries by each news organization). This study found that the best predictor of the sheer amount of CNN coverage accorded to any particular country was that country's level of economic development (as measured by GDP; see Figure 2.5). Wealthy countries received more attention from CNN than poor

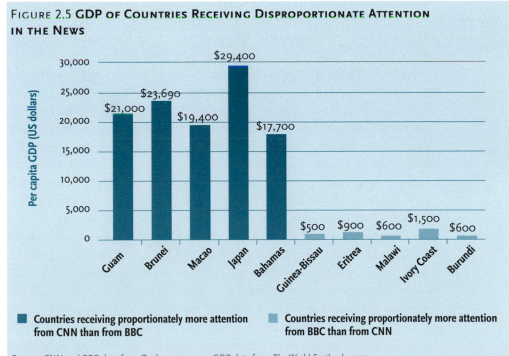

FIGURE 2.5 **GDP OF COUNTRIES RECEIVING DISPROPORTIONATE ATTENTION IN THE NEWS**

■ Countries receiving proportionately more attention from CNN than from BBC

■ Countries receiving proportionately more attention from BBC than from CNN

Sources: CNN and BBC data from Zuckerman, 2003; GDP data from *The World Factbook*, 2005.
Note: Comparison based on multiple years of material on the Web sites of CNN and BBC, current as of October 2, 2004. The top five countries receiving the most disproportionate attention from each network are included here (only countries that had at least one reference from each network are included).

countries. The best predictor of BBC coverage, on the other hand, was the country's population, suggesting a more broad-based allocation of attention to international affairs on the part of the BBC.

Although the evidence is compelling that public television delivers more substantive and global programming than commercial television does, there are shortcomings to the mixed-ownership broadcasting systems common in other industrialized democracies. For example, many Britons object to the mandatory license fee that is imposed on all owners of television sets in the UK to fund the BBC. Furthermore, the share of the audience reached by public broadcasters in mixed-ownership systems—though still respectable, as noted already—is dropping in response to increased commercial offerings and the proliferation of satellite and cable programming. Some evidence suggests, moreover, that programming quality on public television channels is declining because of the increased competition from commercial channels.

Critics of the public-ownership model of television also allege that public funding inevitably compromises the autonomy of the press; that is, news organizations are unlikely to report critically on the government that funds them. An analysis of cross-national variation in press freedom and public ownership shows, however, that this is not the case for Western democracies. When the analysis spans all nations, including those that are undemocratic, we find the expected negative correlation between press freedom and the scope of government-controlled broadcasting (see Figure 2.6).

This result is driven entirely by dictatorships where the media function under strict government controls, essentially acting as propaganda agencies. When nondemocratic regimes are excluded, however, the relationship is reversed, and levels of press freedom are positively correlated with the scope of public broadcasting. This pattern is particularly clear in the case of the Anglo-American democracies. In other words, when only industrialized democracies are considered, press freedom actually *increases* with the level of government-controlled broadcasting. This finding is consistent with Hallin and Mancini's (2004) comparative analysis of European media systems, in which they note that most European democracies with publicly funded television networks have "developed mechanisms to insulate public broadcasting from control by the political majority" (p. 165).

In summary, the structure of media ownership affects news programming. In industrialized democracies where public ownership of at least some television channels is the norm, public affairs programming is more extensive than is the case in the almost purely privately held American media market.

FIGURE 2.6 **FREEDOM OF THE PRESS AND PUBLIC BROADCASTING**

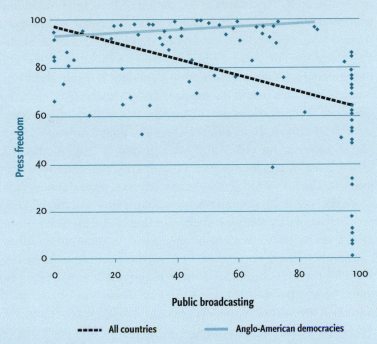

Sources: "Freedom of the press" scores are from the 2004 press freedom index developed by Reporters Without Borders. Countries are assigned scores based on a worldwide survey of journalists, jurists, human rights activists, and researchers. The measure is available for 167 countries (see Reporters Without Borders, 2004). "Scope of public broadcasting" values are from a World Bank study of broadcast media ownership (Djankov, McLiesh, Nenova, & Shleifer, 2001).
Analysis: Note that the slope of the line (representing the relationship between scope of public broadcasting and press freedom) is negative when all countries are taken into account, but positive when only the Anglo-American democracies are considered. In both cases, the relationship is significant ($p = 0.00$ for all countries; $p = 0.04$ for Anglo democracies).

Alternative Approaches to Media Regulation

In addition to the ownership question, different regulatory frameworks have important consequences for the delivery of news programming generally, and specifically for the diversity of political perspectives represented in program content. This is true for print as well as broadcast media, and we will deal with each in turn.

BROADCAST MEDIA

Although the FCC in its early years issued strict (though not always strictly enforced) requirements for public affairs programming by its licensees, most of these no longer apply. From the beginning, broadcasters regularly challenged the FCC regulations as a violation of their First Amendment guarantees of free speech, but the courts generally ruled in favor of the public trustee basis of broadcast regulations. Eventually ideological change at the FCC, and not any judicial mandate, led to weakening of the public service requirements. Under pressure from President Reagan, the FCC adopted a marketplace approach to the media. In essence, the FCC held that the mere existence of competitive media outlets was sufficient to serve the public interest, making it unnecessary to regulate programming.

The scope of the policy shift was substantial. In 1960, the FCC had published a list of the fourteen major elements necessary to serve the public interest. The list included community-oriented programming, political broadcasts, and public affairs and news programs. In 1976, the FCC issued more-precise standards: stations were required to air at least 5 percent local programming and 5 percent informational programming (defined as news and public affairs)—a total of 10 percent nonentertainment programming. In 1984 the FCC abandoned these requirements in favor of looser guidelines, which stated that it was sufficient for stations to "air some programming that meets the community's needs" (Bishop & Hakanen, 2002, p. 264).

In the aftermath of deregulation, television stations increased their amount of local news programming both because local news attracted large audiences (see Chapter 3) and because this sort of programming proved cheap to produce. The typical local newscast, however, lacks meaningful public affairs content.[7] Moreover, local news replaced other forms of public affairs programming. For example, the number of hours per week devoted to non-news public affairs programming across all TV channels in the Philadelphia market dropped from 57.5 in 1976 (before deregulation) to 28.2 in 1985 (after deregulation), and that number fell even further, to 24, in 1997. Nevertheless, the provision of local news has become increasingly important in the FCC's definition of the "public interest" standard.

One of the most important shifts in FCC policy eased the restrictions on concentration of ownership. The National TV and Local Radio Ownership Rules, established in 1941, limited the number of television stations that could be owned by a single entity to seven nationwide, only five of which could be VHF stations (the most common commercial format), and set a similar limit on the number of radio stations. The Dual TV Network Rule, issued in 1946, prohibited any major network from buying another major network, and the Local TV Multiple Ownership Rule (adopted in 1964) limited a broadcaster to just one local station per market, unless there were more than eight stations in that market. Further regulations were implemented in the 1970s limiting cross-ownership of TV stations, radio stations, and newspapers in the same market.

Over time, the multiple-ownership restrictions have been removed. In 1985, the FCC raised the maximum number of TV stations that could be owned by any single entity from seven to twelve. The Telecommunications Act of 1996 further eased the rules by allowing ownership of multiple TV stations, as long as the combined audience of the stations amounted to less than 35 percent of the population. In 2003, the FCC proposed to eliminate all restrictions on cross-ownership within a single market, as long as that market had nine or more TV stations, and to further raise the TV ownership cap from 35 to 45 percent, eventually phasing out TV ownership restrictions altogether. However, this FCC proposal was overturned by a series of court rulings that reinstated the previous ownership limitations.

Quite predictably, the relaxation of ownership restrictions has increased the holdings of the largest owners. As Figure 2.7 shows, the top ten local television station companies increased their combined station ownership almost threefold, from 104 stations in 1995 to 299 stations in 2002. Their combined revenue doubled during the same period.

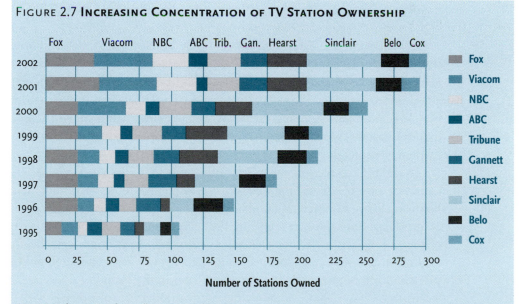

FIGURE 2.7 **INCREASING CONCENTRATION OF TV STATION OWNERSHIP**

Source: Data from Project for Excellence in Journalism, 2004.

The concentration of media ownership in the United States extends well beyond television stations. Large multinational corporations own all categories of media. Rupert Murdoch's News Corporation, for example, currently owns a large number of US cable networks, as well as the terrestrial Fox network, thirty-four Fox-affiliated stations, three movie studios, the Fox Sports Radio network, the *New York Post* newspaper, and several magazines and major publishing houses. As noted by the authors of the Project for Excellence in Journalism (2004c) report:

> In radio, the top twenty companies operate more than twenty percent of all the radio stations in the country; one, Clear Channel, dominates, operating stations in 191 of the 289 Arbitron-rated markets. In local television, the ten biggest companies own 30 percent of all television stations reaching 85 percent of all television households in the United States. In network television, the owners are all giant corporations.

Ownership concentration has also affected the newspaper industry, as we'll discuss shortly.

With so much of the industry controlled by so few, there are good reasons for concern about the supply and quality of news, and about the diversity of voices represented in media programming. According to one well-known critic of American media, "News reporting and commentary controlled by mainstream media companies are the most politically narrow in the democratic world" (Bagdikian, 2000, p. xii).

Research into the effects of ownership on news programming confirms the suspicion that company size is inversely related to quality journalism; that is, the larger the company, the lower the quality. In a comprehensive five-year study of broadcast news quality, the Project for Excellence in Journalism (2003) found that stations owned by small companies (with holdings of three or fewer stations) were 2.5 times more likely to earn an A grade for news quality than were stations owned by the twenty-five largest companies.[8]

In addition to relaxing ownership rules, the FCC has weakened directives that aim to increase the diversity of perspective in news content. The Fairness Doctrine, which required broadcasters to present opposing sides on controversial issues, was repealed in 1987 after broadcasters mounted legal challenges against it. (Other changes in regulation of content, specifically those that deal with candidate access to the airwaves, have also been put in place and will be discussed in more detail later in the chapter.)

In the wake of elimination of the Fairness Doctrine, broadcasts with a partisan slant have increased in frequency and scope. Corporate interests have begun to exert influence over news programming in a number of subtle ways, such as by encouraging journalists not to pursue stories that reflect poorly on their parent corporations, or by imposing programming in keeping with their political preferences. In a recent example, the Sinclair Broadcast Group, whose top executives were major contributors to the Bush 2004 presidential campaign, ordered its sixty-two television stations (which have a combined reach of 24 percent of the national audience) to preempt their regular programming and broadcast an anti-Kerry documentary film a few days before the 2004 presidential election.[9] Sinclair had previously ordered its ABC-affiliate stations not to air an episode (which they denounced as political) of the regular ABC program *Nightline* in which Ted Koppel read the names of all American military personnel killed in Iraq. In similar incidents, the Walt Disney Company refused to distribute Michael Moore's *Fahrenheit 9/11*, and CBS refused to air an anti-Bush ad made by MoveOn.org during the Super Bowl. Thus, media owners increasingly feel free to base programming decisions on their political interests.

Overall, it appears that concern about the impact of deregulation on the quantity and quality of public affairs programming made available to the American public is not misplaced. Clearly, the FCC has transformed American telecommunications policy in ways that significantly decrease the number of voices that have access to the market.

The American experience is hardly unique in this regard; the trend toward broadcast deregulation is global. In Europe, too, ownership rules have been considerably relaxed in recent years, although in most European countries the relaxed regulations are still stronger than those in the United States. In Germany, for example, ownership of television stations is capped at a combined 30 percent of the national audience. In France, no single entity can exercise more than 49 percent control in a company that owns a national television network, with ownership being limited to 15 percent in a second such company, and 5 percent in a third. Furthermore, the presence of public television and radio stations in these countries to some extent counteracts the overall effects of ownership deregulation.

Unlike the American model, the regulatory frameworks of most European countries (and other democracies) take the public service obligations of the media seriously. These countries impose strict programming requirements that apply even to their commercial broadcasters. All European Union countries, for example, have "right-of-reply" laws, which require broadcasters to give people criticized in the media "a right of access to answer criticisms against them" (Hallin & Mancini, 2004, p. 122). In Germany, an internal agreement among all the German states requires any television broadcaster with at least a 10 percent market share to allocate a minimum of 260 minutes of airtime per week to minor political parties. Even in the United Kingdom—which has been criticized for following the US model and dismantling its media regulations in recent years—both the publicly funded BBC and the commercial television stations operate under formal requirements for impartiality and balance in news programming.

Thus, despite the privatization of their broadcast markets, European governments continue to see broadcasting "not simply as a private commercial enterprise but as a social institution for which the state has an important responsibility" (Hallin & Mancini, 2004, p. 161). That responsibility is to ensure that privately owned broadcast outlets, in response to powerful market forces, do not underproduce public affairs programming. This same logic, as we'll see next, is largely mirrored in the regulation of print media.

PRINT MEDIA

In the United States and elsewhere, the print media have never been subject to the same level of regulation as the broadcast media, because the principal rationale for government regulation of broadcasting—that the airwaves are a scarce and publicly owned resource—does not apply to print. Beyond libel laws, regulation of newspaper content has been close to nonexistent. In fact, regulation of American print media has been almost entirely limited to the area of ownership, where the government has applied antitrust laws to promote competition.

Antitrust legislation has been invoked to block the acquisition of one newspaper by another in cases where it has been considered that such mergers/acquisitions would lead to a decrease in competition in the media market, thus potentially harming consumers. In *United States v. Times Mirror Co.* (a case decided in 1967), for example, the court blocked the acquisition of the *San Bernardino County Sun* by the larger *Los Angeles Times* on the basis of the government's argument that the deal would harm competition. Antitrust laws have also been used to prevent newspaper companies from taking anticompetitive measures, such as employing predatory pricing, in which a company prices its product "below cost, usually to run another firm out of business, with the plan of making up the losses later through higher prices" (Lacy & Simon, 1993, p. 200).

The occasional application of antitrust laws has had little impact on the general trend toward concentration of ownership. The lack of effect is partly because the laws have not been rigorously enforced and partly because Congress has exempted newspapers from antitrust provisions in certain situations.[10] Over the years, the newspaper industry has become one of the most monopolistic markets in the American economy.

Historically, American newspaper markets developed on a local level, while those in other Western democracies (most of which are considerably smaller than the United States) developed on a national scale. Only a handful of American newspapers—such as USA Today and the Wall Street Journal—reach a level of distribution that might be described as national; the vast majority are distributed locally. Because the total readership in local markets is small, American newspapers cannot subdivide the market into narrower segments. The importance of advertising to the newspaper industry adds further impetus to reduced competition. Local advertisers, the major source of revenue for newspaper owners, benefit from monopolistic newspaper markets because they reduce the cost per reader. Thus, economic pressures push toward a single newspaper per local market with a catchall audience.

The combination of the inherent tendency toward monopoly in newspaper markets and the lack of a strict regulatory framework has had predictable consequences: namely, a significant drop in competition. Between 1910 and 2000, the number of daily newspapers fell from 2,202 to 1,483. As Figure 2.8 shows, the number of cities with competing daily newspapers dropped sharply during the same period, from 552 in 1920 to just 25 in 1987. The percentage of total circulation attributable to the ten largest newspaper chains in the United States now stands at 51 percent for weekday newspapers and 56 percent for Sunday newspapers. The top twenty-two newspaper chains account for 69 percent of weekday circulation and 73 percent of Sunday circulation.

Only limited research has investigated the effects of ownership concentration on the content of newspapers, and the pattern of results to date is inconsistent. However, the prima facie evidence suggests that the sheer number of voices being represented in the newspaper marketplace has been reduced.

In general, regulation of the print media in Europe has not been as strong as that of the broadcast media. However, some European countries have ownership requirements substantially stricter than those in the United States. In France, for example, a company may not acquire a new publication if the acquisition will push the total daily circulation of all its publications over the 30 percent mark.

An even starker difference between the American and European approaches to print media regulation is the proactive support for diversity in

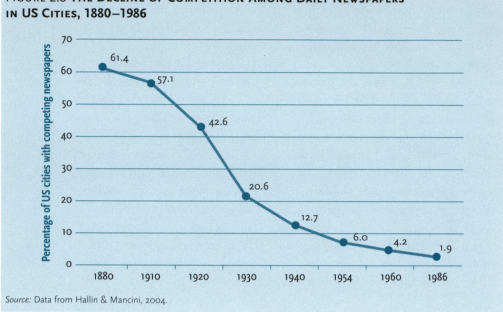

FIGURE 2.8 THE DECLINE OF COMPETITION AMONG DAILY NEWSPAPERS IN US CITIES, 1880–1986

Source: Data from Hallin & Mancini, 2004.

the newspaper market that is provided by European governments, many of which grant direct subsidies to newspapers with the specific aim of increasing diversity. These subsidies seem to have slowed anticompetitive pressures in the European newspaper market. Host (1999, cited in Hallin & Mancini, 2004) estimates, for example, that without subsidies, not a single Norwegian city would have more than one newspaper; with the subsidies, half the cities that had more than one paper in 1972 still had more than one in 1999. It is important to note that, as in the case of public broadcasting, the evidence indicates that newspapers receiving public subsidies are no less likely to play the watchdog role than are newspapers receiving no such subsidies.

Another explanation for the greater competitiveness of European print media markets is the willingness of European newspapers to adopt *self-regulation* practices. In many European countries, there exist strong, institutionalized, self-regulatory bodies that monitor content, and investigate and respond to complaints. These agencies have the power to develop and enforce codes of press ethics. Although some US newspapers have appointed "public editors" or "ombudsmen," there is no formalized interorganizational agency to regulate behavior or serve as a public forum for concerns about the press.

To date, American news organizations have proved reluctant to submit their content to outside review.

In sum, although newspapers are generally subject to less regulation than broadcast media in both the United States and in Europe, the same pattern that holds for broadcasting—stronger regulatory frameworks in Europe aimed at promoting the public good—also applies to the print media. As we'll discuss in the next section, this pattern is repeated in the cross-national rules governing media coverage of campaigns and elections.

Regulating News Media Coverage of Campaigns

As is the case with public affairs programming more generally, the regulatory treatment of the news media has a significant impact on their ability to fulfill the function of providing an electoral forum. And once again, the United States falls short of other industrialized democracies in establishing a regulatory framework that ensures candidate and voter access to the electoral forum.

The equal-time and equal-access rules, which were intended to ensure that the public would have roughly equal opportunity to encounter the perspectives of opposing political candidates, have been rendered meaningless because the FCC now requires broadcasters only to make available time to candidates on equal terms, whatever those terms may be.[11] Thus, whenever a candidate cannot afford to buy the same amount of ad time on a given station as the opponent can (as is often the case for challengers running against congressional incumbents), the rule does not require the station to broadcast that candidate's advertisements for free. The public is effectively denied the opportunity to learn about underfinanced candidates.

In other industrialized democracies, by contrast, access to the electoral forum is not contingent on ability to pay. In every industrialized member of the Organisation for Economic Co-operation and Development (OECD) *other than the United States*, political parties are granted blocks of free airtime for "party political broadcasts" during campaigns. The allocation of airtime is based on an objective formula that differs depending on the country. In the United Kingdom, for instance, the amount of airtime is based on the number of candidates being fielded by each party; in France, broadcasters are obliged to grant equal airtime to candidates, regardless of their prominence or electoral strength. This means that in other democracies, smaller parties, which typically do not have the financial resources available to major parties, are not disadvantaged and still have the opportunity to reach a wide audience through the mass media.

In some instances (such as in the United Kingdom), the party election broadcasts are required to be carried not just by public channels, but also by commercial stations. Moreover, all five British television networks are required to air the party election broadcasts on the same day (although not at the same time), thus increasing the size of the audience. In 2001, 58 percent of the respondents in a British panel survey reported that they had seen at least one party election broadcast, and 37 percent said they had seen one from each of the three major parties.

Not only are political parties guaranteed free airtime, but many countries (including the United Kingdom, France, Ireland, Belgium, Denmark, Spain, and Switzerland) prohibit candidates and parties from advertising on television. There is a stark contrast between American-style media campaigning and the campaigning in countries with free party broadcasts. Setting aside candidates' attempts to influence the content of news in their favor, broadcast campaigning in the United States consists almost entirely of thirty-second paid television ads. In countries with free election broadcasts, in contrast, the blocks of time for campaign messages tend to be considerably longer.

In the United Kingdom in 2001, for example, parties could choose between time slots of two minutes and forty seconds, three minutes and forty seconds, or four minutes and forty seconds. Indeed, British party election broadcasts would seem quite strange to an American audience. They range from plain, straightforward, no-frills presentations—typically featuring the party leader speaking directly into the camera—to more amusing, offbeat presentations from well-known comedians such as John Cleese. Over time, however, as illustrated in Video Feature 2.1, the parties have increasingly resorted to American-style campaign commercials that focus on image and style rather than on the issues.

VIDEO FEATURE 2.1 The Americanization of British Party Election Broadcasts

It is worth noting that election-time media regulations in other democracies apply to more than just broadcast advertising. Many countries regulate the balance of content within television newscasts and election-related special programs. In France, for example, news programs are required to ensure equality between the amount of airtime allocated to members of the government and the amount allocated to opposition parties. In the United Kingdom, all broadcasters (commercial and public) are required to be impartial in their election coverage and to provide for "balance in viewpoints" (McNicholas & Ward, 2004, p. 156). These regulations contrast sharply with the situation in the United States, where "all news outlets, whatever their means of distribution, may cover elections in any way they deem appropriate" (Kaid & Jones, 2004, p. 33).

Candidates and parties in European democracies are thus guaranteed access to the public, and the public, in turn, is guaranteed the opportunity to learn about the full range of available choices. Furthermore, by eliminating the need for candidates to raise money to purchase airtime, the European model allows candidates to focus on more traditional, grassroots forms of campaigning that strengthen, rather than weaken, the role of political parties. And even in the case of broadcast campaigning, the length of the party political broadcasts provides a greater opportunity for candidates to provide important and substantive information to the public, at least in comparison with what is made available in the average thirty-second American political advertisement.

Conclusion

It is clear that there are two conditions under which news media in democratic societies are more likely to make good on their civic responsibilities. The first is a more stringent regulatory framework that requires the media to provide a certain level of public affairs programming. This is the approach adopted in most European democracies, and the evidence shows that European media typically deliver a more robust version of the public forum than that realized in the American market-based approach. Although the laissez-faire approach to media regulation is gaining influence around the world, most industrialized democracies persist in viewing the media in general, and broadcasting in particular, as "an institution whose influence on society is too great to be left under the control of private interests and that must be run under the authority of the state as a representative of the general interest" (Hallin & Mancini, 2004).

The second key condition for helping to ensure that the media meet their civic responsibilities is to afford broadcasters some protection from the ravages of the market. Publicly funded television networks have the necessary cushion to deliver a steady flow of substantive, "hard" news; they need not constantly look at their market share when making programming decisions. Societies in which public television reaches a significant share of the audience are thus more likely to have relatively well-informed and engaged electorates.

Neither the regulatory framework nor market protection conditions hold in the United States. Not surprisingly, American media tend to fall short of expectations; they generally deliver programming that is more entertaining than informative, and instead of acting as a restraint on the actions of government, they frequently toe the official line. The next two chapters will address the weaknesses of contemporary American journalism. In Chapter 3 we'll show how market forces and the norms of professional journalism have combined to undermine the quality of news programming. In Chapter 4 we'll analyze the factors that have undermined the media's ability to play the role of watchdog.

CHAPTER 2 SUMMARY

1. Mass media in democratic societies serve three important functions:

   • Providing an electoral forum for candidates and political parties to debate their qualifications for office before a national audience

   • Contributing to informed citizenship by providing a variety of perspectives on the important issues of the day (the public sphere function)

   • Serving as a watchdog scrutinizing the actions of government officials on behalf of citizens

2. The centrality of the media's role in the political process depends on universal access to media and on the relative strength of other political institutions—political parties in particular.

3. The media became central to US politics in the 1960s, at a time when major changes in the candidate nomination process were weakening political parties. These changes were made possible by the almost universal spread of television occurring at the same time.

4. The American media system (particularly with respect to broadcast media) differs from that of most other industrialized democracies in two respects:

   • It is almost entirely privately owned.

   • Its regulation is relatively weak.

5. Print media, in the United States and elsewhere, have never been subject to the same level of government control as broadcast media.

6. The United States also has weaker regulatory standards governing the coverage of elections. Whereas politicians in the United States must purchase access to the broadcast media (usually in the form of thirty-second campaign commercials), many other democracies grant free airtime to candidates in the run up to elections. Some also have rules governing the balance of viewpoints presented in news during political campaigns.

FURTHER READINGS

Bagdikian, B. H. (2000). *The media monopoly* (6th ed.). Boston: Beacon.

Bennett, W. L. (2003). The burglar alarm that just keeps ringing: A response to Zaller. *Political Communication,20*, 131–138.

Dalton, R. J., & Wattenberg, M. P. (2001). *Parties without partisans: Political change in advanced industrial democracies.* New York: Oxford University Press.

Djankov, S., McLiesh, C., Nenova, T., & Shleifer, A. (2001, June). *Who owns the media?* (Working Paper No. 2620). Washington, DC: World Bank, Office of the Senior Vice President, Development Economics. Retrieved March 14, 2005, from World Bank Web site: http://econ .worldbank.org/files/2225_wps2620.pdf.

Hallin, D. C., & Mancini, P. (2004). *Comparing media systems: Three models of media and politics.* Cambridge, England: Cambridge University Press.

Holtz-Bacha, C., & Norris, P. (2001). To entertain, inform and educate: Still the role of public television? *Political Communication,18*, 123–140.

O'Hagan, J., & Jennings, M. (2003). Public broadcasting in Europe: Rationale, licence fee, and other issues. *Journal of Cultural Economics,27*, 31–56.

Polsby, N. W. (1983). *Consequences of party reform.* New York: Oxford University Press.

Schudson, M. (1998). *The good citizen: A history of American civic life.* New York: Free Press.

Zaller, J. R. (2003). A new standard of news quality: Burglar alarms for the monitorial citizen. *Political Communication,20*, 109–130.

NOTES

1. Note, however, that several studies have found that levels of party membership, and levels of activity by party members, are declining all across Europe.

2. The United Kingdom uses the same system. In a handful of cases in the United States, alternative electoral systems are used. For example, San Francisco voters approved a ballot measure in 2002 to bring in the use of "instant runoff voting" (where voters can specify second preferences that are distributed if no candidate wins a majority) in city elections.

3. Denver, Hands, Fisher, and MacAllister (2003) report, for example, that in the 2001 British general election, fully 17 percent of the electorate were canvassed on their doorsteps. As noted earlier, however, partisan activism is declining around the world, and this figure represents a substantial decline from the 28 percent who were canvassed in 1992.

4. The rationale for the regulation of broadcast media lies in the very technology of broadcasting. Operation of a newspaper printing press does not interfere with any other press. Radio and television, by contrast, are broadcast through signals of a specific frequency and power. Television and radio sets receive these signals on a fixed number of channels, each of which corresponds to the frequency of the signal. The channels have to be sufficiently far apart to avoid interference among the signals. Unlike newspapers, the production of which is not exclusive, with broadcast media "one person's transmission is another's interference" (Krasnow, 1997).

5. It is estimated that approximately 5 percent of televisions in the United Kingdom are unlicensed. Licenses are enforced, on behalf of the government, by private companies, who maintain a database of all addresses in the United Kingdom. It is assumed that there is a television at every address, so any address that does not have a television license is likely to be visited by enforcement agents. In addition to the address database, enforcement agents use electronic detectors to search for unlicensed TVs (by picking up the small amount of energy radiated by traditional television sets), and electronics retailers can be fined if they do not report the addresses of people buying televisions.

6. The "public interest" stipulation was built into the Communications Act of 1934, enacted in response to the increasing congestion of the radio airwaves. Any person who wished to build and operate a transmitter needed to get a license first. The act also created a new agency, the Federal Communications Commission (FCC), to regulate all interstate broadcast communication. The agency was to grant licenses free of charge either on a one-year provisional basis or for a three-year term. At the end of the term the station could apply for renewal. The FCC could deny or modify a license if the station failed to live up to the commission's standards of the public interest. However, the act said little about what constitutes the public interest.

7. For an example of the categories and styles of stories that dominate local news coverage, see Gilliam and Iyengar, 2000.

8. The quality measure was based on performance on a number of criteria: "Cover the whole community; be significant and informative; demonstrate enterprise and courage; be fair, balanced, and accurate; be authoritative; be highly local; presentation; sensationalism" (Project for Excellence in Journalism, 2003).

9. In the aftermath of intense public criticism, threats of viewer boycotts, and a significant decline in Sinclair's stock price, the company reversed course and aired a "news special" called *A POW Story: Politics, Pressure and the Media*, which dealt with "the use of docu-

mentaries and other media to influence voting, which emerged during the 2004 political campaigns, as well as on the content of certain of these documentaries" (Sinclair Broadcast Group, 2004).

10. The Newspaper Preservation Act of 1970 permitted two or more newspapers publishing in the same area (at least one of which is failing) to combine advertising, business, circulation, and printing operations, as long as the news operations (meaning both staff and editorial policy) remained separate.

11. In one example of equal terms, the "lowest unit rate" rule requires that stations offer advertising time to candidates at the lowest rate that they have charged other commercial advertisers during the preceding forty-five days (Kaid & Jones, 2004).

THE MEDIA MARKETPLACE

Where Americans Get the News

HISTORICALLY, WHERE AMERICANS GET THEIR NEWS has depended on the development of new technologies for transmitting information. The earliest newspapers were affiliated with political parties. Their news offerings were unabashedly slanted in the direction of their partisan sympathies. During the latter part of the nineteenth century, however, major improvements in the technology of printing lowered the costs of production. Publishers could reach mass rather than niche or localized audiences, and revenues from advertising far surpassed the subsidies provided by political parties, thus spelling the doom of the partisan press. In 1870, nearly 90 percent of all dailies were affiliated with one of the two major parties. Thirty years later, the figure had been cut in half.

As newspapers began to demonstrate both profitability and political independence, civic-minded publishers and editors began to push for the formal training of journalists. They subsidized the establishment of journalism schools at major universities. By the 1930s, journalism had become professionalized, with appropriate "canons of conduct," including the pronouncement that "news reports should be free from opinion or bias of any kind" (Stevens, n.d.).

The continued success of large-circulation daily newspapers led to gradual consolidation of the industry as local newspapers were acquired by regional and national newspaper chains. Today, most American newspapers are owned by a chain. The six largest newspaper chains (see Figure 3.1) account for more than 50 percent of the total circulation of 55 million.

With the development of radio in the 1920s and the immediate popularity of radio news (spawned by radio's relatively fast-breaking coverage of World War II), newspapers began to surrender their position as the major

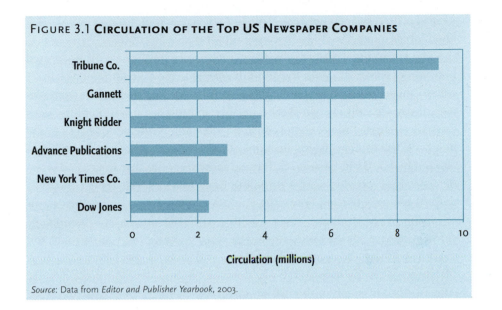

FIGURE 3.1 **CIRCULATION OF THE TOP US NEWSPAPER COMPANIES**

Circulation (millions)

Source: Data from *Editor and Publisher Yearbook,* 2003.

source of news. The arrival of television in the 1950s accentuated this trend, and broadcast news gradually replaced print outlets as the major carriers of news. The national newscasts aired by the three major television networks (ABC, CBS, NBC) soon emerged as the dominant source of daily news. In 1969, at the height of their dominance, the combined audience for the three newscasts accounted for three-fourths of all American households. More people (approximately twenty-five million) tuned in to any one of the network newscasts in the late 1960s than subscribed to the top twenty daily newspapers combined.

The development of cable broadcasting in the early 1980s weakened the major networks' monopoly hold on the television audience. CNN, the first "all news" cable network, was formed in 1980 and was soon followed by Fox, CNBC, and MSNBC. By 2002, 82 percent of American households had access to cable news channels.

A more significant threat to the dominance of network news was the increasing proliferation of local and "soft news" programming. Responding to the low cost of producing local news and the substantial audience demand, station owners began to air multiple local newscasts and hybrid entertainment–news programs each day. In the 1960s most stations broadcast a single evening local newscast; today the ratio of local to national news programming on television is tilted overwhelmingly in favor of the former. In the Los Angeles area, for instance, the three network-affiliated television stations air a total of 7.5 hours of local news each day between 4:00 PM and 7:00 PM.

The recent breakthroughs in digital technology have further transformed how we get our news. With the adoption of the personal computer as a gateway to the outside world, the competition for news audiences has intensified. Today, virtually every major newspaper and television station reproduces its news offerings online, giving consumers instant, on-demand access to the news. We will discuss the implications of information technology for the consumption of news in Chapter 5. For the moment, note that the major Internet portals all provide access to online news sources, but their content is derived exclusively from conventional outlets (newspaper, wire services, or television news). In some cases, such as MSNBC, media and technology companies have joined forces hoping to create synergy between established providers of news content (such as NBC) and technological giants (such as Microsoft). It is too early to tell whether such hybrid news entities will capture a sufficient share of the market to survive.[1]

In the rest of this chapter we will describe the evolution of the national audience for news and changing patterns of news consumption. We will also track changes in the public's evaluations of news; for example, do people believe what they read? Then we'll address the major factors that shape the news. First and foremost are market forces. In a competitive market, audience size is paramount and all news organizations are in a race to increase their market share. Thus, news is produced to entertain rather than inform. Second, the professional norms and values of journalists shape the content of news. The desire to maintain autonomy, for example, has led journalists to cover campaigns from a more interpretive perspective. Rather than simply summarizing the candidates' speeches and advertisements, reporters now focus on the state of the horse race and the candidates' strategies and tactics for winning over voters. Third, the news is inevitably a reflection of organizational processes and routines; the beat system, for instance, ensures a regular supply of news reports from major government agencies.

Audiences

Audience size is everything in the world of news. Since all news outlets (with the exception of National Public Radio and the Public Broadcasting Service) are privately owned, their survival depends on maintaining a loyal audience. Advertising represents the principal source of revenue for publishers and broadcasters. The price of advertising depends on the number of people reached by any given newspaper or television news program. Statistics on newspaper circulation are compiled by the Audit Bureau of Circulations;[2] television news audiences are measured by the A. C. Nielsen Company.[3]

Unlike the situation in Europe, where individual newspapers often command a large share of the national audience, American newspapers circulate on a more modest scale. Today the most widely read American newspaper is *USA Today* (with a circulation of 2.1 million readers). The circulation of the *Wall Street Journal* also tops two million, but it is a specialist provider. *USA Today* can claim to be a national newspaper, but most other dailies are limited to local or regional audiences. The *New York Times* publishes Midwest and West Coast editions, but the majority of its readers are residents of New York. The *Los Angeles Times* attempted to expand its reach by publishing a Washington DC edition, but it failed to attract East Coast readers and was shut down. In general, American newspapers can reach only as far as their advertisers, most of whom are local businesses. New York City department stores have little interest in advertising in the West Coast edition of the *New York Times*.

The historical trend in newspaper circulation is not promising. Unlike broadcast media, newspapers require the audience's undivided attention. Americans' lifestyle and use of time changed dramatically in the latter part of the twentieth century. The marked increase in dual-worker households and the increasing amount of time devoted to work-related activities led to significant declines in newspaper circulation. Today the audience for the ten largest newspapers (see Table 3.1) is approximately fourteen million. This figure is about half of the combined daily audience for *Wheel of Fortune* and *Jeopardy* (27.8 million for the week of November 1–7, 2004).

Unlike newspapers, network television has a nationwide presence. Television programming produced by a network is transmitted across the country by local stations affiliated with that network. Measuring just how many people watch a particular program is the mission of the A. C. Nielsen Company. Nielsen developed the concept of television *rating points*. One rating point generally translates to 1 percent of the viewing audience. Nielsen compiles information from two sources: television diaries maintained by a large and representative sample of households (over five thousand households) and twenty-four-hour metering of television sets (among a smaller subset of households). Each television program broadcast in the United States is identifiable by a unique digital "fingerprint." Nielsen's metering system captures

TABLE 3.1 TOP TEN US NEWSPAPERS

Newspaper	Daily Circulation	Sunday Circulation
USA Today	2,154,539	2,616,824
Wall Street Journal	2,091,062	NA
New York Times	1,118,565	1,676,885
Los Angeles Times	955,211	1,379,258
Washington Post	732,872	1,029,966
New York Daily News	729,124	805,350
New York Post	652,426	437,117
Chicago Tribune	613,509	1,002,166
Newsday	580,069	678,019
Houston Chronicle	553,018	747,404

Source: Editor and Publisher Yearbook, 2003.

this identifying information, making it possible to estimate precisely the number of television sets tuned in to any particular program.[4]

The audience for broadcast news exists at two levels: local and national. The broadcasting industry consists of hundreds of local outlets, many of which are affiliated with a national network, thus enabling them to relay network programming. In exchange, station owners must pay the networks a subscription fee for access to their programming. The three major television networks (and their corporate parents) are ABC (Disney), CBS (Viacom), and NBC (GE). More recently, Congress granted Fox a network license in 1986. Controlled by Rupert Murdoch's News Corporation, Fox has aggressively purchased local stations across the country.

At the local level, the country is divided into 210 local television markets known as *designated media areas*, or *DMAs*. In many cases the DMA corresponds to a metropolitan area, but in less urban parts of the country a DMA may include multiple counties. Whereas California has twelve DMAs, the entire state of Montana has only one. Each DMA consists of a set of antenna-based local television stations licensed by the FCC and assigned to a specific channel.

By the late 1960s, the thirty-minute evening newscasts produced by the major networks had emerged as the industry leader. At the height of their popularity, the three network newscasts attracted a combined daily audience in excess of sixty million viewers. The introduction of cable television, however, inaugurated a period of greater competition within the world of broadcasting. CNN emerged as a reputable supplier of news in the 1980s, employing well-known journalists (many of whom had been let go by the networks) and reaching viewers across the globe.[5]

Although the American audience for CNN (and the other cable networks) is typically less than four gross rating points (GRPs), the market share of cable news providers increases during periods of international tension or conflict. Immediately after the start of Operation Desert Storm in January 1991, CNN reporters Bernard Shaw, John Holliman, and Peter Arnett found themselves the only American television correspondents in Baghdad. As the US bombing of the city began, they broadcast live from the terrace of the Al-Rashid Hotel. Their dramatic reports of the bombing raids were watched by a worldwide audience of more than a billion people from over a hundred countries, including President George H. W. Bush, Saddam Hussein, and other major participants in the conflict, thus guaranteeing the network a place in broadcasting history.

With the institutionalization of cable television, the audience share of network news has gradually declined. Since their heyday, the three nightly newscasts have experienced a ratings decline of nearly 60 percent. The network television audience share fell from 85 percent in 1969 to 40 percent in 2003. The most dramatic declines occurred in the 1990s, considerably after cable television had come of age. Between 1993 and 2003, for instance, the combined audience for the three evening newscasts dropped by nearly 30 percent—from forty-one million to twenty-nine million (see Figure 3.2). It was precisely during this period that the production of local television news surged.

Despite the increasing competition from cable providers, network news remains the single most watched national news source in the United States. In 2004, the combined audience for the three evening newscasts equaled the circulation of the top forty newspapers.

For decades, CBS was considered the premier network newscast. Under the leadership of Edward R. Murrow, the network recruited a stable of distinguished correspondents, including Walter Cronkite, Howard K. Smith, and Eric Sevareid. During much of Cronkite's long tenure as anchorman, the *CBS Evening News* emerged as the perennial ratings winner. Cronkite's retirement in 1981, however, created a more competitive environment, and by the early 1990s the network had fallen to third place in the ratings, trailing both ABC and NBC by a substantial margin. In 2005, the long-standing anchors for NBC and CBS (Tom Brokaw and Dan Rather, respectively) both retired, and ABC's Peter Jennings died (having retired several months earlier), prompting speculation that the network news audience would once again be "up for grabs."

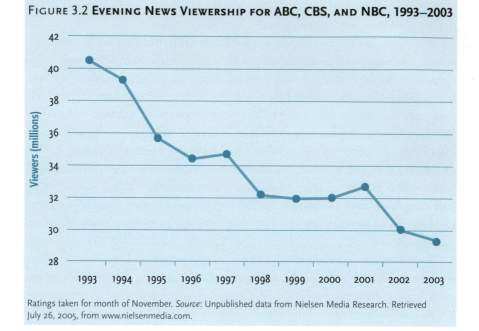

FIGURE 3.2 EVENING NEWS VIEWERSHIP FOR ABC, CBS, AND NBC, 1993–2003

Ratings taken for month of November. *Source*: Unpublished data from Nielsen Media Research. Retrieved July 26, 2005, from www.nielsenmedia.com.

It is important to place the audience for network news in context. Although millions of people watch the evening news, the newscasts are small-fry when compared to reality programming, sports, or prime-time drama. *Survivor, Millionaire,* or *Monday Night Football* outdraws any of the nightly newscasts by a substantial margin. In comparison with entertainment, the demand for public affairs programming is weak. The ten most popular regularly scheduled television broadcasts ever (see Table 3.2) do not include a single news or public affairs program.

The most serious threat to network news today is local news. Station owners have discovered that local news programming can be delivered more or less continuously, and at relatively low cost. Moreover, millions of people tune in because local news provides information that is closer to home, more usable (such as the weather forecast), and entertaining (such as the latest sports results). In market after market, stations have increased the number of programming slots devoted to local news. In New York and Los Angeles, local news runs on a continuous basis between midafternoon and 11:00 PM. In LA, the audience for evening local news aired by the network affiliates generally equals or exceeds the audience for the network's own national news-

TABLE 3.2 **TOP TEN RATED TV PROGRAMS, 1961–2002**

Program	Episode	Network	Date	Rating	Share (%)	Number of Households
M*A*S*H (series)	Final episode	CBS	2/28/83	60.2	77	50,150,000
Dallas (series)	"Who Shot J. R.?"	CBS	11/21/80	53.3	76	41,470,000
Roots (miniseries)	Part 8	ABC	1/30/77	51.1	71	36,380,000
Super Bowl XVI	49ers vs. Bengals	CBS	1/24/82	49.1	73	40,020,000
Super Bowl XVII	Redskins vs. Dolphins	NBC	1/30/83	48.6	69	40,480,000
XVII Winter Olympics	Women's figure skating	CBS	2/23/94	48.5	64	45,690,000
Super Bowl XX	Bears vs. Patriots	NBC	1/26/86	48.3	70	41,490,000
Gone With the Wind (movie)	Part 1	NBC	11/7/76	47.7	65	33,960,000
Gone With the Wind (movie)	Part 2	NBC	11/8/76	47.4	64	33,750,000
Super Bowl XII	Cowboys vs. Broncos	CBS	1/15/78	47.2	67	34,410,000

Source: Data from Nielsen Media Research, unpublished data. Retrieved July 26, 2005, from www.nielsenmedia.com.
Note: Rankings based on surveys taken from January 1961 through August 31, 2002; only sponsored programs seen on individual networks are included, and programs scheduled for less than thirty-minute duration are excluded.

cast (see Figure 3.3).[6] In fact, as we'll describe later in the chapter, the rise of local television news is a compelling case study of how media economics determines media programming.

Ratings are the lifeblood of the broadcasting industry. Advertising revenues for specific television programs fluctuate on the basis of how many people they reach. Nielsen conducts quarterly ratings "sweeps" during the months of February, May, July, and November. The size of the audience during each sweeps period locks in advertising rates for individual programs and stations until the next period. Programs that suffer a decline in their ratings thus stand to lose significant revenue, so broadcast news providers do their utmost to maintain or improve their ratings.

Efforts to monitor online audiences are still in their infancy. Nielsen// NetRatings and other market research companies attempt to track the number of visits to Web sites. Internet traffic is dominated by major portals (such as AOL), e-mail providers (such as MSN), and search engines (such as Yahoo or Google). As we will discuss in greater detail in Chapter 5, the emerging audience for online news is not as large as the audience for shopping, pornography, or other "browsing" activities.

One final point about the supply of news concerns the gradual increase in joint ventures or "cross-media" sources. We have already noted the emerging partnerships between technology and content providers in the case of online news. Similar partnerships have been initiated within conventional media because the FCC has relaxed its "cross-ownership" limits—that is,

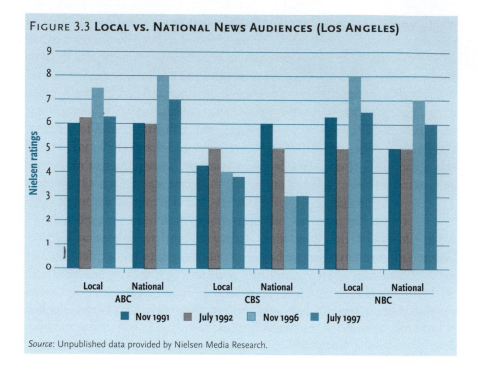

FIGURE 3.3 LOCAL VS. NATIONAL NEWS AUDIENCES (LOS ANGELES)

Source: Unpublished data provided by Nielsen Media Research.

the limits on the number of different news outlets operating within a media market that can be owned by a single entity. In many media markets, the same owner operates both the major newspaper and the top-rated local television station.[7]

The Tribune publishing company became Tribune Broadcasting when it acquired television station WGN (whose call letters stood for the Tribune-owned *Chicago Tribune*, or "World's Greatest Newspaper"). Currently, Tribune Entertainment owns stations in several of the top media markets, including KTLA in Los Angeles, KPIX in New York, and CLTV, the Chicago area's first and only twenty-four-hour all-news local news channel. As the "sister station" of the *Chicago Tribune*, CLTV quickly became a model for content sharing and cross-promotion, with stories and reporters moving seamlessly from print to broadcast outlets.

CREDIBILITY

Audience size is one measure of the demand for news. But does size also imply credibility? Source credibility (believability) is an important indicator of media status and influence; when people perceive news reports to be unbiased and trustworthy, they are more likely to take them seriously (see Chapter 8). Media scholars have tracked the American public's evaluations of media credibility for several decades.

Given the freedom of the American press from government controls and journalists' commitment to objective reporting, we would expect consumers to view the news as generally unbiased. The behavior of practitioners suggests that they take their credibility seriously. A few years ago, CBS anchor Dan Rather agreed to speak at a fund-raising event for the Democratic Party. The ensuing controversy over the appearance of partisan bias led Rather to issue an immediate apology for demonstrating "a lapse of judgment."[8]

An approximate indicator of media credibility is the level of overall public confidence in the press. The General Social Survey, conducted annually by the National Opinion Research Center (NORC) at the University of Chicago, asks a representative sample of Americans for their level of confidence in the media. In 1973, the first year the question was asked, only 10 percent of the public responded "hardly any." By 2000, however, this group had grown to 40 percent of the sample. Although it is true that public confidence in just about every public institution has declined by some 10 points since 1972, it is striking that the news media easily surpassed this trend (see Figure 3.4). The audience may be listening, but it is also increasingly skeptical.

The generic "confidence in the press" question is likely to underestimate the credibility of particular outlets for the well-known reason that people rationalize their own preferences. Many people deride Congress as a corrupt institution but revere their own congressperson as honest and hardworking. Similarly, when people are asked to rate the credibility of the news outlets they rely on, their evaluations are more favorable. The Pew Research Center (2005) has asked Americans to indicate whether they "believe all or most" of the programs offered by well-known news organizations. As Figure 3.5 shows, by this measure a majority of Americans rate most outlets favorably. Television news enjoys a clear credibility advantage over print sources;[9] in fact, CNN and the three major networks are the most credible sources in the United States. Even Fox News, widely disparaged for demonstrating a pro-conservative bias, enjoys *higher* credibility than the major weekly news magazines, *USA Today*, and the *Wall Street Journal*. Not surprisingly, people are also attached to their local news programs (and to a lesser degree their local newspaper); just as many people believe their local station as believe network news.

Although the level of believability accorded to broadcast news is impressive, the trend line is consistent with the downward trend in confidence in

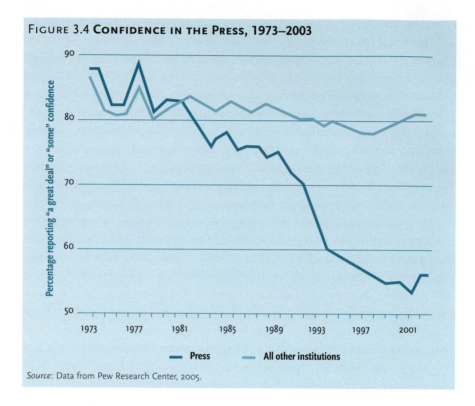

FIGURE 3.4 **CONFIDENCE IN THE PRESS, 1973–2003**

Percentage reporting "a great deal" or "some" confidence

— Press   — All other institutions

Source: Data from Pew Research Center, 2005.

the press. In nearly every case, more Americans believed the news in 1985 than did in 2004. The only exceptions to this trend were the two newcomers to the industry—CNN and *USA Today*—both of which were insufficiently known in 1985 to elicit high ratings. For network news, the average decline in believability between 1985 and 2004 was 18 percentage points. For print media, the decline was even steeper.

A different measure of credibility is the demand for news during times of national or international crisis. When important news stories break, where do people turn first? In the case of the 2003 Iraq War, the data show clearly that people gravitated to more-familiar sources (see Figure 3.6). By a margin of greater than two to one, Americans relied on CBS, NBC, and ABC rather than CNN, Fox, or MSNBC. By this measure of viewer loyalty, the national networks retain a significant advantage over their younger competitors.

Studies of media credibility show one consistent pattern: people who tend to hold strong political views, such as those affiliated with a political

FIGURE 3.5 **BELIEVABILITY RATINGS, 1985–2005**

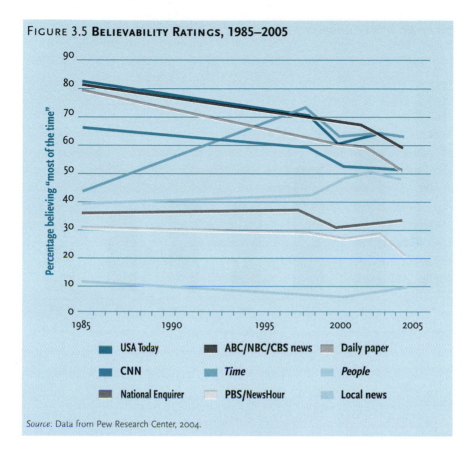

USA Today	ABC/NBC/CBS news	Daily paper
CNN	*Time*	*People*
National Enquirer	PBS/NewsHour	Local news

Source: Data from Pew Research Center, 2004.

party or cause, are especially likely to view the news as biased. Enthusiasm for the "party line" makes partisans dubious of news presentations designed to present a balanced perspective on the day's events. The tendency to believe that "objective" coverage is biased is directly proportional to the intensity of one's political commitments. In fact, research has shown that people with opposing viewpoints, when shown the exact same news report, will each believe that the report is biased in favor of the other side! This is called the *hostile media phenomenon*.

In the United States, support for party orthodoxy is somewhat stronger among Republicans, who represent a smaller and more homogeneous group than Democrats. Accordingly, perceptions of media bias tend to be stronger among Republicans. In Chapter 8 we will demonstrate that Republicans generally dismissed news reports that questioned the validity of the George W.

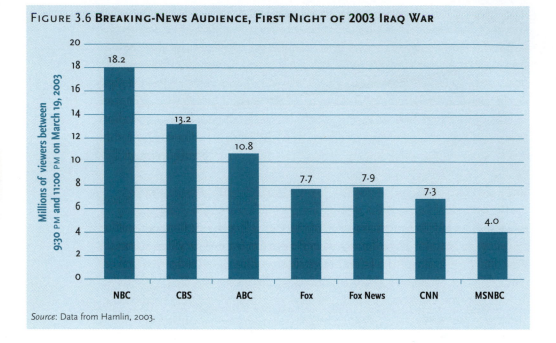

FIGURE 3.6 **BREAKING-NEWS AUDIENCE, FIRST NIGHT OF 2003 IRAQ WAR**

Source: Data from Hamlin, 2003.

Bush administration's intelligence claims concerning Iraq's weapons of mass destruction (WMD). They found it more comfortable to persist in their beliefs that Iraq did have significant WMD quantities. In general, the fact that media credibility is lower among partisans should reassure journalists and others concerned about objectivity and balance in the news; the fact that news reports offend partisans of both the left and the right is in and of itself testimony to objectivity.

> **In Focus: The Hostile Media Phenomenon**
>
> Research has consistently shown that, in general, people who are highly committed to a point of view—strong Democrats or Republicans, for example, or those who are strongly pro-Israel or pro-Palestinian—perceive impartial news stories to be biased in favor of their opponents.

What Gets Reported?

News is meant to be a reflection of reality. The major events and issues occurring in the world at large that are deemed to have consequences for

Americans are the events and issues one expects to encounter in the news. This "mirror image" definition of news stipulates close correspondence between the state of the real world and the content of news coverage. During times of rising joblessness, the news focuses on unemployment; when thousands of Sudanese civilians are massacred, the spotlight shifts to Sudan and to US policy on Africa.

Implicit in the mirror-image definition of news is the well-known asymmetry between newsworthiness and the normal course of events. Events are judged newsworthy only when they deviate from anticipated (everyday) outcomes. Planes that land safely are not news, but planes that crash are front-page news. In general, negative events or outcomes tend to attract greater coverage, for the simple reason that they indicate a deviation from normalcy. News coverage of the economy is sparse during periods of prosperity but abundant during recessions. Politicians who behave as law-abiding citizens attract little attention; the few who break the law elicit volumes of coverage. Gresham's law of news is that negative information always drives out positive information.

The expectation that news organizations behave as mirrors of real-world events is unrealistic on a variety of grounds. Practical considerations make it impossible to cover events at every remote location across the globe, and many issues (such as global warming) do not manifest themselves in the form of observable, concrete events. In other policy areas, indicators of "reality" (such as the level of threat to US national security) are simply unavailable.[10] In these cases, it is impossible to assess the level of correspondence between reality on the one hand, and "mediality" (the "reality" portrayed by the media) on the other.

In the final analysis, the mirror image definition of news is unrealistic because the practice of journalism rests on fallible and culturally determined human judgments. On any given day, thousands of potentially important events occur. It is physically impossible to cover all of them. Editorial selection ("gatekeeping") is the hallmark of news: events are granted coverage in proportion to their newsworthiness. Judgments of newsworthiness are inherently subjective; what's newsworthy to CBS News may be of little interest to All India Television or, for that matter, to the *New York Times*.

Explaining the content of news, therefore, is very much an exercise in understanding journalists' professional values, career incentives, and decision-making processes, all of which affect their behavior and work product. This perspective is generally referred to as the *organizational process* account of news, meaning that the standard operating procedures of news organizations influence what's reported and what's ignored. Thus, to the degree that news reports deviate from "reality," the discrepancy is attributable to organizational procedures and news-gathering routines, and not to the political preferences of journalists.

The major competitor of the organizational process account of news is the standard market-based account of profit-maximizing behavior. As we have noted repeatedly, the media industry in the United States is privately owned. Consumers are free to choose from a wide array of news providers. Facing competition, rational owners prefer to further their own interests rather than to provide public service to the community. The content and form of news coverage are subject to the same logic that drives all other economic activity: minimize costs and maximize revenues.

MARKET PRESSURES

Consider the following facts from the world of broadcast journalism. The award-winning television news program that delivers the most detailed, substantive, and wide-ranging discussion of policy issues is the hour-long newscast produced by the Public Broadcasting Service. This newscast is watched by fewer than three million Americans each evening. *Entertainment Tonight*, the thirty-minute program focusing on Hollywood celebrity news, attracts a daily audience in excess of five million viewers. "Soft" news or reality television programs attract much larger audiences than "serious" news.

The message for news organizations is obvious: make news reports more "interesting." In the last two decades, no matter what the medium, the public affairs content of news has been substantially diluted. Slattery and Hakanen (1994) found, for instance, that news about government and policy fell from 54 to 15 percent in a sample of Philadelphia local newscasts between 1976 and 1992. Even the *New York Times*, which features "All the News That's Fit to Print" as its motto, has had to chart a similar course.

Market pressures are especially intense in the world of broadcast news, where survival must take precedence over informative news reports. Substantive news content and audience size are inversely related. Obviously news producers have to adapt to the competition from soft news, sitcoms, and cable talk shows. They do so by making their own news programs more entertaining and less serious. Patterson's (2000) research shows that one-half of all network news reports broadcast in 2000 had no policy content; in 1980 the figure was approximately one-third. Of the network news reports that aired in the 1980s, 25 percent were sensationalized; by 2003 the figure was 40 percent. Clearly, news organizations have learned that fluff is more profitable than substance.

Journalism was not always so sensitive to the bottom line. In the early days of television news, most senior managers were themselves journalists, with the view that their news programs were to be the very best rather than the most economical. All three network news divisions were "loss leaders" during the 1970s, yet they employed large staffs, maintained bureaus in several countries, and provided what was considered top-notch reporting. In effect, the networks used the vast profits generated by their entertainment programs to subsidize their news divisions. William Paley, the founder of CBS, is said to have remarked to a journalist concerned about the rising costs of the *CBS Evening News,* "You guys cover the news; I've got Jack Benny [a famous entertainer at the time] to make money for me."

As the networks were acquired by conglomerates, the corporate culture changed. The news divisions were expected to make a profit and sink or swim within the parent company. The amount of time reserved for news in the thirty-minute newscast was cut by 10 percent, from twenty-one minutes in 1990 to nineteen minutes in 2002. All three networks were forced to reduce the number of correspondents and close most of their international bureaus. With the end of the Cold War, foreign affairs no longer had a compelling story line ("Could we get along with the Russians?"), and news organizations felt free to scale back their overseas coverage. These measures have created a serious lack of access to international events. In the case of breaking overseas events, American networks typically purchase footage from freelancers or from European network correspondents, with voice-over from the nearest network correspondent. Cost cutting also ushered in the end of serious documentary programming. Hard-hitting investigative documentaries were transformed into up-close interviews with celebrities.

Accentuating the new economic logic was the gradual breakdown of the rigid boundaries in the daily television programming schedule, which restricted local news programs to one thirty-minute slot in the early- and late-evening schedules. Once stations began airing local and soft news programs in multiple time slots, the pressure on network news only intensified.

When the networks were created, their rationale for airing news programs was hardly selfless. Rather, they were required by the FCC to provide a minimal level of public affairs programming in exchange for free use of the broadcasting spectrum. As we documented in Chapter 2, these "public service" obligations have long since been weakened or altogether ignored, making it possible for networks to exist as "all entertainment" entities. A first-rate news division was once a symbol of a network's commitment to public service; today it is a mere cog in the entertainment machine. News is what sells. Several of the most basic principles of serious journalism—worldwide news coverage, multiple correspondents working the same story, and the commitment to getting the story right—all became victims of the new economic logic.

Further compromising the quality of journalism was the acceleration of the news cycle. In the current twenty-four-hour cycle, news organizations face intense pressures to deliver the news faster than their competitors do. The race to be first often requires loosening the standards of journalism; rather than confirming a story with multiple sources, editors routinely accept reports that are poorly substantiated. In a well-known instance of the risks of maintaining "old-fashioned" standards, in 1998 *Newsweek* decided to delay printing its report about new evidence concerning the alleged affair between President Clinton and Monica Lewinsky (the semen-stained dress) because its reporter on the story (Michael Isikoff) had not yet confirmed the material with multiple sources. While *Newsweek* waited, the *Drudge Report* published the story online. It does not pay to be right, if you're last.

Although the conflict between cost-driven journalism and the delivery of hard news is especially pronounced in the world of broadcast journalism, where the financial stakes are much higher, print media have been no less affected. Newspapers have reduced the size of the daily "news hole"—space allocated to current events—in favor of features. On any given day, the reader of the *New York Times* has to wade through sections on technology, food, entertainment, real estate, travel, and more. Newspaper design has been "visualized" with the use of color photography, graphics, and other eye-catching devices. The very same economy measures implemented at the networks—staff cuts, bureau closings, and softening of news content—have been adopted at leading newspapers across the country. The editors of the *New York Times*, for instance, did not notice any conflict between their motto, "All the News That's Fit to Print," and their assigning a full-time correspondent to cover the O. J. Simpson case in 1995. All news organizations, no matter what their prestige or rank in the world of journalism, converged on the O. J. story because it attracted readers. The *Times* simply had no choice; it could either provide intensive coverage of the event or lose readers.

In short, the economic realities of the media business create strong pressures on journalists to cater to the tastes of the median viewer or reader. Programs that are heavy in policy content or in-depth expert analysis will find that their audience has migrated within minutes to the next episode of *Jeopardy*, or to "*Action News* at 6." The proliferation of broadcast outlets and the resulting competition for the attention of the viewing audience spelled doom for "old-fashioned" serious journalism. A new genre of news programs, focusing on the lives of the wealthy and famous, and dwelling incessantly on the mayhem and violence on local streets, created the appropriate fit (for owners and publishers) between economic interests and the delivery of public affairs information.

A Case Study of Local Television News

The rapid emergence of local news programming in the decade of the 1980s is a compelling case study of the responsiveness of news programming to economic constraints. In the 1960s, station owners typically aired old episodes of popular sitcoms (such as *Hogan's Heroes* and *The Beverly Hillbillies*) in the programming slots just before or after the national newscast.[11] Naturally, they paid a significant fee to the syndication company holding the rights to these programs, and the programs tended to attract only modest audiences, so the resulting profit margin was less than station owners hoped it would be.

In the more competitive media markets (Los Angeles and New York), owners noticed that the thirty-minute local newscast proved quite popular with the audience, often drawing in more viewers than the national news. Moreover, the local newscast was inexpensive to produce. The typical local newscast can be staffed by four or five all-purpose correspondents, an anchor or two, a weather forecaster, and a sports correspondent. Local news correspondents, in contrast with their network news counterparts, do not command extravagant salaries. Infrastructure costs for local news programming are similarly limited; for the typical news station, the single most expensive budget item is the monthly lease of a helicopter (to provide immediate access to breaking news). All told, the cost of putting together a local newscast is trivial.

Cost is only half of the programming equation, however. Local news is especially enticing to station owners because they can present the program in ways that bring in large audiences. Not only is local news close to home and the source of both useful (weather forecast, traffic reports) and personally engaging (latest baseball scores) information, but even the public affairs content can be structured to appeal to viewers. It is no accident that the signature "issue" of local news coverage is violent crime. From armed bank robberies to homicides, "home invasions," carjackings, police chases, and gang wars, violence occurs continually in local newscasts. Conversely, little time is devoted to nonviolent crimes such as embezzlement, fraud, or tax evasion, because they lack the "action" to command the attention of the viewing audience. Thus, local news is essentially a televised police blotter: "if it bleeds, it leads" is the motto of local news directors.

Stories about crime focus on concrete events with powerful impacts on ordinary people, convey drama and emotion, and above all, provide attention-getting visuals. The power of this formula is apparent to station owners and news directors in media markets across the country. English-language commercial television stations operating in the Los Angeles market aired a total of 3,014 news stories on crime during 1996 and 1997, of which 2,492 (83 percent) focused on violent crime. The crime of murder, which accounted for less than 1 percent of all crime in Los Angeles County during this period, was the focus of 17 percent of crime stories. In fact, the number of murder stories (510) was equal to the total number of nonviolent crime stories (522) during the period sampled (all figures are taken from Gilliam & Iyengar, 2000).

Although brutal acts of violence are understandably newsworthy, this level of overrepresentation of violent crime is extraordinary. Overall, the Los Angeles study found that the typical thirty-minute local news segment included three distinct reports on crime, totaling to approximately four minutes of coverage (out of twelve minutes devoted to "news"). The results were identical across all six television stations whose offerings were examined. Moreover, violent crime was equally newsworthy in late-afternoon, early-evening, prime-time, and late-night newscasts.

In their preoccupation with violent crime, Los Angeles television stations are not especially distinctive. A recent study of fifty-six different cities by Klite, Bardwell, and Salzman (1997) found that crime was the most prominently featured subject in the local news, accounting for more than 75 percent of all news coverage in some cities.

In sum, low costs and high interest value make local news a winning combination. In response, station owners have increased the supply of local news. More generally, the law of supply and demand has shifted the content of news programming away from relatively serious subjects. Publishers cannot eat Pulitzer prizes and Peabody awards; in order to maintain their competitiveness, they must provide news offerings that attract an audience.

Organizational Processes and Routines

Although the brutal logic of the bottom line goes a long way toward explaining recent trends in the practice of journalism, a fuller understanding of the production of news entails more than a simple exercise in economic determinism. Although news organizations must make ends meet, journalists continue to have considerable leeway to exercise choice, discretion, and control over their work product. Like other professions, journalism has a culture that guides everyday practice. There is a right way and a wrong way. Journalists also pursue professional advancement and recognition. Above all, they rely on a set of conventions or standard operating procedures for uncovering and reporting the news. As we will describe, all these factors leave an indelible imprint on the content and form of news coverage.

In Focus: Influences on What Is Reported

● **Market forces.** As commercial enterprises, news organizations are subject to the same logic that drives all other economic activity: minimize costs and maximize revenues. Soft news attracts much larger audiences than serious news, so producers are under pressure to make their programs more entertaining.

● **Organizational processes and journalistic norms.** Professional norms of autonomy and objectivity in journalism lead journalists to interpretive forms of coverage, emphasizing ad watches, candidate strategy, the horse race, and scandal stories. The routines and procedures followed by news organizations—deadlines in the news cycle, the assignment of reporters to beats, and reliance on official sources—also have substantial impact on the content and form of news, as do the accessibility and appropriateness of competing stories.

AUTONOMY AND OBJECTIVITY AS DOMINANT VALUES

Modern political journalism rests on two dominant values: objectivity and autonomy. In the particular case of election news, as campaigns have become more choreographed and expert at using the press to recirculate their messages, autonomy has upstaged objectivity as the guiding principle of journalists' behavior. In the era before media politics, the press maintained an objective stance on the campaign by providing regular opportunities for *both* candidates to reach their audience. Objectivity simply required equal exposure; the candidates' partisan rhetoric canceled each other out.

In the aftermath of the 1988 campaign, however, the press decided that merely reprinting both candidates' words compromised journalistic autonomy. In that election, the media made the Bush campaign's use of racial imagery in a television commercial (the "Willie Horton" ad) to attack Governor Dukakis's record on crime the major story line of the campaign. The coverage met the standard definition of objectivity: the Bush and Dukakis campaigns were both quoted extensively on the subject of crime and prison furloughs. By their actions, however, journalists elevated the importance of crime as a campaign issue, thus handing Bush (who was more widely seen as "tough" on crime) a significant edge.

Thus, following the 1988 campaign, leading reporters argued that recycling the candidates' message of the day was an inappropriate form of campaign journalism because it made reporters captive to the agenda of campaign consultants. To protect their autonomy, reporters turned to a more analytic form of news coverage that centered on interpretations and analysis of the candidate's actions. Not only was this more aggressive scrutiny of the candidates designed to reduce the likelihood that reporters would be captivated by campaign spin, but it also amplified the voice of the journalist. The campaign correspondent was now a "solo author" of the news, whose own analysis was more newsworthy than what the candidates had to say.

INTERPRETIVE JOURNALISM

The manifestations of the switch from descriptive to interpretive reporting of elections were many. In the first place, reporters were more apt to debunk the candidates' pronouncements. Campaign ads were no longer described exactly as they were; instead, journalists adopted a new genre of reporting— the "ad watch" or "reality check"—in which they dissected and enumerated the specific errors, exaggerations, or undocumented allegations contained in ads or speeches (see Video Feature 3.1). Ad watches soon became a staple of election coverage, with all major news outlets dedicating a full-time correspondent to the task of analyzing the candidates' rhetoric and ads. As noted in Chapter 6, ad watches also changed the behavior of advertisers, but sometimes in a counterintuitive direction.

VIDEO FEATURE 3.1
Policing Campaign Ads

The emphasis on resisting simple regurgitation of the candidates' ads spilled over into daily coverage of the campaign. To a great extent, the older, descriptive mode of coverage consisted of reporting the events of the day, often including verbatim reports of significant amounts of candidate speech. The newer, interpretive journalism also reported on daily events, but in a much different way. Journalists were generally less interested in describing the event and more inclined to use the event as a means of divining the candidates' motives and tactics. Because the focus is no longer on the candidates' positions, reporters today bypass the candidates and turn to a coterie of "experts." The task of the expert is to act as an agent of the reporter and provide the necessary analysis of such questions as why Al Gore went to his opponent's home state of Texas and appeared before a predominantly Hispanic audience, or whether Senator John Kerry's Vietnam service represented a plus or minus for his candidacy.

Thus, the *strategy frame*—analysis of the rationale and strategy underlying the candidate's rhetoric and positions—has emerged as the single most frequent theme in coverage of the political campaign. News is no longer limited to what the candidates say but also reports *why* they say it. The pouring of campaign resources into battleground states, fund-raising tactics, the tone of the advertising campaign, whether "going negative" will help or harm the candidate—all become the stuff of election reports.

The most popular element of interpretive reporting is the state of the horse race. Reporters invariably frame the election not as a contest of ideas or policy platforms, but as a race between two teams, each bent on securing more votes than the other. The bottom-line question at the end of the day is "Who's ahead?" or "Who's scoring more points with the electorate?" Reports on the latest polls or behind-the-scenes efforts to improve the candidates' electoral prospects far outnumber reports on the candidates' worldviews, policy pledges, or previous records of decision making. In fact, the state of the horse race now accounts for more news reports than any other category of news. In some studies, reports on the horse race outnumber reports on the candidates' policy positions by a factor of two to one.

What is especially revealing of the new genre of campaign journalism is the synergy between the professional aspirations of journalists and the competitive pressures of the market. Horse race coverage appears to be a dominant strategy because it satisfies the journalist's need for autonomy and objectivity, it is easy to report, and it sells! All major news organizations now administer their own surveys of public opinion, often once or twice a month. Poll-based coverage is entirely objective; after all, reporters are relaying the results of their own (rather than the candidates') polling, the results are based on representative samples of likely voters, and the journalist or someone in the news bureau with survey and statistical expertise is responsible both for determining the questions to be asked and for tabulating the results (most major news organizations employ a full-time survey researcher to design and interpret their election polls). From the perspective of the reporter, examining the latest poll results on computer and then telephoning a pair of competing experts to get their take on what the results mean for the eventual outcome is much less labor-intensive than following the candidate across the country to extract the message of the day.

Polling also helps make the election more interesting to the audience. The idea that the election is a close race with each side making momentary gains, only to find the race still deadlocked, capitalizes on voters' curiosity and uncertainty over the outcome. People abhor uncertainty; the less clear-cut the eventual result of the election is, the more often they will tune in to news about the race. In fact, some critics have alleged that, during the closing stages of the campaign, media organizations deliberately frame their survey results so as to tighten the race and increase the interest value of their election news.

As the horse race has come to dominate news of the election, coverage of issues has receded into the background. Conventional wisdom holds that issues do not interest the audience. News-reporting organizations cannot protect their market share by covering the candidates' positions on tax cuts or defense. More compellingly, issue information is typically "old" news. Early in the campaign, once the candidate has announced an economic plan, there may be some ripple of news coverage (as was true for Clinton's economic plan in 1992), but as the campaign progresses, the plan is no longer of interest. A candidate's policy stances are never a fresh news item unless there is some discrepancy between the candidate's stated position and the rhetoric or the candidate suddenly reverses position.

Finally, issue-based coverage also weakens the journalist's autonomy from the campaign. Issues are difficult to cover objectively and often leave the reporter open to charges of biased coverage. A spokesperson for the Bush campaign is liable to complain about a story on the Kerry health care plan on the grounds that the story cited a lower total cost than that estimated by the Republicans. Alternatively, the Kerry camp might demand equal time to correct an error in the original report. Given the ambiguity inherent in most policy platforms, virtually anything the reporter says may be disputed as inaccurate or biased. For these reasons, issues are not high-priority items for reporters on the campaign trail.

There is good evidence that the horse race plays well with the audience, while issues do not. Using a multimedia CD as the medium, Stanford University researchers gave a representative sample of "online" American voters a large number of typical news reports (from broadcast and print-based sources) about the 2000 presidential campaign three weeks before the election. The CD was programmed to enable "usage tracking"; that is, the specific pages that participants accessed, the number of times they used the CD, and the length of their CD sessions were recorded.

The CD usage data revealed that news stories focusing on the horse race were the most popular. After adjusting for the location or placement of the news story within the CD (stories that appeared first or second received much more attention than stories that appeared in the hundredth position), the section on the horse race was found to be the most visited section (with an average of nineteen page visits per respondent). Polling-related stories even attracted more attention from CD users than stories focusing on the candidates' personal attributes. In contrast, issue-based stories attracted virtually no attention; the average number of visits to reports covering the candidates' positions on the issues could not be distinguished (with statistical reliability) from zero.

The inevitable consequence of interpretive reporting and the associated fixation on the horse race is a reduced role for the candidates themselves in daily news reports. The candidates still crisscross the country making four or five campaign speeches each day, but their appearances on network television amount to a "bit" role. The disappearance of candidates' voices from daily news coverage of the campaign is striking; in 1968, a viewer of network news could listen to the opposing candidates for over a minute each day (see Video Feature 3.2). By 2000, the daily (total) sound bite was twelve seconds (six seconds per candidate).

VIDEO
FEATURE 3.2
Candidates'
Own Voices
in the News

COMBAT STORIES

Interpretive journalism demands that reporters do their utmost to keep campaigns "off message"—to cut through the spin cycle and expose the unrehearsed candidate, warts and all. The spectacle of Howard Dean ranting to supporters after his loss in Iowa was newsworthy precisely because it appeared spontaneous and unscripted—a candidate revealing his true colors on television. Other opportunities to keep campaigns on the defensive include publicizing inconsistencies between a candidate's record and rhetoric. Al Gore's offhand reference during the first 2000 debate that he had accompanied FEMA's director Jamie Lee Witt on a trip to Texas (when in fact he had accompanied FEMA's deputy director on a trip to New Mexico) spawned a spate of reports on Gore's penchant for exaggeration and dishonesty. During the 2004 presidential campaign, Teresa Heinz Kerry's "shove it" remark to an editorial writer for a conservative Pittsburgh newspaper attracted extensive coverage, only because it clashed with the Kerry strategy of "going positive." To use Ross Perot's apt characterization, "gotcha" journalism is the order of the day.

The degree of conflict between the national press corps and the presidential candidates has reached the point that alternative news programs have emerged as significant outlets for the campaigns. Bill Clinton discovered he could avoid the constant gaggle over the state of his marriage by making the rounds of soft-news programs, where questions were friendlier and he could more effectively control the message. The wisdom of the Clinton strategy is evident from studies that compare the tone of mainstream and nonmainstream news outlets. In the 2000 campaign, Matthew Baum (2005) tracked the coverage of the candidates in national newscasts, interviews with the candidates by "serious" journalists, and interviews by entertainment-oriented talk show hosts. As expected, he found that both Gore and Bush received much "kinder, gentler treatment" in the nontraditional venues (see Figure 3.7).

The one area where the press typically achieves total control over the story line and in many cases inflicts terminal harm to a campaign, concerns allegations of personal misconduct or other signs of unsuitability for office. From 1984, when Colorado senator Gary Hart was exposed as an adulterer; to 1988, when Jesse Jackson was forced to apologize for anti-Semitic remarks; to 1992, when Bill Clinton faced multiple outbreaks of "womanizing" coverage; to 1998, when a young White House intern was sexually linked with President Clinton; to 2004, when Republican senatorial candidate Jack Ryan was forced to withdraw from the race following the disclosure that he had visited X-rated nightclubs—ethical lapses in general and bedroom behavior in particular take center stage in the news coverage of campaigns. The Hart and Jackson episodes are illustrated in Video Feature 3.3.

VIDEO FEATURE 3.3
Feeding Frenzies

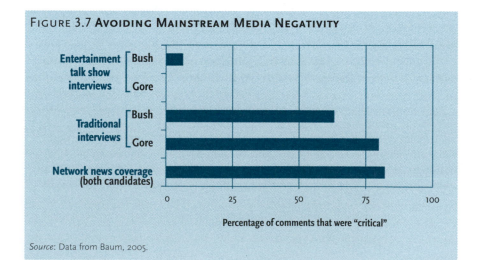

FIGURE 3.7 AVOIDING MAINSTREAM MEDIA NEGATIVITY

Entertainment talk show interviews — Bush / Gore

Traditional interviews — Bush / Gore

Network news coverage (both candidates)

0   25   50   75   100

Percentage of comments that were "critical"

Source: Data from Baum, 2005.

As in the case of horse race news, sex and scandal meet both the economic and the professional aspirations of journalists. Ratings go up, the journalist makes the front page, and the candidate is weakened. Unlike inconsistencies in a candidate's voting record or policy preferences, which might conveniently be attributed to changed circumstances or other complex excuses, it is impossible for candidates to evade responsibility for their personal misconduct. News coverage of the character issue is especially damning because the personal responsibility is unavoidable. All these ingredients, as Howard Kurtz (1999), the media critic for the *Washington Post*, pointed out, made Monica Lewinsky the perfect subject for news coverage:

> And then along came Monica. When Monica Lewinsky first burst into public view on January 21, 1998, the journalists were presented with more than a juicy scandal. It was a chance to convince the public at long last that Clinton was a liar. Whitewater was too arcane? Fundraising too complicated? Here at long last was a plot everyone could understand—a president having a tawdry affair with an intern half his age. And the journalists were right on one fundamental point. The president was lying. It was a legitimate story. The president was under criminal investigation by the independent counsel. But the press went crazy, bonkers, totally over the top. All Monica on the nighttime cable shows with the same cast of characters, all Monica on the Sunday shows, all Monica on the front pages and the magazine covers. And yes, pretty close to all Monica on my CNN program, *Reliable Sources*, where we would critique the all Monica coverage of the other all Monica outlets.

The prominence of the character issue in recent history raises an important historical question: why were reports about the candidates' personal lives missing from the news coverage of campaigns in the 1950s and '60s? It is implausible that the nomination process in those decades produced candidates of such impeccable moral strength that there was simply no basis for questions over their character and integrity. The well-known *New York Times* correspondent R. W. (Johnny) Apple describes his first assignment for the paper as watching the elevators going up to President Kennedy's suite in a New York City hotel. Among the president's visitors was a well-known Hollywood actress. Apple dutifully informed his editor, who showed little interest. By 1980, it would have been impossible to keep this story off the front page!

The character issue was not big news in 1960 because womanizing was deemed not especially unethical or immoral by the all-male press corps. The values of the newsroom led journalists to believe that they had better things to do than investigate the bedroom. The media began to consider marital infidelity unacceptable behavior only after journalism opened its doors to women. The culture of the newsroom changed to acknowledge that candidates' bad treatment of a spouse could be thought to reflect poorly on their candidacy.

As the nonappearance of character stories in the 1950s and '60s suggests, the fact that journalists are trained to suppress their own values when covering elections does not guarantee that these values will not eventually creep into news reports. It is well known that journalists are more likely to identify as Democrats than as Republicans, and critics of the right have long attacked the mainstream media for providing a liberal slant on the news. In fact, however, as we note in the conclusion to this chapter, these fears are misplaced. Most careful analyses of campaign news find few traces of one-sided coverage. Not only are partisan values easy to suppress (by providing candidates equal time), but reporters are especially eager to debunk the "liberal media" hypothesis.

If campaign coverage in the 1950s and '60s reflected the culture of an all-male press corps, more recently the effects of an all-white newsroom were clearer still. Despite some progress, journalism remains a field that underrepresents people of color. In 2001, for example, although 596 minority journalists were hired, 698 left the profession. Overall, minorities made up less than 12 percent of all journalists (compared with 30 percent of the national population), meaning that few media outlets can match the populations they serve in racial or ethnic background.

The insensitivity of reporters to issues of racial bias is especially clear in local television news coverage of crime. We have already noted that local TV stations converged on crime as a means of strengthening their audience appeal. In doing so, they focus on particular "episodes" of crime, which means that, more often than not, the audience is given information about a suspect. In the previously cited Los Angeles study of local news, crime stories provided footage of the suspect—in the form of either a live arrest or a photograph or police sketch of the suspect at large—in more than half the instances. Generally the suspect was either Hispanic or African-American.

Even in the absence of a debate about the accuracy of racial profiling of the crime issue by local newscasts, the daily association of criminal activity with the minority community constitutes strong evidence of racial bias. As community advocates have noted, often vehemently, there is much more to the minority community than violence and crime, but these more positive elements are not news. The all-consuming focus on crime to the exclusion of other activities is equivalent to university administrators' informing the news media only about minority dropout rates while ignoring the awards and distinctions achieved by minority students. Why, then, have local news stations persisted in presenting a clearly one-sided view of racial minorities? The answer is simple: the television newsroom across the country is disproportionately white. The lack of diversity in the newsroom translates into habitual acceptance of news reports that stereotype minorities.

ACCESSIBILITY AND APPROPRIATENESS

Turning to more mundane elements of the organizational process model, the news must often be tailored to the specific needs of news organizations. Accessibility generally refers to the ability to cover stories in timely fashion. In terms of everyday news, there is good reason that Washington DC is the center of the universe for most major news organizations. This is where they station most of their correspondents. The *Los Angeles Times* and *New York Times* both assign more correspondents to Washington DC than to their respective state capitals. As national news organizations, both papers have more interest in the US Congress than in the New York or California legislatures. National news most frequently emanates from the seat of the national government, and news organizations allocate their resources accordingly.

The need for accessibility works as a disincentive for news organizations to cover international news. Most news organizations are hard-pressed to cover developments in Outer Mongolia. In the case of television, the share of international news in the national newscasts has fallen significantly since the end of the Cold War. The likelihood of a newsworthy event occurring in Bangladesh is insufficiently high for the *New York Times* to station a correspondent in that country.

The importance of accessibility to news organizations is a particularly compelling argument against the "news as mirror image" argument. If the news were indexed to an objective indicator of importance, one would expect that, in the case of natural disasters, coverage would be proportional to the number of people who die. Traditionally, the level of coverage of international disasters by the American press was less responsive to the scope of the disaster and more dependent on the distance of the event from Washington DC: the closer the disaster to the United States, the greater the coverage.[12] But more recently, the development of portable communication devices (most notably the videophone) has reduced the costs of overseas coverage. In the aftermath of the major earthquake in Ahmedabad (India) in January 2001, CNN coverage via videophone was instantaneous.

Potential news stories vary not only in their accessibility, but also in their appropriateness, or fit, to the particular mission of news organizations. Developments in the stock market are of greater interest to outlets with a focus on the economy; stories involving nuclear waste are especially newsworthy to news audiences in close proximity to nuclear dump sites. Many news outlets are, in fact, aimed at niche audiences; these outlets necessarily rely on different criteria for judging the newsworthiness of stories. And, as noted already, news organizations treat international, national, regional, and local events differently. A traffic accident is not news for the *New York Times* but may be a candidate for the lead story on New York City local newscasts.

An alternative definition of appropriateness is independent of subject matter or geography. Some news stories are more likely to be covered more or less, simply depending on the medium. Broadcast outlets emphasize certain issues and ignore others, and print media reveal a different set of preferences. In the case of television news, issues that generate compelling visual images are especially appropriate. From the perspective of a television reporter, the presence of a clear story line and the ability to convey the report within two minutes are additional pluses. Conversely, issues that have fewer concrete referents, or "episodes," and that require talking heads are unlikely to be judged broadcast-worthy. Dueling mathematical models of budget deficits and economists' views on macroeconomics may be covered by PBS's *News Hour* but will almost certainly be ignored by network television.

The particular needs of television create a demand for "action" news. During the 1980s, the three networks covered two policy areas—crime and terrorism—more often than any other. This pattern was evident well in advance of the current preoccupation with terrorism. Both issues provided a steady supply of dramatic visual images, a story line consisting of the forces of good versus evil, and an ample supply of individual victims for gut-wrenching interviews. Although the networks aired hundreds of stories on crime and terrorism, they broadcast fewer than fifteen reports on the subject of global warming. The more complex the subject matter is, the less likely it is that the issue will be sufficiently "telegenic."

ROUTINES AND PROCEDURES

News organizations rely on well-developed routines as a means of preidentifying the location of newsworthy events and facilitating their reporters' ability to cover the stories in a timely manner. These routines include establishing deadlines, assigning reporters to news beats, and relying on authoritative sources.

News reports require considerable editing and revision before they see the light of day. Before the Internet, the daily news cycle made it imperative that reporters finalize their stories in time for the publishing deadline. In the case of the evening news, the report had to be filmed, edited, and transmitted to New York well in advance of the 5:30 PM broadcast. In practice, events occurring in the late afternoon were necessarily ignored. Today such late-breaking events still do not make the newscasts, but instead they are posted immediately on the networks' Web sites. As news organizations have replicated themselves online, the news cycle has become compressed. In the views of many, this acceleration of the news cycle has contributed to sloppier journalism. The rush to print or broadcast is often accompanied by an inadequate level of background research and fact checking, as evidenced by the *New York Post*'s mistaken revelation in its July 6, 2004, issue that Congressman Gephardt was Senator Kerry's running mate in the presidential election.

The beat system developed as a way of acclimatizing reporters, allowing them to gain expertise with a particular area or subject matter, and giving them the opportunity to schmooze and develop good relations with key newsmakers. Beats could be defined geographically (such as the West Coast) or topically (for example, health care). In some cases, beats reflect career trajectories; the "prestige" beats are those that guarantee the occupant a regular presence in a paper or broadcast. For national organizations, the three premier beats are the White House, State Department, and Pentagon (sometimes referred to as the *Golden Triangle*); given the newsworthiness of their location, these reporters become household names in a hurry.

Another standard operating procedure of news organizations is to examine and mimic the offerings of the competition. A fixture in any broadcast newsroom is the panel of television monitors playing the newscasts of other stations. As in any other profession, there are leaders and followers. On any typical day, the stories printed on the front page of the *New York Times* invariably appear in the network newscasts. The term *pack journalism* refers to the tendency of high-prestige news organizations to define the daily agenda. Traces of pack journalism are especially visible during the early stages of primary campaigns, when uncertainty over the outcome is the greatest and inexperienced journalists often follow the lead of well-known veterans. In 1968, for instance, in the aftermath of a chaotic Iowa caucus, the scene in the Des Moines newsroom was this:

> Johnny Apple of the *New York Times* sat in a corner and everyone peered over his shoulder to find out what he was writing. The AP guy was looking over

one shoulder, the UPI guy over the other, and CBS, ABC, NBC, and the Baltimore *Sun* were all crowding in behind . . . No one knew how to interpret these figures, what was good and what was bad, and they were taking it off Apple. He would sit down and write a lead, and they would go write leads . . .When he wanted quiet to hear the guy announce the latest returns, he'd shout for quiet and they'd all shut up. (Crouse, 1972, p. 84)

Although *pack journalism* generally refers to a top-down process of influence, at times the logic is reversed and the prestige press chases after purveyors of soft news. Dominick Dunne, who covered the O. J. Simpson case from day one for *Vanity Fair*, emerged as an authoritative source and was quoted extensively in major print and broadcast national outlets.

Sources

Sources are perhaps the most critical elements of the news-gathering process. A basic principle of modern journalism is that news is whatever public officials say it is. As Sigal (1973) states, "Even when the journalist is in a position to observe an event directly, he remains reluctant to offer interpretations of his own, preferring instead to rely on his news sources . . . In short, most news is not what has happened, but what someone says has happened" (p. 69).

Where do reporters go to get the news? In most cases, they do not assemble at the scene of an event, but gravitate instead to sources that can provide authoritative accounts of the event. This practice translates into a dependence on government officials. Most newsworthy issues are the province of government agencies or departments. A famine in Sudan sends reporters straight to the State Department, the latest figures on the trade deficit make the Department of Commerce the news hub, and so on. Even by a conservative count, the overwhelming majority of news stories each day emanates from official sources. In the case of the White House, virtually anything the president does (or fails to do) is news.

Reporters are well aware that official sources often have a vested interest in shaping the news. In the case of obviously partisan sources (such as the chair of the Republican National Committee), reporters maintain their objectivity by relying on countersources from the opposing side of the partisan divide to ensure that the bias is canceled out. However, objective and balanced coverage requires dissent and conflict among official sources. When official sources all speak with one voice, then the press becomes a tool of government. As we will describe in the next chapter, periods of international tension and impending or actual military conflict are typically devoid of open partisan dissent. As a result, at such times reporters become spokespersons for the administration.

The relationship between reporters and sources is complex, often subject to elaborate rituals. In some cases a government official provides information but does not wish to be identified (a "highly placed" source). In other cases, officials seek out reporters to provide information in an attempt either to weaken their policy opponents (the typical case of a "leak") or to test the waters over an impending policy proposal (the "trial balloon"). Shortly before the 2004 Republican National Convention, for example, several news organizations reported that the Bush administration was considering a new space initiative aimed at exploration of Mars. Reaction to these reports was swift and derisive; commentators noted that space exploration seemed an unlikely priority, given that the US budget deficit was at an all-time high. The Bush staff got the message; the president's acceptance speech contained no reference to space exploration initiatives.

In still other cases, the reporter–source relationship becomes a matter of litigation, as in disclosures of information that may threaten national security. The continuing controversy over the revelation by syndicated conservative columnist Robert Novak in 2003 that the wife of a well-known critic of the Bush administration was a CIA agent prompted a grand jury investigation into Novak's source and considerable public speculation about the identity of Novak's "highly placed" source. We defer further discussion of the ways in which official sources attempt to manipulate reporters to Chapter 4.

Conclusion

Contrary to the assertion that the news is simply a mirror image reflection of what happens, we have shown that news content reflects a complex set of interactions between the imperatives of the marketplace and the professional aspirations of journalists. The economic model is by far the more straightforward account: the news is simply what sells. Although there is considerable evidence that economic pressures leave their imprint on the news, there is more to news than the desire to protect the bottom line. No matter what they might say to the contrary, journalists have an agenda; they strive to cover campaigns in ways that maximize their autonomy and, happily for them, increase their own professional visibility.

No one who watches television talk shows will be surprised at the "revolving door" between the regularly invited guests and the list of reporters covering the campaign. Interpretive coverage is defended on the grounds that journalists have a responsibility to protect the public from the machinations of campaign strategists, but it provides considerable side benefits as well. Campaign journalists who project their voices into the news every day not only appear on *Washington Week* or *Larry King Live*; they also command significant book advances from publishers.

One factor conspicuously absent from the commercial-organization process account of news is partisan intent. Contrary to the frequent allegations of ideological bias in news coverage, research suggests that political motives are far less relevant than commercial and organizational pressures.

There are two competing theories of ideologically biased news. Liberal critics see American journalists as captives of their conglomerate owners. The overriding financial interests of corporate owners, in this account, act as disincentives for journalists to write stories exposing questionable business practices, even when these practices harm consumers. Thus, the American media were reluctant to publicize the public health consequences of smoking, for fear of offending an industry that was a major source of advertising revenue.

For every allegation of conservative bias, counterallegations assert that the press is sympathetic to liberal candidates and causes. The media's relentless pursuit of the Watergate scandal led many Republicans to suggest that journalists were motivated by their hostility toward the Nixon administration. Nixon's vice president (Spiro Agnew), for instance, attacked broadcast journalists as "nattering nabobs of negativity" who were out of touch with the "silent majority." (Twenty-five years later, when journalists pursued President Clinton with equal vigor in the course of the Lewinsky scandal, Democrats made much the same argument.) In the eyes of conservatives, the fact that more journalists identify themselves as Democrats than as Republicans is prima facie evidence of liberal bias in the news.

Despite the hue and cry over biased news, the evidence indicates that the American media actually perform quite well according to the criterion of balanced political coverage. Issues and events are typically covered in "point–counterpoint" fashion so that the audience invariably gains exposure to the Democratic and Republican perspective on any given story. Newspaper coverage of American governors, for example, treats incumbents of both parties similarly, providing favorable coverage during periods of falling unemployment and crime rates, but turning critical when real-world conditions deteriorate.

Thus, the real problem facing American journalism is not the intrusion of political motives into editorial decisions, but rather the fact that journalism has become less motivated by the need to inform the public and more intent on taking on dual entertainment and regulatory functions. There is no shortage of compelling factoids on the extent of media shirking. Nationwide, broadcast media offerings in 2003 included less than 1 percent that could be considered (even by a generous definition) public affairs programming, whereas 18 percent was devoted to reality shows and sports events. In the case of local news—admittedly the most deficient outlet—the results are mind-boggling. In 2002, more than half of the top-rated local stations aired newscasts in the seven weeks preceding the election that contained absolutely no reference to the election! By contrast, 70 percent of all network newscasts during the 2000 presidential campaign focused on the horse race. In an ironic role reversal, local television stations in the top one hundred media markets provided more advertising than news during the 2004 campaign.

The fixation on the horse race and strategy catches the attention of the audience while simultaneously providing journalists an edge in their continuing clash with the campaigns to shape the content of the news. In the end, the new style of reporting presents the campaign as theatrics rather than as a genuine clash of ideas. Major campaign events such as debates and conventions are ignored altogether by news organizations with significant market share. Thus, by any stretch of the imagination, modern journalism does not deliver the "marketplace of ideas" that is so vital to the exercise of informed and engaged citizenship. Unfortunately, the verdict is equally pessimistic when we turn to journalism's second potential contribution to the democratic process—namely, serving as a watchdog over the actions of government officials.

CHAPTER 3 SUMMARY

1. Historically, where Americans get their news has depended on the development of new technologies for transmitting information. In the 1920s, radio began to supplant newspapers as the main source of news for most Americans, and radio was itself supplanted by television in the 1950s.

2. The spread of cable television—and more recently the Internet—has transformed the news landscape, but the most serious threat to network news today is local news.

3. The credibility of the media in the eyes of the American public has declined sharply in recent decades.

4. Market forces influence the form and content of news. Market pressures are especially intense in the world of broadcast news, where "soft" news, sitcoms, and reality television shows attract much larger audiences than "serious" news does. News producers adapt to the competition from soft news, sitcoms, and cable talk shows by making their own news programs more entertaining and less serious. The current twenty-four-hour news cycle has also increased pressure, as news organizations strive to deliver the news faster than their competitors do.

5. Organizational processes and the professional principles of journalists also influence what is reported. Modern political journalism rests on two dominant values: objectivity and autonomy. In attempting to protect their autonomy, reporters tend toward a more analytic form of news coverage centered on interpretation and analysis. Ad watches, candidate strategy, the horse race, and scandal stories feature prominently in this kind of coverage.

6. Accessibility and appropriateness also shape news coverage. In terms of everyday news, Washington DC is the center of the universe for most major news organizations and that's where most of their correspondents are stationed (and hence have access to stories). The appropriateness of a story for a particular news outlet also determines whether it will receive coverage; a car crash in Dallas is not news for the *New York Times,* for example. In addition, a story is more likely to be covered by a television news outlet if it generates compelling visual imagery.

7. Finally, the routines and procedures followed by news organizations have substantial impact on the content and form of the news. The pace of the news cycle means that events are more likely to be covered if they occur at some times of the day than at others. Assigning reporters to news beats ensures a steady flow of stories on those beats. And, in covering an event, reporters gravitate to sources that can provide authoritative accounts of the event, which means that they rely on government officials for their information.

FURTHER READINGS

Bagdikian, B. H. (2000). *The media monopoly* (6th ed.). Boston: Beacon.
Baker, C. E. (2002). *Media, markets, and democracy.* New York: Cambridge University Press.

Baum, M. A. (2005). Talking the vote: Why presidential candidates hit the talk show circuit. *American Journal of Political Science, 49*, 213–234.

Crouse, T. (1972). *The boys on the bus.* New York: Random House.

Gilliam, F. D., Jr., & Iyengar, S. (2000). Prime suspects: The influence of local television news on the viewing public. *American Journal of Political Science, 44*, 560–573.

Hallin, D. C. (1986). *The uncensored war: The media and Vietnam.* Berkeley: University of California Press.

Hamilton, J. T. (2003). *All the news that's fit to sell: How the market transforms information into news.* Princeton, NJ: Princeton University Press.

Iyengar, S. (1991). *Is anyone responsible?* Chicago: University of Chicago Press.

Kalb, M. (2001). *One scandalous story: Clinton, Lewinsky, and thirteen days that tarnished American journalism.* New York: Free Press.

McChesney, R. W. (1999). *Rich media, poor democracy: Communication politics in dubious times.* Urbana: University of Illinois Press.

Sigal, L. (1973). *Reporters and officials.* Lexington, MA: Heath.

NOTES

1. After nine years of partnership and the limited success of MSNBC in attracting an audience, Microsoft finally pulled out of the joint venture (Carter, 2005).

2. www.accessabc.com/reader/top100.htm

3. www.nielsenmedia.com/ratings/topnetworktelecasts.htm

4. In recent months Nielsen has had to defend itself against charges of racial bias in audience counts. African-American and Hispanic activists have complained that their communities are underrepresented by Nielsen's metering system, thus resulting in an undercount of the size of minority-oriented programs. The controversy is symptomatic of a more widespread debate provoked by Nielsen data showing that network audiences are diminishing. Naturally, the networks would prefer to see data suggesting the opposite.

5. CNN maintains news bureaus in forty-two countries.

6. The local newscasts used in the comparisons are those that run in the afternoon and evening. The data were provided by Nielsen Media Research.

7. Most media markets resemble oligopolies, with small numbers of news providers controlling the vast share of the market (Baker, 2002; McChesney, 1999).

8. This incident came back to haunt Rather during the 2004 presidential campaign. CBS aired what turned out to be an inaccurate report on President Bush's National Guard service. Critics immediately attributed the report to partisan bias. The blue-ribbon commission that investigated CBS's actions (at the network's own request) concluded that the report was a product of sloppy journalism rather than political bias. Immediately after the release of the report, Rather announced his intention to retire.

9. Respondents are provided with a four-point scale with endpoints of "believe all or most" (of what they encounter in the news source) and "cannot believe." Figure 3.5 shows the sum of the contiguous "all or most" and "almost all or most" categories.

10. In the post-9/11 environment, the US Department of State has attempted to compile statistics on the number of terrorist attacks and casualties on a worldwide basis. As noted in Chapter 4, the department's 2004 report (published in advance of the election) had to be retracted because it was found to underestimate the true level of terrorist activity by a substantial margin.

11. As some scholars have noted, the huge audiences for network news in the 1970s included a nontrivial "inadvertent" component: people who watched the CBS *Evening News* only because they were waiting for their favorite sitcom, which followed.

12. The tsunami coverage of 2004–05 represents an exception to this pattern. The scope of this disaster was so unprecedented that it was the major news story across the world for several weeks.

CHAPTER 4

REPORTERS, OFFICIAL SOURCES, AND THE DECLINE OF ADVERSARIAL JOURNALISM

IN 1974, Bob Woodward and Carl Bernstein, two enterprising reporters at the *Washington Post*, brought about the resignation of an incumbent president. Their systematic exposure of the Watergate cover-up represented the epitome of investigative journalism; a newspaper had single-handedly enforced the standard of honesty in government.

Twenty-four years later, President Clinton emphatically denied allegations that he had had a sexual relationship with a White House intern. His denials were met by an increasingly skeptical press corps, who proceeded to dig deeper into the story and whose efforts ultimately led Congress to initiate impeachment proceedings against the president.

In 2003, the Bush administration decided to invade Iraq, even without the support of key allies and the United Nations. The rationale for American unilateral action rested on two key premises: first, that the regime of Saddam Hussein had the capacity to develop and deliver chemical and biological weapons "in ways that can cause massive death and destruction" (in the words of Secretary of State Colin Powell, speaking at the United Nations in 2003); and second, that the regime was an active collaborator with the Al Qaeda terrorist organization.

What the Bush administration asserted, the press dutifully reported. American journalists accepted the "guilty as charged" claims against Saddam Hussein with little hesitation, despite the opinions of credible international experts to the contrary. One of the country's leading newspapers, the *New*

York Times, published a series of reports that supported the administration's position and used Iraqi expatriates as "corroborating" sources. These same sources (Ahmed Chalabi, for instance) were in fact either employed by American intelligence or harbored aspirations of political power in a post-Hussein Iraq.

The successful invasion of Iraq and overthrow of the Hussein regime was followed by several months of frenzied American efforts to find the Iraqi weapons of mass destruction. Gradually, it became apparent that the weapons did not exist. As for the second alleged threat posed by Iraq—the close relationship with Al Qaeda—the 9/11 Commission and other experts ultimately concluded that, although there were isolated contacts, these did not amount to a "collaborative relationship." Thus, both key premises of the policy of unilateral intervention proved erroneous. Two leading American daily newspapers—the *New York Times* and the *Washington Post*—issued public "apologies" for their failure to investigate the Bush administration's case against Iraq.

What accounts for the striking contrast between the performance of the press during the Watergate and Lewinsky scandals and during the war in Iraq? Why was the press instinctively skeptical when Nixon and Clinton denied wrongdoing, but passively willing to accept the Bush administration's misleading claims concerning the necessity of war with Iraq? The explanation, as outlined in this chapter, is that in matters of national security, the press has been stripped of its ability to act as an adversary of government. Where domestic political events are concerned, the presence of vocal and authoritative critics grants journalists the necessary leverage to question official accounts. On matters of foreign policy and national security, however, critics of government policy tend to fall silent; the press is left with only official sources.

Indexing the News

Inevitably, reporters depend on official sources. Nevertheless, they seek to maintain objectivity in coverage. High-ranking officials, for their part, have a strong political stake in eliciting coverage that reflects favorably on their performance. During political campaigns, these sometimes divergent interests create a basic tension between candidates and journalists that profoundly shapes not only the news coverage of campaigns, but also the content of everyday news as government officials seek to promote their policies while reporters attempt to provide objective and balanced news.

For the press to act as a "fourth branch" of government, journalists must necessarily treat official pronouncements with skepticism. Because they are typically trained as generalists, journalists lack the substantive policy expertise to question or rebut government sources on their own. For critical analysis, they turn to authoritative sources that may provide a fresh perspective on official policies. If the supply of "opposition" sources dries up, journalists have no real choice but to defer to official accounts. The availability of opposition sources generally dwindles in the arenas of foreign policy and national security, especially during periods of national crisis or international conflict. During the heat of crisis, journalists tend to cover the story exactly as it is given to them.

In a news system based on official sources, the "reality" of public policy is the state of official opinion. Reporters attempt to mirror this reality by adjusting their coverage to be in line with the level and intensity of debate among the elites. The higher the level of elite dissent, the easier it is for the reporter to pit competing sources against each other.

In Focus: Indexing the News

Indexing is the process of adjusting coverage of an issue according to the level of disagreement and debate about that issue among policy elites. Indexing is due in large part to the journalistic norms of using official sources and of seeking objectivity by reporting different sides of a debate. If there is conflict among officials, there are opposing viewpoints on which journalists can report and which they can use as a starting point for open debate of the policy in the news. If there is consensus among officials—as there tends to be in foreign policy issues, and particularly in national security crises—there is no reportable conflict, and coverage, when it happens, tends to be deferential.

In practical terms, indexing the news means that the press can represent an adversarial posture only when opponents of government policy outnumber (or prove more vocal than) proponents. On occasions when opponents with stature are not to be found and the government speaks with one voice, the watchdog role falls entirely on reporters. Because reporters have neither the time nor the expertise to critique the views of their sources, elite consensus inevitably slants the news in favor of government policy.

In practice, the indexing system works well for domestic issues (in the sense of allowing reporters to maintain their autonomy from any particular source), but in the domain of foreign policy and national security, it results in near-total official control over the news. For most domestic issues, there exists a variety of politically viable policy alternatives and a corresponding network of competing official sources. Arguments over affirmative action, for instance, range from the complete elimination of race-based preferences to government-funded compensation for the victims of discrimination (such as "reparations"). Any Republican initiative on affirmative action will be met by a chorus of Democratic dissents. Economic issues provide an equally competitive set of sources; as soon as President Bush takes credit for the latest decline in unemployment, the media immediately turn to Democratic officials for the appropriate antidotes (for example, "Last month was fine, but what about the two million lost jobs since Bush took office?").

One layer removed from government, the press can call upon a "second team" of sources drawn from the various think tanks with their stables of former officials, policy entrepreneurs, and academic researchers. Every sound bite from the left-leaning Brookings Institution can be countered by one from the conservative American Enterprise Institute or Americans for Tax Reform. In the case of domestic politics, therefore, journalists have no difficulty resisting official spin. The level of elite disagreement is sufficient to ensure balanced, "objective" reporting.

When foreign policy and national security are the issues of the day, the indexing system breaks down and officials attain substantial control over the flow of news. Traditionally, foreign affairs have not excited partisan divisions; the executive branch enjoys wide latitude to formulate and implement American foreign policy. During the era of the Cold War, for example, there was general bipartisan support for policies designed to resist the spread of international communism. The president exercises tight control over the foreign policy process; White House, State Department, and Pentagon officials offer up a coordinated, uniform take on the events of the day. Moreover, foreign policy events typically occur beyond the geographic reach of most news organizations. Foreign correspondents are few and far between.

The ethnic massacres in the Darfur region of Sudan became a major story for US news organizations only when Secretary of State Colin Powell toured the region in September 2004. Two decades earlier, the deadly famine in Ethiopia came to the attention of Americans only when NBC's London correspondent noticed the vivid footage of starving children in the BBC's coverage of the ongoing humanitarian crisis. These examples illustrate how incumbent officials are typically able to orchestrate the news coverage of foreign affairs.

The state of play between the American press and the foreign policy establishment is exemplified by the treatment accorded the State Department's annual *Patterns of Global Terrorism* report. This report purports to document both the frequency and the severity of terrorist incidents. At the press briefing to announce the release of the 2003 report, Deputy Secretary of State Richard Armitage was on hand to declare, "You will find in these pages clear evidence that we are prevailing in the fight." The data revealed a stunning 40 percent decline in the frequency of terrorist incidents since 2001. According to the numbers, 2003 was the safest year on record since 1969. This rosy assessment of the war against terrorism made big news across the country.

In its April 29, 2004, news story (see Figure 4.1), CNN suggested that the Bush administration was winning the war on terrorism. The following month, in a *Washington Post* op-ed column, two scholars (Alan B. Krueger and David Laitin) identified numerous flaws in the State Department's report. All the observed decrease in terrorist activity had occurred within the category of "nonsignificant" events. Significant terrorist attacks (defined as those causing injury and loss of life) had in fact *increased* by about a third— from 124 in 2001 to 169 in 2003. This revised "scorecard" obviously reflected less favorably on the administration.

In response to the Krueger–Laitin "rebuttal," the State Department was forced to acknowledge the errors and prepare a corrected report. The revised report conceded that the level of terrorism had in fact risen since 2001. To the highest-ranking counterterrorism official in the department, Ambassador J. Cofer Black, the errors represented database problems, not political spin:

> I want to be very clear: we here in the Counterterrorism Office, and I per-
> sonally, should have caught any errors that marred the *Patterns* draft before
> we published it. But I assure you and the American people that the errors in
> the *Patterns* report were honest mistakes, and certainly not deliberate decep-
> tions as some have speculated. (US Dept. of State, 2004)

The case of the botched terrorism report epitomizes press performance in the national security area. The evidence in question was a simple list of events, not complex statistical analysis. The fact that the report failed to include major terrorist attacks that occurred after November 11 (such as the bombing of the British consulate and HSBC bank headquarters in Istanbul, in which twenty-five people died) should have been obvious to anyone with access to a calendar. Reporters initially failed to ask appropriate questions or engage in elementary background research; instead, they deferred to the credibility of the US State Department.

FIGURE 4.1 **CNN COVERAGE OF THE STATE DEPARTMENT REPORT ON IRAQ AND TERRORISM**

CNN.com.

Worldwide terrorist attacks down in 2003

Report: Iraq now 'a central battleground' in war on terror

From David Ensor and Elise Labott
CNN Washington Bureau

WASHINGTON (CNN) -- International acts of terror in 2003 were the fewest in more than 30 years, according to the U.S. State Department's annual terrorism report released Thursday.

The Patterns of Global Terrorism report said ˜ 90 acts of international terrorism occurred in 2003 — a slight drop from ˜ 98 attacks the previous year and the lowest total since 1969.

The figure marked a 45 percent decrease in attacks since 2001, but it did not include most of the attacks in Iraq, because attacks against combatants did not fit the U.S. definition of international terrorism.

Cofer Black, the State Department's ambassador at large for counterterrorism, told a news conference that he attributed the decrease to "unprecedented collaboration between the United States and foreign partners to defeat terrorism."

Source: CNN, 2004.

National Security News: The Triumph of Official Journalism

In comparison with foreign policy, national security matters provide officials with even more control over the press. When the United States resorts to military force, opposing elites generally close ranks behind the president. For fear of appearing unpatriotic, leaders of the "out" party choose not to criticize the administration's actions. The nation—at least as far as the media are concerned—stands united behind the men and women in uniform. Because potential opponents of the use of military force fall silent, the press becomes completely dependent on official spokespersons. In the aftermath of the September 11 attacks, nobody in Washington was willing to question the decision to overthrow the Taliban regime in Afghanistan. And when the Bush administration proposed the USA PATRIOT Act, a measure that would significantly erode Americans' civil liberties, it passed the US Senate by a vote of ninety-nine to one.

NEWS COVERAGE OF THE VIETNAM WAR: A CASE STUDY OF INDEXING

During the early period of media politics in the 1960s, the first real test of the media's ability to challenge official accounts was the war in Vietnam. In August 1964, the Johnson administration claimed that American navy vessels cruising in the Gulf of Tonkin had been deliberately attacked by North Vietnamese gunboats in two distinct incidents. The president ordered retaliatory air strikes and requested a joint resolution of Congress granting him the power to "take all necessary measures to repel any armed attack against the forces of the United States and to prevent further aggression." The Gulf of Tonkin Resolution, passed in 1964 by overwhelming majorities in the House and Senate, became the principal legal basis for expanding US military involvement in South Vietnam.

The news media did little to question the administration's account of the North Vietnamese attacks, instead deferring entirely to the Pentagon. The major American news magazines, for instance, described the attacks as follows:

> As the "night glowed eerily," wrote *Time*, the Communist "intruders boldly sped" toward the destroyers, firing with "automatic weapons," while *Life* had the American ships "under continuous torpedo attack" as they "weaved through the night sea, evading more torpedoes." Not to be outdone, *Newsweek* described "US jets diving, strafing, flattening out . . . and diving again" at the enemy boats, one of which "burst into flames and sank." (Karnow, 1997, pp. 386–387)

Later it was revealed that there was only one torpedo attack and that the Vietnamese gunboats had, in fact, been provoked.

As American military involvement in South Vietnam increased, news organizations assigned reporters to file stories from the immediate vicinity of the conflict. These reporters found themselves relatively free to roam the country in search of news stories. Despite firsthand access to events, press accounts of the war in the early and mid-1960s proved entirely consistent with official US policy. Reporters suggested that the strategy of training the South Vietnamese to defend themselves ("Vietnamization") was working effectively, that heavy losses were being inflicted each day on the communist

Vietcong, and that American bombing of North Vietnam was necessary to disrupt the flow of supplies and personnel down the Ho Chi Minh trail.

Not only was the coverage supportive of stated American policy, but in a harbinger of what would occur later, news reports also avoided details and depiction of military combat. According to Braestrup's (1977) systematic compilation of network news coverage of the Vietnam War, less than 5 percent of all stories that aired on the evening news showed images of battle or American casualties. As described by media critic Michael Arlen (1969), the nightly news provided a

> stylized generally distanced overview of a disjointed conflict which was composed mainly of scenes of helicopters landing, tall grasses blowing in the helicopter wind, American soldiers fanning out across a hillside on foot, rifles at the ready, with now and then [on the sound track] a far-off ping or two, and now and then [as the grand visual finale] a column of dark billowing smoke a half mile away invariably described as a burning Viet Cong ammo dump. (p. 113)

Thus the viewing audience had little reason to be concerned.

As the war continued and the American death toll mounted, the Washington consensus over Vietnam unraveled. Senator Eugene McCarthy, the most vocal critic of the war, challenged President Johnson for the 1968 Democratic presidential nomination. McCarthy's competitive showing in the New Hampshire primary (he received 41 percent of the vote) signaled unambiguously that his antiwar message was politically viable. In mid March, Senator Robert Kennedy entered the presidential race. On March 31, realizing that the unpopularity of the war had made it increasingly difficult for him to wage a winning campaign, President Johnson announced that he would not seek reelection. Suddenly Vietnam had transformed the American political landscape.

The emergence of multiple critics of the war was prompted not merely by the reading of the New Hampshire "tea leaves." There was also high drama in Vietnam. In January 1968, with apparent impunity, the Vietcong launched a full-scale military offensive, including a major assault on the US embassy in Saigon and coordinated attacks on major American military bases across the country. The Tet offensive and the American counteroffensive became huge news stories; images of napalmed villages, dead and maimed civilians, and American troops under intense enemy fire began to air regularly on television news, as illustrated in Video Feature 4.1.

VIDEO
FEATURE 4.1
Vietnam
Coverage,
1968–1970

The Tet offensive and resulting images on the television screen cast serious doubt on the official accounts of the war. Reporters began to question Pentagon officials more aggressively in an effort to contrast the clinical tone of the daily Pentagon briefings with the bloody chaos on the ground. An increasing number of elected officials from both political parties defected to the antiwar position. Mirroring the shift in elite opinion, news reports from Vietnam became less tied to information provided by the US mission in Saigon (whose daily briefings came to be ridiculed as the "Five O'Clock Follies") and more focused on communist successes on the battlefield and the rapidly growing antiwar movement in the United States. By late 1968, the indexing process had kicked in and was producing full-fledged adversarial news.

In summary, news coverage of the Vietnam War provides a clear case of elite opinion leading the news in situations of both consensus and dissent. When Presidents Johnson and Nixon encountered minimal resistance to their military policies, press coverage toed the official line. As soon as well-known Americans made public their opposition to the war and the course of events on the battlefield began to clash with statements from Washington, deferential reliance on official sources gave way to coverage that was more aggressively critical of official policy.

THE LESSONS OF VIETNAM: RESTRICTED PRESS ACCESS

To policy planners in the Defense Department, the lessons of Vietnam were clear: unrestrained battlefield coverage by the media—and especially by television news—could hamstring US strategy, primarily by weakening public support for military conflict. In the future, military officials would need to orchestrate the news more carefully.[1] The first step was to deny reporters access to the war zone, thereby forcing them to rely on official briefings. This more controlled approach was first exercised in 1983 with the American invasion of Grenada.

In October 1983, the elected government of the tiny Caribbean island of Grenada was overthrown by a group of leftist rebels. The former prime minister and several of his associates were killed. The new leaders declared themselves Marxists and appealed to Fidel Castro for assistance. American reaction to the coup was swift and predictable. Washington condemned the developments and declared that the installation of a communist government within the Americas was a violation of the Monroe Doctrine and incompatible with US national security interests. The administration cited the presence of Cuban military "advisors" and their efforts to expand the runways at Point Salines Airport as evidence of the new regime's hostile intent.

The fact that the leaders of the Grenada coup were communists was not the sole basis for intervention. A more urgent concern was the presence of American civilians on the island. St. George's University School of Medicine in Grenada, although unaccredited in the United States, attracted a substantial enrollment of American students. With lingering memories of the 1979 hostage crisis in Iran, the Reagan administration decided to preempt a potential hostage situation by invading Grenada. American marines landed on October 25 (accompanied by a small contingent of soldiers from neighboring Caribbean nations) and arrested the rebel leaders with minimal loss of American life. The original constitution was reinstated.

Major news organizations reacted to the events in Grenada by hurriedly assembling news crews to report from the scene. Hundreds of American reporters attempted to make their way to Grenada. The Pentagon refused to give them access, citing national security concerns. Some newspapers then chartered their own boats in a last-ditch effort to get reporters to the front line. Most of these boats were intercepted and turned back by the American navy. The four American reporters who were based in Grenada accepted an offer from military commanders to file their reports from the USS *Guam*, anchored off the coast of Grenada, only to find that the offer was a hoax. The reporters were prevented from leaving the ship for two days.

In response to mounting media pressure, the Pentagon granted access to fifteen reporters, but they were not permitted to file reports from the immediate area of the fighting. Thus, in the first few days of the conflict, the only information delivered to the American public consisted of official briefings and film clips produced by the military. Finally, five days after the invasion, the military granted general press access to all locations in Grenada.[2]

By preventing the press from covering the invasion and then spoon-feeding images and information that depicted American actions in the most favorable light (such as video of "rescued" American students kissing American soil on their return), the Reagan administration maintained complete control over the story. For the entire period before the president announced on national television that the threat to American security had been removed, American news organizations had been kept in the dark, unable to file independent reports on the situation in Grenada. The president appeared on national television accompanied by the prime minister of one of the neighboring islands, who enthusiastically commended the decisive action taken by the United States. In the days that followed, President Reagan's popularity increased by some 5 percentage points.

Some months after the invasion, several elements of the administration's story line came into question. The airport development was funded by a consortium of European and American companies, as well as by the Cubans. The runway expansion was designed to permit the landing of jumbo jets, thus increasing the volume of tourist traffic. It turned out that the number of Cuban troops in Grenada was less than half that claimed by the administration. The "urgent request" for US intervention from Grenada's neighbors was solicited rather than spontaneous. Several of the American medical students came forward to state that they had never been at risk. By the time these discrepancies came to light, however, the press had turned its attention to other matters and no real harm was done to President Reagan's credibility. From the perspective of the White House, the strategy of restricting press access had its intended effect; the Reagan administration's account of daily events held sway. In the words of former ABC Pentagon correspondent John McWethy:

> When you are in a situation where your primary source of information is the United States government and where, for three days, basically your only source of information except Radio Cuba is the Pentagon, you are totally at their mercy and you have to make an assumption that the US government is telling the truth. You report that Caspar Weinberger, then the Secretary of Defense, says "the fighting was heaviest here," or Weinberger says "the barracks are under siege." Well, you believe it. What are you going to do? You report what he says. (Ansolabehere, Behr, & Iyengar, 1993, p. 197)

THE LESSONS OF GRENADA: MEDIA POOLS

In the aftermath of Grenada and the venting of considerable outrage over "censorship" of the press, the Pentagon was asked to undertake a review of its press access policies. The government appointed a blue-ribbon commission consisting of military and press representatives to study the issue of press access to military combat. The panel recommended a pool system for covering future military operations. The press would be granted access, but only in the form of closely supervised *media pools*—small groups of reporters representing several print and broadcast news organizations who would work under close supervision of the Defense Department. One camera crew, for instance, would provide all the video footage for the major networks.

In Focus: Media Pools

In an effort to limit media access without incurring charges of censorship, the Pentagon revised its policy about media access to war zones in 1989. The press would be granted access, but only in the form of closely supervised *media pools*—small groups of reporters representing several print and broadcast news organizations who would work under close supervision of the Defense Department. The pool reporters' coverage is made available for use by all recognized news organizations.

Initially used in the 1989 American invasion of Panama, the pool system became fully institutionalized in 1991 with the onset of Operation Desert Storm, the campaign to liberate Kuwait from Iraqi occupation. Pool reporters were allowed to cover events in Kuwait, but because they were not permitted to stray from Kuwait City, their independent news-gathering ability was limited to question-and-answer sessions following the daily military briefings. Pooled reports were subject to military approval; in several cases (for example, a story about American pilots watching pornographic videos before their missions), stories were censored or altered. In a telling acknowledgment of the power of visual imagery, photographs of body bags or coffins were prohibited.

In addition to rationing access, the Pentagon gave more careful attention to its choreographed daily presentations for the press. The military officers responsible for briefing the press put on a multimedia performance each day. Not only did film of American "smart" bombs or missiles hitting their intended targets with unerring accuracy demonstrate the military's concern for minimizing Iraqi civilian casualties, but the images also provided compelling material for television newscasts. By relaying the official videos as news, television news spread the message of a clinical and sanitized war effort, devoid of all civilian suffering. In the words of one media critic, "The emphasis was on the nuts and bolts of a sophisticated war machine, but the consequences were never made plain. In other words, television portrayed the war as a war without victims . . . Indeed, the press as a whole bought into the notion that this was somehow a kinder and gentler war" (Dorman, 1997, p. 121).

Another objective of the Pentagon media managers was to elicit news coverage that followed the official story line of Iraq as the transgressor, Kuwait as the victim, and the United States as the law enforcer. Saddam Hussein was depicted as a modern-day Hitler whose occupying forces had engaged in wanton destruction of Kuwaiti natural resources (such as setting oil fields ablaze) and brutal atrocities against Kuwaiti civilians. Adding to the Pentagon's media management efforts, the exiled rulers of Kuwait retained the well-known public relations firm of Hill & Knowlton to spread the word of numerous Iraqi violations of international law during the occupation. In one particularly vicious case, Iraqi soldiers were alleged to have looted a pediatric hospital in Kuwait City and disconnected hundreds of infants from life support equipment. Hill & Knowlton even produced an eyewitness who described the incident in detail to a congressional committee. In contrast to the Iraqis, who were depicted as demonstrating minimal concern for endangering civilian life, the American and coalition forces were portrayed as minimizing "collateral damage" in their bombing of Iraq. Thus, on all fronts, news coverage of the war accentuated the positive.

Once again, official accounts of the war went unchallenged. It was not until several months later that reports surfaced of the failure of several "smart" weapons systems. During the war, the administration claimed that its Patriot missiles had intercepted and destroyed forty-one of forty-two airborne Iraqi Scud missiles. But an independent study by MIT Professors Theodore Postol and George Lewis concluded that the Patriot had failed to disable the Scud warhead in every instance. Contrary to what the videos that were played at the press briefings implied, the coalition bombing campaign had inflicted significant damage to civilian areas of Baghdad. An estimated thirty-five hundred Iraqi civilians were killed (Conetta, 2003). In addition, Hussein's alleged mass murder of Kuwaiti children was retracted; instead of the three hundred alleged victims, only one could be confirmed.

The various "corrections" to the official record were reported by the press, but only long after the war had receded from national attention. The 1992 presidential campaign was under way, and stories about the failing American economy and the surprisingly strong candidacy of an unknown governor from Arkansas took precedence over revised claims of American military and technological prowess or fabricated eyewitness testimony concerning the behavior of Iraqi soldiers.

A REFINEMENT OF MEDIA POOLS: EMBEDDED JOURNALISTS

In the most recent iteration of the national security media script, the Pentagon decided that it was no longer politically feasible to deny American reporters firsthand access to the 2003 invasion of Iraq. In a modernized version of pooled coverage, a select group of American and international correspondents were to be "embedded" with the invading forces. While accompanying the coalition forces into battle, the embedded reporters would be subject to strict restrictions on the content of their reports; they could not, for instance, discuss operational details, nor could they make any slight reference to information that might be of strategic value. These guidelines were enforced; Geraldo Rivera, one of the embedded correspondents for Fox News, was expelled from Iraq for drawing a map of the mission in the sand.

As anticipated by the Pentagon, news reports filed by the embedded correspondents provided close-up and often dramatic footage of American troops in action. The public was given a "live" progress report of the invasion from the perspective of American soldiers, but without coverage of Americans killed in action or of civilians caught up in the fighting. The Project for Excellence in Journalism (cited in Entman, 2004, p. 116) studied embedded correspondents' reports on the major networks; not a single report showed images of people being killed by American soldiers (see Video Feature 4.2).

VIDEO
FEATURE 4.2
Reports from
Embedded
Correspon-
dents in the
Iraq War

Once hostilities commenced, the inability of the press to counter official accounts of daily events was understandable: the Pentagon exercised its monopoly control over information. Briefings by the secretary of defense and other high-ranking military officials were the major sources of news. In the case of American television newscasts, the coverage was thoroughly dominated by current and former government officials. The media watchdog group Fairness & Accuracy In Reporting (FAIR) tracked all references to Iraq in four daily network newscasts (aired by ABC, CBS, NBC, and PBS) over a two-week period that ended one week after Secretary of State Colin Powell's speech at the United Nations in which he insisted that Iraq possessed weapons of mass destruction. During this period, broadcast news reports made reference to 393 sources. As expected, the great majority (68 percent) of the sources were Americans. Even more striking, three-fourths of the Americans interviewed in these programs were current or former government officials. Only one official (Senator Edward Kennedy) was opposed to the war. Even when the networks invited non-Americans, they were drawn overwhelmingly (75 percent) from countries that supported the Bush administration's position on Iraq. Only 4 percent of the foreign sources expressed opposition to the war.[3]

In recruiting their nonofficial sources, the American networks showed only slightly less pro-administration bias. Of the ninety-six private citizens who commented on Iraq, 26 percent expressed skepticism about the war— a level of opposition that considerably understated opposition among the public at large. In contrast to the government sources, who were generally high-ranking officials, half of the nonofficial skeptics were unidentified "persons in the street."

In short, network news coverage of the war during the period when many Americans were uncertain of their position was skewed in the direction of official policy. Even PBS, the network lampooned by conservatives as a left-ist news source, featured a 4-to-1 ratio of war proponents to opponents in their coverage of Iraq. Given the daily exposure to such one-sided coverage, it's no wonder that American public opinion became increasingly supportive of the administration's war plans.

Still more glaring press failures occurred prior to the onset of hostilities. The Bush administration's policy of unilateral intervention rested on the premise that the regime of Saddam Hussein represented a significant military threat to the international community. According to American intelligence accounts, Iraq possessed significant stockpiles of chemical and biological weapons. As Secretary of State Colin Powell stated in his February 2003 address to the UN General Assembly,[4] "There can be no doubt that Saddam Hussein has biological weapons and the capability to rapidly produce more, many more. And he has the ability to dispense these lethal poisons and diseases in ways that can cause massive death and destruction."

What is especially troubling is that these claims went unchallenged by the mainstream press, despite vociferous challenges from credible, international experts. For instance, on the very same day that President Bush referred to Iraqi efforts to obtain uranium for use in the production of nuclear weapons (a claim that was later acknowledged to be false), the deputy head of the UN inspections program held a press conference to debunk the alleged evidence of a renewed Iraqi nuclear program. More generally, months of sustained UN inspections had turned up no traces of the Iraqi weapons of mass destruction. David Kay, one of the UN inspectors later recruited to head the postwar American detection effort (euphemistically titled the "Iraq Study Group"), resigned in January 2004, stating that he did not believe Iraq had stockpiles of chemical or biological weapons.

In short, in the period leading up to war and continuing thereafter, the press had several opportunities to subject the administration's rationale for war to greater scrutiny. For the most part, these opportunities were squandered. Later, as the true extent of the discrepancies between the facts and official accounts became transparent, the *New York Times* and the *Washington Post* issued hard-hitting "apologies" for their generally one-sided coverage. In indicting their own judgment, the *Times* editors were brutally honest:

> The problematic articles varied in authorship and subject matter, but many shared a common feature. They depended at least in part on information from a circle of Iraqi informants, defectors and exiles bent on "regime change" in Iraq, people whose credibility has come under increasing public

debate in recent weeks. (The most prominent of the anti-Saddam campaigners, Ahmad Chalabi, has been named as an occasional source in *Times*
articles since at least 1991, and has introduced reporters to other exiles. He
became a favorite of hard-liners within the Bush administration and a paid
broker of information from Iraqi exiles, until his payments were cut off last
week.) Complicating matters for journalists, the accounts of these exiles
were often eagerly confirmed by United States officials convinced of the need
to intervene in Iraq. Administration officials now acknowledge that they
sometimes fell for misinformation from these exile sources. So did many
news organizations—in particular, this one.

Some critics of our coverage during that time have focused blame on
individual reporters. Our examination, however, indicates that the problem
was more complicated. Editors at several levels who should have been challenging reporters and pressing for more skepticism were perhaps too intent
on rushing scoops into the paper. Accounts of Iraqi defectors were not
always weighed against their strong desire to have Saddam Hussein ousted.
Articles based on dire claims about Iraq tended to get prominent display,
while follow-up articles that called the original ones into question were
sometimes buried. In some cases, there was no follow-up at all. ("From the
Editors," 2004)

Conclusion

The outcome of the indexing system of calibrating the news to represent the
state of elite debate depends on several circumstances. Clearly, when the
focus is on the imminent use of American military force, the president's views
are especially likely to dominate. Reporters feel free to ignore congressional
leaders or international elites as sources because they know that the relevant
decision makers are located at the White House and Pentagon. But when war
is not imminent, when there is no clear security threat, or when American
military power is used to facilitate humanitarian foreign aid (as was the case
in Somalia in 1992), reporters are able to spread their news nets more widely
and the coverage is less biased in favor of the administration.

The outcome of the indexing process also depends on elites' political calculations. When the country is on the verge of war and the conflict has been
broadly portrayed as involving the national interest, critics of the president
risk being seen as unpatriotic. A 1994 study by Zaller shows that congressional Democrats were reluctant to openly question the George H. W. Bush

administration's aggressive response to the Iraqi invasion of Kuwait because they feared reinforcing the stereotype of their party as "soft" on national defense. However, when the president undertakes actions that do not fit the standard script of "good versus evil" or when the president's actions meet with strong international opposition from our traditional allies, as was the case with the Reagan administration's decision to bomb targets in Libya, press accounts tend to be more critical, both because opposing elites are more willing to speak out in opposition and because the press can cite the views of disgruntled American allies.

At other times, despite the prevalence of indexing, the press is able to express muted criticism of official policy. Despite elite consensus on the need for American military action, the press can resort to horse race–type handicapping of the impending hostilities. In the case of the 1991 Persian Gulf conflict, for example, news reports were rife with accounts suggesting that President Bush's political standing and reelection prospects might be seriously jeopardized if Iraqi forces offered stiff resistance or if Kuwait became a "quagmire." Similarly, journalists offered a variety of contextual critiques focusing on possible unintended outcomes of war in the Middle East (such as the elevation of Saddam Hussein to martyr status). However, these manifestations of press objectivity did not venture so far as to question the basic premises of US policy. As Althaus (2003) notes, "No journalist ever questioned the demonization of Saddam Hussein. No journalist ever hinted that the United States had taken an inappropriately aggressive posture toward a regional conflict. . . . At no time did a journalist question whether Iraq's chemical, biological or nuclear capability presented a real threat to the Western world in the foreseeable future" (p. 396).

Finally, there is the possibility that technology may compromise political elites' ability to manage the news. We noted in Chapter 3 that widespread use of videophones has provided reporters with immediate access to breaking events in far-flung locales. And the equally widespread use of digital photography has increased the number of eyewitnesses who may serve as news sources. The graphic photographs of prisoner abuse at Abu Ghraib were taken by American service personnel, who transmitted them via cell phone. Once the photographs had been obtained by the press, the Defense Department was forced to acknowledge the atrocities and begin an official investigation. More generally, immediate access to the scene of an event strengthens journalists' ability to resist the official story line. If "event-driven" reporting becomes more common, the indexing process will no longer produce a one-sided pattern of international and defense-related news.

No matter how balanced the outcome of the indexing process, news coverage that is pegged to official sources threatens the ability of the press to maintain an adversarial stance toward government. During periods of military conflict, the silence of opposition sources inevitably results in a "journalism of deference to the national security state" (Dorman, 1997, p. 124). Even worse, "journalism that indexes debate in Washington violates not just the watchdog ideal, but also the mirror ideal. For under the indexing rule, the journalistic mirror is held up not to reality, but to official interpretations of reality" (Mermin, 1999, p. 145).

We began this chapter by contrasting Watergate with the war against Iraq. The differences between domestic politics and foreign policy are undeniably responsible for the wide gap in press performance in these two instances. International issues have generally proved to be of little interest to Americans, thus encouraging editors to place more emphasis on stories that "sell." But the diminished adversarial capacity of the press can also be attributed to the general development of media politics. That is, the relationship between reporters and government sources has changed substantially since Watergate. Officials in all branches of government have become sensitized to the importance of the media to their ability to govern. Press secretaries, media liaisons, and public relations specialists are now ensconced in every government agency or office. Officials seize every opportunity to present their actions in the most favorable light possible. When news coverage or the course of events is not to their liking, they resort to various strategies (such as leaking information or staging events) for regaining control over the message. These strategies are the subject of Chapter 7.

Before we take up media strategy, however, we must first examine a major change in the media landscape: the proliferation of media sources brought on by the rapid spread of information technology. Chapter 5 will examine the consequences of the revolution in information technology for the practice of media politics. How does the availability of more media choices affect the public's exposure to public affairs programming, and does the rapid spread of the Internet change the way in which political organizations mobilize their supporters for political action?

CHAPTER 4 SUMMARY

1. As coverage of the 2003 invasion of Iraq illustrates, the media tend to be less adversarial in dealing with national security and foreign policy than in dealing with domestic issues.

2. One explanation for the media's less adversarial stance is indexing. In a news system based on official sources, reporters' coverage of issues mirrors the level and intensity of elite debate. The higher the level of elite dissent, the easier it is for the reporter to pit competing sources against each other. Where domestic political events are concerned, the presence of vocal and authoritative critics grants journalists the necessary leverage to question official accounts. On matters of foreign policy, however, critics of government policy tend to fall silent and the press is left with only official sources.

3. National security matters provide officials with even more control over the press. When the United States resorts to military force, opposing elites generally close ranks behind the president, for fear of appearing unpatriotic. Because potential opponents of the use of military force fall silent, the press becomes completely dependent on official spokespersons.

4. After the Vietnam War, the Pentagon and the Defense Department strove to restrict media access to areas of US military action. There was considerable outrage over "censorship" of the press after it was discovered that the Reagan administration had misled the media and the public about the invasion of Grenada. As a result, the Pentagon revised its policy about media access to war zones; the press would be granted access, but only in the form of closely supervised media pools.

5. In contrast to its approach during the 1991 Gulf War, the Pentagon decided that it was no longer politically feasible to deny American reporters first-hand access to the 2003 invasion of Iraq. In a modernized version of pooled coverage, a select group of American and international correspondents were to be "embedded" with the invading forces. The embedded reporters, however, were still subject to severe restrictions on the content of their reports.

FURTHER READINGS

Althaus, S. (2003). When news norms collide, follow the lead: New evidence for press independence. *Political Communication, 20,* 381–414.

Bennett, W. L. (1990). Toward a theory of press-state relations. *Journal of Communication,40,* 103–125.

Cook, T. E. (1994). Domesticating a crisis: Washington newsbeats and the network news after the Iraq invasion of Kuwait. In W. L. Bennett and D. L. Paletz (Eds.), *Taken by storm: The media, public opinion, and U.S. foreign policy in the Gulf War* (pp. 105–130). Chicago: University of Chicago Press.

Dorman, W. A. (1997). Press theory and journalistic practice: The case of the Gulf War. In S. Iyengar & R. Reeves (Eds.), *Do the media govern? Politicians, voters and reporters in America* (pp. 118–125). Thousand Oaks, CA: Sage.

Frenznick, D. A. (1992). The First Amendment on the battlefield: A constitutional analysis of press access to military operations in Grenada, Panama and the Persian Gulf. *Pacific Law Journal,23*, 315–359.

Mermin, J. (1999). *Debating war and peace: Media coverage of U.S. intervention in the post-Vietnam era.* Princeton, NJ: Princeton University Press.

Sigal, L. (1973). *Reporters and officials.* Lexington, MA: Heath.

Zaller, J. R. (1994). Elite leadership of mass opinion: New evidence from the Gulf War. In W. L. Bennett and D. L. Paletz (Eds.), *Taken by storm: The media, public opinion, and U.S. foreign policy in the Gulf War* (pp. 186–209). Chicago: University of Chicago Press.

Zaller, J. R., & Chiu, D. (2000). Government's little helper: U.S. press coverage of foreign policy crises, 1946–1999. In B. L. Nacos, R. Y. Shapiro, & P. Isernia (Eds.), *Decisionmaking in a glass house: Mass media, public opinion, and American foreign policy in the 21st Century* (pp. 61–84). Lanham, MD: Rowman & Littlefield.

NOTES

1. In fact, conclusions about the pivotal role of television news in "turning" public opinion against the Vietnam War are mistaken. In the first place, as described earlier, coverage faithfully reflected the state of American elite opinion. Second, as Mueller (1973) has documented, trends in public support for war were no different for Vietnam and Korea, despite the lack of television coverage during the Korean War.

2. This account rests on David Frenznick's (1992) authoritative history of military–press relations in the United States.

3. The sheer number of sources may underestimate the degree of pro-administration slant in the news. For instance, a 1996 study by Althaus, Edy, Entman, and Phalen of *New York Times* coverage of the 1986 US air strikes against Libya found that foreign sources and American government sources were equally represented in the news. However, the same study documented a more subtle indicator of pro-administration coverage: opposition sources were consistently positioned after administration sources within the same news report.

4. Reproduced at www.whitehouse.gov/news/releases/2003/02/20030205-1.html.

CHAPTER 5

THE RISE OF NEW MEDIA

THE REVOLUTION IN INFORMATION TECHNOLOGY has altered not only the shape of the media landscape, but also the very concept of communication. The traditional forms of communication were either *point-to-point* (between a single sender and recipient) or *broadcast* (between a single sender and multiple recipients). Most senders did not have ready access to broadcast forms of communication and could not reach a significant audience. Traditional media were also limited to a single form (print, audio, or video).

The development of the Internet permitted simultaneous point-to-point and broadcast forms of communication for the first time, and it provided individual users with easy access to an unlimited audience. Every individual on the network of computers making up the World Wide Web is both a sender and a receiver. Any user of the Internet can direct e-mail messages to individual recipients and at the same time communicate with a worldwide audience by hosting a Web site, posting a message on a message board, or participating in an online chat room. Moreover, unlike conventional media, Internet-based communication is multichannel, allowing the free transmission of text, voice, still images, and video.

The pace of the proliferation of information technology has astonished all observers. The Pew Research Center has regularly tracked Americans' use of the Internet since 1995. Survey respondents are asked if they "ever go online to access the Internet and receive e-mail." Even allowing for some inflation in self-reported results, the increase over time in the percentage of Americans who say they go online is striking (see Figure 5.1).

Ten years ago, a mere 14 percent of adult Americans said they used the Internet. By the turn of the century, the figure had more than tripled to half the population. Continuing on this steep slope, between 1999 and 2005 the share

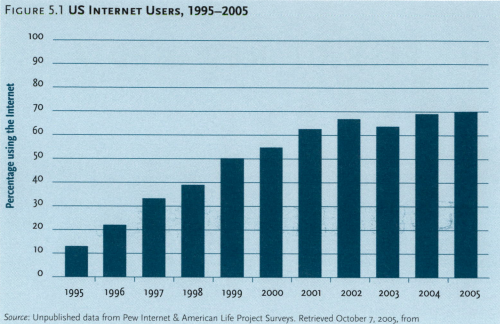

FIGURE 5.1 **US INTERNET USERS, 1995–2005**

Source: Unpublished data from Pew Internet & American Life Project Surveys. Retrieved October 7, 2005, from www.pewinternet.org/trends/uageovertime.xls.

of the online population expanded even further to reach 70 percent. In the span of a decade, self-reported Internet use has increased by a stunning 500 percent.

The availability of information technology to a majority of the population has created a booming Internet economy. In the case of media organizations, hundreds of news sites now compete with each other and with the offerings of political parties, candidates, interest groups, think tanks, and virtually anybody with anything to say about politics. Millions of people visit Internet news sites on a regular basis; as of early 2005, nearly one in three Internet users read a newspaper online. Figure 5.2 lists the ten news sites with the largest weekly traffic, as measured by Nielsen//NetRatings.

Although the numbers suggest that the "legacy" (pre-Internet) news organizations now attract a much larger audience online than in their conventional forms (in the case of the *New York Times*, online "circulation" is nearly ten times greater than print circulation), it is difficult to know the actual extent of online news consumption. Readers of the online edition of the *New York Times* spend an average of fifteen minutes a day on the site.[1] Whether this usage is more or less extensive or efficient than traditional readership and whether it displaces traditional readership is unknown (as we'll discuss).

The proliferation of Internet technology and use is not, of course, confined to the dissemination of news. Any of the major Internet search engines, for

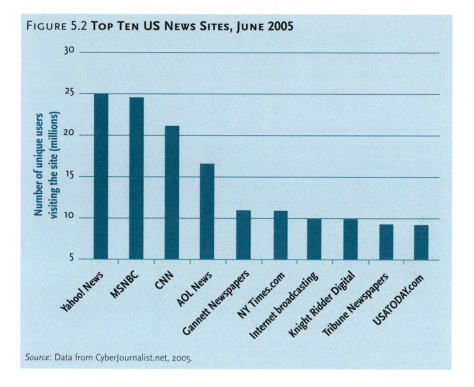

FIGURE 5.2 TOP TEN US NEWS SITES, JUNE 2005

Source: Data from CyberJournalist.net, 2005.

instance, records weekly traffic that far exceeds the online audience for CNN or the *New York Times*. And if we compare news sites with popular shopping sites as a means of assessing competing user interests, we find that the news organizations do not fare well. A typical visitor to eBay, for example, spends more than an hour browsing the site.

Given the speed with which information technology has spread, research into the effects of new media use on individuals, markets, and institutions is still in its infancy. For scholars of media politics, there are two central questions. First, how has increased access to the Internet affected the behavior of consumers of news? Second, what is the potential impact of new forms of "social technology" on the ability of political organizations to recruit and mobilize individual supporters? In the discussion that follows, we will address each of these questions in turn.

Effects of New Media on News Consumers

There are two schools of thought concerning the potential impact of new media on the end user. *Optimists* see technology as a means of revitalizing the public sphere. By providing direct and immediate access to diverging political perspectives, the Internet should enhance the ability of ordinary people to follow events and to participate in the political process. The hope is that even modest levels of online news consumption will build civic awareness and engagement. Former vice president Al Gore epitomized this view when he declared that the coming Internet would bring about "robust and sustainable economic progress, strong democracies, better solutions to global and local environmental challenges, improved health care, and—ultimately—a greater sense of shared stewardship of our small planet."[2]

Skeptics, on the other hand, warn that information technology is no panacea for the limitations of conventional news programming and the weak demand for political information. If "serious" news coverage cannot attract television viewers, why should it draw people online? If Americans are not used to reading or watching foreign media, is there any reason to suppose that they will suddenly access the BBC or the Press Trust of India just because it's possible to do so? Pessimists think not. They believe that the Internet will actually discourage consumers from devoting time to news programming (whether Internet or conventional) in favor of more engaging pursuits, such as online shopping, dating, or keeping in touch. As people become more fluent in the ways of the Web, they may become more personally isolated, preferring "surfing alone" over community involvement or social interaction. Quite possibly, the net effect of technology could be to weaken community and civic engagement.

Quite apart from the question of whether Internet technology will increase or decrease the average time devoted to public affairs content is the question of whether the Internet will, in practice, be used to broaden users' political horizons. Although an infinite variety of information is available, individuals may well sample selectively, limiting their exposure to news or sources that they expect to find agreeable. There is no doubt that the Internet makes available an ample supply of "news" that is not screened for accuracy or objectivity. By turning to biased but favored providers, consumers will be able to "wall themselves off from topics and opinions that they would prefer to avoid" (Sunstein, 2001, pp. 201–202). The end result could be a less informed and more polarized electorate.

A third debate over the potential impact of technology on individuals' civic empowerment concerns inequalities of access. Pessimists argue that the costs of going online, in terms of both money and skills, create striking disparities in access to information. Technology use is significantly correlated with social class and, interestingly, age; the on-ramp to the "information superhighway" is closed to the poor and the technologically less educated, making it less likely that they will be informed on the same level as most Americans.

INTERNET USE AND CIVIC ENGAGEMENT

Just as the advent of television made people less inclined to socialize outside their homes and more inclined to cancel their subscriptions to visually oriented magazines such as *Life*, some scholars argue that the Internet will gradually diminish Americans' participation in other forms of social interaction. Perhaps Americans will become so preoccupied with their private technological spaces that they will have little time to visit with the neighbors, write letters to the editor, or even converse with anybody. It is arguable that, because technology use is an inherently isolated rather than social experience, it will lead to alienation of the individual from the local or national community.

To date, the verdict from the scholarly literature is inconclusive. An early study by Kraut et al. (1998) focused on a group of Pittsburgh-area residents who were given computers and Internet access. Over a two-year period, the researchers found that study participants became less involved in social activities and expressed a higher level of loneliness. These findings were corroborated in a pair of national surveys of the online population. In the first survey, conducted in 1999 by Nie and Erbring (2000), one-fourth of regular Internet users reported that they spent less time (either in person or on the telephone) with friends and family and were less likely to attend events outside the home. This study also found that Internet use seemed to displace the use of conventional news media. A third of the Internet users reported that they spent less time watching television or reading newspapers.

Antisocial effects of Internet use were also uncovered in a 2002 survey by Nie and Hillygus (2002a), which relied on more specific "time diary" questions concerning the respondents' daily activities during various hours of the day. In general, the researchers found that Internet use had substantial displacement effects on "discretionary" activities—those surrounding leisure and media use. Heavy users of the Internet, for example, spent 24 percent less time reading than nonusers did. For television viewing, the displacement effect amounted to 17 percent. Averaged across all free-time activities, Internet users were less active by 21 percent.

Standing in opposition to these findings are several detailed diary-based studies that asked respondents to log their daily activities during all their waking hours. Researchers in these studies typically find that Internet use enhances the use of time rather than displacing it. Regular users of the Internet report that they spend more time conversing with others, attending cultural or sporting events, and reading books and newspapers. Apparently, Internet use makes people significantly more efficient at allocating time (perhaps by increasing the ability to multitask). As Robinson, Kestnbaum, Neustadtl, and Alvarez (2002) summarized the main implication of the diary studies, "Internet users not only do not use news and other media less, but many of them also use print media more and they are more active in a wide variety of other more active, free-time pursuits as well" (p. 26).

Thus, at the level of individuals' self-reported exposure to conventional media and other discretionary activities, the consequences of increased Internet use are unclear. For some, Internet use may free up time for other pastimes; for others, the effect may be the opposite.

BIASED EXPOSURE TO ONLINE NEWS?

For obvious reasons, candidates, political parties, and interest groups have all taken to the Internet to get out their messages, solicit money and other forms of support, and mobilize their members. (We will address the mobilization phenomenon later in the chapter.) The increased volume of online political communication has two immediate consequences. First, conventional news organizations have lost some of their near-monopolistic control over the delivery of public affairs information. Republicans dissatisfied with the *New York Times* coverage of President Bush can turn to the *Drudge Report* or the Republican National Committee Web site for an alternative slant on daily events. In fact, the Pew Research Center's surveys of Internet use show that gathering news is a relevant objective for many Internet users. As Figure 5.3 shows, over 25 percent of Internet users in 2004 reported that they followed news online, representing a fourfold increase since 1995. But at the same time, the largest segment of online Americans has only limited interest in news. Forty percent of the 2004 user group reported that they went online to seek news *at most* once a week.

The second consequence of the increased flow of information is overload. In a world dominated by conventional news sources, the supply of campaign information hardly burdens the typical voter's attention span. The average candidate sound bite in the networks' evening newscasts, for instance, runs for less than ten seconds. New forms of communication not only deliver much larger chunks of campaign information, but they also facilitate consumers' ability to attend to the information selectively. The audience for

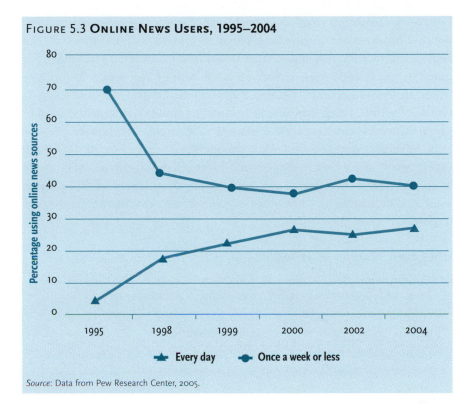

FIGURE 5.3 ONLINE NEWS USERS, 1995–2004

Source: Data from Pew Research Center, 2005.

conventional news programs is hard-pressed to avoid coverage of the candidate they dislike, because news reports typically assign equal coverage to each. When browsing a Web site, on the other hand, users can filter or search through masses of text more easily than in conventional media. Rather than examining the complete collection of speeches found on the "John Kerry for President" Web site, users can seek out Kerry's references to issues of special concern.

In short, as candidates, interest groups, and voters all converge on the Internet, the possibility of selective exposure to political information increases. Given the availability of so much information and so many news providers, the audience must make choices or be overwhelmed. Exactly how do Internet users decide whether the information they're getting is worth considering or should be passed over?

There are three main possibilities. First, people may prefer to encounter information that they find supportive or consistent with their beliefs (the *partisan polarization hypothesis*). For example, Republicans may tune in to

Fox News, Democrats to the *New York Times*. Second, people may pay attention not on the basis of their anticipated agreement with the message, but because of their interest in particular issues (the *issue public hypothesis*). For example, the elderly seek out information bearing on Social Security or Medicare legislation simply because these policies have an immediate impact on their welfare. Third, exposure to political information online may be simply a matter of generic political interest (the *attentive public hypothesis*). Political junkies sample widely while the apolitical majority simply tunes out, except when major events generate a torrent of coverage that is impossible to ignore. From this perspective, multiplying the number of information sources only widens the information gap between the more and the less interested.[3]

In Focus: Theories of Selectivity

● **Partisan polarization.** People prefer to encounter information that supports their beliefs and avoid information that is inconsistent with those beliefs.

● **Issue public.** People seek out information about subjects that are particularly important or interesting to them, and tune out information about other subjects.

● **Attentive public.** People interested by politics tune in to all forms of news, while the apolitical majority pays very little attention to news in any medium.

THE PARTISAN POLARIZATION HYPOTHESIS

Fifty years ago, when campaigns were conducted primarily through partisan channels, voters were thought to simplify their choices by relying on the candidates and positions of their preferred political party. Selective exposure on a partisan basis was considered the principal means by which candidates reached the public; voters were motivated to seek out information that supported rather than challenged their political beliefs.

The notion of partisan polarization was grounded in the theory of cognitive dissonance, which posited that the acquisition of information at odds with one's preexisting beliefs is uncomfortable and therefore to be avoided (Festinger, 1957). Instead, people were thought to prefer acquiring information that would reinforce their beliefs and attitudes. By this theory, for example, Republicans would be expected to avoid news stories critical of President Bush and seek out stories presenting him in a favorable light.

Early studies of political campaigns documented the tendency of partisan voters to report greater exposure to appeals from the candidate or party that they preferred. This pattern of motivated exposure to congenial information sources was thought to explain the surprising finding that campaigns reinforced rather than changed the attitudes of voters. (We will address this finding in greater detail in Chapter 9.) In what would prove to be an early incarnation of concern over the "Daily Me" (a concept we'll discuss in a moment), researchers condemned the preference for congenial information as antithetical to the democratic ideal of informed choice:

> In recent years there has been a good deal of talk by men of good will about the desirability and necessity of guaranteeing the free exchange of ideas in the market place of public opinion. Such talk has centered upon the problem of keeping free the channels of expression and communication. Now we find that the consumers of ideas, if they have made a decision on the issue, themselves erect high tariff walls against alien notions. (Lazarsfeld, Berelson, & Gaudet, 1948, p. 89)

Over the years, scholarship on motivated exposure has yielded mixed results. Although a handful of controlled studies reported the expected result, most did not (for a review of the early research, see Sears and Freedman, 1967). Indeed, even in the famous Elmira study (from which we just quoted—Lazarsfeld, Berelson, & Gaudet, 1948), the researchers actually found that the effect was limited to Republican voters.

More recently, the spread of new media has sparked renewed concerns about motivated exposure to supportive information. Sunstein (2001), for one, describes an ominous scenario in which Internet users customize their contact with the outside world into a "Daily Me." The increased ability to pick and choose among multiple sources is thought to discourage exposure to unfamiliar or disliked perspectives on policy issues. Unlike viewers of television news, who are required to sit through the same uniform supply of stories, Internet users enjoy more control over what they encounter.

The impact of technology on motivated exposure to campaign information was addressed in a study of the 2000 presidential election (Iyengar, Hahn, Krosnick, & Walker, 2005). The researchers produced an extensive and easy-to-use CD-ROM database of information about Vice President Gore and Governor Bush. The CD, which included the complete collection of campaign speeches and televised advertisements from the two candidates, was distributed to a representative sample of online Americans approximately two weeks before election day.[4]

The researchers then tracked individuals' use of the CD electronically so that they could monitor what each person chose to read. The partisan polarization hypothesis predicted that Republicans and conservatives would visit pages featuring Bush more frequently than pages devoted to Gore, while Democrats and liberals would exhibit precisely the opposite tendency. As Figure 5.4 shows, the evidence showed only weak traces of an anticipated agreement bias. Except for strong conservatives, people showed more interest in Gore content. Strong conservatives, however, accessed Bush content significantly more frequently. In terms of party identification, CD use did not differ across Democrats and Republicans; both groups accessed slightly more Gore than Bush pages.

A survey of Internet users during the 2004 campaign also found that partisan preferences have only a limited role in guiding the behavior of online information seekers. The researchers measured Internet users' familiarity with a variety of arguments both favorable and unfavorable to President Bush and Senator Kerry. The partisan polarization hypothesis predicted that Republicans would be aware of only the pro-Bush and anti-Kerry arguments, and vice versa for the Democrats. In fact, the results showed that the largest group of Internet users were unbiased in their awareness of the campaign themes. This "omnivore" group (familiar with both candidates' arguments)

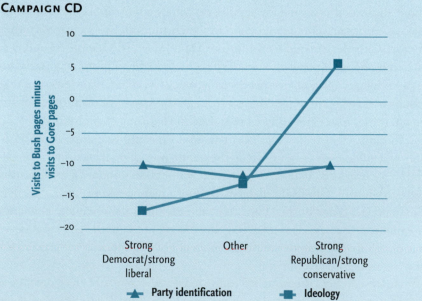

FIGURE 5.4 **PARTISAN-BASED EXPOSURE TO THE 2000 PRESIDENTIAL CAMPAIGN CD**

amounted to 43 percent of Internet users who had a candidate preference. In contrast, "selective reinforcers" (familiar only with the arguments that matched their candidate preference) made up 29 percent of the sample. In another parallel with the CD study, the number of selective reinforcers was substantially higher among Bush voters.

THE ISSUE PUBLIC HYPOTHESIS

An alternative conception of selective exposure is based on differing levels of interest in particular political issues. In their original review, Sears and Friedman identified "utility-based selectivity" as a viable alternative to partisan consistency as a motive for seeking political information. They argued that what individuals paid attention to would depend on how useful they perceived the different pieces of information to be rather than on how much they anticipated agreeing with the implications of the information. In this view, people who derive special benefits from particular government policies are expected to be more inclined to prick up their ears when news programs mention developments concerning these policies (such as the elderly in response to mention of Social Security).

A considerable body of evidence suggests that people do, in fact, allocate their attention according to the personal relevance or utility of information. For instance, Krosnick (1990) has found that people express greater interest in policy issues that touch them directly and toward which they have developed attitudes of great personal importance. To attach importance to a particular policy attitude is to become a member of that policy's "issue public."

The role of issue publics in the consumption of conventional news was examined in a study by Price and Zaller (1993), who carried out several tests of the hypothesis that people whose personal background suggested they might belong to an issue public were more likely to recall news stories bearing on "their" issue. The results indicated only limited support for the hypothesis: in only about half of the tests, the group identified as the issue public had higher recall of stories bearing on that issue.[5]

In a related investigation of issue publics by Iyengar in 1990, recall of television news reports about Social Security and racial discrimination was significantly higher among older and minority viewers, respectively, than among younger and white viewers. In addition to recalling more stories about race, African-Americans proved more informed about matters of civil rights than whites were, despite the latter group's significantly greater knowledge of overall political information. Other scholars have uncovered a similar pattern with gender: on women's issues, women tend to be better informed than men.

The importance of issue public membership to the use of new media was one of the main lessons of the 2000 campaign CD study. The researchers identified eight different issue publics. The "defense issue public," for instance, was identified as all study participants who had served in the military, and the "Social Security issue public" consisted of all retired participants. In six of the eight tests, members of the issue public visited greater numbers of CD pages concerning the issue of interest. When compared with nonmembers, members of issue publics registered more page visits on an order of magnitude ranging from 50 percent (for the "education issue public") to 80 percent (for the "abortion issue public").

As a case in point, Figure 5.5 shows the number of visits to CD pages concerning health care by a variety of health care–related issue publics. The x-axis corresponds to the average number of health-related page visits, and the y-axis divides the "health issue public" into five subcategories: occupation (those who work in the health field versus those who don't), insurance coverage (participants whose health insurance coverage was less than continuous during the preceding year versus those who were continuously insured), membership in a health maintenance organization (HMO members versus non-HMO members), age (participants sixty years and older versus those younger than sixty), and age of parent (those with elderly parents versus those with younger par-

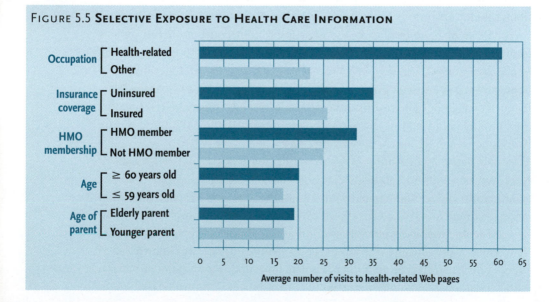

FIGURE 5.5 SELECTIVE EXPOSURE TO HEALTH CARE INFORMATION

Average number of visits to health-related Web pages

ents). In every comparison, the number of accessed health pages was higher among members of the group more affected by health care policy.

THE ATTENTIVE PUBLIC HYPOTHESIS

A third explanation for exposure to news involves neither partisan prefer-ences nor interest in particular issues. According to this account, the act of seeking out political information, online as elsewhere, is simply a matter of generic political interest. People captivated by politics tune in to all forms of news, while the apolitical majority tunes out politics in favor of online bar-gain hunting, for example. From this perspective, the Internet will simply widen the information gap between the more and less interested.

In the area of conventional media use, the Price and Zaller study des-cribed earlier reported evidence consistent with the "rich get richer" pattern. They found that respondents with a higher level of education (education is an indicator of political attentiveness; that is, people who are more educated tend to be more interested in politics) remembered all news stories better. These investigators concluded that "someone who is generally well-informed about politics will tend to be well-informed about whatever the news media also cover, whether the trials of Hollywood celebrities or the latest arms control proposals" (Price & Zaller, 1993, p. 157). Other studies reach similar conclusions, suggesting that people who attend to political information are generalists, soaking up whatever is available, rather than ideologues looking for ammunition to strengthen their arguments or specialists interested in particular issues.

In the case of new media, we would expect the tendency for information to be disproportionately distributed among the more educated to be magni-fied. Virtually every study of Internet use has documented that educated and more-affluent Americans are more likely than their less-advantaged counter-parts to be online. In the 2000 election, the voters most likely to report going online to get campaign information were college graduates and those with a strong interest in politics. In fact, the education and interest advantage in Internet exposure to campaign information was almost identical to the advan-tage in newspaper use.

Overall, the evidence suggests that exposure to political information is determined by multiple factors: the desire to learn about politics generally, to learn about issues of special interest, and, at least among Republicans and conservatives, to learn about a favored candidate. It is difficult to dismiss this last finding as idiosyncratic to recent campaigns because the very same pattern of anticipated agreement-driven selective exposure among Republicans and conservatives was apparent in the Lazarsfeld, Berelson, and Gaudet study of the 1948 election. Perhaps conservatives and Republicans have more-intense partisan preferences and are less inclined to consider opposing perspectives. Whatever the explanation, the pattern of greater partisan bias in exposure to information on the political right deserves further investigation.

Impact of the Internet on Campaign Organizations

As we have noted already, candidates are attracted to media outlets in direct proportion to the size of the media audience. In the early days of the Internet, when the online population numbered fewer than one in ten Americans, most campaigns felt it unnecessary to establish a Web presence. As the technology spread and innovative new forms of "social software" emerged, however, so too did the incentives for Internet-based campaigning.

In principle, campaigns can harness the immense networking power of the Internet to accomplish multiple campaign objectives, including fund-raising, increasing the candidate's visibility and likability, and most critically, recruiting and mobilizing a cadre of activists. To date, the impact of new media has been greatest on the goal of mobilization. Other facets of the campaign remain grounded in conventional (especially broadcast) media because there are still more voters to be reached in front of their television sets than at their computers. (Exactly what campaigns do to reach voters is the subject of Chapter 6.) Nonetheless, the networking advantages of the Internet have already transformed the conduct of campaigns.

Before the Internet, candidates recruited volunteers and raised money by making phone calls, sending mass mailings, or going door to door. These old-fashioned forms of mobilization and fund-raising were both capital- and time-intensive; successful campaigns had an existing organization, professional (paid) staff, and access to phone banks or mailing lists of prospective supporters. Candidates themselves might spend long hours on the phone with prospective donors. The amount of time between the initial contact and receipt of a financial contribution might take weeks or even months. These infrastructure costs made it nearly impossible for lesser-known and cash-strapped candidates to develop and manage a hard-core group of activists.

By lowering the cost of communication, the Internet has transformed the political arena by enabling any campaign, no matter how large its electoral constituency, to assemble a network of supporters. Any candidate with the ability to mount a basic Web site can instantly sign up volunteers and send them assignments for upcoming events, thus developing the nucleus of a viable field organization. Once formed, these groups become "smart mobs"— capable of acting in a coordinated manner, despite the absence of any face-to-face contact (for examples of smart mobs in action, see Rheingold, 2002). In effect, the Internet lowered the eligibility requirements for groups to engage in collective action.[6] For large and small campaigns alike, the Internet is a public good that can be exploited with minimal marginal costs.

The first campaign to take advantage of the Internet to organize its supporters was the 1998 Jesse Ventura campaign for governor of Minnesota. Running as the Reform Party candidate, Ventura was heavily outspent by his Republican and Democratic opponents (Norm Coleman and Hubert H. Humphrey III, respectively). But Ventura's campaign launched a Web site (see Figure 5.6) in early 1998 (at a monthly cost of under thirty dollars) and began to develop a statewide e-mail list of volunteers. The list was used to publicize information about local organizational meetings; one such meeting drew a standing-room-only crowd of more than 250 people.

Taking further advantage of its statewide network, the Ventura campaign scheduled a seventy-two-hour "Drive to Victory" caravan tour of the state.

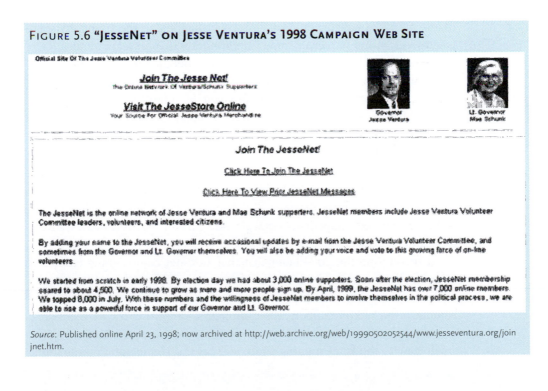

FIGURE 5.6 "JESSENET" ON JESSE VENTURA'S 1998 CAMPAIGN WEB SITE

Source: Published online April 23, 1998; now archived at http://web.archive.org/web/19990502052544/www.jesseventura.org/join jnet.htm.

Because supporters had been informed in advance of the candidate's appearance in their area, the tour attracted large, enthusiastic crowds, thus raising the candidate's media profile. Simultaneously, the campaign used its online network to raise much-needed funds. Online contributions to the Ventura campaign amounted to a third of its total fund-raising.

Despite being outspent and outstaffed by his opponents (the campaign had only one paid staff member, the campaign manager), Ventura was elected governor. It is difficult to say precisely how much difference Ventura's use of technology made to the upset victory. After all, his unusual persona and career as a professional wrestler combined to make him a highly visible candidate, and his antigovernment, populist platform resonated well in a state with a long history of supporting progressive reformers. In one respect, however, the pay-off of using technology was clear: young people, who are most likely to be reached online, turned out to vote in large numbers. Over half of them voted for Ventura—more than enough to account for the margin of his victory.

The success of the Ventura campaign made it clear to campaign operatives that the Internet could and should be exploited for political action. By 2000, all reputable candidates had elaborate, interactive Web sites and e-mail lists of prospective supporters. Among the presidential contenders, it was John McCain who became the poster boy for use of the Internet (see Figure 5.7). Capitalizing on McCain's special appeal to the young, his campaign went online to recruit some fifteen hundred volunteers in advance of the New Hampshire primary. The campaign scheduled regular online "chat" encounters with the candidate. In one such session, five hundred people each paid a hundred dollars for the privilege of submitting an e-mail question to McCain. Overall, the McCain campaign set a new record (four million dollars) for electronic fund-raising.

Despite McCain's stunning victory in the New Hampshire primary, his candidacy proved short-lived. George W. Bush rebounded from New Hampshire and soundly defeated McCain in South Carolina. Shortly thereafter, McCain withdrew from the race. But once again, an "insurgent" candidate had demonstrated competitiveness with the help of a relatively modest investment in new media.

It was during the 2004 campaign that Internet campaigning came into its own. Governor Howard Dean tied his presidential candidacy inextricably to the Internet. Although Dean was eventually forced to withdraw from the campaign for lack of support, his campaign's innovative use of technology contributed to his meteoric rise from the relatively unknown governor of a small state to the front-running contender for the Democratic nomination.

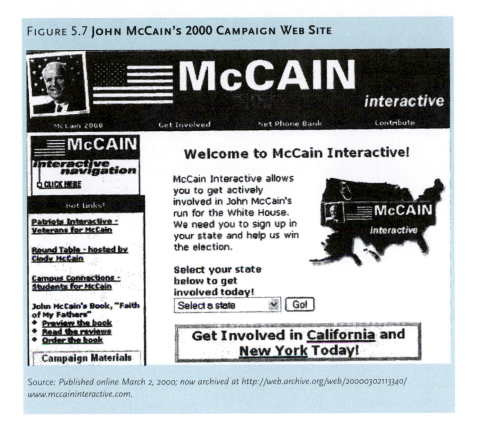

FIGURE 5.7 JOHN MCCAIN'S 2000 CAMPAIGN WEB SITE

Source: *Published online March 2, 2000; now archived at http://web.archive.org/web/20000302113340/ www.mccaininteractive.com.*

The Dean campaign hired a full-time Internet consultant. The first step was to use the networking portal Meetup.com to recruit Dean supporters from across the nation. Meetup is designed to create local groups for people with common interests, whether that interest is witches, cricket, or Howard Dean for president. The Dean campaign used Meetup to schedule face-to-face meetings across the nation, several of which were attended by the candidate himself. For the campaign, mailing out campaign materials was the only cost of maintaining this network of activists.

By July, the Dean Meetup group had grown to over 60,000 members, and membership peaked at 189,000 shortly before Dean withdrew in February 2004.[7] The Dean Web site served as the hub for the online campaign. Visitors were urged to "stay connected" and were informed about local Meetup groups and upcoming campaign events (in addition to the standard position papers, press releases, and televised advertisements). The Dean campaign also initiated the popular Weblog "Blog for America" (which is still active but is now known as Democracy for America[8]). By December 2003, with twenty-nine hundred entries and over thirty thousand spontaneous comments, the blog had become required reading for the national press corps.

While organizing "Deaniacs" nationwide, the Dean campaign also demonstrated considerable prowess at online fund-raising. In one instance, the campaign responded to a Bush–Cheney two-thousand-dollar-a-plate dinner (which raised $250,000) by hosting an online "eat in" challenge featuring a Web page with an image of Dean eating a turkey sandwich and a "contribute now" button. In response, ninety-seven hundred people visited the page, and the campaign netted over $500,000. In the second quarter of 2003 alone, the campaign took in more than seven million dollars.

The Dean campaign also relied on online polling to take the pulse of supporters. In one case, the campaign even scheduled an online referendum on whether Dean should opt out of the public financing provisions of the campaign (thus enabling him to raise and spend unlimited amounts of money). A majority of his supporters voted for opting out, and no sooner had the campaign announced the results than it began to solicit contributions from those who voted. Another widely publicized online poll was sponsored by the liberal-leaning issue advocacy group MoveOn.org. MoveOn held a "virtual primary" in June 2003. More than three hundred thousand people voted. Given the ideological leanings of the group, it was not surprising that the two most liberal candidates in the Democratic field finished first (Dean) and second (Kucinich), respectively. Despite the wholly nonrepresentative nature of the result, the MoveOn primary attracted considerable media coverage, thus further cementing Dean's stature as the leading Democratic contender.

Given the Dean campaign's effective use of the Internet to mobilize supporters, why did he fail to win even one primary?[9] Dean's extensive network of online volunteers did not translate into an outpouring of primary votes. In the language of social scientists, the Dean campaign was doomed by a "self-selection bias." The American techno-literati, most of whom were eager to drive Bush from the White House and who seized the opportunity to volunteer for Dean, were much too small a group to swing even a small-state primary. In other words, the Deaniacs were not representative of Democratic primary voters. A Pew Research Center survey of Dean activists found that 54 percent had attended graduate school (for all Democratic activists, the comparable figure was 11 percent) and that they were significantly more liberal and anti-Bush than mainstream Democrats were. Dean's candidacy itself was clearly faithful to his supporters, but it also made Dean less appealing to most Democratic voters.

Thus the main lesson of 2004 was that, although the Internet provides a cost-efficient means of developing a network of campaign workers and donors, it is not yet the best platform for candidates to appeal for votes. It is one thing to develop an electronic network of enthusiastic supporters; it is quite another to attract enough votes to win a primary election. As of 2004, the Internet was not yet competitive with television as a way of communicating with rank-and-file voters.

Conclusion

The scholarly evidence concerning the emerging role of the Internet in American public life does not support the dire forecasts that the Internet will create virtual "gated communities" of polarized groups. The research shows instead that what people see or read in news presentations—both conventional and online—is not motivated solely, or even primarily, by the desire to track sources with which they are likely to agree. Some people (conservatives in particular) do tend to gravitate to a "preferred" provider, but others consume news because they are generally interested in politics, or select content on the basis of its relative interest or utility.

Although partisan values exert only limited influence over people's choices of news sources, these values do have more powerful effects on what people do with information they do encounter, either willfully or inadvertently. As we will describe in Chapter 8, partisans tend to ignore or discount highly publicized facts when these facts are at odds with their political preferences. In 2004, Republicans refused to acknowledge that President Bush's decision to go to war in Iraq was based on inaccurate intelligence, despite an avalanche of news stories calling the intelligence reports into question.

Quite apart from the ambiguous verdict of the scholarly literature, there is another reason to be optimistic about the potential impact of the technological revolution on the political process. We have already documented that media-based campaigns fail to deliver substantive information. In place of the candidates' positions and past performance on the issues, news coverage gravitates inevitably toward the more "entertaining" facets of the campaign: the horse race, the strategy, and whenever possible, instances of scandalous or unethical behavior. Against this backdrop, technology at least makes it possible for voters to bypass or supplement media treatment of the campaign and access information about the issues that affect them.

Rather than waiting (typically in vain) for news organizations to report on the issues they care about, voters can take matters into their own hands and seek out information about the candidates' positions on these issues. This form of motivated exposure is hardly an impediment to deliberation: paying attention to what the candidates have to say on the issues facilitates issue-oriented voting; paying attention to the media circus does not. Thus, there is some reason to hope that the spread of new forms of unmediated communication will provide a better way to inform and engage voters. We will elaborate on this theme in Chapter 11.

Finally, the brief case studies of candidates who have successfully organized campaigns on the Internet make it clear that technology, in this respect at least, has leveled the campaign playing field. Even the poorest candidate has the capacity to publicize a candidacy and solicit support online. As the examples of Ventura, McCain, and Dean suggest, an Internet presence can, virtually overnight, help candidates establish a viable campaign organization. As technology spreads even further, and the next generation of software makes possible even closer contact and cooperation among like-minded individuals, we may expect the Internet to play a pivotal role in American campaigns. But for the moment at least, as will be described in Chapter 6, to campaign for votes, candidates still use relatively old-fashioned approaches, relying on conventional media.

CHAPTER 5 SUMMARY

1. The development of information technology and the spread of new media have changed the communication landscape. Traditional forms of communication were either point-to-point (between a single sender and recipient) or broadcast (between a single sender and multiple recipients). New media—particularly the Internet—have broken down those distinctions. Any Internet user can send e-mail messages to individual recipients and at the same time communicate with a worldwide audience by, for example, hosting a Web site. Moreover, unlike conventional media, Internet-based communication is multichannel, allowing the intermingling of text, voice, still images, and video.

2. There is contradictory evidence as to whether use of the Internet displaces, or merely supplements, the use of other media and other social tasks more generally. Some studies have shown that Internet users become

less likely to engage in social activities and devote less time to traditional media. Other studies have found that that frequent Internet users spend more time conversing with others, attending cultural or sporting events, and reading books and newspapers.

3. The Internet has greatly increased both the amount and the variety of material available to the public, as well as consumers' control over the information to which they're exposed. There are three main theories about how people choose which political communications they will attend to:

- The *partisan polarization theory* suggests that people prefer to encounter information that they find consistent with their beliefs. Some fear that, if partisanship is the dominant basis of selectivity, the spread of new media will lead to political polarization, since liberals and conservatives will both have greater ability to select information sources that they agree with and ignore others.

- The *issue public theory* suggests that people seek out information about subjects that are particularly important or interesting to them, and tune out information about other subjects. Evidence for this type of selectivity has been more consistent than that for partisan polarization.

- The *attentive public theory* suggests that the act of seeking out political information is simply a matter of generic political interest. People captivated by politics tune in to all forms of news, while the apolitical majority tunes out politics.

4. The widespread proliferation of the Internet has increased its use in political campaigns. It has been used to great effect to boost candidates' profiles, build grassroots organizations, and raise funds—especially by "outsider" candidates.

FURTHER READINGS

Bimber, B. (2003). *Information and American democracy: Technology in the evolution of political power*. New York: Cambridge University Press.

Lazarsfeld, P. F., Berelson, B. R., & Gaudet, H. (1948). *The people's choice*. New York: Columbia University Press.

Nie, N., & Hillygus, D. S. (2002). The impact of Internet use on sociability: Time-diary findings. *IT & Society, 1*(1), 1–20.

Price, V., & Zaller, J. (1993). Who gets the news? Alternative measures of news reception and their implications for research. *Public Opinion Quarterly, 57,* 133–164.

Rheingold, H. (2002). *Smart mobs: The next social revolution.* Cambridge, MA: Basic Books.

Robinson, J. P., Kestnbaum, M., Neustadtl, A., & Alvarez, A. (2002). Information technology and functional time displacement. *IT & Society, 1,* 21–36.

Sears, D. O., & Freedman, J. L. (1967). Selective exposure to information: A critical review. *Public Opinion Quarterly, 31,* 194–213.

Sunstein, C. (2001). *Republic.com.* Princeton, NJ: Princeton University Press.

NOTES

1. All figures are from Nielsen//NetRatings for the week ending July 4, 2005 (see Cyber-Journalist.net, 2005).
2. From *Remarks prepared for delivery by Vice President Al Gore, International Telecommunications Union, Monday March 21, 1994.* Retrieved October 7, 2005, from www.ifla.org/documents/infopol/us/goregii.txt.
3. It is well known that interest in politics and other indicators of engagement in civic life are strongly correlated with education and socioeconomic status. In one sense, then, the measure of political interest is an indicator of access to and proficiency with information technology.
4. Production of the CD was made possible through the generous support of the Pew Charitable Trusts, the Carnegie Corporation, and the active cooperation of the Bush and Gore campaigns. Produced by the Political Communication Lab at Stanford University, the CD was entitled "Vote 2004: Presidential Candidates in Their Own Words" and was distributed broadly to the general public, as well as to the study participants. The CD is available at http://pcl.stanford.edu/campaigns.
5. Some of the authors' indicators of issue public membership were, at best, approximations. For example, "reading a great deal of international news in the newspaper" was treated as indicating membership in the issue public for international events.
6. The Internet does not necessarily reduce the inequality in organizational capacity. Larger groups that invest more heavily in customized technology, for instance, may reap even larger benefits than those using cruder and more publicly available electronic tools.
7. Dean was not the only candidate to network online. John Kerry was quick to follow Dean as a client of Meetup.com, and the Wesley Clark campaign formed the "Clark Community Network." Not to be outdone by the Democrats, the Bush–Cheney campaign also developed a proprietary electronic networking system. Their Web site included an online invitation system, downloadable flyers, and a searchable zip code directory that allowed users to locate other supporters in their area. For a more detailed description of the various campaigns' online efforts, see Samuel, 2004.
8. www.democracyforamerica.com
9. After withdrawing from the race, Dean did win his home-state primary.

CHAPTER 6

CAMPAIGNING THROUGH THE MEDIA

IN THE WEEKS LEADING UP to the 1948 election, President Truman crisscrossed the country on his campaign train, making daily appearances before enthusiastic crowds of voters. Shaking hands, kissing babies, and greeting voters were standard practice in the era of in-person, retail politics.

By 1960, the rapid spread of television had altered the behavior of candidates. Personal appearances were time-consuming for the candidates and attracted only the most faithful of partisans. Most Americans, especially those lacking a strong party affiliation, stayed away from campaign events. These same people, however, watched lots of television. Candidates soon realized that television provided efficient access to a national audience. Unlike personal appearances, with their idiosyncratic hit-or-miss quality (attendance at an event might be cut in half by bad weather), televised news programs attracted a more predictable audience.

As a campaign medium, television provided still further advantages, including the ability to deliver different messages and appeals, depending on the needs and interests of particular television markets. Most notably, the medium of television advertising guaranteed campaigns maximum control over the content and form of their message. Unlike speeches, there would be no hecklers interrupting an ad and distracting voters from the candidate's appeal. Unlike news coverage, there would be no editor selecting the particular sound bites actually aired. Unlike debates, there would be no hovering journalists probing for weaknesses, or opponents standing ready to pounce on any misstatement of fact. From the perspective of candidates, television seemed to have it all.

Beginning in 1952, presidential campaigns began to experiment with different forms of television-based campaigning. Ads appeared in 1952. During the 1960 presidential campaign, John Kennedy and Richard Nixon debated each other on four occasions before an average audience amounting to 60 percent of the population. By 1968, campaigns were designed explicitly for television, and no serious campaign was without its cadre of full-time, highly paid media strategists. As Roger Ailes, the well-known Republican consultant (now the CEO of Fox News) declared, "This is the beginning of a whole new concept. This is it. This is the way they'll be elected forevermore. The next guys will have to be performers" (Wisconsin Public Television, 1998–2001).

Candidates perform on two parallel stages, corresponding to *free media* (news coverage) and *paid media* (advertising). In most statewide and congressional races, advertising tends to dominate news as the principal stage, for the simple reason that these campaigns attract only sparse news coverage. In the case of the 2002 race for governor of California, to cite a recent instance, less than 1 percent of all local news that was broadcast in the month of October focused on the election. Unable to crack the newsworthiness barrier, gubernatorial candidates are forced to invest heavily in advertising. In the 2002 California race, incumbent Gray Davis and his challenger, Bill Simon, together spent ten million dollars on ads.

In contrast to statewide or congressional races, presidential races enjoy virtually unlimited news coverage, making the ad campaign only a small trickle in the cumulative message stream. This does not mean that advertising strategy is unimportant in presidential races. Far from it; the continuous and often acrimonious conflict between journalists and candidates over the content of news coverage has only intensified the importance of advertising as the one truly "unmediated" form of campaign speech.

In this chapter we will address three forms of contemporary media campaigning: the candidates' efforts to exploit press coverage, their advertising strategies, and their performance in televised candidate debates.

Strategies for Managing the Press

In the ideal campaign, each candidate hopes to enjoy a regular stream of favorable news coverage while the opponent either suffers from inattention or is portrayed in unflattering terms. In this scenario the news media would play the role of a credible spokesperson for the campaign. The professional norms governing journalism make it almost certain that reporters will refuse to act as campaign agents. As we noted in Chapter 3, the practice of interpretive journalism requires journalists to dismiss the candidate's rhetoric out of hand. The need to make news entertaining and eye-catching is a further drag on the candidates' ability to insert their messages intact into the news stream. The latest position paper on combating international terrorism might contain a myriad of specific proposals, none of which can be conveyed in a ten-second sound bite.

In the real world, a variety of factors influence the ability of a campaign to "spin" the press. We begin with the worst-case scenario and then describe a series of specific strategies that provide campaigns at least some leverage over the content of the news.

In Focus: Strategies That Candidates Use to Manage the Press

- Avoid behavior that calls into question your suitability for office.
- Don't waffle or "flip-flop" on the issues.
- Make sure journalists have low expectations concerning your chances of victory.
- Schedule events strategically to maximize their newsworthiness.
- When leading in the polls, restrict journalists' access.
- "Go local" to avoid critical coverage from national news organizations.
- Feed the press titillating but critical information concerning your opponent.

AVOIDING FEEDING FRENZIES

The ability of a campaign to influence the press is at a low ebb in races where the media scent evidence of personal misbehavior or "character" issues. When candidates demonstrate obvious personal flaws, they are completely at the mercy of the media. Given the premium value of the character story, the ensuing "feeding frenzy" can prove fatal. As mentioned in Chapter 3, Gary Hart's 1988 presidential campaign effectively ended the day the *Miami Herald* broke the news of his overnight stay at Donna Rice's condominium. Four years earlier, Senator Joseph Biden was forced to withdraw from the Democratic primary race when news reports disclosed that he had knowingly delivered the very same speech given by British Labor Party leader Neil Kinnock. More recently, Jack Ryan, the 2004 Republican candidate for the US Senate from Illinois, dropped out of the race less than a week after allegations by his ex-wife that the couple had frequently visited risqué nightclubs where, on occasion, he had asked her to "perform" for the patrons.

In less scandalous circumstances, it is imperative that the candidates not behave in ways that raise doubts about their personal makeup. The storm of critical news coverage aimed at Governor Howard Dean following the Iowa caucuses was self-inflicted. His impassioned concession speech—dubbed the "Dean Scream"—was replayed incessantly in the following days and interpreted by the pundits as symptomatic of Dean's unstable personality and lack of self-control.

DEALING WITH THE OBJECTIVITY IMPERATIVE

On the substantive or "performance" side of the ledger, it is rare for a candidate to eke out an edge in news coverage. Unlike character issues, which tend to be viewed in black-and-white terms (a candidate is either an adulterer or happily married), the candidates' credentials and positions on the issues represent a gray zone—there are no clear winners and losers. Journalists purport to be self-consciously objective in their discussion and take pains to provide "point–counterpoint" reporting. The rare occasions when the norm does not preclude one-sided coverage arise either when one candidate has a clear-cut advantage over the opponent or, as we will discuss here, when a candidate makes a major misstatement of fact or reverses course on a matter of public policy.

The coverage of the 2004 presidential candidates' war records provides an example of the infrequently experienced comparative advantage scenario. During the 2004 primary season, Senator Kerry enjoyed a favorable balance of news over President Bush because of their contrasting records on Vietnam. Kerry had volunteered for a particularly dangerous assignment (patrolling the Mekong River, one of the deadliest war zones), and won several awards for heroism and bravery under fire. For his part, President Bush had joined the Texas Air National Guard, but the actual extent of his weekend service remains unclear.

Kerry's advantage on the war record story proved short-lived. The commitment to balanced coverage is so compelling that this phase of reporting was followed almost immediately by several reports highlighting Kerry's later involvement in the antiwar movement. The *New York Times* and other major newspapers published photos of Kerry in close proximity to "Hanoi Jane" (the actress Jane Fonda, then a leading antiwar activist). The call of objectivity had been answered.

As in the case of character-related news, the candidate's pronouncements on policy issues may provide journalists with a convenient excuse to attack. A candidate whose words and deeds are inconsistent or who revises a previously stated position is a ripe target for critical scrutiny. Senator

George McGovern, the Democratic presidential candidate in 1972, was widely criticized for dropping Senator Tom Eagleton as his running mate after the press revealed that Eagleton had once been treated for clinical depression. A similar media cloud enveloped Senator John McCain when, in 2000, somewhat inconsistently with his campaign theme of being a "straight talker," he aired a television commercial comparing his Republican opponent George W. Bush to Bill Clinton. Journalists were quick to point out that McCain's use of negative advertising revealed him as just another cynical candidate.

Playing the Expectations Game

Recognizing the difficulty of directly influencing the content and tone of news coverage, the candidates have recently turned to more-subtle media strategies. One is to try to influence reporters' treatment of their electoral prospects. We have seen that the state of the "horse race" is the foundation of campaign news. In the early stages of the primary campaign, favorable coverage of the candidate's position in the race can prove pivotal; candidates thought to be doing well (thanks to press reports) can use their standing to attract additional financial contributions and, as several scholars have documented, to attract even more voters in upcoming primaries.

Senator Kerry's trajectory in the 2004 race provides a classic example of the power of electoral momentum. In the months before the Iowa caucuses, Kerry was dismissed as an underachieving contender whose national poll numbers remained steadily in the single digits and whose finances were so shaky that he had to take out yet another mortgage in order to compete in Iowa. Given this baseline, Kerry's victory in Iowa was equivalent to a home run: he had defied journalists' expectations. The Iowa results elicited a wave of favorable coverage, Kerry went on to win New Hampshire, and eventually he captured the Democratic nomination quite handily (see Chapter 9).

Setting journalists' expectations is crucial during the early days of the primary season. Campaign spokespersons typically downplay poll results that show their candidate comfortably ahead in Iowa or New Hampshire, in the hope that the outcome will be more surprising and hence covered more extensively and favorably. Conversely, campaigns sometimes attempt to persuade reporters that the opponent has a substantial lead when they know that the poll numbers represent a short-term blip that will inevitably wear off. Shortly after Kerry picked John Edwards as his running mate in 2004, Matt Dowd, the chief strategist for the Republican National Committee, released a statement to the press claiming that the Bush campaign expected to be trailing in the polls by as much as 15 points after the Democratic convention. Not to be outdone, Mark Mellman (Kerry's pollster) responded by noting that, because voters had made up their minds relatively early in 2004, Kerry's convention "bounce" would necessarily be small. Both Dowd and Mellman knew full well that the increase in a candidate's support following the convention is a short-term "bubble" effect and that the two conventions generally neutralize each other, restoring the status quo that existed before the conventions.

MANAGING EVENTS

The "nuts and bolts" of press management is the strategic scheduling of events. Put simply, events must be designed and scheduled to attract maximal news coverage. In the days of old-fashioned descriptive journalism, the selection of the vice presidential candidate was delayed until the convention because the nominee was assured adequate coverage in advance of the convention. The increased resistance of the press corps to campaign spin has forced candidates to use the announcement of the vice presidential selection as a media opportunity.

Rather than wasting the vice presidential selection by announcing it during a period of ordinarily high media coverage (the convention), the announcement is now made considerably in advance of the convention so as to capitalize on the news and analysis that follows. John Kerry announced his selection of John Edwards on Monday, July 5, 2004, three weeks before the Democratic National Convention. The duo immediately left on a multistate bus tour, riding a crest of publicity sparked by the surprise announcement. A similar logic prompted Clinton and Gore to embark on their bus tour the minute they exited the 1992 Democratic convention.

Nominating conventions were once significant opportunities for the candidates and their allies to posture at length before a nationwide audience. Since the advent of primaries, however, conventions have become ceremonial occasions with no possibility of delegations walking out in protest or the eruption of heated arguments over the platform—either of which might pique the media's attention. In contrast to the 1968 Democratic convention in Chicago, which precipitated a full-scale riot in the streets of Chicago, present-day conventions are tame affairs. Speakers are screened to ensure that dissent or strident partisanship (which may throw off independents) is minimized.

The 1992 Republican convention, generally considered a poorly managed affair, violated the basic rule of projecting an image of party unity when it included prime-time speeches by dissident voices. Pat Buchanan, who had challenged Bush in the Republican primaries, described the Clinton–Gore campaign as advocates of "radical feminism" and "the homosexual rights movement." Marilyn Quayle, the vice-president's wife, though less strident, commended "stay-at-home" moms for furthering family values.

The trade-off of scripted conventions is reduced press coverage. Gavel-to-gavel coverage was last provided in 1976. Since then, television coverage of the conventions has been sporadic. In 2004 the three major networks allocated each convention three hours of total coverage over three days (at the least desirable prime-time slot of 10:00 PM).[1]

The reduced newsworthiness of the convention has forced campaign strategists to work harder for news coverage. The appearance of celebrities (such as Arnold Schwarzenegger) attracts news, but the overall theme of party unity tends to dampen press interest. In an unusual move designed to stimulate media interest, the Republicans decided to hold their 2004 convention in early September rather than the usual July–August timing. Their choice of New York as the host city was not coincidental with the change in schedule. President Bush's advisors realized that the third anniversary of the 9/11 attacks would provide them with a convenient photo opportunity immediately following a convention dominated by terrorism and national security as the Bush campaign's signature issues. The decision to delay the convention is a textbook example of the strategy of "riding the wave"—coordinating the campaign with events of consequence so that the campaign will benefit from the additional coverage elicited by the newsworthy event.

In Focus: "Riding the Wave"

Riding the wave refers to the way candidates seek to coordinate their campaigns with external events of consequence so that the campaign will benefit from the additional media coverage elicited by newsworthy events. In the aftermath of the September 11 attacks, for example, the 2002 campaigns featured frequent references to the threat of terrorism and the need for US military preparedness.

REGULATING ACCESS

Providing the press with access to the candidate is an important ingredient of campaign management. On the one hand, there is the "open door" strategy, designed to maximize the candidate's availability. As one might expect, this strategy is favored by candidates who trail in the polls, who typically lack the resources to engage in advertising. When more competitive or emerging as the front-runner, the candidate limits access. The candidate may make the campaign's press secretary available for questioning, but does not appear in person. The most extreme form of attempts to restrict press access is the "Rose Garden Strategy" named for incumbent presidents who enjoy such substantial leads in the polls (for example, in the 1972, 1984, and 1996 elections) that the candidate prefers to ignore the press altogether. Thus, there is an inverse relationship between press access and electoral standing. Candidates throw themselves at the press (such as Senator McCain's "straight talk express" in 1992) when they anticipate that every additional news report may help them gain on their opponents, but they maintain a closed-door posture and ration information more sparingly once they attain a more competitive position in the polls.

Exactly the same ritual is played out in the context of debates. Front-runners are loath to participate in debates at all, but trailing candidates seek to have as many debates as is humanly possible. Arnold Schwarzenegger, the prohibitive favorite to win the candidate selection phase of the California recall election, condescended to participate in just one debate; his handlers explained his absence from the remaining debates by citing the rigors of his campaign schedule.

When candidates regulate their access, the principle of risk aversion dominates their behavior. Candidates who are ahead in the polls know that they represent appropriate targets and that the press will adopt an even more aggressive and skeptical posture when covering them. For the leading candidates, therefore, less press access is better than more.

PLAYING ONE SOURCE AGAINST ANOTHER

The abundance of reporters covering a major campaign provides candidates with the option of awarding access to sources on the basis of the anticipated "quality" of their coverage. The Clinton campaign emerged from the 1992 primaries with a number of serious character-related liabilities, any one of which could have erupted into a full-scale press crisis. The Whitewater scandal, the Gennifer Flowers affair, the state of the Clinton marriage, and Clinton's draft deferment were all red meat to the national press corps. No serious news organizations would cover Clinton without making reference to these nagging questions.

Rather than subject the candidate to this line of potentially damaging coverage, the Clinton campaign decided to schedule appearances on programs not typically associated with national political news. Clinton played the saxophone on *The Arsenio Hall Show*. His candidacy was the subject of an hour-long special on MTV (during which he was asked about his use of marijuana and responded, "I didn't inhale"). The Clinton team also arranged for the candidate to provide in-person interviews with local anchorpersons at every campaign stop. In short, the campaign was able to shield the candidate from the hostile posture of the national press by cultivating less prominent news outlets.

For a local television correspondent, an exclusive interview with a presidential candidate offers significant professional prestige; for candidate Clinton, the naïveté and inexperience of "outer ring" reporters allowed him to dominate the interviews, avoid all reference to his troubled past, and stay "on message"—that is, hammer away on the state of the national economy. What was the end result? A steady stream of favorable news reports that, according to Clinton insiders, allowed the candidate to transform his image from "Slick Willie" to the candidate with a plan to rejuvenate the economy.

The use of local news to spearhead the campaign message not only offers the candidate greater control over the message, but also makes for a better fit between the message and the audience. In presidential campaigns, candidates visit states that are up for grabs, not those that are firmly in the grasp of either party. The issues that concern voters are not the same in all battleground states. Disposal of nuclear waste, for instance, is a major concern for residents of New Mexico (the location of a major federal nuclear waste site); when campaigning in Wisconsin, where dairy subsidies are a major source of farmers' income, the candidate must demonstrate expertise on matters of agriculture policy. Local news, which is typically an intrastate medium, allows candidates the ability to switch messages depending on the local context.

DUELING PRESS RELEASES

A final element of press relations takes its cue from advertising. Candidates continually react to each other's statements and actions, mainly in the form of competing press releases. Each campaign maintains a "war room" to research and uncover weaknesses in the opponent's record. As soon as Kerry selected Edwards as his running mate in 2004, the Republican National Committee issued a detailed list of the North Carolina senator's "liberal" votes in the Senate. Republicans also noted Cheney's superior government experience, to which charge the Kerry–Edwards team responded with the retort that Vice President Cheney was in fact the president. These dueling press releases were designed to offer the media a coherent story line for the day's coverage. In fact, in the aftermath of the selection of Edwards, the "experience" theme was featured prominently in several stories covering the campaign. Thus, a significant amount of daily news coverage can be attributed to the candidates' strategists. Both teams maintain a complete roster of "analysts" to represent them on the talk radio and cable television circuit.

The fact that both campaigns are sifting through each other's actions and words with an eye on particularly newsworthy items creates a form of "balanced news"; when one side successfully plants a story, the other side is typically asked to react. Sometimes a candidate uses the opportunity to rebut the original story. On May 3, 2004, the Democrats issued a release while President Bush was on a bus tour of the Midwest focusing on jobs and the economy. They pointed out that Bush's bus was made by Prevost, a Canadian company. For good measure, they noted that Senator Kerry's bus was made in the United States. This story was reported by several major news organizations. As Kerry spokesperson Phil Singer put it, "Seeing the president drive around in this Canadian-made luxury bus is just another reminder of George Bush's failed economic policies" (Allen & Balz, 2004). The next day it was the Republicans' turn: "Kerry Rode in Prevost Bus Earlier This Year!" trumpeted the Republican National Committee release. This latest addition to the story was dutifully reported the next day: "Bush, Kerry Tour Buses Made in Canada."

As this example illustrates, a first principle of press management is the immediate rebuttal of unflattering stories in the news. Seeking to counter the series of reports about Kerry's combat experiences in Vietnam, the Bush campaign contacted veterans who had witnessed Kerry participate in protests against the Vietnam War. The campaign then made available the dates of the protests and the contact information of eyewitnesses. A more surgical strike was carried out by the Dukakis campaign in the 1988 primaries when they provided a videotape of the "plagiarized" speech given by Senator Biden, with the intention of aborting his campaign. The existence of the videotape was uncovered not by the press, but by the "opposition research" crew within the Dukakis campaign.

Campaign press releases are designed not only to show the candidate in the most favorable light, but also to help simplify the reporter's task of sorting out the various events, announcements, messages, and retorts that make up the daily news cycle. Campaigns are careful to synchronize their daily activities around a common principle or theme, in the hope that reporters will find it more convenient to organize their coverage around the "message of the day." Naturally, the press staffers are well aware of the special needs of the broadcast media and maintain a steady supply of colorful comments from their candidate suitable for inclusion as sound bites in the national newscasts.

In sum, candidates are no longer in a position to manufacture news. Since 1988, the press has become more combative and less willing to recycle the candidates' rhetoric. In response, candidates have taken a series of steps all meant to focus the attention of reporters on subjects that they consider advantageous: from the candidate's plan to revive the economy to misstatements by the opponent, they offer up their version of the message of the day in the hope of providing reporters with a story line they can't resist. When the national press corps proves insufficiently malleable, candidates turn to less prestigious news outlets where they are assured of gentler treatment.

Advertising Strategy

Unlike press management, where success requires campaigns to cater to the needs and values of journalists, advertising provides candidates with a much more "direct" route to the minds of voters. There is a significant trade-off, however: advertising is unmediated, but it is also a much less credible messenger than news reports are.

Effective advertising is not simply a question of designing a persuasive and memorable campaign jingle. The overall game plan is to strengthen the sponsoring candidate's "market share." That goal may be accomplished by adjustment in the advertising message to the stage of the campaign and to the specific attributes of the candidates in the race. In addition to synchronizing the advertising message to the context, campaigns must decide on the precise mix of affirmative messages in favor of the candidate (positive advertising) and negative messages designed to increase voter aversion to the opposing candidate. The extensive use of negative appeals is the hallmark of political advertising. Commercial advertising stays positive; automobile companies and department stores rarely criticize their competitors. Political advertising is different: candidates frequently attack their opponents.

TARGETING THE AUDIENCE

Television advertising takes different roles over the course of the campaign. Before we spell out the temporal contours of advertising strategy, it is important to understand that advertising is a highly targeted form of communication, no matter what the stage of the campaign. Unlike brand-name product appeals, which air on a national basis, political advertising is much narrower in scope. As the use of local news illustrates, candidates are interested primarily in reaching voters whose preferences may be pivotal to the outcome of the race. Senator Kerry had little interest in any of the California media markets in 2004 because he fully expected to win the state by a comfortable margin. Conversely, even the most optimistic Democratic strategist will avoid wasting advertising dollars in Texas, where the probability of a Democratic victory is near zero. By this logic, approximately thirty-five states are off the advertising table. Residents of these strongly "red" (Republican) or "blue" (Democratic) states typically see no presidential ads at all. The remaining states, however, are blanketed with advertising (see Figure 6.1).

The strategy is no different in statewide races. Counties or areas that are heavily Democratic or Republican are bypassed; instead, the candidates invest in markets where a small movement in the numbers can make the difference between winning and losing. In California, for example, voter preferences in the Bay Area are too one-sided to warrant an ad campaign, so candidates for statewide office concentrate on the Central Valley and the densely populated and more competitive Southern California markets.

In addition to singling out particular locations, campaigns engage in a different form of targeting designed to maximize the impact of advertising. For advertising to work, the audience must include adults who intend to vote. Clearly, advertising during children's programs would be meaningless, and advertising on MTV would be just as irrational, given the low rate of turnout among youth. Ideally, the ad would air during a program that drew likely voters. Local news, a form of programming that has enjoyed steady increases in viewership, provides just such an audience; people sufficiently motivated to watch the news are also likely to vote. The first half of the local newscast is thus a prime time slot for campaign advertising; the audience is tuning in to the top stories of the day, and their attention has yet to wander. Campaigns also rely heavily on "news adjacencies"—time slots just before or just after a local newscast. In some battleground states, the most desirable advertising slots (during local newscasts in particular) are booked ninety days in advance. Residents of Michigan or Wisconsin—at least those who watch television regularly—are sometimes exposed to the same ad so frequently that they claim they can recite the text in their sleep!

One other overarching factor affects candidates' use of advertising: the state of the campaign budget. Advertising is the single largest expenditure in

FIGURE 6.1 TARGETING VOTERS IN THE 2004 PRESIDENTIAL CAMPAIGN

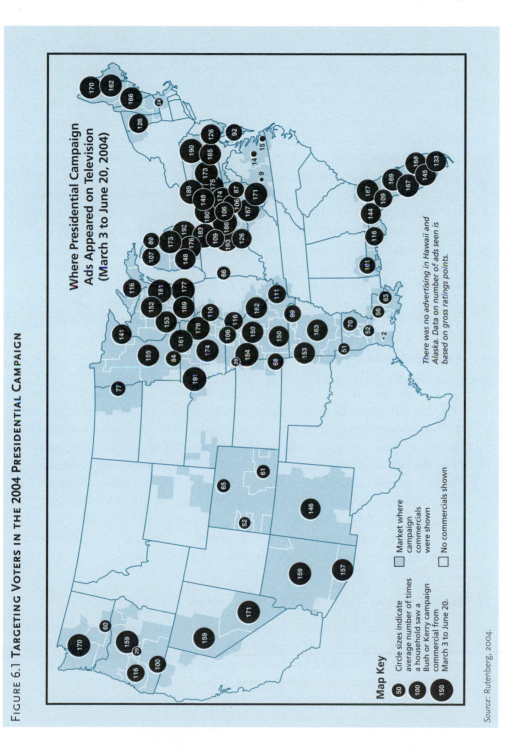

Where Presidential Campaign Ads Appeared on Television (March 3 to June 20, 2004)

There was no advertising in Hawaii and Alaska. Data on number of ads seen is based on gross ratings points.

Map Key

Circle sizes indicate average number of times a household saw a Bush or Kerry campaign commercial from March 3 to June 20.

50 100 150

☐ Market where campaign commercials were shown

☐ No commercials shown

Source: Rutenberg, 2004.

most major campaigns. A single airing of a thirty-second commercial during a 6:00 PM newscast in the two biggest television markets (New York City and Los Angeles) costs approximately seven thousand dollars. In contrast, candidates can run the ad ten different times for that amount in Las Vegas, and more than twenty times in South Dakota or Montana. Thus, allocating resources into ad campaigns depends not only on geography (targeting battleground states) but also on cost considerations. Residents of smaller media markets are likely to receive greater amounts of advertising simply because candidates get more for their advertising dollar.

Given the cost, campaigns attempt to reach as many likely voters as possible with each of their ads. The basic unit of exposure to advertising is the *gross rating point*, or *GRP*.[2] GRPs are scored to reflect the percentage of the media market that is exposed to the ad. Buying a hundred GRPs for an ad, for instance, would mean one exposure for each viewer; a thousand GRPs would mean that viewers would see the ad ten times. In recent years, with the increased proliferation of cable and satellite channels, consultants have been forced to ratchet up their ad buys to fight channel and advertising "clutter." In the 1990s, for instance, running a single ad five times was considered the norm. Today, an ad is likely to air ten times.

Ad buying is more art form than science. Depending on the ad, the stage of the campaign, and the scale of the budget, buyers might opt for the same level of GRPs throughout the campaign or, more likely, vary their buys to synchronize exposure to the ad campaign with the level of news coverage. The expectation is that candidates get more bang for their advertising buck when the campaign is in the news. This logic also influences the content of advertising. When a particular issue or event grabs the headlines, the candidates tend to incorporate that issue into their ads. In the 2001 and 2002 election cycles, for example, it was no surprise—given the exposure following 9/11—that the most popular spokesperson for Republican candidates across the country was New York City mayor Rudy Giuliani.

PLANTING THE SEED: EARLY ADVERTISING

VIDEO
FEATURE 6.1
Introducing
the
Candidate

Early in the campaign, advertising introduces the candidate to the electorate. Biographical spots focus on the candidate's personal background and record of public service. Military service is especially noteworthy as an indicator of fitness for office, as the images in Video Feature 6.1 reflect. For candidates who cannot claim to have risked their lives for the nation, alternative "qualifications" include humble beginnings, the ability to overcome adversity, strong family ties, and adherence to a core set of political principles. By focusing on personal virtues, campaigns attempt to instill confidence in the candidate's suitability for public office.

In nonpresidential races, where candidates might be unknown to voters, the first goal of the ad campaign is more mundane—namely, a boost in the candidate's name recognition (see Video Feature 6.2). In some cases, biographical spots focus specifically on the candidate's name. Ed Zschau and Wyche Fowler, both little-known candidates for the US Senate in 1986, opened their campaigns with ads that simply explained the correct pronunciation of their names. In politics, familiarity is a necessary condition of electability; voters are disinclined to vote for a name they do not recognize.

VIDEO FEATURE 6.2 Promoting Name Recognition

IMAGE VERSUS ISSUE SPOTS

Once they have provided voters with a snapshot of their lives, candidates move on to their credentials. *Image ads* maintain thematic continuity with the biographical message by presenting the candidate as a likable human being with a strong sense of public service. *Issue ads* are more substantive and either focus on the candidate's past experience and record in public life, or outline the candidate's positions on major policy issues.

The relative importance of image and issue advertising depends on the electoral context. In 1984, the Cold War had ended and voters felt secure on the economic front. This atmosphere of political tranquility was captured by the Reagan campaign in what is generally considered the classic image ad. Labeled "Morning in America," the ad listed President Reagan's accomplishments against a background of idyllic rural landscapes and smiling children. Four years later, Vice President Bush aired a textbook example of an issue ad, calling into question Governor Dukakis's credentials on the issue of national defense. Video Feature 6.3 recalls these two ads.

When voters are concerned about the state of the country, both incumbents and challengers turn to issue ads. As President George H. W. Bush found out in 1992, voters who were worried about losing their jobs were relatively forgiving of a challenger with questionable personal attributes; they made their choices based more on questions of performance. The "Slick Willie" nickname applied to Bill Clinton was not as relevant as "It's the economy, stupid."

VIDEO FEATURE 6.3 Image and Issue Appeals

From the beginning of campaign advertising, image ads have inevitably portrayed the candidate as a "man of the people." American voters do not take kindly to millionaire candidates from privileged backgrounds. The focus on the common touch is ironic; most presidential candidates are members of a distinctly elite group with appropriate prep school and Ivy League credentials. One of President George H. W. Bush's greatest liabilities during the 1992 campaign was that he personified the gulf between the well-to-do and middle-class America. In a well-circulated story, the president was said to have expressed his delight with the advanced technology of price scanners at a local supermarket, thus revealing his utter unfamiliarity with grocery store shopping.[3]

Issue ads fall into two broad classes: performance messages touting the sponsoring candidate's experience and proven accomplishments as a public servant (see Video Feature 6.4), and policy messages summarizing the candidate's preferences on public policy. Campaigns featuring an incumbent invariably gravitate to performance themes. In presidential and gubernatorial contests, voters habitually frame the choice as a referendum on the performance of the incumbent. Challengers broadcast ads suggesting that the incumbent has weakened the economy, or that the administration has done nothing to make the world more secure from terrorism. Conversely, incumbents are quick to take credit for economic growth, balanced budgets, reductions in crime, or other such indicators of effective governance.

VIDEO
FEATURE 6.4
Performance
Messages

ISSUE OWNERSHIP

Policy advertising follows a simple formula: highlight the candidate's positions, but focus only on issues where your candidate is favored. This directive has two specific implications: First, do not publicize your support for unpopular or controversial positions (that task will be taken up by your opponent). Second, single out issues on which you and, more important, your party are seen as more likely to provide relief. In sum, parties and candidates often "own" certain issues, and these owned issues are featured in campaign advertising.

Issue ownership is a by-product of American political culture. Long before they reach voting age, most Americans are socialized to associate each party with a set of interests and, by inference, with a set of issues or problems on which they will deliver. In general, "Republican-owned" issues include national security, defense, and foreign affairs. That is, the public typically assumes that Republicans are better able to deal with these issues than Democrats are. Conversely, voters favor Democrats on most "quality of life" issues, including job and income security, health care, and social welfare. Of course, the public rates the two parties evenly on certain other issues, such as balancing the budget and strengthening the public schools.

In Focus: Issue Ownership

Issue ownership refers to the fact that the public considers each party to be more capable on different issues; for example, Republicans are thought to perform better in the area of military and defense policy, and Democrats are considered more favorably on issues such as education, Social Security, and the like. Candidates tend to campaign on issues that their party owns because their message is more credible when consistent with the stereotype of the party.

How did voters rate the parties on the salient issues in 2004? In California, a recent poll (see Figure 6.2) showed that Republicans owned terrorism and Democrats were preferred on health care, but neither party could claim ownership of the economy.

The Bush campaign in 2004 attempted to capitalize on its reputation by making the war on terrorism the centerpiece of the campaign. The first round of Republican ads, released on March 5, 2004, made frequent references to 9/11 and terrorist threats. Later in the campaign, the Bush team produced "Wolves" (see Video Feature 6.5), an ad that attacked Senator Kerry as being weak on defense. Interestingly, this ad borrowed heavily from "Bear in the Woods," President Reagan's 1984 ad promoting a strong military posture vis-à-vis the Soviet Union. For its part, the Kerry campaign followed the

VIDEO FEATURE 6.5 Advertising on Owned Issues

FIGURE 6.2 **CALIFORNIANS RATE THE PARTIES**

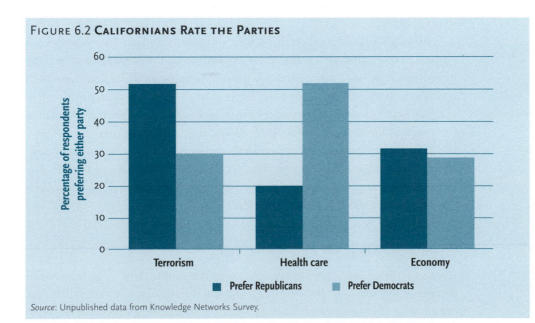

Source: Unpublished data from Knowledge Networks Survey.

standard Democratic script and promoted Kerry's positions on job loss and health care while attacking Bush as a stooge of the wealthy.

The principle of issue ownership extends to attributes of the candidate other than party affiliation. Gender is an especially visible attribute, and American culture provides ample cues about the traits of males and females. Given these widely held gender stereotypes, male and female candidates have reason to project their masculinity and femininity, respectively. "Masculine" issues such as defense, terrorism, and crime resonate well for a male candidate; child care and matters of educational policy confirm voters' beliefs about the credentials of a female candidate (see, for example, Video Feature 6.6).

VIDEO
FEATURE 6.6
Hillary
Rodham
Clinton on
the Issues in
the 2000
Senatorial
Campaign

Between "owned" issues are policy areas in which neither party enjoys a decisive advantage. These can be seen as "leased" issues on which parties can claim short-term occupancy, depending on the nature of the times or the track record of particular candidates. The Bush administration's policy of preemption and the massive intelligence failure on which the policy rested provided Kerry with the opportunity to challenge Bush on the issue of national security. Similarly, the Enron scandal and other instances of corporate corruption allowed Democrats to exploit white-collar crime as a political issue. On the other side, President Bush's successful efforts to enact comprehensive school reform in Texas and the passage of the No Child Left Behind Act during his first term gave him sufficient credibility to contest the issue in 2004.

Although leased issues attract ads from both candidates, the principle of playing to one's strengths creates few opportunities for candidates to engage in an exchange on issues. Advertising campaigns generally do not resemble a dialogue between the competing candidates. Instead, they typically offer two essentially unrelated streams of messages. Candidates prefer to talk past each other in the hope of promoting their comparative advantages.

There is one notable exception to this pattern. The frequent use of negative advertising means that the attack–counterattack spiral is a typical outcome of ad campaigns. Before we discuss negative advertising, however, let's look at another strategy of agenda control.

WEDGE APPEALS: US VERSUS THEM

Consider the following scenario. As the traditional kickoff of the 2004 fall campaign approached, the economy remained stagnant, the federal budget deficit had ballooned, and American troops were dying every day in Iraq. Obviously this state of affairs represented a serious liability for President

Bush. Boxed in by the war on one side and the domestic economy on the other, the only recourse seemed to be to introduce so-called wedge issues into campaign discourse. *Wedge issues* are designed to pit groups against each other, to appeal to voters' sense of group identity. (As we'll discuss, gay marriage became the wedge issue of the day in the 2004 election.) When candidates turn to wedge appeals, it is generally a tacit acknowledgment that they are losing the debate on generic issues.

Race and ethnicity are the most powerfully divisive issues in American politics. From the Civil War through the passage of landmark civil rights legislation in the 1960s to current debates over affirmative action and reparations, Americans have been consistently divided by race. One set of wedge appeals seeks to capitalize on this racial division. Typically, the strategy is used by Republican candidates, who hope to attract white Democrats and independents on the basis of their opposition to race-based policies such as affirmative action in employment and diversity credits in college admissions.[4]

In recent years, the emergence of immigration-related issues has injected a parallel Latino-versus-Anglo divide into campaigns. In this case, the strategy is for candidates to position themselves as opponents of immigration. When California governor Pete Wilson ran an ad in 1994 that began with the line "They keep coming," most Californians immediately understood what he meant. In short, wedge appeals based on race or ethnicity are aimed at capturing white votes by depicting the candidate as taking a stand against the threatening demands of blacks or Hispanics. The appeal is either explicit— as in the case of immigration or affirmative action—or implicit, as in the case of crime, drug abuse, or law and order.

Cultural identity, or "family values," provides an alternative basis for dividing voters. Initially introduced by President Nixon in 1968 as an appeal to conservative southern Democrats, based on Republican opposition to school busing, the "family values" slogan has since broadened into a code word for general conservatism and opposition to nonmainstream lifestyles. A call for family values is generally interpreted as opposition to abortion, feminism, gay rights, and sex education in the public schools.

For President George W. Bush, the family values theme represented a clear advantage in 2004. In February of that year, the decision by the mayor of San Francisco to issue same-sex marriage licenses attracted considerable media attention across the country. It was not coincidental that the Republican-controlled Senate took up the proposed constitutional amendment banning same-sex marriage (framed by Republicans as the amendment to "save traditional marriage") two weeks before the Democratic convention. They hoped to elevate family values as a criterion for differentiating between Kerry and Bush.

Conservative groups placed measures banning same-sex marriage on the November ballot in eleven states (including the key battleground states of Ohio and Oregon).[5] Moral issues became a battle cry for conservative Republicans, many of them Evangelical Christians. In fact, the response "moral issues" was checked as the "most important issue" in the 2004 exit poll by over 20 percent of voters. This group voted for President Bush by a four-to-one margin.

Explicit appeals to wedge issues were made in both the 1988 and 1996 presidential campaigns, in which crime and illegal immigration, respectively, were major issues (see Video Feature 6.7). Given the one-sided nature of the 1996 election, it is unlikely that Senator Robert Dole's attempts to run on the immigration issue had any role in the outcome. In August 1988, however, the airing of the notorious "Willie Horton" ad attacking Michael Dukakis for his support of prison furlough programs was thought to have played a major role in the Bush campaign's ability to overcome what was then a double-digit deficit in the polls.

Although recent presidential campaigns have steered clear of race-based wedge appeals, the same cannot be said of candidates for statewide office. In 1990, conservative Republican senator Jesse Helms was locked in a close race with Democrat Harvey Gantt (the African-American mayor of Charlotte, North Carolina). During the closing days of the race, Helms released an ad opposing the use of affirmative action in employment decisions. This "White Hands" ad (see Video Feature 6.8) is credited with producing a significant surge in white support for Helms. Eight years later the tables were turned. Opponents of Proposition 209, a measure to end affirmative action in California, aired an ad featuring David Duke, a well-known member of the Ku Klux Klan, in the hope that the negative imagery of hooded Klansmen and cross burnings would weaken moderate whites' support for the measure. The strategy failed, and Proposition 209 passed easily.

In recent campaign cycles, immigration has emerged as a significant electoral issue in many states. Given that California has a Hispanic population amounting to one-third of its population, and considering the state's proximity to Mexico, it is not surprising that California is in the thick of the battle to limit immigration. To illustrate how immigration has affected the political scene, in the following section we will examine the 1994 race for governor of California between incumbent Republican Pete Wilson and Democratic challenger Kathleen Brown.

"THEY KEEP COMING"

As governor of California, Pete Wilson faced a challenging reelection campaign in 1994. The state was in the throes of a severe recession, with an

VIDEO
FEATURE 6.7
Dividing by
Race and
Ethnicity

VIDEO
FEATURE 6.8
Affirmative
Action as a
Wedge Issue

accompanying exodus of companies and jobs. Wilson faced a popular and well-known Democrat—State Treasurer Kathleen Brown. Naturally, Brown's ads emphasized the recession, Wilson's inability to bring relief to the state, and her own economic expertise. With this theme, she established a substantial lead over Wilson.

Recognizing that a debate over the state of the economy was a hopeless cause, Wilson campaigned as a crime fighter and an opponent of illegal immigration. He linked his candidacy to two well-known statewide propositions: 184 and 187. Proposition 184, known as the *three-strikes* measure, was approved by a landslide margin (72 to 28 percent). Proposition 187, which proposed limiting or eliminating illegal immigrants' eligibility for a variety of government services, also attracted majority support. As Video Feature 6.9 shows, the Wilson campaign invested heavily in advertising on both issues.

VIDEO FEATURE 6.9 Changing the Subject in the 1994 California Gubernatorial Campaign

Wilson's efforts to shift the agenda were aided by the Brown campaign, which engaged Wilson on the issue of crime despite Brown's opposition to the death penalty. In a strategic error, Brown preempted Wilson on crime by airing a "Willie Horton"–like critique of Wilson's decision to parole a violent offender. This ad provoked a series of ads on the subject of crime (see Video Feature 6.10).

Thanks to Brown's tactical error, the California electorate was exposed to a genuine "dialogue" on the issue of crime and punishment. Voters' impressions of the candidates became increasingly linked to their positions on crime. On this issue, most voters (including many Democrats) favored Wilson over Brown. Brown's support eroded (see Figure 6.3) and Wilson was reelected by a comfortable margin.

VIDEO FEATURE 6.10 Advertising Dialogue in the Brown/ Wilson Race

The success of the Wilson campaign suggests that ethnicity is still a potent divider in American politics. Republicans are able to attract white voters by representing themselves as being opposed to policies widely perceived as contrary to whites' interests.

Negative Advertising

In recent years, research on the subject of negative campaign advertising has become a growth industry. As we have noted, a striking attribute of political advertising campaigns is the heavy reliance (at least in comparison with product advertising campaigns) on so-called negative or attack advertising. Although the number and ratio of positive to negative ads varies across campaigns, there can be no denying that political advertising is a relatively hostile and impolite form of discourse. In contrast to normal discourse, which is char-

FIGURE 6.3 EROSION OF SUPPORT FOR BROWN IN THE 1994 CALIFORNIA GUBERNATORIAL CAMPAIGN

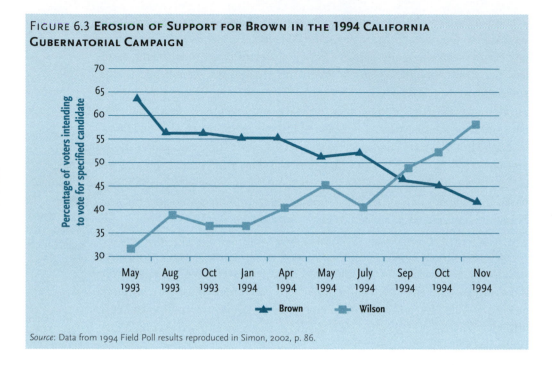

Source: Data from 1994 Field Poll results reproduced in Simon, 2002, p. 86.

acterized by a positivity bias (we normally greet others with a smile and a cheery hello), candidates tend to dwell on the flaws—either personal or substantive—of their opponents. In some cases, advertising campaigns devote all their resources to questioning the opponent's fitness for office. It has reached the point where candidates routinely air ads attacking their opponents for running negative campaigns.

Certainly criticism, counterargument, and rebuttal are legitimate and essential ingredients of fair political debate. In the context of political advertising, however, it is possible for a candidate to focus exclusively on defining the opponent while remaining silent about his own suitability for office. Gray Davis was reelected governor of California in 2002 using just this strategy. Davis spent millions attacking his Republican opponent (Bill Simon) as a wealthy and corrupt businessman with no political experience. But even before Simon won the Republican nomination, Davis spent millions on ads attacking Simon's Republican rival, Richard Riordan (see Video Feature 6.11). As the mayor of Los Angeles, Riordan had accumulated an impressive record in office, was well known, and could appeal to moderate voters. Realizing that Riordan would be a more dangerous direct opponent, Davis broadcast

VIDEO
FEATURE 6.11
Attacks by
the Davis
Campaign in
the 2002
California
Gubernatorial
Race

ads attacking Riordan for his frequent policy reversals on abortion (a charge likely to resonate with conservative Republican voters). Subject to attacks from both Davis and Simon, Riordan's poll numbers dropped and Simon won the primary.

In the end, though, did the Davis strategy really work? It can't be disputed that Simon defeated Riordan in the primary and Davis easily defeated Simon in November. However, having campaigned against both Riordan and Simon without giving voters a single affirmative reason to reelect him, Davis was vulnerable to a rising tide of political discontent that was orchestrated by Republican activists into a full-scale recall campaign. Lacking public support, Davis was ousted from office less than a year after his reelection.

NEGATIVE THEMES

Negative campaigns run the gamut from direct attacks on the personal attributes of a candidate to ads linking the candidate with unsavory groups or causes. Typically, consultants differentiate between character assassination in which the opponent is depicted as an immoral human being and performance critiques that focus on the candidate's record. Personal attacks are standard fare in lower-level races. As one moves up the political ladder, attack ads become more performance-oriented. In 2000, for instance, the Gore campaign lampooned Governor Bush's credentials on education by pointing out that Texas schools ranked forty-ninth on basic indicators of school achievement.

The most common genre of political attack is the "flip-flop" ad: Candidate X voted yes in 2002, but no in 2004, for example. In 2004, the Bush campaign repeatedly juxtaposed Kerry's criticisms of the Iraq War with his Senate vote authorizing the war. This line of attack is thought to be especially effective because it resonates with voters' stereotypes of politicians as insincere and willing to say anything to get elected. In one of the most negative campaigns for US Senate (which occurred in 1994), Republican challenger Michael Huffington ended each of his attack ads on incumbent Dianne Feinstein with this punch line: "Dianne Feinstein, the candidate who'll say anything to get elected." Not to be outdone, Feinstein adopted an equally pungent sign-off: "Michael Huffington, a Texas millionaire that Californians can't trust."

An especially effective attack on a candidate's record is the "guilt by association" spot. Criticizing a candidate for having voted to weaken the Patriot Act is unlikely to have much impact because most voters are not very familiar with that act. Linking the candidate with Osama bin Laden, however, would make it crystal clear that the candidate is soft on terrorism. In 1996, the Clinton campaign repeatedly portrayed Senator Dole as out of touch with majority opinion by depicting him side by side with House Speaker Newt Gingrich.

REACTIVITY: ATTACKS PROVOKE COUNTERATTACKS

The prominence of negative appeals in campaign advertising can be attributed to several factors. Politics is seen as a dirty business, and the public is cynical about the motives and behaviors of candidates for office. In this context, an attack is more credible than a message promoting a candidate's virtues. Equally important, bad news and conflict are far more newsworthy than good news and civility are. The ripple effect of negative advertising can be considerable. That is, attacks are especially effective in attracting press coverage; in fact, campaigns often schedule a press conference to announce their latest attack ad.

Sometimes the ad is merely a ruse designed to titillate the press, and no airtime is purchased. The Republican National Committee (RNC) announced the hard-hitting anti-Clinton "Soldiers and Sailors" ad to the press in 1996, and the attack was summarized and critiqued in all the leading outlets, but the ad was never actually aired. From the perspective of the Dole campaign, putting Clinton's penchant for sex scandals on the front pages was well worth the criticism of releasing "misleading" information. More recently, a group funded by Republican donors (Swift Vets and POWs for Truth, a group of veterans who served in Vietnam on US Navy "Swift Boats") aired an ad in 2004 accusing Senator John Kerry of lying about his military record in Vietnam.

Although the amount of money invested in both of these ads was trivial, the sponsors attracted a torrent of news reports across the country simply because their message was so controversial. As Figure 6.4 shows, the "Swift Boats" ad not only generated an avalanche of newspaper reports within the United States, but it also attracted considerable attention in the international press. For the media, personal attacks are big stories.

The most compelling explanation of negative campaigning is that one attack invites a counterattack, thus setting in motion a spiral of negativity. Among campaign professionals, a fundamental principle is that the attacked candidate must punch back, and the sooner the better. In this sense, at least, negative campaigns amount to a debate.

We know of very little good scientific evidence on the efficacy of counterattacks, but the anecdotal evidence is consistent with the view that they work. In 1988, Michael Dukakis enjoyed a substantial lead over Vice Presi-

VIDEO
FEATURE 6.12
Character
Attacks

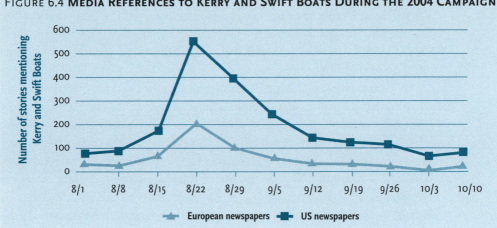

FIGURE 6.4 **MEDIA REFERENCES TO KERRY AND SWIFT BOATS DURING THE 2004 CAMPAIGN**

dent Bush following the Democratic nomination. The Bush campaign then released a series of negative ads attacking Dukakis on crime (including a version of the previously discussed "Willie Horton" ad) and the polluted state of Boston's harbor. Inexplicably, the Dukakis campaign ignored these attacks, even though they were highly controversial and the subject of interminable news coverage across the country. Eventually Bush was able to catch Dukakis in the polls, and he went on to win the election.

Since 1988, campaign strategists have become convinced of the necessity to mount counterattacks. Clinton's advisors saw to it that every attack in 1992 was rebutted, in some cases even before the Republican ad hit the airwaves. Rapid response became the hallmark of advertising strategy, thus accelerating the pace at which ad campaigns arrived at the negative–negative endgame. One of the major themes in postmortems of the 2004 campaign concerned the Kerry campaign's unwillingness to rebut the Swift Boat allegations. According to Kerry pollster Mark Mellman, the campaign was hesitant to counter the attacks, for fear of adding credibility to the charges.[6]

In one of the few controlled studies to examine the value of counterattacks, Ansolabehere and Iyengar (1995) compared the vote shares of candidates who responded to an opponent's attack either by running a positive ad or by attacking the attacker. Respondents in these studies watched the initial attack and the attacked candidate's response. Applying this method to two statewide campaigns, the authors showed that the attacked candidate was significantly better off to counterattack. Moreover, they also demonstrated that support for the attacked candidate who responded with a positive ad dropped substantially among voters who shared the attacked candidate's party. That is, Democrats were less enthusiastic about voting Democratic when the Republican attacked and the Democrat countered with a positive message. Overall, Ansolabehere and Iyengar's results show clearly that rational candidates should counterattack.

The extensive use of negative campaigning raises serious questions about accountability in campaign discourse. Journalists can be sued for knowingly printing inaccurate information about public figures with intent to harm. The "victims" of negative advertising campaigns, on the other hand, only have recourse to the dictum of more speech—in this context, counterattacks. The lack of accountability for the use of misleading or inaccurate attacks is compounded by the frequent use of surrogates rather than the candidate as the messenger. In general, the more personal or controversial the attack, the less likely it is that the sponsoring candidate will appear in person. In the 2004 campaign, the most hard-hitting attacks on President Bush were delivered not by John Kerry, but by liberal interest groups such as MoveOn (see Video Feature 6.13).

VIDEO
FEATURE 6.13
MoveOn.org
Attacks on
President
Bush

As a means of making candidates more responsible for their advertisements, reform-minded groups have been urging the passage of legislation that makes the connection between specific ads and the sponsoring candidate more transparent. Their efforts succeeded in 2003 when Congress adopted a provision requiring presidential candidates to appear on-screen

---

In Focus: Campaign Advertising Strategies

- Target voters who may be pivotal to the outcome of the race—that is, voters in states or regions considered competitive.

- Advertise during programs watched by those likely to vote (such as during local news shows).

- Ride the wave" by connecting advertising to issues or events in the headlines.

- Use biographical spots early in the campaign to introduce the candidate; then move on to image and issue ads.

- Take advantage of "issue ownership."

- Use wedge appeals when necessary.

- Go negative to generate media coverage and be credible to voters, and use surrogates to deliver the most controversial claims.

- When attacked, mount a counterattack.

in their ads while stating "I'm Candidate X, and I approved this message." Because candidates can no longer rely on surrogates to do their dirty work for them, we may anticipate that the negativity quotient in campaign advertising will fall. At the very least, the "in person" rule is likely to deter campaigns from engaging in character-related attacks.

Direct Mail as an Alternative to Televised Advertising

For nonpresidential candidates, especially those running in geographically compact districts, televised advertising is an inefficient medium. The Los Angeles media market includes all or part of seventeen congressional districts. New York City provides even less overlap between the media market and political district boundaries. The audience for New York City television includes voters in three different states (New York, New Jersey, and Connecticut). A congressional candidate who advertises on Los Angeles TV, or a candidate for governor of New York who buys time on New York City stations is paying top dollar (New York and Los Angeles are the two most expensive markets in the country) to reach people who cannot vote for her.

In "congested" markets such as Los Angeles and New York, candidates rely on a more precise method of reaching voters: direct mail. Mail is the most extensive form of advertising in congressional and other "localized" campaigns. Direct mail is big business; in California alone, there are some seventy-five registered mail consultants, and total expenditures on mail amounted to nearly twenty million dollars in 1998. As in the case of television advertising, mail consultants are affiliated by party; they work exclusively for Republicans or Democrats.

Direct mail is utilized by all candidates, from the top of the ticket to the bottom. In some cases, mailers may focus on an individual candidate, but more commonly they urge the voter to support an entire slate. So-called slate mailers are typically financed by state party organizations, but they are also published by private campaign consultants, some of whom mail millions of pieces per election.

Slate mail is the most economical form of political advertising. Not only does it maximize the ability of the candidate to target the message to voters (as opposed to nonvoters), slate mail also allows several candidates to share in the cost of advertising. For candidates whose budgets do not run into several millions of dollars (virtually every candidate for county or local office), slate mail is the only advertising medium.

Because slate mailers usually feature candidates for several offices, lesser-known candidates benefit from their association with more visible candidates and causes. For instance, in the midst of the impeachment proceedings against President Clinton, a 1998 mailer sent to California Democrats featured the slogan "end the Washington witch hunt."

One final advantage of direct mail, at least from the candidate's perspective, is that the message is generally ignored by the news media. Candidates often resort to using misleading, unsubstantiated, and even flat-out false allegations against opponents.

In the final analysis, despite widespread concern that political ads trivialize democracy and transform campaigns into shouting matches, they remain an essential form of campaign communication. In the era of interpretive journalism, ads represent the only unmediated form of communicating with voters. Not surprisingly, candidates use the opportunity to extol their own virtues and denigrate their opponents. If voters seem more responsive to a particular form of advertising, rational candidates converge on that form.

Attempts to regulate the content and form of campaign advertising are exercises in futility. As an ingredient of political speech, advertising is fully protected by the First Amendment. In races with evenly matched candidates, voters encounter countervailing and retaliatory messages; that is, the campaign creates a free flow of information. As for the notion that voters need protection from ad campaigns, it suffices to note that voters are not fools. Recognizing the nature of the medium, they discount ads appropriately. The evidence on the effects of exposure to advertising presented in Chapter 9 demonstrates that the principal effect of advertising is to make fellow partisans more enthusiastic about the sponsoring candidate. Seen in this light (preaching to the choir), efforts to police campaign advertising and monitor the accuracy of the charges and countercharges seem both elitist and excessive. Not only do ad watches have the potential to recycle the message in the guise of a news report, but they are just as lacking in accountability as the ads themselves. And who watches the ad watchers?

Campaign advertising is expensive. Except for presidential candidates, whose campaigns are paid for by public funding, all candidates must raise large sums of money if they are to engage in advertising. Since 1972, the total amount of money expended on campaigns has increased tenfold, reaching a billion dollars in 2002. The huge sums of money involved and the resulting preoccupation with fund-raising have provoked considerable discussion about the role of money in politics. Should candidates who accept money from contributors return the favor by voting for legislation supported by the donors? Does the high cost of campaigning create the appearance that candidates are "bought" by powerful interests, thus compromising the political process? These and other questions have propelled campaign finance reform to the forefront of the policy agenda.

Campaign Finance Reform: A Brief Overview

The present era of campaign finance reform began in 1971 with the passage of the Federal Election Campaign Act (FECA), whose stricter requirements concerning the disclosure of sources of campaign funding played a role in the Watergate scandal. The remaining provisions of the 1971 FECA never took effect, because Watergate prompted their replacement by the 1974 FECA amendments. Those amendments remain the backbone of federal campaign finance regulation.

Aside from disclosure, the 1974 amendments contained three broad categories of regulation: limits on the size of contributions, limits on the amount of spending, and limits on public financing. The limits on how much a campaign could spend were supplemented by limits on how much candidates could spend of their own money on their campaigns, and on how much outsiders could spend independently to help the candidate. The contribution and spending limits applied to all federal candidates, but the public financing was available only for presidential elections. Public funds matched private contributions in presidential primaries, and the public funds were supposed to pay all the costs of the national nominating conventions and of the presidential general-election campaigns. The Federal Election Commission (FEC), with members appointed by the president and by party leaders in the House and Senate, was created to administer the new law.

The first challenge to campaign finance regulations was considered by the US Supreme Court in 1976 in *Buckley v. Valeo*. The Court ruled that all three forms of spending limits were violations of the First Amendment guarantee of freedom of speech. In an oft-quoted passage, the Court said, "The concept that government may restrict the speech of some elements of our society in order to enhance the relative voice of others is wholly foreign to the First Amendment" (*Buckley v. Valeo*, 1976, pp. 48–49). Although the Court thus rejected promotion of equality as a justification for speech restrictions, it gave more credence to the goal of preventing corruption (such as the buying of influence) and the appearance of corruption. That goal justified the limits on the size of contributions by individuals, political action committees (PACs), and other entities.

The Court rejected challenges to most other parts of the law, including the disclosure and public financing provisions. Furthermore, even spending limits could be constitutional, if they were conditions attached to the voluntary acceptance of benefits received from the state, such as public financing. However, the Court found that the ability of congressional leaders to appoint members of the FEC violated the separation of powers required by the Constitution. Congress quickly amended the law in 1976 to allow the president to appoint all the members. By custom ever since, the president has deferred to the leadership of the other party on half the FEC appointments.

An additional set of FECA amendments was enacted in 1979. In an attempt to strengthen the role of party organizations, Congress excluded "party-building activities" such as get-out-the-vote efforts and administrative upkeep from regulation. This provision became significant in later years as parties took advantage of the party-building exclusion to raise unlimited amounts of contributions known as *soft money*.

Federal campaign law then remained stable for nearly a quarter of a century. Campaign practices evolved, however, usually to the discomfort of reform activists, who tended to be Democrats. The first major development was the rise of business-oriented PACs during the 1970s. As is often the case with political reform, this development contained some irony, in that it had been labor unions, not corporations, that had pressed Congress to make clear the legality of PACs in the 1974 amendments. But business took the most advantage. Four major types of organizations sponsored PACs in the 1970s: unions, corporations, trade groups, and ideological groups. All were significant, but it was the corporate PACs that grew the fastest and raised the most money.

Nevertheless, the PAC situation eventually stabilized, and in the meantime, activists became preoccupied with a new development: independent spending. Because the Supreme Court had upheld limits on the size of contributions but protected the right to independently spend unlimited amounts for a candidate, some organizations found that, to have a noticeable effect on elections, they had to turn to independent spending. In particular, certain conservative PACs had considerable success in 1978 and 1980 using independent spending to defeat incumbent Democratic senators. Reformers who were Democrats clamored for control of independent spending for both partisan and ideological reasons. But by 1982, Democratic senators had learned how to defend themselves against attacks driven by independent spending. Reformers' attention turned to the issue of soft money and, later, to the related issue of "issue advocacy."

Soft money has been defined in various ways. Its original meaning was money that political parties could raise and spend that was exempt from the disclosure requirements and, especially, the contribution limits imposed by

FECA. Now the term often denotes campaign money that is exempt from limitation, whether or not it is spent by a party. Concern over soft money began to be expressed in the 1980s and grew steadily through the mid-1990s. Despite the reformers' concern, however, soft money does not appear to have played a major role until the 1996 election.

To understand *issue advocacy*, which also emerged as a major issue in 1996, we must go back to the Supreme Court's decision in *Buckley v. Valeo*. The FECA definition of campaign expenditures turned on whether money was spent for a "political purpose," a term that the Court regarded as unduly vague. To avoid that vagueness, the Court in *Buckley* interpreted FECA to cover only expenditures for speech that expressly urged the election or defeat of a clearly identified candidate. Phrases like "vote for Smith," "defeat Lopez," or "reelect the president" would qualify. Ads referring to candidates but not containing express advocacy were referred to as *issue ads* or *issue advocacy*, and they were not covered by FECA.

The Court itself admitted in *Buckley* that the narrow definition of what was included as a campaign expenditure would allow evasion of the campaign law. Nevertheless, and perhaps surprisingly, for about two decades very little advertising took advantage of this loophole. But the new possibilities of both soft money and issue advocacy exploded in 1996.

In that year, parties began raising soft money in much larger amounts than in the past, much of it in contributions of six or seven figures. Furthermore, much of the soft money was more directly related to particular federal campaigns than it had been before. The clearest and most important example was issue advertising that targeted particular candidates but that evaded regulation because it did not use words such as "vote for" or "defeat."

In addition to the explosion of soft money raised by parties, the 1996 election saw a new large-scale use of issue advertising by nonparty groups. Unions paid for ads attacking Republican candidates, and business funded ads attacking Democrats. Unlike the use of soft money by the parties, nonparty issue advertising evaded not only the contribution limitations and prohibitions, but also the disclosure requirements.

Soft money and issue advocacy expanded dramatically in 1996 and grew even more in subsequent elections. Reformers, who in the early and mid-1990s had been proposing broad new campaign regulations that were going nowhere in Congress, began focusing on soft money and issue advocacy. They enjoyed widespread support from the press, but the passage of legislation might not have been possible if not for a political boost from scandals that erupted early in 2002 regarding fraudulent accounting practices of Enron and other large corporations.

The legislation, passed by Congress in 2002 and signed by President George W. Bush, was known as the McCain–Feingold bill in the Senate and the Shays–Meehan bill in the House. Its official name is the Bipartisan Campaign Reform Act (BCRA), which is a misnomer because, despite support from a few prominent Republicans, such as Senator John McCain, it relied primarily on Democratic support.

Although BCRA doubled the limit on contributions from individuals to federal candidates from one thousand dollars to two thousand dollars, virtually all the remaining provisions consisted of new or tightened regulations. These regulations cover a wide variety of subjects, but the most important provisions are aimed at parties (and therefore at soft money) and at issue advocacy.

The BCRA method of dealing with soft money is rather severe. All money raised by parties at the national level has to be *hard money*—money raised within the federal contribution limits and subject to federal prohibitions, such as those against corporate and union contributions. This restriction applies even to money raised for purposes far removed from campaigns, such as building party headquarters. Furthermore, restrictions on state and local parties are greatly tightened. Suppose, for example, that a state party spends a hundred thousand dollars on get-out-the-vote activity. Prior to BCRA, a formula would be applied to determine the portion of the expenditure attributable to federal races. If that portion were 40 percent, then forty thousand dollars of the state party's expenditure would have to be paid for out of contributions raised within the federal limits and prohibitions, but the remaining sixty thousand dollars would be subject only to whatever limits were imposed by state law. Under BCRA, all the funds must come from hard money if the ballot contains any federal candidates at all.

BCRA's approach to issue advocacy is equally broad, but also surprisingly incomplete. In order to deal with the vagueness that caused problems in *Buckley*, BCRA creates a new category called *electioneering communications*, consisting of any broadcast advertising that identifies a federal candidate and is run within thirty days before a primary or sixty days before a general election. Electioneering communications must be disclosed and must be paid for out of hard money. The concept sweeps broadly because it includes not only ads clearly targeted at the campaign, but other ads that mention, say, the president or a senator while debating a particular legislative or policy controversy having no direct relation to the campaign. On the other hand, all nonbroadcast advertising and all advertising more than a month or two before the election are excluded.

It remains to be seen whether BCRA will have its intended consequences. It overcame a major hurdle in 2003 when the Supreme Court upheld, by a five-to-four vote, all of its major provisions in *McConnell v. Federal Election Commission*. *McConnell* and other recent decisions have caused speculation that the Court might be ready to overrule portions of *Buckley* to permit more-stringent campaign finance regulation. Indeed, among legal scholars, even some friendly to regulation have questioned the Court's casual approach to First Amendment concerns in *McConnell*. However, with the retirement in 2005 of one member of the *McConnell* majority, Justice Sandra Day O'Connor, the future direction of the Court's treatment of campaign finance is anyone's guess.

Despite BCRA's early success in court, it had little impact on the money chase in the 2004 elections. To the surprise of some, parties were able to make up for the loss of large contributions by raising increased amounts of hard money, partly with the aid of relatively small donations raised through the Internet. But the large donors, blocked from giving to the parties, found a new vehicle in the so-called *527 groups* (named after the section of the Internal Revenue Code under which they are organized). George Soros and other wealthy Democrats announced that they would be contributing millions to 527s in their efforts to defeat President Bush, and the Republicans were quick to follow suit. Most analysts agree that the 527 groups are evidence of the perverse consequences of campaign finance regulation. By eliminating soft money raised by political parties—whose role in the electoral process is essential and legitimate—reformers have encouraged the development of a class of groups with no electoral accountability whatsoever.

In addition to the rise of the 527s, tighter campaign finance restrictions may be a cause of increased incumbency advantage in congressional elections. Incumbents are reelected more than 90 percent of the time, primarily because they are more well-known to voters than their challengers are. Incumbents receive regular media exposure and various other perks (free use of television studios to produce videos, multiple trips to their district, costs of mailings to their constituents covered by taxpayers, etc.) that contribute to their greater visibility. Placing equal limits on challengers' and incumbents' fund-raising inevitably has unequal consequences because challengers need to spend more money to overcome the incumbent's considerable recognizability advantage.

Another drawback of BCRA is its incredible complexity. It used to be said that if you wanted to run for office, the first thing you had to do was hire a lawyer. In this post-BCRA era, probably your lawyer will have to hire a lawyer, because only a few specialists have a firm grasp on the ins and outs of the new legislation. Although the effects are hard to quantify, campaign finance regulation of this order of magnitude may tend to discourage some people from becoming active in politics, as candidates, party officials, or activists.

Candidate Debates

The final element of campaign strategy in the post-television era concerns debates. On September 26, 1960, an audience of seventy million gathered around their television sets to watch the first of four debates between John Kennedy and Richard Nixon. Nixon was in poor health and appeared without makeup (thus revealing that he had not shaved). Kennedy, in contrast, appeared tanned, fit, and youthful. Audience reaction to the historic debate was remarkably one-sided; a significant majority gave the nod to Kennedy (see Chapter 9). In future debates, candidates would be more attentive to matters of appearance and imagery.

Oddly enough, debates occur more frequently in primary than in general-election campaigns. In the 2003–04 Democratic primary and preprimary seasons there were so many debates and "joint appearances" on the schedule that the candidates found it difficult to carry on with their normal activities (fund-raising).

The term *debate* is something of a misnomer when applied to campaigns. It is true that the audience observes the candidates answering questions and offering summary introductory and closing statements, but these resemblances to conventional debates are superficial. In fact, debates—at least those occurring in the fall of election years—are closely managed by the candidates so as to maximize their ability to score points with the relevant "judges"—namely, the viewing audience. From the subject matter of the questions, to the identity of the questioners, the dates, and even the details of the shape of the stage and the podiums, campaigns control the protocol. The Clinton campaign, for instance, pushed hard for adoption of a "town hall" format in the 1992 campaign; the Bush campaign, knowing that its candidate was more reserved and less apt to connect with ordinary people, argued in favor of the more conventional panel of questioners. In the end, the town hall format was used for one debate and the other two debates relied on the conventional panel of questioners.

A recurring issue with televised candidate debates concerns eligibility. Major party candidates may participate, but all minor party candidates are excluded. In fact, the reason for the suspension of debates between 1964 and

1976 was that the television networks (who were then the principal sponsors) were legally bound to include minor party candidates under the provisions of the FCC's Fairness Doctrine. If one candidate was offered ninety minutes of prime-time exposure, then all other candidates for the same position were entitled to similar treatment. In 1976, the rule was evaded and the debates resumed by use of a third-party sponsor—the League of Women Voters. The League invited only the major party candidates, giving the networks the freedom to televise the debates as a newsworthy event. Today, organization of the debates is in the hands of a nonpartisan commission on presidential debates. The commission has formulated a set of criteria for eligibility, the most notable of which is that a candidate must demonstrate a level of public support (in reputable polls) of at last 15 percent. By this standard, virtually all third-party candidates are excluded.

With the advent of cable television and the greater freedom afforded the viewing audience, presidential debates no longer attract the great majority of people watching television at the time. As Figure 6.5 shows, the size of the debate audience has declined substantially from its peak in 1960. If we translate the Nielsen ratings into millions of viewers, the loss of viewers amounts to twenty million between 1960 and 2000. Clearly, the television audience has deserted the debates in favor of more entertaining fare. The declining trend in audience size also applies to less "substantive" programming, such as the World Series and Academy Awards, suggesting a generalized fragmentation of the national television audience. In 2004, the unusu-

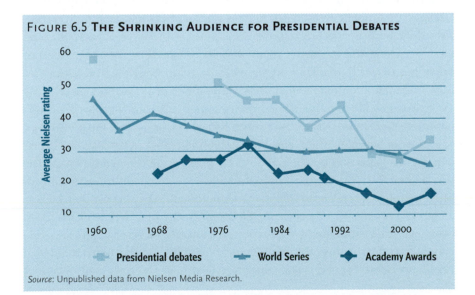

FIGURE 6.5 **THE SHRINKING AUDIENCE FOR PRESIDENTIAL DEBATES**

Average Nielsen rating

60 — 50 — 40 — 30 — 20 — 10

1960   1968   1976   1984   1992   2000

Presidential debates   World Series   Academy Awards

Source: Unpublished data from Nielsen Media Research.

ally high level of interest in the campaign reversed the long-term trend, and the average debate audience was the largest recorded since 1992.[7]

Even with their diminished share of the audience, debates reach a much larger number of voters than any single advertisement or news report can. For the candidates, the benefits (and risks) of performing before fifty million viewers mere weeks in advance of the election are huge. Campaigns understandably go to great lengths to prepare their candidates. They suspend the travel schedule, hold no other events, and devote several days to preparation, even to the extent of holding full-scale dress rehearsals.

The fact that the debates are far from spontaneous exchanges does not seem to have reduced their credibility with the public. In comparison with television ads and news reports, debates are easily the most favorably evaluated form of campaigning. Nearly one-third of the electorate reported that they took debates into account in 1996 and 2000. Surveys also indicate that, unlike advertising and news coverage, which the public dismisses as unhelpful to the task of voting, large majorities rate the debates as either "very helpful" or "somewhat helpful."

From the candidate's perspective, the benefits of debates include an opportunity to demonstrate their fitness for office: their command over the issues, their demeanor under duress, their sense of humor, and their ability to deal with conflict. The principal risk is that they will say or do something that makes them look less than "presidential." Their first priority, accordingly, is to avoid committing a *gaffe*—a major misstatement of fact. The best example of such a misstatement occurred in the 1976 foreign policy debate between incumbent Republican Gerald Ford and Democrat Jimmy Carter. President Ford incorrectly asserted that the countries of Eastern Europe were generally free of Soviet domination—a statement that he made not once, but twice. Remarkably, as we will discuss in Chapter 9, this blunder had no immediate impact on viewers' evaluations of Ford and Carter.

Scoring points with undecided voters sometimes calls for more than verbal fluency or command over the subject matter. Candidates must also convey cues concerning their personality, feelings, and people skills. When Michael Dukakis was asked in 1988 if his position on the death penalty (he was opposed) would change if his wife Kitty were raped and then murdered, his relatively calm response led many commentators to suggest that he was a cold fish, incapable of expressing emotion. In the first debate of the 2000 campaign, Vice President Al Gore repeatedly cut off Governor Bush's answers, generally coming across as an arrogant know-it-all. At the nonverbal level, President George H. W. Bush committed a gaffe in the town hall debate of

1992; obviously uncomfortable with the format and the proceedings, the president was seen studying his watch, thus conveying the impression that he found the discussion, which concerned mostly middle-class worries, of little interest. His son committed a similar faux pas in 2004, when he reacted to criticism from Senator Kerry by repeatedly scowling into the camera (see Video Feature 6.14).

In nonpresidential campaigns, debates contribute little. It's not that candidates for statewide office do not debate. They do, and frequently. But voters have little opportunity to view these debates because they are rarely televised in prime time. In a study of statewide campaigns in ten states, the Committee for the Study of the American Electorate found that two-thirds of the debates were televised, but only half were shown on network affiliates with large shares of the audience. Debates between candidates for the US House were even less newsworthy—only 30 percent were televised.

VIDEO
FEATURE 6.14
Nonverbal
Debate
Gaffes

Conclusion

The basic objective of any campaign strategy is simple: maximize the number of positive messages about yourself and the number of negative messages about your opponent. Given the role of the press, candidates can no longer expect reporters to do their bidding. As a result, the campaigns have taken to more subtle forms of spin, from staging events to uncovering newsworthy information concerning opponents. On the advertising front, candidates attempt to promote their candidacies with personal and performance-based appeals. More often than not, advertising campaigns do not address the same issues; instead candidates "talk" past each other, each emphasizing their respective strengths. In the case of negative campaigns, the candidates engage in a debate of sorts, not concerning the strengths of their policy proposals, but over the veracity and fairness of the charges and countercharges they hurl at each other. Finally, debates provide candidates with opportunities to "close the deal"—to demonstrate to voters that what they see in the ad campaign is what they get for real.

CHAPTER 6 SUMMARY

1. Media-based campaigns take place on two stages: free media (news coverage) and paid media (candidate advertisements). Presidential races

enjoy virtually unlimited news coverage, making the ad campaign only a small trickle in the cumulative message stream; advertising strategy is still extremely important to presidential candidates, however, because it represents their only opportunity to present their case unfiltered by journalists. In the case of nonpresidential races (congressional, gubernatorial, etc.), paid media dominate because news coverage is sparse.

2. Although advertising provides candidates with much greater control over their message than news coverage does, there is a significant trade-off; advertising is a much less credible messenger than news reports.

3. Candidates take numerous steps to focus news coverage on subjects that they consider advantageous:

- Candidates try to avoid the media "feeding frenzies" that arise whenever they demonstrate a personal or character flaw.

- Candidates can gain an advantage in coverage if the opponent makes a major misstatement of fact or reverses course on a matter of public policy.

- Campaigns often attempt to set low expectations about their candidates' prospects or standing—especially during the primary season—so that any level of achievement above this low baseline will be more surprising to journalists and hence covered more extensively and favorably.

- The "nuts and bolts" of press management is the strategic handling of events, which are scheduled in such a way as to maximize press coverage.

- Campaigns regulate media access to candidates on the basis of the candidate's standing in the polls; candidates who are trailing may follow an "open door" strategy with the press; candidates who are ahead tend to severely limit media access.

- Candidates can limit the access of journalists who are more likely to be critical, while devoting time to outlets more likely to provide favorable coverage. Campaigns dogged by critical coverage may try to shield the candidate from the national press by cultivating less-prominent outlets, such as local news and talk show formats.

- Candidates react to each other's statements and actions on a continuous basis, mainly in the form of competing press releases. Campaigns research the opponent's record and monitor the opponent's actions and words, with the aim of pouncing on any particularly newsworthy item.

4. Candidates follow several strategies in designing their advertising campaigns:

- Campaigns aim their advertisements at voters whose preferences may be pivotal to the outcome of the race—that is, voters in states or areas considered competitive.

- Candidates change the content and tone of their advertisements over the course of the campaign, from biographical spots early in the campaign to image and issue ads later.

- In their advertising campaigns, candidates emphasize issues on which they enjoy an advantage over their opponent. A particularly important aspect of this strategy is issue ownership.

- Candidates may also use wedge appeals in their advertising, particularly if they are losing the debate on generic issues. Wedge issues are designed to pit groups against each other, to appeal to voters' sense of group identity.

- A striking attribute of political advertising campaigns is the heavy reliance on negative or attack advertising.

- Negative ads dominate both because they tend to be more newsworthy than civil discourse and because the public's low opinion of politicians makes attacks on opposing candidates more credible than promoting one's own virtues. Furthermore, among campaign professionals a fundamental principle is that a candidate must punch back when attacked.

- Candidates often use direct mail to target voters more effectively. Direct mail is especially important in lower-level races, where TV advertising is inefficient,

5. Advertising is expensive and necessitates the raising of huge sums of money for political campaigns. In recent decades, concern about the role of money in politics has led to several attempts at campaign finance reform. In most cases, however, these attempts have merely encouraged campaigns to find loopholes and new, creative financing techniques.

6. Another important element of campaigns is the candidate debates. Campaigns closely manage debates to maximize their candidates' ability to score points with the viewing audience.

FURTHER READINGS

Ansolabehere, S., & Iyengar, S. (1995). *Going negative: How attack ads shrink and polarize the electorate*. New York: Free Press.

Bartels, L. M. (1988). *Presidential primaries and the dynamics of public choice*. Princeton, NJ: Princeton University Press.

Jacobson, G. C. (1997). *The politics of congressional elections* (4th ed.). New York: Longman.

Lau, R. R., Sigelman, L., Heldman, C., & Babbitt, P. (1999). The effects of negative political advertisements: A meta-analytic assessment. *American Political Science Review, 93,* 851–875.

Petrocik, J. R. (1996). Issue ownership in presidential elections, with a 1980 case study. *American Journal of Political Science, 40,* 825–850.

Popkin, S. L. (1994). *The reasoning voter: Communication and persuasion in presidential campaigns* (2nd ed.). Chicago: University of Chicago Press.

Shaw, D. R. (2006). *The race to 270: The electoral college and the campaign strategies of 2000 and 2004*. Chicago: University of Chicago Press.

NOTES

1. The networks were quick to point out that this limited coverage did not amount to an abdication of their civic responsibility, stating that they intended to provide gavel-to-gavel coverage on their online subsidiaries!

2. A GRP is defined as the sum of all Nielsen rating points (one Nielsen point is approximately 1 percent of the media market in which the ad airs) for the programs in which the ad was placed.

3. After the campaign, the story was exposed as Democratic spin; no such event occurred.

4. Because there are more Democrats than Republicans in the national electorate and the Democrats have traditionally enjoyed near-unanimous backing from the African-American community, the incentive to use wedge appeals based on race is especially enticing for Republican candidates.

5. It is too early to tell whether these ballot measures had any impact on the presidential vote. All eleven measures passed, however, suggesting that the median voter is to the right of the center on issues involving gay rights.

6. Mellman made his comments at a conference on the 2004 election held at Stanford University on November 9, 2004.

7. The debate audience is drawn disproportionately from the ranks of the politically engaged—partisans, the educated, and people over the age of forty.

CHAPTER 7

GOING PUBLIC

Governing Through the Media

IT USED TO BE that when an election was over, the winning candidates took office, put away their campaign paraphernalia and rhetoric, and got down to the serious business of governing. For a US president, this meant cultivating majority support in Congress for the key provisions of the presidential platform. The White House became the center of serious behind-the-scenes negotiations. The end result was the passage of legislation that reflected and accommodated competing interests. In the pre-media era, an essential element of presidential leadership was the ability to create winning coalitions from across the party or ideological divides.

Amassing support for the president's proposals typically required both patience and a horse trader's knack for compromise. Presidents with extensive personal networks on Capitol Hill (Lyndon Johnson, for example), were in the best position to readily elicit bipartisan support. In the Johnson era, conservative southern Democrats would support civil rights legislation in return for increased defense spending directed to southern states. This "bargaining" model of policy making rested on face-to-face communications among a relatively small group of elites who felt a common sense of obligation to place the interests of the nation ahead of the narrow confines of party or ideology.

Of course, bargaining among the elites did not guarantee sound policy. "Pork barrel" considerations typically trumped cost–benefit analysis of political problems as the basis for compromise. Powerful committee or subcommittee chairs could see to it that a significant share of federal spending was deposited into the pockets of their constituents. Despite these flaws, however, the bargaining model did, for the most part, result in smoothly functioning governance. The federal budget, for instance, was routinely enacted into law in advance of the fiscal-year deadline.

As elections became more media-centric, the president's increasingly important role as direct spokesman to the public began to alter the policy-making process. Rather than dealing directly with congressional leaders, presidents preferred to influence them indirectly by making them respond to "the people." As political scientist Samuel Kernell (1986) defined the new approach, "It is a strategy whereby a president promotes himself and his policies in Washington by appealing to the American public for support" (p. 2).

The increased reliance on the modern bully pulpit of television intensified partisan conflict and ill will, making it more difficult for rival elites to engage in good-faith bargaining. The more confrontational atmosphere in Washington led to the shutdown of the federal government on seventeen occasions between 1977 and 1995 because of irreconcilable policy differences between the president and Congress over the federal budget. In most cases, federal offices were closed for only a day or two. In 1995, however, in the longest shutdown in history, involving eight hundred thousand federal employees, essential government services were unavailable for twenty-two days because President Clinton and the Republican-led Congress could not reach agreement on lifting the federal debt ceiling as a precondition for passage of the budget. Gridlock rather than compromise had become the order of the day.

The deterioration in the relationship between competing elites can be attributed in significant part to media-based electoral campaigns. When hard-edged rhetoric and often personal attacks are directed at opponents during the campaign, it becomes difficult for elected leaders to extend the olive branch once the election is over. Incumbents must look over their shoulders constantly, for fear of offending potential donors to their next campaign, or of casting a vote that might become the focus of the next round of attack ads. More generally, the very same tools and strategies that are used to win the election are now applied for purposes of policy making. "Going public" has gradually superseded give-and-take bargaining as the preferred approach to governance.

In Focus: Going Public

Going public is a strategy used by presidents and other politicians to promote their policies by appealing to the American public for support. If a president enjoys strong public support, that popularity creates an important bargaining advantage. A president with a high level of public approval can often count on being able to persuade a few members of the opposition who may fear that they will not be reelected if they take a stand against a well-liked president.

The central ingredient of going public as a strategy of leadership is the cultivation of public approval. Given the overriding importance of reelection to the strategic calculations of elected officials, the most basic consideration is to avoid offending the voters. A president's popularity creates an important bargaining advantage; a president who enjoys a high level of public approval can count on being able to persuade a few members of the opposition. When the public backs the president, the president's credibility is enhanced; members of Congress are more likely to defer to the president's legislative proposals because they fear that the potential costs of opposition are too high. As Brody (1991) puts it, popularity enables the president to "achieve his program, keep challengers at bay, and guide his and other political leaders' expectations about the president's party's prospects in presidential and congressional elections" (p. 4).

The effects of a president's popularity on the ability to garner legislative support are most evident when the president's proposals address issues that are salient to the public but concern subject matter about which the public possesses little information. For example, the public is unanimously in favor of policies that reduce terrorism but has little ability to discriminate between the pros and cons of military intervention versus economic development as possible solutions. In such circumstances, presidential rhetoric has a double-barreled effect: it makes the targeted issues more prominent for the public, and it makes Congress more responsive to the president's proposals.

Conversely, a president buffeted by allegations of illegal or immoral behavior will be much less effective at pushing through a legislative program. Nixon's credibility with Congress was minimal once the Watergate allegations began to hold the public's attention. Overall, the evidence suggests that going public is an indispensable ingredient of presidential influence with Congress. According to Canes-Wrone (2001), "modern presidents systematically achieve policy goals by promoting issues to the public" (p. 326).

Ronald Reagan's presidency provided a number of illustrations of a popular president's power to persuade. Reagan had defeated incumbent president Jimmy Carter on a platform of smaller government and tax cuts. Reagan's first budget proposal (1981) called for unprecedented cuts in social welfare programs, coupled with significant increases in defense spending. On both counts, the budget was an abomination to congressional Democrats, who still controlled the House. Undeterred, Reagan embarked on a systematic media campaign to promote the budget. The president gave several speeches across the country urging citizens to convey their support for his budget to their congressional representatives. The speeches were carefully designed (with catchy sound bites) to attract coverage from local and network news-casts. Reagan also made it plain that he would personally campaign against any Democrats who might vote against his budget. Here's how David Gergen (Reagan's director of communications) described the closing stages of the campaign:

> We learned about it (the impending congressional vote on the budget reso-lution) the next day . . . Reagan was flying off to Texas. I was back at the White House, and we worked it out by sending statements to the plane for Reagan to make a planeside statement in time to get it on the evening news. We wanted to give it hype, to elevate the issue on the evening news so that the nation was getting a message. We were calling the press and doing what-ever we could to build the issue. At the same time, the political office went to work, notifying all their allies around the country, bringing the calls and pressure onto Congress as quickly as possible. (Hertsgaard, 1988, p. 120)

Reagan's strategy paid off. Despite the radical nature of his proposals and the deep hostility of congressional Democrats to the Reagan agenda, the budget was passed. Recognizing President Reagan's considerable appeal to the voting public, a sufficient number of Democrats voted against their party. Fear of angering voters rather than some form of political inducement had become the basis for creating policy coalitions in government. Directly appealing to the public had replaced negotiations among elites as the basis for governance.

The transition from a style of governance based on negotiations among elites to one based on media-oriented appeals can be attributed in part to the growing prominence of media professionals in the electoral process. Increasingly, political appointments have come to be distributed among the members of the winning campaign team, rather than among party supporters. Key campaign professionals have taken up positions in the executive branch with the principal agenda of ensuring the president's reelection. At the other end of Pennsylvania Avenue, members of Congress have behaved in similar fashion, recruiting political operatives for their office staffs whose major responsibility is to prepare for the next campaign.

Once appointed to office, media professionals have continued to serve by exploiting their expertise in dealing with the media and the public, and they have focused less on building coalitions among elites or on developing substantive policy initiatives. Hamilton Jordan, President Carter's campaign manager and White House chief of staff, was a stark example of this type.

Because Jordan had no contacts in Congress and engaged in little outreach, and because the president's popularity with the public eventually suffered under the pressure of the Iran hostage crisis, most of President Carter's legislative proposals were ignored or defeated.

The many repercussions of going public as a way of governing are taken up in detail in Chapter 10. In brief, the consequences include a preoccupation with media relations and public popularity. In the case of the president, close control over news coverage, especially symbolism—pomp and ceremony—is the order of the day, and few resources remain for developing and pushing through policy proposals.

The remainder of this chapter will discuss the role of public communication by the president today. Why is communication with the public so essential? What are the key forms of presidential communication and why?

Presidential Communication

The conventional wisdom in Washington is that going public is indeed essential to political success. As explained by President George W. Bush's political guru Karl Rove:

> I think in the post-1980 era we all owe it to [Michael] Deaver who said turn off the sound of the television and that's how people are going to decide whether you won the day or lost the day, the quality of the picture. That's what they're going to get the message by, with the sound entirely off. I think that's simplistic, but I think it's an important insight. There's a reason why the old saw, a picture is worth a thousand words, how we look, how we sound and how we project is important. So winning the picture is important. (Kumar, 2003, p. 321)

Validating Rove's analysis, recent presidents have all adapted their behavior to harness the power of television. Exercising control over the media message rather than cultivating good relations with Congress has become an absolutely essential element of presidential leadership. Herbert Hoover's media staff consisted of a single assistant for press relations. In the 1950s the White House media operation expanded to include the press secretary, the press secretary's deputy, and five secretarial employees. Forty-five years later, the vast White House media complex (see Figure 7.1) has fifty full-time employees and five distinct organizational branches within the White

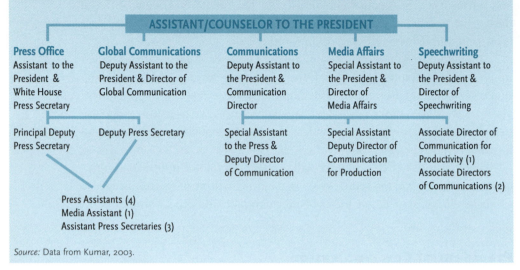

FIGURE 7.1 MEDIA OPERATIONS IN THE GEORGE W. BUSH WHITE HOUSE

ASSISTANT/COUNSELOR TO THE PRESIDENT				
Press Office	**Global Communications**	**Communications**	**Media Affairs**	**Speechwriting**
Assistant to the President & White House Press Secretary	Deputy Assistant to the President & Director of Global Communication	Deputy Assistant to the President & Communication Director	Special Assistant to the President & Director of Media Affairs	Deputy Assistant to the President & Director of Speechwriting
Principal Deputy Press Secretary	Deputy Press Secretary	Special Assistant to the Press & Deputy Director of Communication	Special Assistant Deputy Director of Communication for Production	Associate Director of Communication for Productivity (1) Associate Directors of Communications (2)
Press Assistants (4) Media Assistant (1) Assistant Press Secretaries (3)				

Source: Data from Kumar, 2003.

House counsel's office. Clearly, the strategy of going public has magnified the function of press management in the contemporary presidency.

THE PRESIDENT'S MEDIA MANAGERS

The nerve center of the executive branch's communication efforts is the Office of the Press Secretary, commonly referred to as the *press office*. The office has five distinct branches, of which Press and Communications are the most significant. These are headed by the press secretary and communications director, respectively, both of whom play a pivotal role within the administration. The press office issues all press releases and responds to inquiries from the national media. The Office of Communications is responsible for planning the president's media appearances, including press conferences and other public events. The communications director is also responsible for coordinating the message of the various spokespersons throughout the administration. The Office of Media Affairs provides the same services as the Office of Communications, but for the benefit of local and regional news outlets. Finally, the Office of Global Communications provides "strategic direction and themes" to government agencies (such as the Voice of America) that produce information and media content for overseas audiences.[1]

The communications director is responsible for overseeing the production and release of information throughout the administration. Given the number of agencies and offices that deal with the media, message coordination is often impossible. Getting the federal government to speak with one voice is the goal, but more often than not, there are inconsistencies and "misstatements" that must be explained. Unlike the press secretary, who acts mainly as a conduit between the press and the White House, the communications director is more of an "ideas person," a strategist who seeks to define and market the president's image. Gerald Rafshoon, Jimmy Carter's communications director, instructed the president to carry his own bags when disembarking from Air Force One. This advice was meant to help Carter project a "man of the people" image.[2] Fearing Ronald Reagan's penchant for off-the-cuff remarks, communications director Michael Deaver prohibited the press from asking questions during photo ops.

The press secretary, the president's point person for dealing with the national media, is much more likely to occupy the spotlight. The press secretary (or the secretary's deputy) conducts two daily press briefings for the White House press corps. On occasion, the press office also arranges special background briefings (usually by a policy specialist) for reporters. In addition, there are more informal "off the record" sessions between reporters and administration officials. Behind the scenes, the press office regulates journalists' access to the White House (by issuing credentials) and maintains the elaborate on-site facilities necessary for journalists to transmit their news reports.

The position of press secretary imposes difficult demands on the incumbent, who often has to walk a tightrope between meeting the political objectives of the White House staff ("spin and more spin") on the one hand, and maintaining journalistic credibility on the other. As a member of the president's inner circle, the press secretary is expected to do as much as possible to score points for the administration. Some press secretaries engage in so much spinning, however, that they find themselves facing an increasingly disbelieving press corps. During the closing stages of the Watergate scandal, relations between Nixon's press secretary, Ron Ziegler, and the press corps became so strained that deputy press secretary Gerald Warren was frequently asked to stand in at the daily press briefing.

Other press secretaries lose the confidence of the press because it is widely known that they are not part of the president's inner circle. As media management becomes critical to the effectiveness of the presidency, reporters have adapted by more aggressively challenging the press secretary at the daily briefings and other appearances. According to Ari Fleischer (President George W. Bush's first press secretary), the resulting pressures are so intense that no press secretary can hope to serve out a full four-year term (Auletta, 2004).

The more effective press secretaries, while enjoying the trust and confidence of the White House political operatives and the president, have maintained an "objective" posture with the press. Mike McCurry, press secretary to President Clinton, was able to draw on his reputation as a straight shooter to weather the storms of the Monica Lewinsky scandal, when all too often he was forced to claim ignorance in response to reporters' questioning. In the text on page 175, McCurry describes his daily routine as press secretary.[3]

As the complexity of the White House media apparatus suggests, managing the press has become a key function within the administration. Going public requires that the administration orchestrate the news media to present a consistently positive image of the president. At the same time, as outlined below, the president must be protected against being put on the defensive by aggressive or unexpected questioning of actions taken.

GETTING THE MESSAGE OUT

There are three distinct media opportunities that presidents may pursue. In each case, the amount of resources invested varies with the payoffs: the number of people who can be reached and the degree of control over the message. In the ideal scenario (from the president's perspective), the president would command a nationwide news audience and be granted free rein to influence public opinion, unimpeded by skeptical reporters or critical commentary from opposing elites. Over the years, as media audiences have changed and the national press corps has adopted a more critical perspective, presidents have taken to travel and speechmaking as their principal communication strategies. The presidential press conference, once prized as an opportunity to demonstrate the president's leadership before a captive audience, has all but fallen into disuse.

NEWS COVERAGE
As Mike McCurry points out in the speech excerpted on the following page, the president is the focal point of the national government. Given reporters' reliance on official sources, the president can count on regular and sustained news coverage from all forms of news media. Studies of national news repeatedly demonstrate the visibility of the White House. In the case of

A Day in the Life of the Presidential Press Secretary

The hardest part of the job is to just get on top of the flow of information that is crushing, all-consuming, surrounding you every waking moment of the day with some new plotline that you have to think about. Because part of the problem is that the White House has become, for most of the US press corps, the prism through which every story anywhere can sometimes be seen. I don't know if, when Princess Diana died, what was that a Saturday night? It was like a Saturday night that she died in Paris. And it was awful and tragic but I was watching a ball game or something. And I suddenly got this flood of calls at home from angry network executives saying "Your people said they won't open up the White House press office so we can go live from the White House." And I said, "Well, what does the White House have to do with Princess Diana dying in this car accident?" But the immediate thought was that this big, significant, huge moment had to be reflected through this stage that most Americans associate with big events. If it's a big event, clearly the White House has something to do with it. . . . But anyhow, the reality is that every single day everything happening in the world is going to at least be a possible source of questions in the White House.

I'd get to work about 7, 7:30 and then start a process by which the White House would decide, well, what's the news we want to make today versus what's the news that's coming at us because that's going to be the agenda of the press corps that day and how do you reconcile the two and how do you make some guess over which is going to top the other? Because a successful day for the White House was a day in which the story that we put out there and wanted to drive made the network news that night and was the dominant focus of the press corps that day versus some other storyline that presented us with more risk and less advantageous coverage of our own point of view. . . .

But the press corps would then come into my office in the West Wing and we would sit and go through our schedule, and they would want me to try to react to any breaking news or anything that had happened overnight or if some big news

Mike McCurry

organization had a big story on the front page that day they would want an initial reaction to that story. This was the working briefing. It was off-camera and we did not make a transcript of it. At that first briefing of the day, it was perfectly legitimate for me to say, "I'll do that question at 1 o'clock," because that would then give me time to research what the right answer was.

At some point every morning I would either see Clinton or swing by the Oval Office and kind of walk through my briefing book and say, "Here's what we are going to say about this, that or the other," and he would kind of like dial me one way or the other. If he wanted me to be sharper or more provocative on one point, or usually he would dial me in the other direction and want me to tone it down and not be as pithy or as partisan as probably my own instinct would have had me be. But he kind of got me where he wanted me to be as I articulated an answer. And then when I would give the briefing for the press at 1 o'clock, I would then spend the next hour cleaning up whatever messes I had created or get more information or trying to deal with the immediate aftermath of the briefing, and then just a lot of one-on-one work with reporters to get additional information for them. . . .

And then everybody would kind of watch the news collectively at 6:30 and 7, and that was your report card at the end of the day because either your story made it and you got that out there, or something else came in to dominate the storyline about the White House that day.

Source: From a speech at Stanford University on May 8, 2001.

New York Times coverage between 1950 and 1997 (see Figure 7.2), the share of front-page news accorded to the president was initially below the level of coverage accorded to Congress. Beginning with the election of John Kennedy, however, presidential coverage increased and reached the level of congressional news. By the late 1970s, the president was clearly the principal source of news; averaging across the presidencies from Carter to Clinton, presidential coverage exceeded congressional coverage by a significant margin ($p < .01$).[4]

Executive power is especially pronounced in the arena of foreign policy. By virtue of the president's constitutional prerogatives as commander in chief, the president is unquestionably the principal source of news on American foreign policy. When we examine news reports about foreign policy (see Figure 7.3), the dominance of the president is apparent: since Reagan, the president's share of foreign affairs news coverage has been at three times the level of congressional coverage. Foreign policy news, for all practical purposes, is presidential news.

Unfortunately, there is no comparable database for broadcast news coverage of the president (archived videotape recordings of network news began

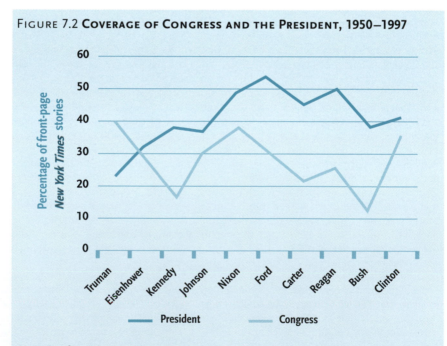

FIGURE 7.2 **COVERAGE OF CONGRESS AND THE PRESIDENT, 1950–1997**

Percentage of front-page New York Times stories

President — Congress

Source: Data from Policy Agendas Project, 2004.

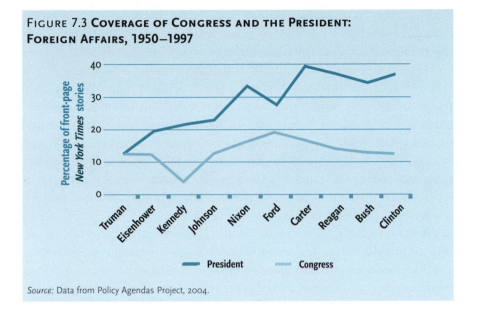

FIGURE 7.3 **COVERAGE OF CONGRESS AND THE PRESIDENT: FOREIGN AFFAIRS, 1950–1997**

Source: Data from Policy Agendas Project, 2004.

only in 1968). In tracking CBS News coverage between 1968 and 1978, Grossman and Kumar (1981) found that the network devoted substantial attention to the executive branch, even more so than print news did. On average, CBS aired four news reports each day on the president, amounting to approximately 20 percent of the newscast.[5]

Clearly, the president can command the attention of the national media at will. But does the president also influence the story line? Studies of news content suggest that news coverage of incumbent presidents follows the same pattern as coverage of presidential candidates—evolving from generally positive coverage in the 1960s and '70s to more interpretive and critical coverage in the 1990s. In Grossman and Kumar's 1968–78 comparative study of *Time*, the *New York Times*, and CBS News, favorable coverage of the president exceeded unfavorable coverage by a wide margin in both print outlets. Only in the case of CBS was the assessment mixed: the network aired an equal number of positive and negative reports (Grossman & Kumar, 1981, p. 256). Although the content of the CBS News reports was mixed, the accompanying visual imagery was invariably flattering: 40 percent of the pictures used in the newscasts were positive, and only 8 percent were negative (p. 258). Thus the evidence suggests that, during this period at least, the efforts of the White House media apparatus paid rich dividends.

Over time, as journalists learned to resist the persuasiveness of media consultants and press secretaries alike, news reports began to take on a sharper tone. Presidents Bill Clinton and George W. Bush both elicited news coverage that proved more critical than complimentary. Even though it is acknowledged that the press and the political opposition generally defer to the president's proposals during the first few months of an incoming administration (the so-called honeymoon period), Clinton and Bush were not treated kindly by the press during their first hundred days in office. According to a study by the Project for Excellence in Journalism (2001), network news coverage of Clinton was more negative than positive by a margin of 6 percent (28 percent negative, 22 percent positive); and for Bush, positive and negative reports aired with equal frequency.

The increasingly negative tone of press reports is symptomatic of decreased presidential control over the national press. In response, presidents and their media advisors have pursued alternative media strategies. They have frequently left Washington on speaking trips to areas where they hope to attract more sympathetic coverage from local and regional news outlets.

SPEECHMAKING

Speechmaking is a relatively recent form of presidential leadership. The framers of the Constitution did not expect the president to interact with the public. They preferred that the president spend the time in office deliberating with Congress and other leaders. During the early days of the republic, presidential speechmaking was limited to formal presentations to Congress.[6]

With the rapid development of radio in the twentieth century and the gradual enfranchisement of adult voters, presidents took to communicating with the public on a regular basis. The use of presidential rhetoric to rally public opinion was pioneered by Teddy Roosevelt, whose frequent appeals for public support proved instrumental in his efforts to persuade Congress to enact significant "trustbusting" legislation. A few years later, Franklin Roosevelt introduced his "fireside chats" held before a nationwide radio audience. These were occasions for Roosevelt to explain what his administration intended to do to combat the Depression. He used these addresses to mobilize support for key provisions of his New Deal.[7]

With the advent of television, the audience at the president's command climbed still further. A prime-time speech carried by all three of the networks might reach as many as 60 percent of all American households (see Figure 7.4). The period of the late 1960s—when network television was the

FIGURE 7.4 **HOUSEHOLDS WATCHING PRESIDENTIAL PRIME-TIME APPEARANCES, 1965–1994**

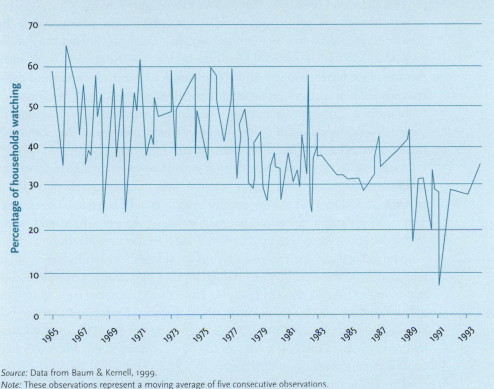

Source: Data from Baum & Kernell, 1999.
Note: These observations represent a moving average of five consecutive observations.
A moving average has the effect of smoothing a data series.

dominant media source—is referred to as the "golden age of presidential television" because presidents could count on a massive captive audience for their speeches. Of course, presidents were quick to exploit this opportunity; in 1970 alone, Nixon delivered nine major policy speeches in prime time.

The ability to reach a majority of the American public through prime-time appearances has proved especially useful when presidents become embroiled in controversy (see Video Feature 7.1). In the aftermath of revelations that members of his staff had arranged for arms to be sold to Iran and had then diverted the proceeds of the sales to the right-wing Contra rebels in Nicaragua, Ronald Reagan delivered a prime-time address assuring the public that he was indeed awake at the steering wheel. In the aftermath of Hurricane Katrina and the inadequate relief efforts mounted by the federal government, President Bush reassured the nation that New Orleans would

VIDEO FEATURE 7.1 Presidential Speech-making as a Form of Damage Control be rebuilt and that the reconstruction efforts would address the issues of poverty and racial inequality that had become highly visible.

Of course, the golden age of television proved short-lived. With the growth of cable networks, not only did people have the ability to tune out the president, but the commercial pressures on the major networks were sufficient to deter the regular provision of free airtime. Since the advent of cable television, the president's prime-time opportunities have shrunk to the annual State of the Union address and, on occasion, prepared remarks on a topic of unusual importance (such as President Clinton's apology to the nation for his behavior related to his affair with Monica Lewinsky).

Deprived of the captive nationwide audience, presidents have turned to other media venues. Local and regional audiences, particularly those living in critical battleground states, are the new targets of presidential rhetoric. This "narrowcasting" approach to going public is designed to attract favorable coverage in areas that could prove pivotal in the next election.

The behavior of the two most recent presidents reveals the new look of going public. President Bush made seventy-five appearances outside Washington in the first six months of 2004. The majority of these trips (forty-two of seventy-five) were aimed at voters in swing states. President Bush was following the example of his predecessor; eight years earlier, President Clinton had embarked on fifty-eight trips in his first six months in office—45 percent of them to battleground states.

Presidents are especially prone to travel in election years, and they increasingly choose to speak about the state of the economy. Given the importance of economic conditions to voter decision making, the president's election year speeches typically sound an optimistic note concerning the economy. The frequency of presidential speechmaking also responds to the state of the economy. During periods of economic distress, presidents typically turn up the volume of their economic message.

In sum, speechmaking remains the major form of presidential communication, but presidents have substituted local for national audiences. In the golden age of network television, presidents could count on unmediated access to the whole country, thanks to the programming monopoly enjoyed by the three television networks. Today, with the proliferation of television channels and programming choices, the president is no longer a major draw on national television. In response, presidents have taken to playing local and regional venues. Unlike the more aggressive and skeptical national press corps, local reporters are typically more malleable and willing to accept the tone of the president's rhetoric.

THE PRESS CONFERENCE

Like speechmaking, presidents' use of the press conference has evolved in response to the risks and rewards of the medium. When the prime-time audience was there for the taking, the benefits of reaching the entire nation outweighed the risks of appearing before a group of seasoned reporters who were all bent on asking the toughest question. With the loss of the national audience, however, the risks of committing a gaffe or appearing uninformed have deterred modern presidents from holding frequent press conferences.

Prior to the development of the press conference, presidents generally granted interviews to reporters and editors on an ad hoc basis. Teddy Roosevelt attempted to systematize the process by increasing reporters' access to the White House while maintaining tight control over their stories. Calvin Coolidge flatly refused to take questions from reporters. Warren G. Harding was willing to take questions, but only if they were submitted in advance.

A more open posture toward the press was the hallmark of the first Franklin Roosevelt (FDR) administration. Under FDR, the press conference became the principal source of news; in fact, FDR still holds the record for the number of scheduled press conferences—more than the combined total of all his successors!

Holding press conferences during prime time was the brainchild of the Kennedy administration. Kennedy's advisors were well aware that Kennedy's telegenic characteristics would impress the audience. When Pierre Salinger (Kennedy's press secretary) first announced the plan, it was met with uniform derision from the press establishment (which was dominated at the time by newspaper reporters). Still, the first-ever televised press conference attracted more than four hundred reporters, and the president's remarks were watched by an audience in excess of sixty million.

Despite the 1960s transformation of the press conference into a television spectacle, the institution has since fallen out of favor. Reporters' interests in catching the president in a moment of spontaneity clash with White House objectives of scripting the president in the best light possible. At press conferences, the risks are high that the president might misspeak or be put on the defensive by a tough line of questioning. Even as accomplished a public speaker as President Reagan stumbled on several occasions, demonstrating that he did not know the answers to important questions, and that his command of the facts was, at best, limited.[8] To be revealed as ignorant on national television, of course, is not likely to impress voters.

To reduce the risks of appearing inept, presidential staff personnel have attempted to choreograph presidents' appearances. Presidents Ford, Carter, and Reagan all staged elaborate "dress rehearsals," attempting to fine-tune their answers to anticipated questions. The press office is intimately familiar with most White House reporters and, on the basis of the daily press briefings, can reliably predict what individual reporters might ask. Larry Speakes, press secretary to Reagan, claimed that "out of 30 questions and follow-ups the press would ask, we might fail to anticipate one. And often, we could even predict which reporters were going to ask which questions" (Ansolabehere, Behr, & Iyengar, 1993, p. 114).

The press office often takes advantage of journalistic competition by "planting" questions. The term *planting* refers to the practice of getting a pliable reporter to ask a "softball" question provided by the White House. In exchange, the reporter might be awarded a significant journalistic coup (such as an exclusive interview with the First Lady). Although it is difficult to demonstrate the frequency of planted questions, it is generally accepted that all administrations engage in the practice. Planting questions was fairly common during the Eisenhower and Johnson administrations; Eisenhower's press secretary often received questions in advance from reporters, allowing the president to call on a specific reporter and deliver a prepared answer. President Johnson is said to have instructed his staff to arrange a press conference in which all the questions were planted.

A clearer case of planted questions, though not in a national press conference, occurred in December 1990 during a telephone question-and-answer session between President George H. W. Bush and newspaper reporters in Southern California. Not realizing that his microphone was live, the president complained aloud that one of the questions was not "in the right order." In another instance illustrating White House influence over press conferences, President George W. Bush recognized a relatively unknown Web journalist (Jeff Gannon) in the first national press conference after his reelection in 2004. The question Mr. Gannon put to President Bush was not exactly "objective":

> Senate Democratic leaders have painted a very bleak picture of the US economy. Harry Reid was talking about soup lines and Hillary Clinton was talking about the economy being on the verge of collapse. Yet, in the same breath, they say that Social Security is rock solid and there's no crisis there. You've said you're going to reach out to these people. How are you going to work with people who seem to have divorced themselves from reality? ("Bush Expounds on Theme of Freedom," 2005)

Even with all the preparation, however, press conferences can prove damaging to the president's image. Perhaps the most extreme case of presidential blundering occurred during a Reagan press conference held in early 1987 after disclosure of the Iran–Contra scandal. The president's answers to the questions were so frequently confused and inaccurate (for example, he indicated that Israel had not been involved in the transaction) that the press office took the unprecedented step of issuing a news release immediately following the conference—even before the networks had concluded their coverage—"clarifying" the president's remarks.

Recent presidents have adopted several routines to help bolster their performance at press conferences. They typically make an opening statement in the hope of setting the agenda for reporters' questions. They may also schedule the event on short notice. The most extreme case of this tactic was one occasion in which President Johnson held a press conference without notice to reporters, addressing only those who happened to be present in the White House press room at the time. Presidents have also taken to sharing the spotlight by holding joint press conferences (usually with a visiting foreign leader). This approach not only shifts the burden of performance from the president, but it also permits the administration to present the image of a unified front.

Despite their considerable ability to stage-manage the event that is afforded them by their position, presidents have concluded that the risks of frequent press conferences outweigh the benefits. The overall trend is one of fewer press conferences per month. Although Presidents Bush Sr. and Clinton both held more conferences than their predecessors, in the case of the former at least, most of the occasions were reserved for discussion of foreign affairs, a subject on which Bush was especially authoritative. Naturally, the press office sought to minimize Bush's exposure to "tough" questions on domestic issues; between 1989 and 1991 Bush answered a total of four questions on AIDS and two questions on the widespread bankruptcy of savings and loan institutions.

When we limit the count to televised prime-time press conferences and "solo" appearances by the president (see Figure 7.5), the aversion of recent presidents to the process is quite clear. Only Reagan, the "great communicator," appeared in prime time with any regularity, and as noted earlier, he did so with mixed results. Since Reagan, presidents have increasingly taken to sharing the spotlight with others (in most cases, visiting foreign heads of state). The number of solo press conferences has declined precipitously.

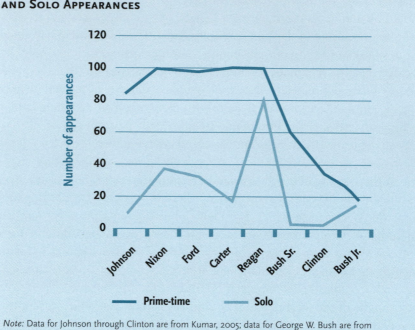

FIGURE 7.5 PRESIDENTIAL PRIME-TIME PRESS CONFERENCES AND SOLO APPEARANCES

Note: Data for Johnson through Clinton are from Kumar, 2005; data for George W. Bush are from www.whitehouse.gov/news/releases and cover the period January 2001 through December 2005.

In short, the recent history of the presidential press conference illustrates the fundamental tension in the relationship between the national press and the president. Reporters crave information, particularly information that is objective and free of political spin or distortion. Presidents demand control over the story. Today, in the era of interpretive reporting, the risks of critical news coverage have come to outweigh the benefits of television exposure. As a result, the frequency of the presidential press conference has decreased dramatically.

ALTERNATIVES TO THE PRESS CONFERENCE
Instead of subjecting themselves to the entire White House press corps, presidents often negotiate appearances on individual television programs or grant interviews to small groups of reporters. President Reagan granted more than two hundred private interviews to reporters during his first term. Question-and-answer sessions with local reporters (sometimes referred to as *end runs*) are particularly rewarding from the administration's perspective because local reporters are more easily impressed than their Washington counterparts.

When the White House loses control over the message, as is the case during major scandals (such as the affair between Clinton and Monica Lewinsky) or policy debacles (such as the Enron collapse), the president may be forced to engage in a variety of "fire-extinguishing" maneuvers. Such measures might include scheduling newsworthy events on diversionary issues (for example, inviting injured servicemen to the White House for an awards ceremony), and putting the best possible interpretation on controversial events (such as saying that President George W. Bush was unaware of any terrorist plans to attack the United States prior to 9/11). On other occasions, the president may attempt to seize the initiative by making a solo appearance on a highly rated news program. In the aftermath of the invasion of Iraq and the failure to discover Iraqi weapons of mass destruction, for example, President Bush decided to appear on *Meet the Press* to defend the administration's actions and explain the many inconsistencies between his pre- and postwar rhetoric.

Sometimes the White House responds to press criticism more combatively, by attempting to repudiate particular reports or questioning the motives of the reporter or outlet. The Bush White House responded to the CBS News report on the president's National Guard service by calling into question Dan Rather's objectivity (Rather had once spoken at a Democratic fundraiser) and journalistic competence. In the face of these attacks on Rather's objectivity—as well as a firestorm of criticism for its sloppy reporting—CBS decided to postpone until after the 2004 election a *60 Minutes* segment investigating the Bush administration's claims concerning Iraqi weapons of mass destruction.[9]

Overall, there can be no denying the inherent newsworthiness of the presidency. Presidents are not so much subjects of news coverage as they are sources of news about the actions of the federal government. Presidential media management is essentially a process of spoon-feeding: the president gives a speech or holds a press conference, and reporters write stories about what the president had to say. The president stages a photo opportunity with a visiting foreign dignitary, and images of the two leaders appear on the evening news. Of course, as we will demonstrate in Chapter 8, the power to shape the news is tantamount to shaping the public's perceptions of the president.

In Focus: Three Principal Forms of Presidential Communication

● Attracting news coverage

● Making speeches

● Holding press conferences

The Public Congressperson

The president is not alone in seeking to use the media for political gain. Everyone else in Washington plays the same game. However, members of Congress find it more difficult to achieve media leverage because there are so many of them, each promoting a different story or angle. Reporters are much more likely to gravitate to a story that can be personalized and that offers a clean "story line." Reports on parliamentary procedures or legislative protocol typically do not meet the requirements of appropriateness, making it difficult for journalists to put the legislative branch in the spotlight.

COMMITTEE HEARINGS

Committee hearings provide the best opportunity for congressional media coverage. The subject matter is timely, the number of congressional participants is relatively small, and in many cases the witnesses who appear have considerable "star" power. As early as the 1950s, congressional hearings attracted national television coverage. The first televised hearings were organized by Senator Estes Kefauver's special Senate committee investigating the influence of organized crime. Shortly thereafter, Senator Joseph McCarthy's hearings on security lapses at military installations (the Army-McCarthy hearings) became big news and led eventually to the end of McCarthy's crusade to root out American communists. In the 1970s, the spotlight was directed at the House Judiciary Committee proceedings to consider the impeachment of President Nixon. By the late 1970s it was clear that regular television coverage of Congress would facilitate the policy and electoral interests of members and also enable the public to monitor the actions of their representatives. C-SPAN coverage of the House began in 1977, followed by Senate coverage in 1986.

Even though hearings provide committee members much-needed national exposure, the fact that legislative committees represent a wide range of political preferences makes it difficult for Congress to compete with the president. Whereas the White House provides a solo speaker, congressional committees represent a chorus. The famous "Hill–Thomas" hearings provide a striking case of the more confused nature of the congressional message.

In 1991, President George H. W. Bush nominated Clarence Thomas for the US Supreme Court. Senate Democrats had challenged the nomination on a number of grounds, including Thomas's weak judicial credentials, his stance on abortion, and his record as head of the Equal Employment Opportunity Commission (EEOC). When a young African-American college professor (Anita Hill) publicly accused Thomas of sexual harassment, the possibility of lukewarm support from within the black community appeared to doom the nomination. The confrontation, featuring sexually explicit material, made for dramatic television (see Video Feature 7.2). On the first day (a Friday) the television audience numbered thirty million viewers. Over the following weekend, the networks cut away to their regularly scheduled sports programming, leaving PBS to cover the hearings. The interest in the controversy was so intense that PBS achieved its largest audience ever; more people watched the hearings than watched college football, the baseball playoffs, or the NFL.

VIDEO
FEATURE 7.2
The 1991
Hill–Thomas
Hearings

Despite the intense and potentially damaging media coverage, Thomas was confirmed. Opponents of the nomination had no common argument. Some Democrats took issue with his pro-life stance; others singled out his handling of age discrimination cases at the EEOC, the ambiguity of his testimony, or his lack of judicial experience. On the other hand, the president offered a succinct defense of his nominee as a deserving minority candidate who had acquired his credentials through effort and hard work. Against this simple theme of mainstream American individualism, the Democratic message—"Some of us think he's not qualified. Some of us don't like him because he may not be pro-choice. Some of us think he lied to us. And some of us think he's just fine."—was no match (Ansolabehere, Behr, & Iyengar, 1991, p. 119).

A textbook case of a legislative leader's exercise of going public was provided by Republican congressman Newt Gingrich in 1994. Realizing the importance of a unified and defining message for Republican candidates, Gingrich drafted a ten-point "Contract with America" representing the conservative legislative agenda of House Republicans. Each agenda item was given an appropriately catchy label ("Fiscal Responsibility Act," "American Dream Restoration Act," etc.). The contract was signed by 433 of the 435 Republican candidates running for the House in 1994. In effect, Gingrich nationalized the 1994 elections by providing each Republican candidate with a common theme.

Although it is hard to know just how much the contract influenced voters, the results of the 1994 election were spectacular: the Republicans picked up more than fifty seats and became the majority party in the House for the first time since 1954. Gingrich himself became the House Speaker, but his efforts to implement the provisions of the contract met with mixed success. President Clinton vetoed most of the bills, others became the basis

of protracted budget disputes (some of which shut down the federal government), and still others were watered down before being passed. Nevertheless, in a testament to the perceived effectiveness of the Republicans' 1994
strategy, House Democrats in 2004 considered a similar statement of intent,
designed to help them reclaim their majority status. As one Democratic
leadership aide put it, "We're recognizing that in a world of sound bites we
really are far behind and we're playing catch-up. We're trying to come up
with a very succinct way of explaining who we are and what we stand for"
(Billings, 2004).

POLICY VERSUS ELECTORAL GOALS

Political scientists generally assume that the overriding aspiration of all legislators is political survival or reelection. A secondary aspiration is moving up
the legislative hierarchy and becoming known as an effective legislator with
high-profile committee memberships or leadership assignments. In the pre-
media days, congressional representatives worked their way up the career
ladder by acquiring seniority, and by currying favor with party and committee leaders (which meant obediently voting the party line). Today the road to
legislative success is much more likely to include maintaining a media profile. Congressional press secretaries are now ubiquitous; their principal role
is to flood the media with daily press releases claiming credit for Congressperson X's legislative accomplishments.

In line with their career objectives, legislators typically seek out two forms
of press coverage. First, they hope to attract attention for their legislative
performance: sponsoring important legislation, shepherding bills through the
intricacies of the legislative process, and eventually getting bills enacted into
law. Policy or performance coverage is more likely to come from the national
press or from regional outlets with full-time Washington correspondents. We
noted earlier that Congress was on a par with the presidency in the pages of
the *New York Times* until the 1970s; most of this coverage focused on substantive issues (civil rights legislation, the "great society" programs, the war
on poverty, etc.). National media recognition is likely to boost a congressperson's reputation and leads to increased influence with party leaders.

National reports dealing with matters of public policy are unlikely to
reach a congressperson's home district or state. The goal of reelection can
best be served by local news. Most local television stations do not have full-
time Washington correspondents. Instead, they subscribe to a video wire

service that feeds cookie-cutter reports to multiple stations across the country. Wire services have a strong economic incentive to provide congressional news with a local angle because they are paid by the report. Members of Congress can take advantage of this system by creating an appropriate local angle—by inviting local VIPs to testify at committee hearings or by holding a press conference to announce the funding of local programs.

Of course, members of Congress with legislative influence are better able to attract local coverage. In Arnold's 2004 study of newspaper coverage, members of Congress holding leadership positions were assigned substantially more print coverage than were rank-and-file members. Newspapers also assigned greater coverage to more-senior legislators.

Which of the two branches of Congress is better able to generate news? The smaller size of the Senate, coupled with the greater prestige of the office, grants senators a distinct advantage. In Tim Cook's (1998) comparative study, almost all senators (90 percent) were interviewed on network news at least once; for House members, only one-third were given similar treatment.

One form of notoriety that members of Congress would do well to avoid is involvement in scandal or being the target of ethics-related investigations. To be the subject of an investigation is to be featured in the news. Moreover, reporters seem inclined to test the hypothesis that congresspersons implicated in ethics violations are vulnerable at the polls; coverage of the allegations therefore usually continues well into the campaign (Arnold, 2004, p. 47). For instance, the 2006 Republican primary for the House seat held by Texas Congressman Tom DeLay attracted significant press coverage because of his resignation from his position as House majority leader in the aftermath of allegations that he had violated campaign finance regulations.

The ability to attract news depends not only on the degree to which members of Congress "make news," but also on the nature of the media market in the areas that they represent. In Los Angeles or New York, an individual representative rarely makes the news, simply because the competition for coverage is too intense; to give one of the seventeen Los Angeles–area House members a story in the *Los Angeles Times* is bound to generate complaints of favoritism from the remaining sixteen. When the *Times* has provided such coverage, it has generally been buried in the "Metro" rather than the national section (Arnold, 2004, p. 67).

The problem is especially acute in broadcast news. Local newscasts in the Los Angeles area rarely mention a congressperson by name, because then they would be obliged to provide coverage of all the others in their viewing area. In Vinson's 2003 study of Los Angeles local news, not a single congressional representative or senator appeared in the news over a four-week period. Thus, "incongruent" media markets—areas where a media outlet is shared by multiple elected officials (the classic case is New York City, where media serve residents of three different states)—generate fewer local reports on incumbent legislators.

Members of Congress who attract media attention by virtue of their constituency service or their legislative accomplishments can be said to have earned their publicity. In other cases, however, a congressional representative can elicit news coverage on nonsubstantive grounds, either by staging an event with considerable human interest (such as Ohio Congressman Tony Hall's twenty-two-day hunger fast in 1993, aimed at drawing attention to the problem of hunger in the United States) or by exploiting the media's penchant for covering stories involving sex, sleaze, or scandal. Senator Arlen Specter of Pennsylvania has earned a justifiable reputation as the "tabloid king" of Congress. In 1985, while presiding over a subcommittee investigating the effects of pornography on women, Specter called Linda Lovelace, Veronica Vera, and Seka—all famous pornographic movie actresses—as key witnesses. Of course, the hearings attracted more reporters than any other Washington event that day. Drawing a similar level of attention was the extensive media coverage (including live ESPN coverage) of the 2005 hearings on steroid use by major-league baseball players.

In sum, elected officials' ability to lead depends increasingly on their public image. Presidents and members of Congress invest heavily in efforts to attract media coverage and to shape the media message. Favorable coverage is seen as contributing to public approval, and public approval is thought to strengthen the official's hand in Washington. In comparison with Congress, the president enjoys significant media advantages: the presidential office is the classic authoritative source, and the president is one person rather than an impersonal institution. Legislators can also generate news, but their multiple messages often amount to a confusing jumble, making it difficult for them to compete with the executive branch's message of the day.

When reporters prove less than malleable, the White House often resorts to old-fashioned public relations. In several recent instances, federal agencies provided "video news releases" having the appearance of a news report, distributing them as news items to local television stations across the country. In the case of one such news release plugging the 2004 Medicare prescription drug plan, the announcer signed off as "Karen Ryan reporting from Washington." This particular video appeared in more than fifty different local newscasts. In an effort to promote the No Child Left Behind Act, officials at the Department of Education took a similar course: they paid Armstrong Williams, a conservative African-American commentator, to write columns and make speeches supporting the bill. In these instances the federal government retained Ketchum Communications, a leading public relations firm, to produce the video material and recruit Mr. Williams as the spokesperson for No Child Left Behind.[10]

The Rise of Issue Advertising

The president and members of Congress are not the only media players. The identical strategy of making and shaping the news is pursued by the vast army of interest groups intent on influencing public policy. During policy debates, it is not unusual for organized interests on either side to take to the airwaves in an effort to signal their position. The "Harry and Louise" ad campaign successfully mobilized opposition to the Clinton health care reform package in 1993 (the American Health Security Act). The ads featured a middle-class couple who spoke out against the Clinton plan on the grounds that it would create a massive bureaucracy. At the time the ads appeared (September 1993), Americans supported the Clinton plan by a two-to-one margin. After approximately fifteen million dollars worth of exposure to Harry and Louise (concentrated in Washington DC and a few other markets), the Clinton proposals suffered a substantial erosion of public support.

Interest groups air ads not because they think the advertising will persuade decision makers. Rather, they hope to get the attention of the news media and frame the policy debate in terms of their own choosing. In the case of the "Harry and Louise" campaign (see Video Feature 7.3), the story line in each ad—the creation of a bloated health care bureaucracy—became the story line in the press and the rallying cry of the Republican opponents. The ads became even more newsworthy when President Clinton and the First Lady attempted to rebut them. In the end, the reform bill was voted down, sending First Lady Hillary Clinton into involuntary retirement as the administration's point person for health care reform.

Video Feature 7.3
Issue Ads

The effectiveness of the original "Harry and Louise" campaign in 1993 has prompted multiple repeat appearances by the couple. In an ironic role reversal, Harry and Louise reappeared in 1998, but this time on behalf of people without health insurance. In the new ads, the couple lamented the "epidemic" of uninsured families and lent their support to a plan that offered government health insurance vouchers for low-income groups coupled with tax credits to small businesses.[11]

Issue advertising has also played a major role in the ongoing efforts to regulate the tobacco industry. In 1998 the US Senate defeated a bill that would have raised the tax on a pack of cigarettes by more than a dollar and granted the federal Food and Drug Administration wide regulatory authority over all tobacco products. The bill also would have imposed restrictions on cigarette advertising. Manufacturers would have been subject to stiff financial penalties if youth smoking rates did not decrease to specified levels over the coming years. The tobacco companies launched a major advertising offensive against the bill. Invoking a familiar Republican theme, the ads suggested that the cigarette tax was just another case of Washington's "tax and spend" appetite. The convenience store industry (which derives most of its revenue from cigarette sales) also weighed in, claiming that the bill would amount to a "devastating disaster" for family-owned convenience stores. Framing the bill as a tax increase and harmful to small business not only had the effect of weakening public support for the legislation, but it also helped create a defensible "cover story" for Republicans voting against the bill.

As the health care reform and tobacco legislation cases both illustrate, issue advertising is the modern version of old-fashioned lobbying. Interest groups opposed to policy legislation relay their preferences to policy makers in the form of television ads. As soon as President Bush nominated Justice John Roberts to fill Sandra Day O'Connor's seat on the Supreme Court in 2005, groups for and against the nomination took to the Washington DC airwaves (see Video Feature 7.4). One particular ad—aired by the abortion rights group NARAL Pro-Choice America—misleadingly suggested that Roberts supported groups that used violence against abortion clinics: "Supreme Court nominee John Roberts filed court briefs supporting violent fringe groups and a convicted clinic bomber. America can't afford a justice whose ideology leads him to excuse violence against other Americans." As might be expected, the controversy generated by these claims resulted in front-page coverage across the country.

Unlike conventional lobbying, which is aimed exclusively at public officials, issue advertising is designed to influence both elite and mass opinion. By framing the Clinton health care proposals as attempts to create health care by bureaucracy, the 1993 Republican ad campaign stirred up public opposition to the bills, thus providing wavering or undecided members of Congress the impetus to join the opposition. In the current debate over Social Security, supporters of President Bush's private retirement accounts hope to

VIDEO FEATURE 7.4
Issue Ads For and Against Justice Roberts

persuade Republican-leaning members of the AARP[12] to desert, thus weakening the AARP's influence with Democratic legislators.

Conclusion

The power of elected officials to govern depends increasingly on their public image. The number of people who support the president is a key barometer of the president's persuasiveness in Washington, and maintaining a high level of popularity requires close attention to the media. Presidents and their advisors strive to capitalize on the inherent newsworthiness of presidential speeches and press conferences to focus the media spotlight on "success stories," while avoiding reference to issues or outcomes that cast aspersions on the president's leadership. In recent years, speeches have replaced press conferences as the president's principal media opportunity because they provide the president with more control over the message. In general, media management has become central to effective governing.

The focus on using media relations to maintain a high level of public approval is not without cost. At the very least, the time and effort devoted to working the press detracts from elected leaders' ability to develop and implement policy initiatives. Moreover, the fear of alienating public opinion may be additional disincentive for leaders to tackle difficult problems that may require the prescription of "bitter medicine" (such as higher taxes). These and other ways in which going public affects the policy process are described in Chapter 10.

CHAPTER 7 SUMMARY

1. Going public is a strategy used by presidents and other political actors to promote their policies by appealing to the American public for support. Given the overriding importance of reelection to the strategic calculations of elected officials, a president's popularity creates an important bargaining advantage; a president who enjoys a high level of public approval can often count on being able to persuade a few members of the opposition.

2. The effects of a president's popularity on the ability to garner legislative support are most evident when the president's proposals address issues

that are salient to the public but concern subject matter about which the public possesses little information (such as the best way to combat terrorism).

3. The White House media complex has become a vast operation, with fifty full-time employees and five distinct organizational branches. Two of the main players are the communications director and the press secretary:

   • The communications director, who seeks to define and market the president's image, is responsible for overseeing the production and release of information throughout the administration.

   • The press secretary, who conducts daily press briefings for the White House press corps, must walk a tightrope between meeting the political objectives of the White House staff ("spin and more spin") and maintaining personal credibility with the media.

4. Presidents have three distinct media opportunities: attracting news coverage, making speeches, and holding press conferences.

   • Given reporters' reliance on official sources, the president can count on regular and sustained news coverage from all forms of news media.

   • In response to the increased negativity of news coverage and the decrease in the size of the audience for national television appearances, presidential speeches around the country have become more common as presidents hope to attract more sympathetic coverage from local and regional news outlets.

   • With the decrease in size of the national audience, presidents have lost the incentive to make themselves available for tough questioning by the press; the risks of committing a gaffe or appearing uninformed have deterred modern presidents from holding frequent press conferences.

5. As alternatives to the three main approaches to gaining exposure in the media, presidents often negotiate appearances on individual television programs or grant interviews to small groups of reporters (preferably local reporters, who are more easily impressed and controlled than their Washington colleagues are). These strategies are particularly useful and common when the White House has lost control over the message, as is the case during major scandals.

6. Like the president, members of Congress seek to use the media for political gain, with two particular goals: reelection, and moving up the legislative hierarchy. Members of Congress (particularly in the House of

Representatives) find it much more difficult to garner media attention than the president does, however, because there are so many of them and each is promoting a different story or angle, and because legislative dynamics do not make for clean, easily explicated story lines.

7. Legislators typically seek out two forms of press coverage. First, with the aim of boosting their reputation and increasing influence with party leaders, they hope to attract attention from national and important regional news outlets. Second, with the goal of reelection in mind, they target local news in their home districts.

8. Interest groups intent on influencing public policy pursue the same strategies that elected officials use for making and shaping the news. During policy debates, organized interests on either side often take their case to the airwaves, with the aim of framing the policy debate in terms of their own choosing and garnering public support for their position.

FURTHER READINGS

Arnold, R. D. (2004). *Congress, the press, and political accountability*. Princeton, NJ: Princeton University Press.

Auletta, K. (2004, January 19). Fortress Bush: How the White House keeps the press under control. *The New Yorker*. Retrieved March 28, 2006: www.newyorker.com/fact/content/?040119fa_fact2.

Baum, M. A., & Kernell, S. (1999). Has cable ended the golden age of presidential television? *American Political Science Review, 93*, 99–114.

Canes-Wrone, B., & de Marchi, S. (2002). Presidential approval and legislative success. *Journal of Politics, 64*, 491–509.

Cook, T. E. (1998). *Governing with the news: The news media as a political institution*. Chicago: University of Chicago Press.

Kernell, S. (1986). *Going public: New strategies of presidential leadership*. Washington, DC: Congressional Quarterly Press.

Kumar, M. J. (2003). The White House and the press: News organizations as a presidential resource and as a source of pressure. *Presidential Studies Quarterly, 33*, 669–683. [7]

Tulis, J. K. (1987). *The rhetorical presidency*. Chatham, NJ: Chatham House.

Wildavsky, A. (1991). The two presidencies. In S. Shull (Ed.), *The two presidencies: A quarter century assessment* (pp. 11–25). Chicago: Nelson-Hall.

NOTES

1. The fifth office (Speechwriting) is entrusted with drafting the president's speeches and public remarks.

2. According to *New York Times* columnist William Safire, the bags were in fact empty.

3. Mike McCurry served as President Clinton's press secretary from 1995 to 1998. Before that he served as spokesperson for the Department of State from 1993 to 1995, and as director of communications for the Democratic National Committee from 1988 to 1990.

4. The *New York Times* data quoted throughout this discussion come from the Policy Agendas Project (2004) at the University of Washington. The data were originally collected by Frank R. Baumgartner and Bryan D. Jones, with the support of National Science Foundation grant number SBR 9320922, and were distributed through the Center for American Politics and Public Policy at the University of Washington and/or the Department of Political Science at Pennsylvania State University. Neither NSF nor the original collectors of the data bear any responsibility for the analysis reported here.

5. The 20 percent figure is based on the assumption that a typical network newscast includes between twenty and twenty-five reports.

6. In fact, one of the articles of impeachment brought against President Andrew Johnson alleged excessive use of rhetoric. Specifically, he was accused of "intemperate, inflammatory and scandalous harangues . . . [and of being] unmindful of the high duties of his office and the dignities and proprieties thereof" (Tulis, 1987, p. 91).

7. Roosevelt broadcast thirty fireside chats between 1933 and 1944.

8. As we noted earlier, President Reagan's fondness for off-the-cuff remarks led the White House to implement the "Deaver Rule" (named for Michael Deaver, the President's communications director), which stipulated that no reporter was permitted to ask Reagan questions during photo opportunities. The networks initially threatened to boycott these sessions if the rule was enforced, but NBC capitulated immediately and within two days the rule was in force.

9. In the era of televised press conferences, presidents could retaliate against the authors of particularly critical news reports by deliberately ignoring their questions.

10. The political fallout from the Armstrong Williams and fake news release episodes included a warning from the Government Accountability Office (the investigative arm of Congress) that federal agencies must clearly disclose that they paid their spokespersons or "reporters." The warning went on to state, "While agencies generally have the right to disseminate information about their policies and activities, agencies may not use appropriated funds to produce or distribute pre-packaged news stories intended to be viewed by television audiences that conceal or do not clearly identify to the audience that the agency was the source of these materials" (Kornblut, 2005).

11. Not content with their work in the health field, the couple has also starred in ad campaigns addressing the issues of encryption and, more recently, human cloning. In 1998, they appeared in ads that opposed government restrictions on the export of US encryption technology (on behalf of US technology companies). Later, in a 2002 ad campaign aired in Utah and Washington, the couple spoke out in favor of human cloning (and in opposition to the Bush administration's efforts to ban cloning).

12. Originally called the American Association of Retired Persons, this organization now goes by just its initials: AARP.

CHAPTER 8

NEWS AND
PUBLIC OPINION

DESPITE THE FIXATION of politicians on their public image as presented by the media, the conventional wisdom in academic circles until quite recently has been that the media's influence on public opinion is somewhere between weak and nonexistent. Scholars have long bought into the doctrine of *minimal consequences*.

What can explain the astounding divergence between the observed behavior of practitioners and the judgment of scholars? The paradox of so much media campaigning with so little apparent effect is, in part, a question of definition. Communication scholars initially conceptualized media effects simply as changes in voter preference; no other outcomes were recognized as evidence of media influence. Against this standard, evidence that campaigns reinforced rather than altered voters' preexisting partisan sentiments was taken as a symptom of minimal effects.

Over time, researchers began to incorporate other measures of influence instead of relying simply on evidence of change in voter preference. When additional indicators were included in research studies—for example, changes in the prominence of particular political issues and in the weight ascribed to particular issues in evaluations of candidates—the effects of media campaigns quickly became more apparent. The earlier verdict that mass media exerted minimal consequences on public opinion was a result of not only a limited definition of *effects*, but also a methodological artifact. As in all social scientific fields, there are multiple possible approaches to studying a phenomenon of interest (in this case the political effects of media on citizens). The doctrine of minimal consequences was predicated on decades of survey research. Unfortunately, survey research simply lacks the power to detect traces of influence, because it cannot assess causation. More recent scholarship has increasingly turned to experimental methods, which, unlike survey research, provide unequivocal evidence of causal impact.

To illustrate the difference in the power of survey and experimental methods, consider, for example, a scholar who wants to find out whether watching a negative campaign advertisement has any influence on voter turnout. In this case, intention to vote is the *dependent variable*, the variable that the researcher believes might hinge on or be influenced by some other, *independent variable*, such as watching the negative campaign ad. The researcher can use either surveys or experiments to investigate whether the independent variable (watching the negative campaign ad) has any effect on the dependent variable (intention to vote). For a survey, the researcher might select a representative sample of citizens and ask them whether they saw the negative campaign ad and whether they intended to vote. For an experiment, the researcher might select a group of citizens, show half of them—selected at random—the ad while showing no ad (or a positive ad) to the other half, and afterward ask the citizens in both groups whether they intend to vote.

Both research methods (surveys and experiments) have strengths and weaknesses, which we will discuss in detail. In short, though, experiments are especially powerful for detecting causation. By contrast, surveys lack the ability to detect causation, but their results can be generalized more easily to larger populations.

Unlike other areas of mass communication, such as marketing, the field of political communication (particularly in its earlier years) relied predominantly on survey research. For reasons that we will discuss, surveys are notoriously imprecise instruments for detecting media or campaign effects. As soon as scholars increased the power of their methodology by turning to experimentation and more elaborate survey designs, the balance of evidence turned in the direction of maximal rather than minimal consequences. Thus, any account of the development of research on media effects must cover both changing conceptualizations of media influence and advances in the methodologies employed in research on mass communication.

Conceptualizations of Media Influence

Serious research into the effects of mass communication can be dated to about the 1930s, following the large-scale spread of radio. Political events in Europe, most notably the rapid development of extremist political parties in

Germany and Italy, prompted widespread speculation that public opinion could easily be swayed by demagoguery or xenophobic appeals. To horrified observers in the United States, Hitler and Mussolini appeared to be the products of effective propaganda. If the Nazis and Fascists could move public opinion so successfully, might the American public be equally susceptible to extremist appeals? Answers to these questions were of considerable interest to senior administrators in the US Department of Defense (DOD), who in the late 1940s commissioned a series of studies to understand the dynamics of propaganda campaigns.

The DOD-sponsored research was carried out by a group of social psychologists at Yale University. The leader of the group, one of the founding fathers of the field of media effects, was Carl Hovland. Hovland's team designed a series of experiments to identify the conditions under which people might be persuaded to change their positions on social and personal issues (Hovland, Janis, & Kelley, 1953; Hovland, Lumsdaine, & Sheffield, 1949). Their research program, which remains a backbone of the literature on media effects, was guided by an overarching analytic framework known as *message learning theory*. Attitude change, according to this theory, depends on source (who), message (what), and receiver (whom) factors (which will be discussed in more detail later in this chapter).

While developing the essential ingredients of message learning theory, Hovland's team was especially interested in Defense Department movies that were meant either to encourage young men to enlist or to boost civilian morale. Through experimental research they found that, although the films were informative, they generally failed to shift attitudes toward the war or willingness to volunteer for military service. Thus, the team concluded that concerns over the power of propaganda seemed unfounded.

Following World War II, scholars turned their attention to the persuasive effects of political campaigns. Social scientists at Columbia University and the University of Michigan undertook large-scale survey studies of attitude change over the course of several presidential campaigns, expecting to find widespread political conversion (Republicans deciding to vote Democratic or vice versa) resulting from campaign messages. The survey evidence, however, showed no traces of last-minute shifts in opinion. In fact, voters who followed campaigns the most closely were the least likely to be influenced.

The 1948 results proved to be no fluke. A series of election studies—carried out between 1948 and 1960—all reached the conclusion that political campaigns persuaded almost no one (for a summary of the evidence, see

Klapper, 1960). People who intended to vote Democratic or Republican at the start of the campaign generally became all the more convinced of their preference. Only a handful of voters switched from one candidate to the other. Thus, any concept of an all-powerful media gave way to the idea of minimal media effects.

Naturally, these results eventually caused scholars to question whether persuasion was, or should be regarded as, the only indicator or criterion of media influence. Researchers began to change their approach. Rather than asking, "What do people think?" researchers focused on asking, "What do people think *about*?" Changes in the political agenda became the operative definition of media influence. The media were thought to act as gatekeepers— selecting some issues for presentation and ignoring others—rather than as marketers of specific points of view.

As scholars began to test and refine the idea of agenda setting by the media, they discovered that the process of defining the political agenda did, in fact, contribute to attitude change or persuasion. Consider the case of the 2004 election. Voters were subjected to extensive news coverage of terrorism, the war in Iraq, and the state of the American economy. In response, the public deemed those issues to be among the most important facing the nation.[1] Because national security and the economy proved so prominent, voters focused on the candidates' relative ability to deal with those issues. In other words, the doctrine of agenda control holds that the more news coverage is assigned to an issue, the more weight voters will accord that issue when evaluating the candidates. This extension of the agenda-setting logic (which we will take up later in this chapter) is called the *priming effect* of news coverage.

The gradual extension of the agenda-setting argument to the determination of voter choice in effect delineated a process of indirect persuasion. If, by increasing the visibility of a particular issue, campaigns also make voters more attached to that issue as a basis for voting, for all practical purposes the effect is equivalent to persuasion. Substitution of the criteria on which candidates are evaluated produces a different bottom-line choice. Thus the theoretical orientation of research on media effects turned full circle. In the early days of mass media, researchers set out with a notion of powerful media capable of altering all manner of social and political attitudes. In the aftermath of repeated failures to document widespread persuasion during campaigns, scholars assigned media a more limited agenda-setting function. Eventually, scholars realized that agenda setting and priming could generate effects that were similar to persuasion.

THE CHOICE OF METHODS

Just as the concept of media influence has waxed and waned, so, too, has the debate over the appropriate tool kit for measuring the effects of the news media. Within the field of mass communication are two distinct methodological traditions: experimentation and survey research. Each tradition is associated with a set of distinctive results. The discovery of agenda-setting and priming effects resulted primarily from the extensive use of experimental methods; the earlier period of minimal consequences, on the other hand, was marked by exclusive reliance on surveys. This pattern suggests a general effect caused by the methodology itself—namely, that experimental and survey studies lead to diametrically opposing conclusions about the effects of mass communication.

The impact of methodological choices on research findings was first identified by Hovland (1959). After enumerating the complementary strengths and weaknesses of experiments and surveys, Hovland warned that exclusive use of one or the other would inevitably lead to biased results. Accordingly, the optimal research strategy was a combination of survey and experimental methods. Here we retrace and update Hovland's classic analysis.

IDENTIFYING CAUSES: THE ADVANTAGE OF EXPERIMENTS

The major advantage of the experiment over the survey—and the focus of the discussion that follows—is its ability to isolate the effects of specific components of political messages. Consider the case of political campaigns. At the aggregate level, campaigns encompass a set of messages, channels, and sources, all of which may influence the audience, often in inconsistent directions. The researcher's task is to identify specific causal factors and specify the range of their relevant attributes.

What was it about the infamous "Revolving Door" advertisement that is thought to have moved so many American voters in 1988? Was it, as widely alleged, the race of Willie Horton, whose crimes the ad highlighted? Alternatively, was it the violent and brutal nature of his behavior, the fact that he was a convict, the dramatic voice-over used in the ad, or another factor? By manipulating the possible causal attributes, experiments make it possible to isolate the explanation. Surveys, on the other hand, can only provide evidence on self-reported exposure to the causal variable in question; respondents are unlikely to remember even whether they saw a particular campaign commercial, let alone its unique features. (In fact, as we will discuss, many people do not even accurately report whether they have seen an ad, watched the news, or voted.)

Experimentation is the method of choice in every scientific discipline, therefore, because the researcher can tightly control the phenomenon under investigation. Potential causal factors can be switched on and off. Consider the key phenomenon of media exposure. The experimenter can measure exposure with almost total precision because she creates it. Using random assignment, she can ensure that the treatment group (those exposed to the message) and control group (those not exposed to the message) will be similar on average; for example, the two groups will have approximately the same proportion of Democrats and Republicans.[2] Thus there can be no doubt that any observed difference between the treatment and control groups after the experiment was caused by the manipulation and nothing else.

Using the context of the 1990 gubernatorial campaign between Republican Pete Wilson and Democrat Dianne Feinstein, Ansolabehere and Iyengar (1995) manipulated the negativity of the candidates' advertising on the environment and examined the effect of this manipulation on intention to vote. In the "positive ad" condition, the sponsoring candidate was depicted as being opposed to offshore oil drilling; in the "negative ad" condition, the sponsor's opponent was said to be in favor of offshore drilling. This difference in the candidate's position was accomplished by the substitution of three words into the soundtrack of a thirty-second commercial—*yes* for *no*, and *will destroy* for *will preserve* (see Video Feature 8.1). Because this was the sole difference between the conditions and because study participants were randomly assigned to either condition, the researchers could attribute any observed difference between the conditions to negativity. The experiment showed that participants who watched the negative version of the ad were less likely to report that they intended to vote in the election.

VIDEO FEATURE 8.1 Experimental Manipulation of Advertising Tone

Experimental studies, of course, do have their own limitations. Long considered the Achilles' heel of experiments, the problem of generalizability—that is, being able to generalize the results observed in an experiment to the population as a whole—manifests itself at three levels: mundane realism, sampling bias, and the nonrandom basis of media exposure in the real world. In the sections that follow, we'll look at each of these.

MUNDANE REALISM

Because of the need for tightly controlled stimuli, the setting in which the typical laboratory experiment is conducted is often quite different from the setting in which subjects ordinarily experience the "target" phenomenon. Although asking subjects to report to a location on a university campus may be convenient for the researcher, it is also a highly unnatural environment for watching television or for other types of activities that are of interest to political-communication researchers. The artificial properties of laboratory experiments are likely to influence the behavior of participants. In order to avoid the reactivity of the laboratory setting, researchers have increasingly turned to so-called field experiments, in which the procedures and settings more closely reflect ordinary life (providing subjects with a milieu that better matches the setting of their living room or den, for example).

In general, building realism into experimental designs necessitates some loss of experimental control. Watching treatments in a mock living room means that some subjects may not pay attention to the stimulus, for example, just as many people zone out when watching TV at home.

Sampling Bias

The most widely cited limitation of experiments concerns the composition of the subject pool. Typically, laboratory experiments are conducted on "captive" populations—for example, college students who must serve as guinea pigs in order to gain course credit. College sophomores may be a convenient subject population, but they are hardly representative of the general population; they have been found, for example, to have less resolute attitudes and a stronger tendency to comply with authority than do older adults. College sophomores might be persuaded by a stimulus, but what about likely voters?

One solution to the sampling problem is to transport the experiment to public locations and recruit participants from nonstudent populations. Ansolabehere and Iyengar, for instance, administered their experiments on campaign advertising at three different shopping malls in and around Los Angeles, and they offered a financial incentive to attract participants.

Fortunately, technology has both enlarged the pool of potential experimental participants and reduced the per capita cost of administering subjects. Today, it is possible to use traditional experimental methods online. The advantages of using the Internet as the experimental "site" include the ability to reach diverse populations without geographic limitations, since subjects can easily "self-administer" experimental manipulations in their own homes. The increased generalizability of experiments administered online, however, again involves the trade-off of a loss of experimental control (because researchers cannot ensure that all subjects are exposed to the treatment under the same circumstances or in similar environments).

Self-Selection

An especially important difference between experimental and real-world contexts concerns the nature of exposure to media messages. The defining advantage of the experiment is that exposure is made equivalent to a lottery, thus guaranteeing equivalence between the experimental and control groups. In the real world, however, exposure to political messages is far from a lottery. Some people get the message, others do not; and the distinction is based on self-selection. The audience for news consists disproportionately of relatively attentive voters, and the increased level of consumer choice only makes it easier for less interested voters to tune out. Thus the challenge facing experimental researchers is to design communication-related manipulations that more closely reflect processes of self-selection by the audience.

One approach is to give participants some control over their exposure to the experimental treatment. As discussed in Chapter 5, in one experiment, Stanford researchers mailed a campaign CD to a representative sample of registered voters just before the 2000 presidential election. Not all participants who received the CD actually used it. In fact, fewer than half of them did.[3] The nonusers were considered the control group. Those who used the CD were significantly more interested in the campaign and more likely to vote than the control group. Was it the use of the CD that stimulated their interest in the campaign, or the reverse? The researchers were able to disentangle the effects of CD use from self-selection through a statistical technique that matched the CD users with members of the control group.[4] As we will discuss in Chapter 11, these "matched" results showed a significant effect of CD use on voter turnout and interest in the election.

In summary, the experiment is unsurpassed in its ability to isolate cause from effect. By physically manipulating the causal factor and holding all other factors constant, the researcher provides unequivocal evidence of causation. At the same time, by maximizing control, the researcher necessarily sacrifices realism, often casting doubts on the generalizability of experimental results to the real world.

GENERALIZABILITY: THE ADVANTAGE OF SURVEYS

Surveys are almost the exact complement of experiments: they yield evidence that is ambiguous with respect to causation, but that may be confidently generalized. For communication scholars, the most fundamental weakness of the survey is that it provides little control over the key phenomenon of media exposure. In the experimental context, exposure is turned on or off; in the survey context, it is approximated by the request that participants reconstruct their past behavior. In the closing days of a campaign, for instance, respondents might be asked to recall which political commercials they watched on television. Survey researchers treat respondents' self-reported exposure to campaign communication as a substitute for actual exposure. Accordingly, the standard test for campaign or media effects is to compare voting choice or candidate preference across respondents who self-report high or low levels of exposure to the campaign. If those with higher levels of self-reported exposure are more likely to prefer one candidate over another (all other factors being equal), the researcher concludes that this preference was due to exposure to the campaign.

The assumption that self-reported exposure is an accurate approximation of actual exposure is problematic on several grounds. People have notoriously weak memories for past events, especially when the "event" in question concerns an encounter with a political campaign or media message. In the experiments conducted by Ansolabehere and Iyengar, over 50 percent of the participants who were actually exposed to an advertisement were unable a mere thirty minutes later to recall having seen the advertisement. On the other side of the coin, survey respondents tend to err in the opposite direction, often overreporting exposure, possibly because they feel that these affirmative responses speak well of their civic virtue. For example, although ratings data showed that only 6 percent of adults listen to NPR at least once per week, fully 35 percent of respondents in a 1989 National Election Studies pilot study reported that they did so (Price & Zaller, 1993). Inaccuracy in self-reports necessarily weakens the ability of survey researchers to detect media effects.

Even more problematic for the survey researcher is the fact that self-reported media use is typically a by-product of the very same political attitudes that are considered effects of media consumption. Those who remember encountering political messages (candidate ads, for example)—and therefore are likely to report having seen them when asked about it in a survey—are likely to be those who are already highly politically engaged. People who are not already interested in politics are less likely to pay attention to campaign ads that appear when they are watching television, and therefore are unlikely to remember—and report—having seen them.

The fact that those who are highly politically engaged are more likely to report exposure to political messages has predictable consequences for research on media effects. In experiments that manipulated the tone of campaign advertising, researchers found that exposure to negative messages discouraged turnout (Ansolabehere & Iyengar, 1995). On the basis of self-reports, however, survey researchers concluded the opposite—that exposure to negative campaign advertising stimulated turnout (Wattenberg & Brians, 1999). But was it recalled exposure to negative advertising that prompted turnout, or the greater interest in campaigns among likely voters that prompted higher recall? When statistical techniques were used to control this problem, the sign of the coefficient for recall was reversed, indicating that those who recalled negative advertisements were less likely to intend to vote (see Ansolabehere, Iyengar, & Simon, 1999). Unfortunately, most survey-based analyses fail to disentangle the reciprocal effects of self-reported exposure to the campaign and partisan attitudes/behaviors.

Over the years, survey design has improved, survey measures of media exposure have become more finely calibrated, and scholars have become more adept at data analysis. Panels (before and after surveys) and aggregate time-series designs make causal inferences from the results much more reliable. In the 2004 election, for instance, researchers interviewed a large number of respondents on a daily basis to yield evidence that spanned the entire life of the campaign (Johnston, Hagen, & Jamieson, 2004). Because respondents were interviewed more or less continuously from the earliest stages of the campaign, the researchers could aggregate respondents into precise temporal groupings corresponding to "before" and "after" major events. Not surprisingly, work based on longitudinal surveys replicates several experimental findings of significant campaign effects. All told, these significant methodological advances have strengthened survey researchers' ability to detect media effects.

Surveys do have their advantages. A relatively small sample yields evidence about a much larger population because the respondents can be a microcosm of the entire population rather than just college students. Estimates based on probability samples come very close to approximating the "true" value of a particular population parameter. In addition to providing generalizable evidence, surveys are less intrusive than experiments. Answering the phone is a routine task for most people, compared with visiting the local college campus, as subjects still must in the case of many experiments.[5] Survey responses are less likely to be contaminated by the novelty of the situation.

COMBINING EXPERIMENTAL AND SURVEY APPROACHES

Given the complementary strengths and weaknesses of experiments and surveys, the least biased methodology for the study of communication effects is to combine the two. Using experiments in tandem with surveys, as Hovland (1959) put it, amounts to "the royal road to wisdom." Over the years researchers have come to heed Hovland's advice. Their tool kit now includes experiments, quasi experiments, telephone surveys, in-person surveys, and, most recently, Web-based surveys.

Methodological advances and the adoption of multimethod research strategies have gradually eroded the "minimal consequences" verdict in the scholarly literature. Today, it is generally acknowledged that media presentations leave their mark on the audience and that media campaigns can affect the outcome of an election. We will summarize the evidence on the effects of news presentations on public opinion in the next section of this chapter. Then, in Chapter 9, we'll turn to the effects of campaigns.

In Focus: Methodological Trade-offs

Surveys and experiments each have strengths and weaknesses as methods of establishing the nature of relationships between independent and dependent variables. By giving the researcher greater control, *experiments* provide the most unambiguous evidence of causation. Because of issues of mundane realism, sampling bias, and self-selection, however, the results from experimental studies often cannot be generalized to the real world.

Surveys do not have such generalizability problems. Because they rely on self-reported data (which are inaccurate because of errors of memory and self-presentation biases), however, they often fail to reveal the true relationships between cause and effect.

Varieties of Media Effects

Ordinary people encounter the political world only through what they see and read about in the media. This dependence has motivated political elites to invest heavily in efforts to shape the content of the news. As we'll describe in this section, this strategy is not irrational; what appears in the news does influence the state of public opinion.

LEARNING

The dissemination of public affairs information is considered a basic responsibility of the news media in democratic societies. By tuning in to the news, Americans can acquire factual information about the course of events—for example, that the number of American soldiers killed in Iraq has passed the two thousand mark, or that President Bush has nominated a new Supreme

Court justice. However, as we will note shortly, the media do not write on a blank slate. Voters' partisan beliefs affect their willingness to learn.

One of the most striking characteristics of American public opinion is that it does not appear to rest on a command of political facts. Americans offer opinions about candidates or issues even when they possess minimal amounts of information. Examples abound: one month after the Republican sweep of the 1994 congressional elections, 57 percent of the electorate could not identify Newt Gingrich and a majority had never heard of the "Contract with America" (which we discussed in Chapter 7). In January 1994, two years after he took office as secretary-general of the United Nations, a mere 10 percent of the American public could identify Boutros Boutros-Ghali. The same number could identify John Major one year after he was elected prime minister of the United Kingdom.

There are several explanations for the unusually high level of political ignorance in the media-richest society on Earth. Americans' relative affluence is thought to contribute to their inattentiveness to politics. For most citizens, decisions made in Congress or the state legislature have little impact on their daily lives. The benefits of knowing who does what in government are minimal. Hence, voters may consider it unnecessary—even irrational—to accumulate large amounts of political information.

A variation on the "rational ignorance" theme is that people do not need facts to express "informed" opinions. The public is able to arrive at reasonable approximations of informed political decisions using shortcuts, or *heuristics*, such as voting on the basis of their liking or disliking of the groups that support a particular candidate or cause, or supporting a candidate because of that candidate's standing in the polls. Although not all scholars agree that the public's use of heuristics produces opinions equivalent to opinions that are based on hard factual information,[6] opinions and voting behavior are undeniably much less affected by information per se than by relevant cues.

Other scholars believe that the explanation for Americans' low level of information about current events is that people use relevant pieces of information to make appropriate changes in their opinions and attitudes, but then discard the information. On hearing that Candidate X voted against tax cuts, a conservative voter may shift opinion of Candidate X in a more critical direction. Later, the voter can remember the change in opinion, but not the information that prompted it to be updated.

A different explanation for widespread civic ignorance concerns the performance of the media. One reason that Europeans are significantly more informed about politics than Americans are may have to do with the quality of news programming (see Dimock & Popkin, 1997) that they encounter on a daily basis. According to this view of the situation, Americans are less informed because they are exposed to less substantive news programming.

It is unclear whether broadcast or print sources are more informative. In a study of the 1972 presidential election, regular newspaper readers acquired more information than irregular readers did, but there was no parallel difference between frequent and infrequent viewers of television news (Patterson & McClure, 1976). Other studies, however, have questioned the greater information value of print over broadcast news. Mondak (1995) found that, if respondents' education and prior political knowledge were taken into account, exposure to a major local newspaper did little to boost knowledge of national or international politics. Price and Zaller (1993) found that self-reported exposure to television news was associated with higher levels of knowledge about current affairs than was exposure to newspapers.

Most research on civic information has focused on mainstream news sources. In recent years, however, soft news and infotainment programs— such as the late-night talk shows and Comedy Central's *The Daily Show*— have become increasingly important as sources of political information, particularly for young people. In a 2004 survey of media use by the Pew Research Center for the People and the Press, 21 percent of people aged eighteen to twenty-nine claimed to have regularly learned something about the election from comedy TV shows, and 13 percent reported that they had obtained some election information from late-night TV shows.

Evidence concerning the extent to which people acquire information from nontraditional news media is just as mixed as the evidence from mainstream media studies. Some researchers suggest that soft news programs, by presenting political issues in a more entertaining format, also inform their audience. According to Baum (2002), the growing popularity of soft news outlets means that "many otherwise politically inattentive individuals are exposed to information about high-profile political issues, most prominently foreign policy crises, as an incidental by-product of seeking entertainment" (p. 91). Other studies, however, have found little evidence of "incidental learning" from soft news sources.

Overall, the jury is still out on whether exposure to the news contributes significantly to factual information about politics. The American public's low level of knowledge can be attributed not only to the increasingly nonsubstantive content of news programming, but also to the lack of incentives for becoming informed, and the easy availability of psychological cues that allow individuals to form opinions despite their lack of information.

AGENDA CONTROL

As casual observers of the political scene, most Americans notice only those issues that are in the news; events, issues, and personalities not covered by the media might as well not exist. What the public notices becomes the principal basis for their beliefs about the state of the country. Thus, the relative prominence of issues in the news is the major determinant of the public's perceptions of the problems facing the nation (see, for example, Dearing & Rogers, 1996; McCombs & Shaw, 1972). The media's issue agenda becomes the public's agenda. This is particularly true in the case of national and international issues, about which the public has almost no opportunity to learn from firsthand experience.

The famine that devastated Ethiopia in the early 1980s provides a clear example of the public's responsiveness to the media agenda. Although the famine had persisted for many months with loss of life in the thousands, most Americans were completely unaware of the issue until it finally attracted attention from the news media in October 1984. Once the spotlight was turned on, there was an outpouring of relief efforts. As the executive producer of NBC's *Today* show commented, "This famine has been going on for a long time and nobody cared. Now it's on TV and everybody cares. I guess a picture is worth many words" (Boyer, 1986, p. 293).

> **In Focus: Agenda Setting and Priming**
>
> The central idea of *agenda setting* is that, by giving differential attention to certain issues, the media set the agenda of public discourse. That is to say, by covering some issues and ignoring others, the media influence which issues people view as important and which they view as unimportant.
>
> An extension of agenda setting, *priming* refers to the way in which the media affect the criteria by which political leaders are judged. The more prominent an issue becomes in the public consciousness, the more it will influence people's assessments of politicians.

The relationship between news coverage and public concern has come to be known as the *agenda-setting effect*. An early statement of the hypothesis was formulated by B. E. Cohen (1963): the media, Cohen said, "may not be successful most of the time in telling people what to think, but it is stunningly successful in telling its readers what to think *about*" (p. 13). The first study to test for the effect was conducted by McCombs and Shaw (1972) in the context of the 1968 presidential campaign. They surveyed a random sample of Chapel Hill (North Carolina) voters, asking them to identify the key campaign issues. Simultaneously, they monitored the news media used by residents of the Chapel Hill area to track the level of news coverage given to different issues. They found almost a one-to-one correspondence between the rankings of issues based on amount of news coverage and the number of survey respondents who mentioned the issue as important.

Although evidence of agenda-setting effects of media coverage is plentiful, some scholars have suggested that the convergence of the public and the news media on the same issue agenda may result simply because both respond to the same real-world events, and *not* because the media is influencing the public. This explanation is unlikely to be correct, however, because most political issues can be experienced only through exposure to the news. How would ordinary voters know about global warming, for example, without encountering any discussion of the problem in the news?

The case of crime provides a striking example of public concern and real-world indicators moving in opposite directions. As Figure 8.1 shows, the FBI nationwide violent crime index has declined significantly since the early 1990s. Despite the reduction in crime, the percentage of the public that

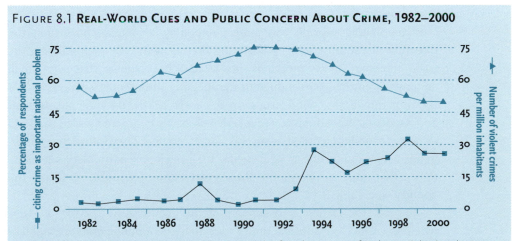

FIGURE 8.1 REAL-WORLD CUES AND PUBLIC CONCERN ABOUT CRIME, 1982–2000

Source: Data from the Gallup "most important problem" series (taken from the University of Washington Policy Agendas Project Web site: www.policyagendas.org/datasets/index.html) and FBI violent crime index (available at www.fbi.gov/filelink.html?file=/ucr/cius_01/xl/01tbl01.xls).

viewed crime as an important national problem increased substantially during this same period. Not coincidentally, the decade of the 1990s witnessed a dramatic increase in the availability of local television news, which is likely to feature stories on crime. Figure 8.1 suggests, at least in the case of crime, that public opinion is more responsive to what appears on the television screen than to the state of the real world.

Survey-based studies of agenda setting have difficulty establishing the direction of causality. That is, some scholars suggest that the correlation between the media and public agenda reflect editors' decisions to run stories on issues deemed important by the public, rather than the other way around. Researchers have attempted to tease out the direction of causality by tracking changes in public opinion and news coverage over time, thus establishing whether it is the media that leads public concern or vice versa. In one such study—the first to test for "feedback" from the level of public concern to news coverage—the authors found no traces of shifts in the amount of news devoted to the economy induced by changes in public concern for economic issues (Behr & Iyengar, 1985). The authors thus effectively dismissed the possibility that news panders to the concerns of the audience. The same study, however, also showed that television news coverage of economic issues predicted the level of public concern for these issues independent of real-world economic conditions. The researchers concluded that correspondence between the media and public agendas was not a result of the fact that both were responding to the same real-world conditions.

Experiments provide the most compelling evidence concerning the direction of causality in agenda setting by the media. By manipulating the issue content of news programs, researchers have shown that even small amounts of coverage are enough to significantly shift people's perceptions of the importance of various issues. In the early 1980s, for example, Iyengar and Kinder (1987) administered a series of experiments that varied the level of news coverage accorded to several "target" issues. They found that participants who watched one story every day for a week on a particular issue came to see that issue as one of the three most important problems facing the country (see Table 8.1).

Overall, the evidence in support of the agenda-setting effect is overwhelming. One-shot surveys, time-series analysis of public opinion, and laboratory experiments all agree on the finding that issues in the news are the issues that people care about.

TABLE 8.1 AGENDA SETTING BY NETWORK NEWS: CHANGES IN THE
PUBLIC'S PERCEPTION OF THE IMPORTANCE OF A PROBLEM

Experiment	Problem	Percentage of Viewers Naming the Problem as One of the Country's Most Serious		
		Before the Experiment	After the Experiment	Change
2	Defense	33	53	+20*
	Inflation	100	100	0
	Pollution	0	14	+14*
8	Arms control	35	65	+30*
	Civil rights	0	10	10*
	Unemployment	43	71	+28*
9	Unemployment	50	86	+36*

Source: Data from Iyengar & Kinder, 1987.
*The reported change is statistically significant.

SETTING THE ELITE AGENDA

The effects of news coverage on the perception of which issues are important extend beyond the mass public. The fact that ordinary citizens care
about an issue is of considerable interest to policy makers, who view public
opinion as a strategic resource. Policy makers know that when the media
spotlight is aimed at a particular issue, they are likely to have greater success
in proposing or moving along legislation on that issue, because it is more difficult for those who might normally try to block such efforts to do so when
the public is clamoring for action. Legislators interested in regulating the
tobacco industry, for instance, are more likely to propose policy initiatives
designed to curb smoking when health issues are moving up the public
agenda. In fact, as Baumgartner and Jones (1993) have demonstrated, congressional hearings on the public health consequences of smoking were pre-
ceded by periods of relatively heavy media coverage of the issue. Across a
variety of policy issues, Baumgartner and Jones found that the frequency of
congressional committee hearings on particular issues over time corresponded to the level of news coverage. As Figure 8.2 shows, hearings on
environmental issues were scheduled more frequently when the state of the
environment attracted more attention in the pages of the *New York Times*.

A study by Wood (1999) found that the relationship between media
attention and elite attention to issues differs across policy areas. On foreign
policy issues, as well as some domestic issues (such as crime and education),

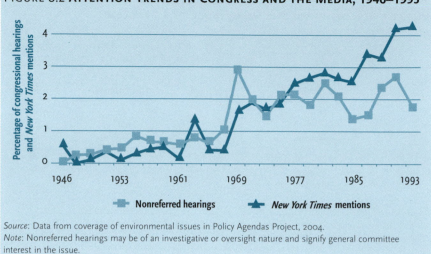

FIGURE 8.2 ATTENTION TRENDS IN CONGRESS AND THE MEDIA, 1946–1993

■ Nonreferred hearings   ▲ *New York Times* mentions

Source: Data from coverage of environmental issues in Policy Agendas Project, 2004.
Note: Nonreferred hearings may be of an investigative or oversight nature and signify general committee interest in the issue.

the president responded to the level of media attention. In domestic policy areas, however, the relationship was reciprocal, with the level of media attention also responding to the level of presidential attention.

Thus, media coverage not only moves public concern, but also motivates policy makers to take action. And because political elites (most notably the president) are the primary generators of news stories, they are in an especially advantageous position to simultaneously influence the media and public agendas.

PSYCHOLOGICAL ACCOUNTS OF AGENDA SETTING

Scholars have identified at least two psychological mechanisms that influence agenda setting. First, people may respond to news coverage because the issues receiving attention in the news are more likely to be "top-of-the-head"—that is, coming to mind more quickly and easily—and are therefore more likely to be cited when respondents are asked to name important national issues. If every newspaper headline and every TV news report you saw prominently featured a story on Iraq, it would not be surprising if that were the first thing that sprang to mind if somebody asked you to name the problems facing the country today.

An alternative perspective treats agenda setting as a more thoughtful process. In this view, people treat journalists as credible sources for judging the importance of issues. When a particular issue receives regular and high-profile coverage, citizens surmise that it must be an important issue for the nation.

Researchers studying agenda setting have also looked at the conditions that underlie the media's ability to shape the public's priorities. Such factors include the personal relevance of the issue and the visibility of the coverage. In general, the more prominent the coverage given an issue is, the more likely it is that that issue will move up the public agenda. Front-page news, newspaper stories accompanied by photographs, and lead stories in television newscasts tend to be particularly influential. This could be taken as evidence in favor of the "thoughtful" account of agenda setting. On the other hand, the greater impact of front-page and lead-story coverage might indicate that the public's attention to news is so limited that they notice only glaring headlines or lead-story coverage.

Some individuals are more responsive to the media agenda than others. In general, the further removed an issue or event is from direct personal experience, the weaker the agenda-setting effects of news coverage are. In other words, when an issue is in the news, people personally affected by it are the first to have their agendas set by that issue. Iyengar and Kinder (1987) found, for example, that after being exposed to broadcast news reports detailing the financial difficulties of the Social Security fund, elderly viewers were much more likely than their younger counterparts to name Social Security as one of the most important problems facing the country.

PRIMING EFFECTS

Beyond merely affecting the perceived importance of issues, news coverage influences the criteria that the public uses to evaluate political candidates and institutions—a phenomenon known as *priming*. An extension of agenda setting, priming is a process by which news coverage influences the weights that individuals assign to their opinions on particular issues when they make summary political evaluations, such as which candidate deserves their vote. As Ansolabehere, Behr, and Iyengar (1993) put it, "Priming refers to the capacity of the media to isolate particular issues, events, or themes in the news as criteria for evaluating politicians" (p. 148).

In general, the evidence indicates that, when asked to appraise politicians and public figures, voters weight their opinions on particular policy issues in proportion to the perceived importance of those issues: the more prominent the issue, the greater the impact of opinions about that issue on the appraisal (for reviews of priming research, see Krosnick & Kinder, 1990; and Miller & Krosnick, 2000). If crime is the issue receiving the most attention in the news, for example, people will be more likely to support the candidate or public official who they think is best able to deal with crime.

Priming effects can be especially important during election campaigns. The closing days of the 1980 presidential campaign provide an especially dramatic example of priming. With less than a week to go before the election, the polls showed Jimmy Carter and Ronald Reagan to be dead even. Suddenly, the Iranian government offered President Carter a last-minute proposal for releasing the Americans whom they had held hostage for over a year. Carter suspended his campaign to devote full attention to these negotiations. The hostage issue and the progress of the negotiations became the major news story of the day. The media's preoccupation with the hostage story caused voters to seize upon the candidates' ability to control terrorism as a basis for their vote choice. Given his record in office, this logic proved disadvantageous to President Carter.

Similar volatility in the public agenda bedeviled President George H. W. Bush in the 1992 election. In the previous year, as he presided over the successful liberation of Kuwait from Iraqi occupation, his popularity ratings had soared to 90 percent. Following the end of the Gulf War, news coverage of the economy drowned out news about military and international issues; on economic issues, voters preferred Clinton over Bush by a wide margin. Had the media played up military or security issues, of course, it's likely that the tables would have been turned.

A recent instance of priming comes from the post-9/11 era. Prior to the terrorist attacks, President George W. Bush's overall popularity was closely tied to perceptions of his performance on economic issues (see Figure 8.3). After September 11, 2001, and extending through 2003, Bush's popularity moved more closely in tandem with public assessments of his performance on terrorism. Terrorism and national security had replaced the economy as the yardstick for judging Bush's performance. Only in 2004, after the onset of the presidential campaign, were economic performance and overall performance again linked. Our analysis of presidential popularity in Chapter 10 reinforces this finding. There we show that, following the 9/11 attacks, news coverage of terrorism became the single most important determinant of Bush's public approval.

As already noted in Chapter 6, voters' tendency to focus on highly visible issues creates strong incentives for candidates to introduce issues on which they enjoy an advantage. September 11 gave George Bush a significant advantage over John Kerry on national security. Among the exit poll respondents who cited terrorism as the most important issue facing the country, 86 percent said they voted for Bush. Among voters concerned about the economy, however, 80 percent said they voted for John Kerry. As these data

FIGURE 8.3 **PRESIDENT BUSH'S POPULARITY**

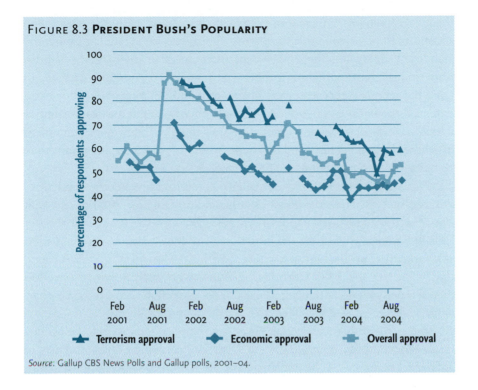

Source: Gallup CBS News Polls and Gallup polls, 2001–04.

suggest, elections often turn on the issue that voters find most important. Had the state of the economy been more prominent, Kerry would likely have been elected. Conversely, if voters had been even more preoccupied with terrorism, Bush would have won by a landslide.

Media priming effects have been documented in a series of experiments and surveys targeting evaluations of presidents and lesser officials and covering a variety of attitudes, including assessments of incumbents' performance in office and ratings of their personal attributes. Overall, news coverage of issues elicits stronger priming effects in the area of performance assessments than in the area of personality assessments.

A special case of priming concerns the phenomenon of "momentum" in primary elections. News coverage during the early primaries tends to focus exclusively on the state of the "horse race." Because horse race coverage is so pervasive (as explained in Chapter 3), primary voters are likely to rely heavily on information about the candidates' electoral viability when making their choices. In a study of the 2004 primary campaign, researchers found that the single most important determinant of Democrats' primary-vote preference between Senators John Kerry and John Edwards was perception of the two candidates' personalities (Luskin, Iyengar, & Fishkin, 2005). The second most powerful predictor of vote choice was the candidates' electoral viability. Viability was more important to voters than the candidates' positions on major issues, including the war in Iraq and outsourcing of American jobs. But among voters who were given ample information about the candidates' positions on the issues, "policy agreement" (defined as the extent to which a voter's own opinion on major issues matched the voter's perception of where the candidates stood on these issues) proved more important than viability as a determinant of candidate preference.

Priming can also lead citizens to give greater weight to other evaluative criteria, such as character traits. Druckman and Holmes (2004) found that President Bush successfully used his 2002 State of the Union address for "image priming," increasing the influence of trait evaluations (strong leadership, integrity) on his approval rating. Similarly, Mendelsohn (1996) found that voters (in the 1988 Canadian election) who were heavily exposed to media reports were more likely to base their vote choice on candidate character evaluations, and less likely to base them on issues.

Just as the influence of news coverage on the state of the public agenda is conditioned both by properties of news stories and by characteristics of individual members of the audience, the ability of the news to prime political evaluations is similarly tempered. Not surprisingly, priming effects peak when news reports explicitly suggest that politicians are responsible for the state of national affairs, or when they clearly link politicians' actions with national problems. Thus, evaluations of President Reagan's performance were more strongly influenced by news stories when the coverage suggested that "Reaganomics" was responsible for rising American unemployment than when the coverage directed attention to alternative causes of unemployment.

In another parallel with research on agenda setting, individuals differ in their susceptibility to media priming effects. Miller and Krosnick (2000) found that priming effects occurred only among people who were both highly knowledgeable about political affairs and highly trusting of the media. Iyengar and Kinder (1987) found that partisanship affected the issues on which people could be primed: Democrats tended to be most susceptible to priming when the news focused on issues that favor Democrats, such as unemployment and civil rights; and Republicans were influenced most when the news focused on traditional Republican issues, such as national defense.

In sum, people use patterns of news coverage as an indicator of the state of the nation. Issues and events in the news are deemed important and weigh heavily in evaluations of incumbent officials and political candidates.

As is clear from the way in which President George H. W. Bush benefited from media coverage of the 1991 Gulf War and then suffered from coverage of the economy, priming results equally from news of political successes or news of political failures. Priming is a double-edged sword.

FRAMING EFFECTS

The term *framing* refers to the way in which opinions about an issue can be altered by emphasizing or de-emphasizing particular facets of that issue. Framing theory was developed by the psychologists Amos Tversky and Daniel Kahneman, who showed that choices could be reversed if outcomes were simply defined as potential gains or losses. A program that would certainly save two hundred out of six hundred people from an outbreak of a rare disease, for example, was chosen by a majority of subjects over an alternative with the identical outcome that was couched in terms that made it seem more risky ("a one-third probability of six hundred people saved"). But when the choice was presented in terms of loss (four hundred deaths for sure, or a two-thirds probability of six hundred deaths), the majority now preferred the riskier-seeming alternative (see Tversky & Kahneman, 1981). Similar presentation effects occur in surveys. Trivial changes in the wording of survey questions can bring about large shifts in public opinion; for example, people respond far less charitably when asked about the desirable level of government aid for "people on welfare" than when asked about aid for "poor people."

Media researchers have identified two distinct types of framing effects: equivalency framing effects and emphasis framing effects. *Equivalency framing effects* involve "the use of different, but logically equivalent, words or phrases" to describe the same possible event or issue; *emphasis framing effects* involve highlighting different "subset(s) of potentially relevant considerations" of an issue (Druckman, 2001a, pp. 228, 230).

The previous example—"people on welfare" versus "poor people"—belongs more in the category of *emphasis* framing because the two phrases emphasize different aspects of poverty (whereas referring to poor people puts the focus on the plight of the less fortunate, referring to welfare brings up the question of whether government has the responsibility to take care of them, as well as the negative stereotype that Americans have of people on the dole). Other examples of documented emphasis framing effects include presenting a Ku Klux Klan rally as either a free speech issue or a public safety issue (subjects reported higher levels of support for allowing such a rally when it was framed as a free speech issue) and presenting gun control as either an individual rights issue or a public safety issue. Because equivalency framing is rarely possible in real-world political contexts, emphasis framing effects are most relevant to our purposes here—and the issue of who is responsible for national problems is a particularly important case, as we will now discuss.

In Focus: Framing

Framing refers to the way in which the media, by highlighting some aspects of an event or issue and ignoring others, can influence how people think about that event or issue. Changing the "manner of presentation" of a news story can result in a very different audience perception of that story.

News coverage of political issues comes in two distinct genres of presentation corresponding to thematic and episodic news frames. A *thematic* news frame places a public issue in a general context and usually takes the form of an in-depth, "background" report. An example of thematic framing would be a story about a war that addressed the historical context of the relations between the two sides, the factors that contributed to the current conflict, and so on. *Episodic* framing, on the other hand, depicts issues in terms of individual instances or specific events—the carnage resulting from a particular terrorist bombing, for example. Episodic coverage typically features dramatic visual footage and pictures; thematic reports tend to be more sedate, consisting primarily of "talking heads."

In the United States, episodic framing is by far the predominant mode of presentation in news stories, largely as a result of market pressures. The preponderance of episodically framed news has serious political repercussions, for it affects viewers' attributions of responsibility for political issues. Most political issues are capable of being viewed either as the creations of societal and/or governmental forces, or the result of private actions of individuals. Rising unemployment, for instance, might be attributed to the changing nature of the job market, or to government economic policies (societal responsibility). Alternatively, unemployment might be attributed to the unwillingness of the unemployed to work for low wages (individual responsibility). The tendency of people to attribute responsibility to societal or individual factors depends, in part, on how television frames political issues.

In a series of experimental studies (see Iyengar, 1991), viewers exposed to thematic framing attributed responsibility for issues to government and society. Following exposure to news reports about increases in malnutrition among the US poor, participants in the study discussed poverty in terms of inadequate social welfare programs; confronted with news accounts of the shrinking demand for unskilled labor, participants described unemployment as a result of inadequate economic policies or insensitive public officials; and provided with news reports on increasing rates of crime in the inner cities, participants cited improved economic opportunities for the under-privileged as the appropriate remedy for crime. Thus, when television news coverage presented an analytic frame of reference, attributions of responsi-bility—both for causing and curing national problems—were societal in focus.

When provided with episodic news, however, viewers attributed respon-sibility not to societal or political forces, but to the actions of particular indi-viduals or groups. For example, when poverty, crime, and terrorism were depicted in episodic terms, viewers attributed causal and treatment respon-sibility primarily to poor people, criminals, and terrorists. In response to news stories describing particular illustrations of national issues, viewers focused on individual and group characteristics rather than on historical, social, political, or other general forces.

The importance of episodic and thematic news frames extends beyond viewers' attributions of responsibility. In each of the framing experiments (and in replications with national survey data), individuals who attributed responsibility for national issues to general societal factors were found to be significantly more critical of the performance of elected officials than were individuals who attributed responsibility to nonsocietal factors. Thus, tele-vision news is generally a significant asset for incumbent officials; the pre-dominance of event-oriented and case study news coverage tends to insulate them from any rising tide of disenchantment over unemployment, poverty, corporate corruption, or other such problems. In contrast, when television casts its coverage in thematic terms, issues are more likely to become cam-paign ammunition with which to attack incumbents.

More recent work has extended analysis of the episodic frame to local news coverage of crime (see Video Feature 8.2). Typically, local crime reports provide a physical description—and perhaps a police sketch, or even secu-rity camera footage or an old mug shot—of the suspect. The visual empha-sis of television, and the focus of crime reports on particular offenders, means that, as depicted in the news, the principal determining factor of criminal behavior appears to be race (since race is something that is clearly evident in a news report, whereas poverty and other social factors obviously are not). Episodic framing thus necessarily introduces racial stereotypes into

VIDEO FEATURE 8.2 Episodic Versus Thematic Framing of Crime

the public's understanding of crime. Viewers are compelled to evaluate their racial beliefs in light of what seem to be empirical realities. Lacking the focus on an individual suspect or perpetrator, by contrast, thematic framing directs the viewers' attention to alternative and more contextual accounts of crime.

Experiments by Gilliam and Iyengar (2000) further demonstrate that the race of the suspect in episodic crime reports is a meaningful cue. Using computer-based editing techniques, the researchers presented the *same* individual as either a white or an African-American male suspect (see Video Feature 8.3). Their results showed that when the suspect depicted in the news was African-American, the number of viewers who endorsed punitive criminal justice policies increased significantly. In addition, exposure to the black suspect strengthened viewers' racial stereotypes (ratings of blacks as lazy and unintelligent) and their hostility to black leaders such as Jesse Jackson.

VIDEO
FEATURE 8.3
Race
Manipulation
in Crime
News Study

Racial stereotypes, particularly those associating crime and race, are also exploited by politicians (hence the rise of wedge appeals, as discussed in Chapter 6). Not only does exposure to information about crime influence viewers' attitudes toward crime and race, but it can also prime racial stereotypes as a basis for judging the performance of elected officials or for choosing between candidates for elective office. In a recent study, Mendelberg (1997) found that, among voters who watched the infamous 1988 "Willie Horton" advertisement, racial prejudice was more closely linked to their attitudes about civil rights and social welfare policies than among voters who did not view the ad. Similarly, Nelson and Kinder (1996) found that frames that focused attention on the perceived beneficiaries of a policy (such as homosexuals in the case of AIDS spending) increased the importance of attitudes toward that group in determining attitudes toward the policy.

Some news frames originate with the media themselves (as by-products of news production processes). Episodic coverage is one such media-generated frame, since in most cases it results from the organizational and commercial pressures on news organizations. Other frames are inserted into the news by politicians and candidates in pursuit of political advantage (as in the case of the Horton ad used by the George H. W. Bush campaign). If politicians can increase their support by using appeals—either explicit or coded—to racial prejudice, it is only to be expected that such appeals will become even more frequent during political campaigns.

Frames can occur on a number of levels as well. Political elites generate frames both on the level of individual issues (for example, is spending on social welfare an equality issue or an economic issue?) and on the level of elections. Campaigns often amount to framing battles between parties, each fighting to define the election in terms of the issues or concerns on which they enjoy a strategic advantage (Republicans have been very successful, for example, in framing elections in terms of values).

Frames that originate with the media also occur on a number of different levels. On one level, what the media tend to cover and not cover over the long term amounts to a frame; in campaign coverage, the heavy emphasis on candidates' strategy and poll standings overwhelms coverage of their issue positions, thus framing elections—and politics more generally—in terms of superficial rather than substantive matters (Cappella & Jamieson, 1997). Indeed, in some ways a specific medium could itself be considered a frame; for example, television—as a visual medium—tends to focus attention on superficial aspects of political presentations, such as candidate appearance or demeanor. The media generate frames on the within-story level, too, as can be seen in the case of the distinction between thematic and episodic coverage.

Like agenda setting and priming, framing effects are conditioned by individual and contextual factors. Source credibility (believing a source to be knowledgeable and/or trustworthy) has been shown to be necessary for framing effects to occur. Researchers have also demonstrated that, when given an opportunity to deliberate on issues, people are less susceptible to framing. People are more likely to accept frames that are congruent with their political predispositions. This finding is consistent with the finding, mentioned earlier, that Republicans and Democrats are each more easily primed by issues traditionally associated with their own parties. Findings concerning the role of political knowledge are more ambiguous, with some studies finding the less informed to be more open to framing effects, and others finding them to be less so.

In summary, despite mediating factors on both contextual and individual levels, the manner in which the news media frame issues and events affects the public in a number of important ways. Politicians fight to frame issues and elections in terms that are advantageous to themselves. The news media assist them in their task, focusing on nonsubstantive facets of elections and presenting individualistic rather than contextualized accounts of political issues that discourage citizens from holding politicians accountable for national problems.

PERSUASION EFFECTS

Persuasion is typically defined as "attitude change." As discussed at the outset of this chapter, early political-communication researchers, looking for evidence of reversals in voter preference, found little evidence of persuasion effects. However, attitude change does not necessarily mean converting from one candidate or one side of an issue to the other. For example, persuasion can involve switching from having no opinion at all to having an opinion, or from having a weak opinion to having a strong opinion, or from not intending to act on an opinion to intending to act. Television news coverage of the abortion issue might encourage viewers to alter their position from uncommitted or "slightly pro-choice" to "strongly pro-choice." A political advertisement might induce some undecided citizens to vote for a particular candidate. News reports on business activity might increase consumer confidence in the economy. And under certain circumstances, people may reverse their preferences or opinions.

Communication theorists typically analyze persuasion situations from the perspective of "who says what to whom." Thus, the major determinants of attitude change are source, message, and receiver characteristics. Applied to politics, the sources are either the news media in general, particular news organizations, or candidates and political parties. Message-related factors might include the particular subject matter of a news report (crime versus the economy), the content of news reports (such as reports suggesting that Iraq was involved in the 9/11 attacks versus reports suggesting that it wasn't), or the tone of a candidate advertisement (positive versus negative appeals). Receiver factors include a wide variety of political predispositions (is the voter Republican or Democrat?) and general background characteristics (is the voter young or old, more educated or less?). As we will describe, the evidence suggests that political persuasion, like persuasion in other contexts, requires a set of joint contingencies among message, source, and receiver factors.

RECEIVER-RELATED CONTINGENCIES

In his classic paper on persuasion effects in campaigns, Converse (1962) demonstrated that the most and the least attentive strata of the electorate remained equally stable (unpersuaded) over the course of political campaigns. The former group encountered a host of campaign messages, in the form of either news reports or candidate advertisements, but rejected most of them. This is because attentiveness is associated with partisanship: those most likely to tune in to campaigns are strongly Republican or Democratic in affiliation. The less attentive, on the other hand, are drawn disproportionately from the ranks of nonpartisans. Although willing to consider any campaign message, they encounter none.

Political campaigns thus typify the "golden mean" maxim of attitude change theorists: voters at the upper end of the attentiveness curve cannot be persuaded because they already have strong preferences; those at the bottom cannot be persuaded because they are never exposed to political messages. Therefore, the middle strata of political engagement—citizens who are moderately interested or informed—are the most influenced by campaigns. Those who paid no attention to news during the 2004 presidential campaign, for instance, would have had no exposure to the "Swift Boats" ads attacking John Kerry's veracity (discussed in Chapter 6) and could not possibly have been persuaded by them. Strong Democrats and Republicans, two groups that were especially likely to have heard about the ads, would have been equally unpersuaded—the former because they rejected the ads as just another Republican attack on their candidate, the latter because they were already staunchly anti-Kerry. However, weak Democrats and Republicans who were only mildly interested in the campaign but who saw the ads could have been swayed to vote against Kerry.

The opposing effects of exposure and acceptance on susceptibility to persuasion help explain why reinforcement rather than persuasion is the typical outcome of political campaigns. Voters' partisan loyalties provide a filter for interpreting campaign messages: messages that oppose viewers' attitudes are actively resisted; those that agree with viewers' attitudes are accepted. Of course, nonpartisans are far less attentive to campaigns than partisans are; nonpartisans' attitudes remain unaffected because they are unaware of what the candidates are saying. Thus, as we will demonstrate in greater detail in Chapter 9, the principal effect of campaigns is to push Republicans and Democrats farther into their respective camps.

SOURCE- AND MESSAGE-RELATED CONTINGENCIES

While accepting the premise that exposure to and acceptance of persuasive messages are both conditioned by specific properties of receivers, some scholars have uncovered a different family of interactions—this time between message and source factors. Their argument is that persuasion effects depend on the degree of fit between the "what" and "who" factors. Readers should recognize this argument as none other than the strategy of issue ownership. That is, Republican candidates are more persuasive when they (the source) discuss issues on which Republicans are generally preferred (the message), and the same is true for Democrats and their preferred issues.

Ansolabehere and Iyengar (1995) experimentally tested for the interaction of source and message factors. The identical advertisement (on unemployment or crime) was attributed to either the Democratic or the Republican candidate running for US Senate in California. Whereas exposure to the unemployment ad elicited greater gains for the Democratic candidate, exposure to the crime ad did the same for the Republican candidate. In a related study, voters rated campaign ads aired by presidential candidates Dole and Clinton during the 1996 presidential campaign. Republicans were more likely to rate Dole's ads as informative (and less likely to rate them as misleading) when the ads addressed "Republican" issues (Iyengar & Valentino, 2000). Conversely, Democrats were more impressed by Clinton's ads dealing with "Democratic" issues. Thus the parties' policy reputations are tantamount to assessments of source credibility.

The logic of differential source credibility extends easily to attributes of the candidates other than their party affiliation. Gender is an especially visible attribute, and the popular culture provides several cues about the traits of males and females—cues that are amply reinforced by the media's depiction of female candidates (Kahn, 1994). Given the availability of gender stereotypes, certain issue messages might be expected to have differential effects across male and female candidates. In fact, the evidence reveals that "masculine" issues such as defense or crime are especially persuasive as campaign material for male candidates, whereas preschool funding and other matters of educational policy work well for female candidates.

In short, persuasive messages are not encountered in a vacuum and must blend in with voters' partisan motives and attitudes. Persuasion effects are thus inherently interactive—involving interactions between the message and the source, interactions between the message and the partisan values of the receiver, or higher-order interactions that also capture individual differences in exposure to campaign messages.

Conclusion

Writing eighty years ago, Walter Lippmann (1922, 1925) offered a series of remarkably foresightful comments about the nature of American democracy. First, he warned that the great majority of American citizens were too apathetic and uninformed to govern themselves. Lacking firsthand knowledge, the public had no recourse but to rely on the "pictures in their heads" when attempting to make sense of political issues and events. Second, he warned that opportunistic political elites could take advantage of citizens' apathy and dependence on the media to manipulate public opinion to their advantage.

The evidence summarized in this chapter matches the first part of Lippmann's argument quite closely. Ordinary citizens are preoccupied with their personal lives and pay little attention to public affairs. Among the advanced industrialized democracies, the United States exhibits an unusually low level of civic literacy. Unable to weigh the pros and cons of policy debates, citizens make do with what they have: the images and sound bites transmitted by the media. They follow the lead of news programming when asked to identify the important issues of the day. Those who influence the media agenda also hold a great deal of power to mold public opinion because issues in the news become the principal yardsticks for evaluating public officials. The impact of media messages on political attitudes, however, is limited by the audience's partisan predispositions.

Taken cumulatively, the evidence indicates that media presentations achieve considerable influence over public opinion. When journalists parrot the views of political elites—as is the case during periods of military conflict—they allow elites to bolster their popularity and gain an important strategic advantage in the policy arena. In Chapter 10, we will demonstrate that fluctuations in presidential popularity have become less dependent on the state of the American economy and more dependent on media coverage—a finding we take as suggestive of Lippmann's "manufactured consent" hypothesis. First, however, in Chapter 9 we'll consider the impact of political campaigns on election outcomes.

CHAPTER 8 SUMMARY

1. As a result of a limited conceptualization of media effects (defining them only in terms of persuasion) and a reliance on survey methodology (which tends to underestimate media effects), political-communication researchers for a long time held that media effects were minimal. Methodological advances (including wider use of experiments), along with a broadened definition of media effects, have since led scholars to acknowledge that media presentations can make a difference in politics.

2. Surveys and experiments, the two methods used to study media effects, each have strengths and weaknesses. Experiments give researchers control over the stimuli to which study participants are exposed, allowing them to isolate causality, but the results from experiments cannot be

easily generalized. Surveys, on the other hand, are highly generalizable, but inaccuracy in participants' self-reports weakens the ability of survey researchers to detect media effects.

3. A variety of media effects on citizens have been examined by researchers:

- *Learning.* By tuning in to the news, Americans can acquire factual information about events. However, many studies have shown Americans to be severely lacking in political information.

- *Agenda setting.* The term *agenda setting* describes the way in which the media set the agenda for public opinion by highlighting certain issues and ignoring others.

- *Priming.* An extension of agenda setting, priming is the way in which the media affect the criteria by which political leaders are judged. The more prominent an issue becomes in the public consciousness, the more that issue will influence people's assessments of politicians, candidates, and other public figures.

- *Framing.* By highlighting some aspects of an event or issue and ignoring others, the media can influence how people think about that event or issue.

- *Persuasion.* Although most early studies on media effects failed to find evidence of persuasion, the media do have some persuasive influence—especially when the definition of persuasion is not limited to conversion from one candidate or one side of an issue to the other.

FURTHER READINGS

Berelson, B., Lazarsfeld, P. F., & McPhee, W. (1954). *Voting.* Chicago: University of Chicago Press.

Cappella, J., & Jamieson, K. H. (1997). *Spiral of cynicism: The press and the public good.* New York: Oxford University Press.

Cohen, B. E. (1963). *The press and foreign policy.* Princeton, NJ: Princeton University Press.

Dimock, M. A., & Popkin, S. L. (1997). Political knowledge in comparative perspective. In S. Iyengar & R. Reeves (Eds.), *Do the media govern? Politicians, voters and reporters in America* (pp. 217–224). Thousand Oaks, CA: Sage.

Druckman, J. N. (2001). On the limits of framing effects: Who can frame? *The Journal of Politics, 63,* 1041–1066.

Gilliam, F. D., Jr., & Iyengar, S. (2000). Prime suspects: The influence of local television news on the viewing public. *American Journal of Political Science, 44,* 560–573.

Hovland, C. L. (1959). Reconciling conflicting results derived from experimental and survey studies of attitude change. *The American Psychologist, 14,* 8–17.

Iyengar, S. (1991). *Is anyone responsible?* Chicago: University of Chicago Press.

Iyengar, S., & Kinder, D. R. (1987). *News that matters: Television and American opinion.* Chicago: University of Chicago Press.

Johnston, R., Hagen, M. G., & Jamieson, K. H. (2004). *The 2000 presidential election and the foundations of party politics.* New York: Cambridge University Press.

Popkin, S. L. (1994). *The reasoning voter: Communication and persuasion in presidential campaigns* (2nd ed.). Chicago: University of Chicago Press.

Price, V., & Zaller, J. (1993). Who gets the news? Alternative measures of news reception and their implications for research. *Public Opinion Quarterly, 57,* 133–164.

Zaller, J. R. (1992). *The nature and origins of mass opinion.* New York: Cambridge University Press.

NOTES

1. Of all respondents in CNN's 2004 election exit poll, 34 percent cited terrorism or the war in Iraq as the most important issue, and 20 percent cited the economy or unemployment (www.cnn.com/ELECTION/2004/pages/results/states/US/P/00/epolls.0.html).

2. Of course, as in any probabilistic outcome, there is some chance (typically small) that the two groups might not be equivalent.

3. The researchers were able to identify the CD users on the basis of the "tracking file" that showed their number of page visits.

4. The general idea behind matching is straightforward: although respondents have self-selected into the treatment, after we control for factors that predispose participants to accept or refuse treatment, the outcomes of interest and treatment are no longer confounded. That is, if we have data on variables that determine whether the treatment is received (covariates), we can overcome the failure of random assignment into treatment or control groups and recover an unbiased estimate of the treatment effect. In particular, we can form *matched comparisons* of treated participants and controls (matching on the covariates); averaging over these matched comparisons produces an unbiased estimate of the causal effect of treatment (for details, see Abadie & Imbens, 2002; Imbens, 2003; Rosenbaum & Rubin, 1983).

5. Perhaps the imposition of answering the phone is not so trivial. The response rate in most major surveys has dropped in recent years and now approaches 30 percent.

6. Critics of the "heuristics as equivalent to information" argument cite evidence showing that, when voters are made to acquire factual information, they express opinions that are often significantly different from the opinions they held previously. We will discuss this evidence in Chapter 11.

APPENDIX TO CHAPTER 8
A CASE STUDY OF RECEIVER-RELATED CONTINGENCIES: PARTISAN DIFFERENCES IN ACCEPTANCE OF IRAQ WAR MESSAGES

Although partisans may not be sufficiently motivated to seek out only supportive information, they are fully prepared to protect their beliefs from unwanted information. People ignore, discount or actively resist information that is inconsistent with their partisan preferences—a phenomenon that scholars refer to as *selective perception*. One of the most striking examples of such biased processing of persuasive messages occurred in the aftermath of the invasion of Iraq. At that time, a majority of Republicans continued to subscribe to beliefs that were contrary to the facts (for example, that the United States had discovered weapons of mass destruction in Iraq) but consistent with their support for the Bush administration. Democrats, on the other hand, were open to information suggesting that the Bush administration's rationale for war was based on false premises.

News coverage of the war in Iraq changed dramatically from 2003 to the weeks leading up to the 2004 election. Immediately prior to the invasion, as we described in Chapter 4, news media unanimously reported that Iraq possessed significant stockpiles of weapons of mass destruction (WMD) and that Saddam Hussein had aided the participants in the 9/11 terrorist attacks. Once the Hussein regime had been toppled and the task of rebuilding Iraq had begun, however, the content of the news changed.

Democratic leaders began to attack the president over the chaos and bloodshed in Iraq. The 9/11 Commission and congressional committee hearings provided documentation that the administration's intelligence on weapons of mass destruction and Iraqi connections to Al Qaeda were false. The Duelfer Report, delivered by Charles Duelfer to Congress in October 2004, repudiated virtually every prewar intelligence claim.[1] The report concluded that Iraq's WMD and nuclear programs had been effectively destroyed during the 1991 Gulf War and that the regime had not undertaken any effort to restart them. And there was no evidence of any official Iraqi contacts with the Al Qaeda organization. Thus, as Duelfer testified (Priest & Pincus, 2004), "We were almost all wrong." As elite discourse on US intelligence turned critical, so, too, did news coverage.

The Duelfer Report was treated as a major event by the national press. The report generated more than 250 stories in American daily newspapers in the first week of October alone. Democrats took the opportunity to ratchet up their criticism of the Bush administration's Iraq policy. By late October, there was general agreement (at least among experts) that Iraq did not possess significant stockpiles of weapons of mass destruction and that Iraq was not a "co-conspirator" in the 9/11 attacks.

Given the trend in the content of the news—from strongly supporting the administration's claims concerning Iraq before the invasion, to rebutting those claims with increasing frequency following the invasion—we might expect to observe increased public awareness of the inaccuracy of the intelligence claims. If people were reading or listening to the news objectively, we should expect a gradual pre- to postinvasion increase in the number of Americans who believed that the United States did not have evidence connecting Iraq with the 9/11 attacks. The onset of news reports contradicting the administration's prewar claims should have informed the public. In fact, as we will describe, increased exposure to the "faulty intelligence" story made only the Democrats more informed.

Surveys tracking public opinion on the war in Iraq included a variety of questions designed to reveal the public's beliefs about the military and security threats posed by Iraq. We focus on one particular question (mainly because it was asked most frequently) in our quest for evidence of differential persuasion. This question concerned the claim that Iraq had collaborated with the 9/11 attackers; respondents were asked, "Is it your impression that the United States has or has not found clear evidence in Iraq that Saddam Hussein was working closely with the Al Qaeda terrorist organization?" Prior to 2004, we may treat "has"—the official position of the Bush administration—as the dominant message emanating from news reports. Beginning in late 2003, however, in response to the 9/11 Commission hearings and other events, "has not" became the overwhelming story line in the news. Did the marked shift in the content of the news affect what Americans believed? The trend in respondents' answers is graphed in Figure A8.1.

Before the invasion of Iraq, a majority of Americans believed there was evidence connecting Iraq to terrorists. Over time, in response to events in the news, this group became smaller, falling to 38 percent of the sample just

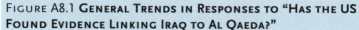

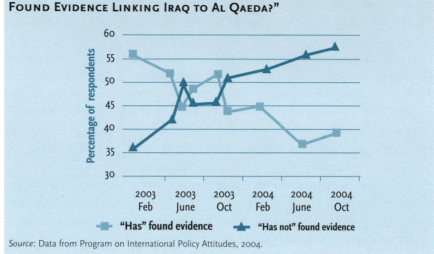

FIGURE A8.1 GENERAL TRENDS IN RESPONSES TO "HAS THE US FOUND EVIDENCE LINKING IRAQ TO AL QAEDA?"

Source: Data from Program on International Policy Attitudes, 2004.

before the election. Conversely, the percentage of the public that was aware of the facts grew by 20 points between February 2003 and October 2004. Thus the original ratio of 56 to 36 in favor of the "has" response was exactly reversed, becoming 38 to 57. News coverage had changed what the public believed, but a significant number of Americans went into the election accepting false premises.

The nearly 40 percent who stated that the United States had found evidence of a link between Saddam Hussein and Al Qaeda must not have been paying attention to the news, or they were tuning in to news sources that minimized the discrepancy between postinvasion events and preinvasion claims, or they were simply motivated to deny the validity of news reports so as to protect their political preferences (for a complete analysis of the relationship between misperceptions on Iraq and political preferences; see Kull, Ramsay, Subias, Weber, & Lewis, 2004). Did Bush supporters ignore the revelations in the media to remain steadfast in their belief that the United States had the evidence, while Democrats welcomed the news and changed their beliefs accordingly? The answer, as Figure A8.2 shows, is clearly yes.

A look at Figure A8.2 suggests that Republicans and Democrats did not encounter the same news stories! A majority of the Democrats doubted the administration's claims in early 2003 well before the media began to propagate the "has not" story. By October 2004, however, 82 percent of Democrats

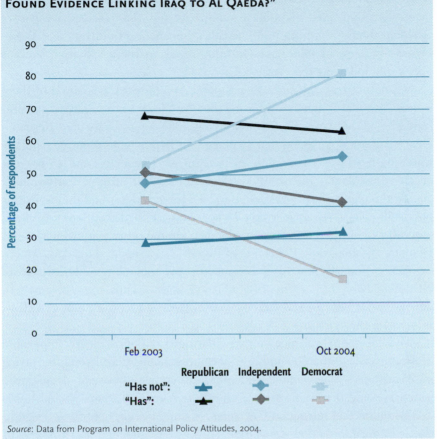

FIGURE A8.2 **PARTISAN-LINKED TRENDS IN RESPONSES TO "HAS THE US FOUND EVIDENCE LINKING IRAQ TO AL QAEDA?"**

Source: Data from Program on International Policy Attitudes, 2004.

believed there was no evidence to support the Hussein–Al Qaeda link. Independents were also influenced by the media message; the percentage of participants responding "has not" increased by nearly 10 points. There was no change, however, within the ranks of Republicans. Two-thirds of them remained adamant in the belief that Saddam Hussein was connected to 9/11. Clearly, the news about Iraq produced much bigger changes among Democrats than among Republicans; the "has not" slope is steepest for Democrats, nearly flat for Republicans.

How can we explain the contradictory responses of Democrats and Republicans to the same media message? When news reports supported the position of the Bush administration, Democrats persisted in believing that there was no evidence; when the media disclosed that the Democrats were correct, Republicans persisted in believing otherwise. There are two plausible explanations. First, Republicans may have resorted to selective exposure to shield themselves from the "bad news" emanating from Iraq and Washington—perhaps by increasingly turning to "sympathetic" sources, such as Fox News, following the invasion.

We do not have adequate longitudinal data to test this claim, but there is no shortage of evidence suggesting that Fox News has emerged as the preferred broadcast source for Republicans. A 2004 survey by the Pew Research Center, for example, found that 35 percent of Republicans reported regularly watching Fox News, while only 21 percent of Democrats (and 25 percent of all respondents) did so (Pew Research Center, 2004). Furthermore, among the regular Fox News watchers, 52 percent described themselves as politically conservative, while only 13 percent described themselves as liberal (and 30 percent said they were moderate). On the other side, 28 percent of Democrats, versus only 19 percent of Republicans, reported regularly watching CNN; and 19 percent of Democrats said they commonly listened to NPR, while only 13 percent of Republicans said so. Thus, there is some tendency for Democrats and Republicans to gravitate to different broadcast sources for their news.

The differential reliance on particular news outlets is clearly implicated in Americans' information and misinformation about Iraq. Even after taking into account socioeconomic and other differences between people who watch Fox and those who watch other networks, Kull, Ramsey, and Lewis (2003) found that relying on Fox News, in and of itself, contributed significantly to misinformation about Iraq. Those who depended on Fox News as their main source of news were the most misinformed about important aspects of the Iraq situation—including the questions of weapons of mass destruction and terrorist links—and those who depended on NPR or PBS were the least likely to be misinformed.

Not all of the difference between Bush and Kerry supporters, however, can be explained by selective exposure. First, despite their differential reliance on specific sources, many Democrats and Republicans were still exposed to the same news sources: 45 percent of Republicans and 46 percent of Democrats reported that they had "read a newspaper yesterday," and a comparable number of Republicans (31 percent) and Democrats (36 percent) reported regularly watching the nightly news of one of the three major networks (Pew Research Center, 2004). In addition, evidence suggests that Bush and Kerry supporters were exposed to the same information, no matter which source they were using. Equal numbers of Bush and Kerry supporters (82 and 84 percent, respectively) accurately perceived the position of the Bush administration on Iraqi weapons of mass destruction, as well as the administration's position on the links between Saddam Hussein and the 9/11 terrorists (Program on International Policy Attitudes, 2004).

The most compelling explanation of the substantially varying levels of misinformation among Republicans and Democrats is not selective exposure to, but selective acceptance of, the news message. Partisan values provide people with the wherewithal to resist information that runs contrary to their beliefs and opinions. In 2003, a majority of Democrats were not prepared to accept the intelligence claims offered by the administration, despite the wholly uncritical coverage provided by the media. In late 2004, most Repub-

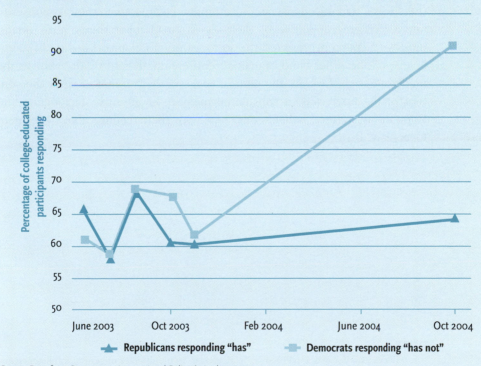

FIGURE A8.3 **CONSISTENCY IN BELIEFS OF ATTENTIVE REPUBLICANS AND DEMOCRATS AS GAUGED BY RESPONSES TO "HAS THE US FOUND EVIDENCE LINKING IRAQ TO AL QAEDA?"**

Source: Data from Program on International Policy Attitudes, 2004.

licans were not prepared to accept the deluge of news coverage that questioned the validity of the administration's claims. Thus, there was virtually no change in Republican beliefs between 2003 and 2004, but a there was a twenty-two-point increase in the percentage of Democrats who believed there was no evidence to link Iraq with the terrorist attacks.

We can carry the analysis of partisan differences in susceptibility to persuasion one step further by comparing the beliefs of the most attentive Republicans and Democrats (using education as a surrogate for attentiveness to news). In Figure A8.3, we graph the percentage of college-educated Democrats and Republicans expressing beliefs consistent with their party identification. The Democratic line reflects the "has not" response; the Republican line corresponds to the opposite position. The results are striking.

The level of partisan consistency in beliefs about Iraq as a terrorist state remained identical through 2003: some two-thirds of educated Democrats and Republicans gave *opposing* answers to the question about Saddam Hussein's involvement in 9/11. Between August and October 2004, the period characterized by heavy news coverage critical of the administration's claims, there was a striking change among attentive Democrats in their responses to news coverage supportive of their views. In October they almost unanimously (91 percent) rejected the administration's claims. Educated Republicans, on the other hand, remained entirely unaffected by the shift in the media message. Overall, the pattern suggests that no matter what the content of the news was, a substantial majority of attentive Democrats and Republicans offered beliefs consistent with their feelings about President George W. Bush.

NOTE

1. Charles Duelfer was appointed "special advisor" to the director of central intelligence and charged with preparing a report on Iraq's WMD program. His report is available at www.cia.gov/cia/reports/iraq_wmd_2004.

CAMPAIGNS THAT MATTER

CANDIDATES SPEND MILLIONS OF DOLLARS on political campaigns and deploy small armies of professional consultants hoping to gain a competitive edge. But in the end, would they have been any worse off without this investment? Do campaigns really make a difference?

This chapter begins by providing an overview of two competing perspectives on this question and suggesting how these disparate perspectives may be reconciled. We then turn to the dynamics influencing voter behavior, the role of campaigns in providing civic education, and factors influencing voter turnout.

Political Context Versus Campaign Effects

There are two competing perspectives on the question of how much campaigns matter. In the "minimalist" view typically advanced by academics, political campaigns represent "sound and fury signifying nothing." The evidence shows that, at least in the case of presidential elections, the results can be predicted with a high degree of accuracy from indicators of economic growth and public approval of the incumbent administration: changes in gross national product (GNP) during the preceding twelve months or the level of public approval of the incumbent president four months before the election are relevant to election outcomes; day-to-day tactics of the candidates in October seemingly are not. At the very least, this evidence suggests that the general political and economic context in which elections occur is just as important as anything the candidates themselves might do or say over the course of the campaign.

The view from the trenches is quite different. Campaign consultants claim considerable prowess in improving their clients' electoral prospects. By their account, well-executed campaigns can produce a significant increase in the candidate's level of support. They claim that the level of political advertising, the candidates' travel schedules, their verbal dexterity and their demeanor in the debates make all the difference to voters. The theory is that "image" matters; therefore, image is what campaigns seek to create, using intensive interventions.

Mounting evidence supports the existence of campaign effects. Typically a presidential candidate's visit to a state generates considerable media publicity and increases that candidate's support statewide. But an opposing candidate who arrives the very next day creates an equally powerful ripple in the opposite direction. It seems that day-to-day tactics can significantly move public opinion; however, if campaigns have similar levels of resources (in terms of both funding and professional expertise), any short-term shifts in voter support cancel each other out over the course of the campaign.

Between the strictly context-driven and "engineered" explanations of electoral outcomes is a more realistic middle ground. Every election occurs within a distinct political context to which the candidates adapt their messages. During the recession of 1992, Americans' general sense of economic insecurity led the Clinton campaign to adopt "It's the economy, stupid" as its core message and mantra. In 2004, in the aftermath of the 9/11 attacks and the first stages of the war in Iraq, President Bush ran for reelection on the grounds that he had made the country more secure from terrorist attacks. Both campaign messages reflected a then-current larger political context to which the candidates had to respond. Economic messages were profoundly relevant in 1992, but less so in 2004, even though outsourcing had become a prominent economic issue by that time.

No matter what the nature of the current political context is, a perennial element of campaigns is the track record of the candidate or party in power. Voters tend to rely on their assessments of the incumbent's performance as a guide for choosing between the candidates. In their eyes, the state of the country reflects either favorably or unfavorably on the incumbent. Ronald Reagan understood the intuitive appeal of this psychological barometer when he asked voters, "Are you better off today than you were four years ago?"

However, well-entrenched perceptions of the state of the nation and the qualities of the incumbent administration do not make campaign strategies irrelevant. To the contrary, campaign professionals know full well that voters care about the current political context, and they therefore design their messages accordingly. They position their clients to capitalize on what voters deem important. Thus, in any given campaign, exposure to the candidates' messages makes voters even more reliant on the underlying "fundamental" or contextual forces.

VOTER DYNAMICS: FORECASTING PRESIDENTIAL ELECTIONS

Political scientists have devised a variety of statistical models for forecasting the results of presidential elections. In most cases, the forecasts combine the incumbent's popularity with the state of the economy. The dynamic underlying the forecasting models is exactly as implied by Reagan's rhetorical ploy—namely, the logic of reward or punishment based on the incumbent's stewardship of the country. Voters are expected to reelect the incumbent during times of economic growth but opt for change during times of distress.

Forecasters capture this logic by incorporating some measure of public support for the incumbent (typically the incumbent's standing in "trial heat" polls on Labor Day or the percentage of the public who approve of the president's job performance) with standard indicators of economic performance. The economic indicators are generally recorded considerably in advance of the campaign; examples include change in real gross domestic product (GDP) during the second quarter of the election year, consumer satisfaction with personal finances in the second quarter, or the percentage change in gross national product between the fourth quarter of the preceding year and the second quarter of the election year.

Basing their predictions on a combination of incumbent approval and the past state of the economy, the forecasting models have accumulated an impressive track record: with the exception of the 2000 election (which was the closest on record), the models have accurately predicted the winner in elections from 1948 to 2004 with only a small spread between the predicted and actual results. If we consider the performance of the forecasts over time, however, the 2000 and 2004 presidential elections proved the least predictable. Averaged across all the models, the margin of error for the 2000 and 2004 elections was nearly 5 points. For elections between 1960 and 1996, the average error amounted to less than 2 points. Thus the trend suggests increased volatility in voter behavior, perhaps in response to the events and story lines of the campaign.

The overall correspondence between the state of the economy in the months preceding the election and the fate of the incumbent party's presidential candidate is graphed in Figure 9.1. Clearly, favorable economic con-

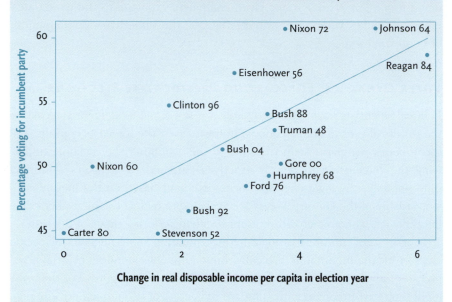

FIGURE 9.1 **THE ECONOMY AND THE VOTE FOR PRESIDENT, 1948–2004**

Source: Data from Bureau of Economic Analysis, available at John Zaller's Web page: www.sscnet.ucla
.edu/polisci/faculty/zaller/1.%20Dataprep2000.xls.

ditions benefit incumbents. On the basis of this particular model (devised
by political scientists John Zaller and Larry Bartels), President Bush won
reelection in 2004 by almost exactly the expected margin, given the state of
the economy (Bartels & Zaller, 2001).

Given the strong "anchoring" role of economic circumstances, one way
to assess the influence of campaigns is to consider the deviations from the
forecasted result. Figure 9.2 presents these deviations for the Zaller–Bartels
forecasting model.

In historical context, Al Gore was—as widely asserted in the media—an
underachieving candidate. Gore's share of the vote was some 5 points below
his expected share. Others who fared worse than they should have include
President George H. W. Bush in 1992, Gerald Ford in 1976, Hubert Humphrey
in 1968, and Adlai Stevenson in 1952. On the positive side, Presidents
Nixon (1972), Clinton (1996), and Eisenhower (1956) all beat the forecast.
Overall, Figure 9.2 suggests that, at the margin, campaigns produce relatively small deviations from voting that is based solely on the state of the
economy.

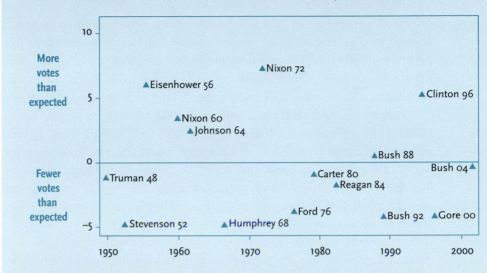

FIGURE 9.2 INCUMBENT PARTY CANDIDATES' PERFORMANCE, 1950–2000

Note: Candidates above the horizontal line did better than expected, given the economy. Candidates below the line underperformed, given the economy.

The Influence of Campaigns

The fact that presidential elections generally follow the "reward–punish" rule is not, in and of itself, an argument against the influence of campaigns. First, when the contest is competitive and the candidates are separated by only a few points in the polls, the efforts of campaign strategists may make all the difference between winning and losing. Trailing in the key battleground states in the closing weeks of the 2000 campaign, the Bush campaign outspent the Gore campaign on the airwaves and narrowed the gap. Second, as we will discuss, considerable evidence suggests that exposure to campaign messages encourages voters, especially those with lower levels of political interest and motivation, to behave in ways that are exactly as anticipated by the forecasting models.

Contrary to the conventional wisdom, the evidence suggests that campaigns do not manipulate voters into supporting the candidate with the most attractive appearance or compelling advertisements. Instead, one of the principal effects of campaigns is to bring candidate preferences into line with the voter's sense of party identification. By the end of the campaign, very few partisans contemplate voting for the out-party candidate.

In the rest of this chapter we will look at the ways in which campaigns influence voters. After presenting the evidence concerning the reinforcing effects of campaigns, we will turn to the ways in which campaigns attract so-called swing, or undecided, voters. Typically lacking an attachment to a party, these voters are susceptible to image- and issue-oriented appeals. They might vote for the candidate deemed more trustworthy, or the candidate who stands for policies that more closely approximate their own preferences.

Next we will take up the educational or civic impact of campaigns. Presumably the onslaught of advertising, news coverage, and partisan rhetoric adds something to voters' store of knowledge about the candidates and the issues. The evidence suggests that voters do indeed learn from campaigns, but that they find it easier to learn about image than about issues. In the case of primary elections, voters are especially likely to gain information about the question of *viability*—a candidate's ability to win. The proliferation of early primaries and the fact that primary voters cannot fall back on their party affiliation creates the possibility of significant bandwagon effects by which voters flock to candidates who demonstrate vote-getting prowess in the early primaries.

Finally, we will address the role of campaigns in influencing the level of voter turnout. In recent cycles, both parties have invested significant resources in the "ground game"—contacting their potential supporters and getting them to the polls. For voters who may be less than enthusiastic about politics, get-out-the-vote efforts can be especially effective. While striving to increase turnout among their supporters, campaigns may simultaneously take steps to discourage would-be opponents from voting. One of the objectives of negative campaigning is to make undecided voters cynical about both candidates, thus weakening their incentive to vote.

Voting as an Expression of Partisanship

Decades of research into why individuals vote the way they do has made it abundantly clear that party affiliation is the single most important determinant of vote choice. Most Americans are socialized into identifying with one of the two major political parties even before they enter kindergarten. This basic sense of loyalty to the party sticks with individuals through their entire lives. In the jargon of voting research, party identification is the *long-term* influence on elections; year in and year out, Americans vote according to their standing commitment.[1] Contrary to popular accounts, party identification is alive and well within the electorate; if anything, party-line voting is on the increase.

Of course, not all Americans claim to identify with a political party. As Figure 9.3 shows, a third of the electorate rejected partisan labels in 2000, preferring to call themselves *independents*.[2] For this pivotal group, the voting decision varies from election to election—hence their designation as *swing voters*. Swing voters might choose candidates on the basis of their positions on the issues, or according to their assessments of incumbent performance. More likely, swing voters are attracted to a candidate on personality grounds; they are willing to vote for someone they believe is a strong leader, with the necessary experience, or alternatively, a person of impeccable character. In short, swing voters choose on the basis of candidate and not party considerations. We will consider the evidence concerning candidate-based voting shortly.

Going into the campaign, Democrats and Republicans have a predisposition to support their nominee. Except when the party nominates a candidate who is so unrepresentative of rank-and-file voters (such as Goldwater in 1964, McGovern in 1972), the great majority of partisans can be counted on to vote "correctly." As the case of the missing Iraqi weapons of mass destruction indicates, partisans interpret campaign events and messages in

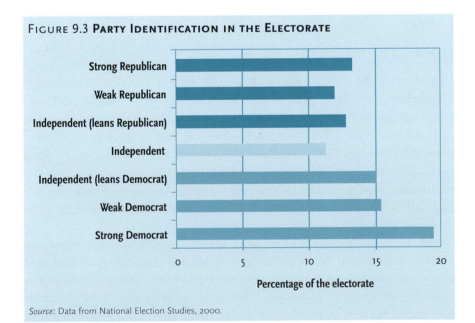

FIGURE 9.3 **PARTY IDENTIFICATION IN THE ELECTORATE**

Percentage of the electorate

Source: Data from National Election Studies, 2000.

ways that confirm rather than contradict their sense of political identity. For Democrats, candidate John Kerry was a patriotic American who put his life on the line in Vietnam; for Republicans, he was a "flip-flopper" who exaggerated his service in Vietnam and then betrayed his fellow veterans by joining the antiwar movement. Over the course of the campaign, the pressure to maintain consistency between party affiliation and beliefs about the candidates makes partisans increasingly likely to vote for their nominee. Exposure to the campaign thus reinforces party loyalty.

Unlike partisans, independents enter the campaign with an open mind. As the campaign progresses, they encounter information and form impressions of the candidates. When the information flow is relatively balanced (an equal number of favorable and unfavorable encounters with both candidates), nonpartisans may remain undecided until the very last moment. In other cases, when one candidate generates more favorable messages than the opponent, independents are persuaded accordingly.

Thus, campaigns have multiple objectives. The first is to ensure that their partisans remain steadfast ("holding the base"). The second is to attract a sufficient number of independents to win them a plurality. Implicit to both of these goals is the task of informing voters about the personal characteristics, political credentials, and policy visions of the candidates. Finally, campaigns seek to optimize turnout by encouraging supporters and discouraging opponents and would-be opponents from voting.

HOLDING THE BASE

Beginning in the 1940s, large-scale sample surveys noted that campaigns induced very few voters to cross party lines. Instead of converting partisans, campaigns made Republicans even more enthusiastic about voting Republican, and Democrats all the more inclined to vote Democratic. The reinforcement effect means that campaigns typically polarize the electorate along partisan lines.[3] As the campaign progresses and more voters encounter the candidates' messages, they increasingly come to behave in line with their party affiliation, their evaluations of the incumbent administration, or their assessments of the state of the country.

In the 1988 presidential campaign, for instance, Republican candidate George Bush trailed Michael Dukakis by double digits in June and July. Once the campaign began in earnest, more and more Americans reacted in a partisan manner; those whose standing connections were predominantly Republican became more likely to declare their intention to vote for Bush.

As a result, the gap between Bush's expected support (based on voters' partisan predispositions) and his actual support narrowed. This trend is graphed in Figure 9.4.

This chart shows that, in early June, Vice President Bush was clearly failing to attract the votes of Republican and Republican-leaning voters. Shortly before Labor Day, however, most Republicans were in the Bush camp, and during the last weeks of the campaign, voters behaved as partisans. In effect, exposure to the campaign made voters' choices more predictable. What was only "soft" support (or indecision) for Bush in June and July had solidified by October and November.

A simpler barometer of partisan reinforcement in campaigns is to track the number of voters who say they intend to vote for their party candidate. Using national surveys conducted over the entire period of the 1988, 1992, and 1996 presidential campaigns, researchers found that the level of party voting increased steadily with time, generally peaking by October (see Figure 9.5). A few weeks before the election, strong partisans (those who claim they are "strongly" affiliated with their party) were almost unanimously behind their candidate (with levels of party voting in excess of 90 percent). Note that the

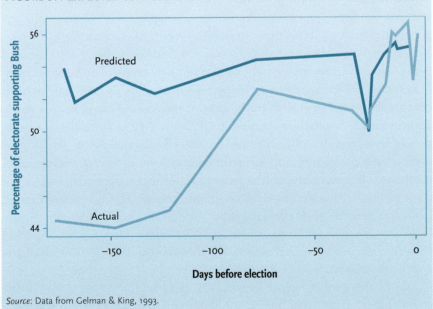

FIGURE 9.4 EXPECTED VS. ACTUAL SUPPORT FOR GEORGE H. W. BUSH IN 1988

Percentage of electorate supporting Bush

Predicted

Actual

56

50

44

−150   −100   −50   0

Days before election

Source: Data from Gelman & King, 1993.

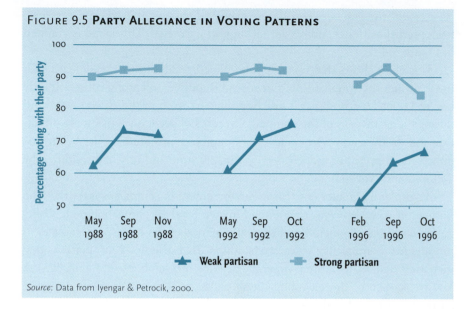

FIGURE 9.5 **PARTY ALLEGIANCE IN VOTING PATTERNS**

Source: Data from Iyengar & Petrocik, 2000.

reinforcing effect of the campaign proved much stronger among voters whose sense of party loyalty was ambivalent (people who said that they were only "weak" Republicans or Democrats). Weak partisans registered larger increases in support for their nominee; over time they tended to catch up with their more intense teammates. By October, the gap between strong and weak partisans was significantly narrowed. As the election approached, more than 70 percent of the weak partisans were prepared to vote for their candidate.

The pattern shown in Figures 9.6 and 9.7 suggests that voters' sense of partisanship is activated or strengthened through exposure to specific partisan messages or events. Both campaign advertisements and televised debates contribute to reinforcement. In the case of the former, exposure to a single advertisement is sufficient. During the 1990 and 1992 campaigns, Ansolabehere and Iyengar (1995) conducted several experiments in which they inserted a campaign ad into a fifteen-minute local newscast. Residents of southern California watched the newscast and then completed a survey of their political attitudes. Overall, exposure to the political ad proved persuasive—the percentage of the sample reporting that they would vote for the candidate featured in the ad increased by 7 percent. However, almost all of the effect occurred among viewers who shared the party affiliation of the sponsoring candidate.

When the ad was from a Democratic candidate, the Democrats in the study responded favorably, but independents and Republicans were unmoved.

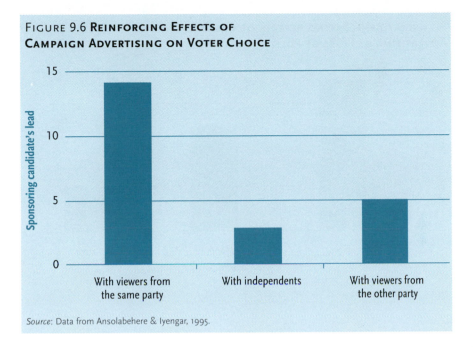

FIGURE 9.6 **REINFORCING EFFECTS OF CAMPAIGN ADVERTISING ON VOTER CHOICE**

Source: Data from Ansolabehere & Iyengar, 1995.

Similarly, when the sponsor was Republican, the ad produced significant gains primarily among Republican voters. Averaged across studies, the effect of watching an ad among "in-party" viewers was a 14 percent increase in support for the sponsoring candidate. Thus the benefits of advertising were concentrated among partisans. Over time, as more and more voters encounter ads, members of the electorate are increasingly pushed into their respective partisan camps.

What is especially revealing about the experimental studies is the relationship between the reinforcing effects of advertising and voters' level of political interest (see Figure 9.7). Consider an intense Republican who follows the campaign religiously. She is so enthusiastic that her preferences need no reinforcing. On the other hand, a more lukewarm partisan may not be particularly familiar with the candidates or the issues. For this voter, a television advertisement may provide the necessary spark to "fire up" partisan sentiments. The reinforcing effects of campaigns, accordingly, should be especially pronounced among the less motivated and attentive partisans.

This graded pattern of reinforcement effects by level of interest is precisely what occurred in the advertising experiments. As Figure 9.7 shows, the persuasive effects of exposure to a television commercial were concentrated among the less interested partisans. For Democrats with a relatively

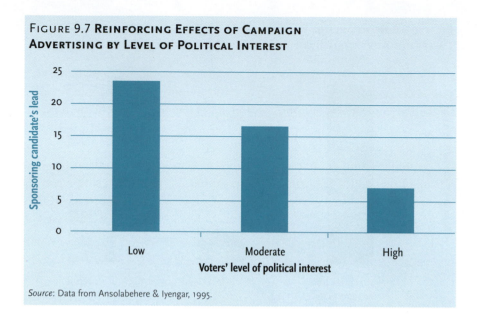

FIGURE 9.7 REINFORCING EFFECTS OF CAMPAIGN ADVERTISING BY LEVEL OF POLITICAL INTEREST

Voters' level of political interest

Source: Data from Ansolabehere & Iyengar, 1995.

high level of political interest, encountering an ad from a Democratic candidate represents overkill: they are already committed to the Democratic candidate. For the less motivated partisan, however, advertising provides a necessary wake-up call; among this group, candidates can increase their level of support by up to 20 percent.

As in the case of advertising, the evidence suggests that voters react to televised debates not as objective "judges," but rather as partisan fans. No matter how poorly their candidate might perform, that candidate is deemed to have outdebated the opponent. Perceptions of who won the debate (in a general election), for all practical purposes, are proxies for voters' party affiliation.

The most extreme case of selective perception occurred in 1976 in a debate between Gerald Ford and Jimmy Carter (Video Feature 9.1). During the debate, as noted in Chapter 6, Ford was asked a question about American policy concerning the Soviet-controlled nations of Eastern Europe. He replied that the United States did not tolerate Soviet interference in the affairs of sovereign states and that the countries of Eastern Europe were free of Soviet control.[4]

By any standard, Ford's statement represented a major gaffe. The Soviets exercised tight control over Eastern European governments at the time and, as the Czechs learned in 1968 (and the Hungarians before them in

VIDEO

FEATURE 9.1

Ford–Carter

Debate, 1976

1956), any attempts at autonomy would be crushed by Soviet military might. President Ford seemed blissfully unaware of recent history. But despite this blunder, polls conducted immediately following the debate showed that voters' support for the candidates remained unchanged. Democrats felt that Carter had won the debate, and by equally wide margins, Republicans gave the nod to Ford. It was not until several days later, in the aftermath of extensive press coverage of Ford's debate misstatement that Carter eked out a small lead over Ford in the polls.

A similar blunder, although of a different variety, occurred in the first debate of the 2000 campaign (Video Feature 9.2). In addition to continually interrupting Governor Bush and making clear his irritation with Bush's answers, Vice President Gore casually stated that he had accompanied FEMA (Federal Emergency Management Agency) Director James Witt on a tour of Parker County, Texas—an area devastated by wildfires. The vice president had misspoken; he had not accompanied the FEMA director on that particular tour.[5] The Republicans seized upon this error and other misstatements (including one concerning his grandmother's out-of-pocket expenses for prescription drugs) as further evidence of Gore's penchant for exaggeration and bravado. Fanned by Bush campaign press releases, a secondary "debate" over Gore's veracity burst out in the media, especially on talk radio. Gradually a significant number of swing voters came over to Bush on the grounds that Gore played fast and loose with the facts.

VIDEO FEATURE 9.2 Bush–Gore Debate, 2000

These episodes can be generalized to all debates. Viewers evaluate what the candidates say depending on their party. Even when candidates commit a major faux pas, or demonstrate considerable ignorance about the state of the world, they manage to hold on to the support of their partisans. It takes a significant mistake, and one that generates considerable buzz in the media before debates have an impact on voters' evaluations of the candidates.

In Focus: The Reinforcement Effect

One of the primary effects of campaigns is *reinforcement*, bringing voters' candidate preferences in line with their party identification. As a campaign progresses and more voters encounter the candidates' messages, they are increasingly inclined to vote for their party's candidate. By the end of the campaign, very few partisans contemplate voting for another party's candidate. Thus the reinforcement effect means that campaigns typically polarize the electorate along partisan lines.

Overall, the evidence on reinforcement indicates that, contrary to conventional wisdom, media-based campaigns do not manipulate voters. Instead, campaigns steer voters in the direction of their respective parties, encouraging them to vote in accordance with their core political loyalties. Reinforcement of partisanship is a far cry from manipulation.

Attracting Swing Voters

For partisans, the candidates can do little wrong. Independents, however, are more open-minded and, depending on the course of a campaign, can be moved in either direction. Once candidates have secured their base, they direct their overtures at this group.

The most important clue to the behavior of independent voters concerns their impressions of the candidates' personalities, especially the traits of competence and integrity. To be seen as intelligent, decisive, and knowledgeable is a prerequisite for attracting voter support. The candidate's moral bearings are also relevant; Senator Edward Kennedy was unable to mount a successful run for the presidency in 1980 because large numbers of the public questioned his integrity in the wake of the notorious Chappaquiddick incident.[6]

In Focus: Swing Voters

Swing voters are voters who lack strong partisan ties and who are therefore considered "up for grabs" in elections. Because voters with partisan affiliations reliably support their party's candidate, often swing voters are the target of most campaign activity. Swing voters are most likely to base their choices on their impressions of the candidates' personalities, especially the traits of competence and integrity.

As we noted in Chapter 6, advertising early in a campaign tends to portray the candidate as a pleasant, upstanding, experienced problem solver. A favorable personal image can go a long way among independent voters. Independents were drawn to John F. Kennedy's youthful charisma, Jimmy Carter's image as a hardworking and honest public servant, Reagan's charm and strong values, and George W. Bush's "average guy" demeanor. Conversely, they were turned off by Michael Dukakis's lack of personal warmth, by President George H. W. Bush's apparent lack of concern for the welfare of working people, and by Al Gore's arrogance and inconsiderate behavior in the first debate of the 2000 campaign. In all these instances, images of the candidates' personal traits were one-sided.

In general, voters do not care equally about all facets of a candidate's character. Depending on the circumstances, they seize upon particular traits. In 1992, President George H. W. Bush was a decorated war hero with an unblemished personal life. His opponent, Bill Clinton, had not only managed to avoid military service, but was also dogged by allegations of womanizing and marital infidelity. During the debates (Video Feature 9.3), President Bush repeatedly reminded voters of Clinton's history, but to no effect. For most voters, even though Bush was apparently the more trustworthy candidate, Clinton was perceived as the more able manager, who would turn around the economy. Because voters assigned higher priority to competence over integrity, Clinton won despite his unfavorable image on the latter.

VIDEO FEATURE 9.3 Bush–Clinton Debate, 1992

In addition to responding to their impressions of the candidates' personalities, swing voters may base their choices on a more substantive evaluation that focuses on the candidates' policy platforms. In the idealized case, an "issue voter" is one who holds preferences on policy issues and who is aware of both of the major candidates' positions on these issues. Assume that voter Smith is pro-choice, supports affirmative action, and opposes American military intervention in Iraq. In the 2004 election, Smith would have concluded that Kerry was the closer candidate on all three issues and cast his vote accordingly.

Voting on the issues requires relatively well-informed and opinionated voters. As we will note in the next section, however, relatively few Americans are capable of casting strictly issue-based votes. Many voters do not have a clear preference on any given issue, and even more are unaware of the candidates' positions. The media's penchant for covering the horse race does not make the task any easier. And when voters have the opportunity to watch the candidates debate the issues, they are drawn to evidence of personality rather than ideology. The 1960 debates between Kennedy and Nixon (Video Feature 9.4) were thought to have given Kennedy an advantage because viewers were drawn to the visual contrast between the youthful-looking and tanned Kennedy and the pale, sickly Nixon. Among people who listened to the debate on the radio, however, it was Nixon's debating skills that made an impression.[7]

VIDEO FEATURE 9.4 Kennedy–Nixon Debate, 1960

In a recent experimental re-creation of the first Kennedy–Nixon debate (Druckman, 2003), one group watched on television while another was given only the audio track. As expected, the television group was more likely to rely on image factors (such as integrity) when considering the candidates' performance in the debate. The radio group, on the other hand, took into account both image and the candidates' positions on the issues. This study confirms that the visual imagery provided by candidate debates encourages voters to focus on personality-related rather than issue-related considerations when evaluating the candidates.

An additional set of candidate attributes can come into play, especially during nonpresidential campaigns, in which news coverage and other forms of campaign communication tend to be less prevalent. In state and local races, clearly visible physical attributes, such as the candidate's gender, ethnicity, or physical attractiveness, may influence their level of support. Female candidates, for instance, run well among women, as do black candidates in districts with large numbers of African-American voters. Because the decibel level of the campaign is lower, voters lack information about the candidates' personal attributes or policy positions. They make do by inferring these attributes from the candidate's gender or ethnicity. Extrapolating from cultural stereotypes, for instance, they may view a female candidate as caring and compassionate, and more willing to support government funding for child care and nutrition programs. Conversely, male candidates tend to be seen as strong leaders who are more likely to support a "tough" stance on issues of national security.

EDUCATING VOTERS

Partisan voters have a convenient basis for voting, even without the benefit of specific information concerning the candidates and the issues. Independents, however, are not similarly equipped. For independents to express a vote preference, they must first acquire a basic impression of the candidates. Campaigns facilitate this task by delivering information about their candidate's personal background and positions on major issues. Gradually voters develop differentiated, though not necessarily accurate, images of the candidates.

There are three levels of relevant candidate information. At the most basic level, voters must recognize the candidates' names. Voters are unlikely to select a candidate whose name they encounter for the first time on the ballot. In presidential campaigns, the candidates typically achieve universal name recognition (either through news coverage of their candidacies or by using biographical advertisements) by the time they are officially nominated in late summer. In lower-level races, however, candidates tend to be less visible and must expend more effort to achieve public familiarity. The fact that incumbents have much higher levels of name recognition than their challengers, as we noted in Chapter 6, makes for an inherently unequal contest.

Incumbents attempt to preserve their tactical advantage by limiting their participation in debates, thus denying their lesser-known opponents much-needed opportunities to catch up.

Although it helps to be recognized, candidates cannot count on mere familiarity as a basis for voter support. They must flesh out their candidacies by telling voters about their experience and qualifications (competence), moral values, and concern for the needs of ordinary people (trustworthiness). As demonstrated in Chapter 6, early advertising is designed to provide voters with an image of the candidate as a likable person capable of political leadership.

The final layer of campaign information concerns the candidates' positions on the issues. Given the penchant of the news media to downplay issues at the expense of the horse race and character-related stories, it is not surprising that acquiring information about the candidates' stances on major issues is the most difficult task confronting voters. Not only do they infrequently encounter issue information, but they also lack the sophistication and motivation to know where to find this information (such as at the candidates' Web sites). Compounding the problem, the candidates are often deliberately ambiguous in their messages, hoping to attract votes from both sides of a contested issue.

Unlike the case with issues, voters have little difficulty forming impressions of the candidates' personal qualities. The percentage of voters who can offer an opinion about presidential candidates' intelligence, sincerity, honesty, or other related attributes generally rises dramatically during the initial stages of the campaign. Of course, the learning trajectory varies, depending on the visibility of the candidate and the attentiveness of the voter. Household names such as Ronald Reagan, George H. W. Bush, and Walter Mondale all entered the race with universal name recognition. Others, such as Jimmy Carter (initially referred to as "Jimmy Who?") and Bill Clinton, had to build up voter familiarity through early primary successes. Once again, incumbents enjoy a substantial advantage. At the outset of the 2004 campaign, for instance, almost all Americans could rate President George W. Bush's personal attributes, but only a bare majority could do the same for Senator Kerry and the rest of the Democratic field. Unlike Senator Kerry, who had to invest substantially in biographical ads, President Bush could proceed directly to discussing the issues.

The ability to learn about the candidates' traits also depends on just who is tuning in to the campaign. Voters with higher levels of interest and stronger partisan preferences are more likely to acquire opinions about the candidates

and at a relatively earlier stage. In general, campaigns only widen the knowledge gap between the haves and the have-nots.

Figure 9.8 shows the level of public familiarity with the candidates' personal traits at the outset of the 2004 campaign. The graph shows the percentage of voters who could rate Bush and five of the Democratic candidates
as "sincere," "intelligent," and "someone who thinks as I do."

In December 2003, 90 percent of the public "knew" about Bush's sincerity,
intelligence, and responsiveness to ordinary people. Among the Democrats,
Howard Dean and Al Sharpton were the only candidates for whom a majority
of voters had formed any impression. Kerry and Edwards were relative un-
knowns. Two months later, however, the average proportion of respondents
with opinions about Kerry's and Edwards's traits had reached 60 percent (a significant increase of more than 15 percent). Kerry was still less familiar to voters than President Bush, but at the observed rate of learning, the president's
advantage would be neutralized by September. For the rest of the Democrats,
whose media profiles were more modest, the learning curves were flatter. Dean,
Clark, and Sharpton registered much smaller gains than Kerry and Edwards.

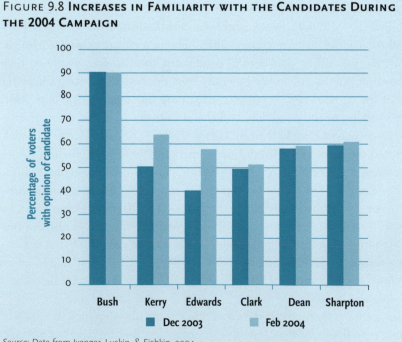

FIGURE 9.8 INCREASES IN FAMILIARITY WITH THE CANDIDATES DURING
THE 2004 CAMPAIGN

Source: Data from Iyengar, Luskin, & Fishkin, 2004.

One reason that voters find it generally easier to acquire personality impressions than policy impressions of the candidates is that the former task is equivalent to the everyday process of forming impressions of friends, neighbors, or colleagues. Small and colorful snippets of information, telltale incidents or events, and the candidate's demeanor at an interview or debate all fuel inferences about personality (a phenomenon psychologists call the *fundamental attribution error*). In 1976, President Gerald Ford's unfamiliarity with Mexican cuisine (Ford neglected to remove the husk from a tamale before biting into it at a televised rally in San Antonio) was interpreted by Hispanic voters as revealing insensitivity to their needs. In 1980, Ronald Reagan insisted that a New Hampshire Republican primary debate be open to all the candidates (breaking his earlier pledge to debate only George Bush). Bush, who had agreed only to a one-on-one debate with Reagan, refused to participate. When the moderator of the debate asked the "uninvited" candidates to leave, Mr. Reagan strode over to the podium, grabbed the microphone and proclaimed, "I paid for this microphone, Mr. Green." To voters, his actions conveyed an image of decisiveness and conviction.[8] In 1996, when Republican candidate Bob Dole stumbled and fell off a speaker's platform at a campaign event, the incident immediately raised alarm about Dole's age and fitness.

In contrast with matters of personality, voters generally take much longer to become aware of the candidates' positions on policy issues. By normal standards, issues are considered the most appropriate criteria for evaluating candidates. Against this standard, American campaigns are woefully inadequate; voters tend to be poorly informed at the start of the campaign, and their ignorance persists.

Voters remain ignorant of the candidates' positions even when the candidates address particular issues at length. In the 2004 primary campaign, American intervention in Iraq and the outsourcing of American jobs were central issues. Howard Dean catapulted to the top of the Democratic field in advance of the primaries because he was the first to come out against American intervention in Iraq. Later, John Edwards mounted a strong challenge to John Kerry, using the outsourcing of American jobs as his signature issue. As Figure 9.9 shows, however, the level of public awareness of the candidates' positions on these two issues was slight.

With the solitary exception of President Bush's position on unilateral military intervention, only a minority of the public could accurately identify candidates' positions on the issues. Perhaps because of the stridency of his message, Dean's position was initially more widely recognized than the posi-

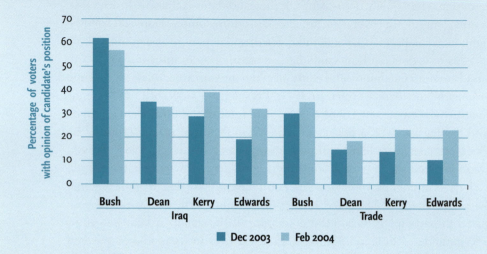

FIGURE 9.9 **CHANGES IN AWARENESS OF CANDIDATES' ISSUE POSITIONS**

Source: Data from Iyengar et al., 2004.

Note: These data are based on a representative sample of approximately five hundred adult Americans who were interviewed in December 2003 and February 2004. The sample was drawn from the Knowledge Networks panel and comprised the control group in a study designed to assess the effects of online deliberation on voter information.

tion of either Kerry or Edwards. Two months later, the number of voters able to identify Kerry's position had increased significantly (by 10 points), making Kerry the most recognized Democrat. Edwards's position on the issue also had become significantly more visible. In comparison with President Bush, however, Kerry and all the Democrats trailed by substantial margins.

Relative to the question of military intervention, the issue of free trade versus protectionism remained invisible. In December, the proportion of voters able to identify the Democrats as protectionists was about 10 percent. President Bush's well-publicized support for free trade was recognized by a mere 30 percent of the public. Two months later, as a result of the Democratic primary campaign, the gap between Bush and the two leading Democrats had narrowed. Overall, however, fewer than one in three Americans could identify the views of the major candidates on this issue. Despite the amount of rhetoric devoted to the trade issue during the early primary campaign, information about the candidates' positions had not trickled down to the level of the ordinary voter.

Voter unfamiliarity with the issues at the outset of the campaign changes little as an election draws near. A study of the 1988 presidential campaign (Buchanan, 1991) compared the number of voters who became reasonably informed about issues that received either extensive press coverage (such as taxes and capital punishment) or minimal coverage (such as the line-item veto and federal tax credits for day care). Between September and October, voters became more informed (on average) about where Vice President Bush and Governor Dukakis stood on the high-visibility issues by a margin of 10 percent. For low-visibility issues, the comparable level of learning was only 3 percent. A mere two weeks before the election, only 29 percent of the public had heard of Bush's pledge to be the "education president." Similar levels of ignorance applied to the Dukakis position on defense: only 30 percent were familiar with his proposals to strengthen US conventional forces.

Despite everything we've said up to this point, the public's unfamiliarity with the candidates' policy positions should not be overstated. Although voters may be unfamiliar with the details of the party platforms, they can compensate through their familiarity with the groups and interests that stand to gain from Democratic or Republican policies—for example, blue-collar workers and senior citizens in the case of Democrats, business interests and fundamentalist Christians in the case of Republicans. They are also aware of the broad policy emphases of the political parties. A majority, for instance, correctly recognize that Democrats are more sensitive to unemployment than Republicans, and Republicans are seen as more likely to adopt policies that minimize inflation. Thus, although information about specific pledges may be missing, voters do have a "gut" sense of the candidates' ideology and general policy orientation.

In summary, campaigns seek to flesh out voters' impressions of the candidates. The task is generally easier in the case of personality because voters infer or form impressions from casual incidents and isolated pieces of information. In the case of issue positions, voters tend to be aware of the candidates' overall vision of government, but most people remain uninformed about candidates' specific policy positions.

Learning and Momentum in Primary Campaigns

Primary elections represent a special case of campaign effects. The principal determinant of vote choice—party identification—is no longer applicable. With a relatively large field of sometimes unfamiliar candidates, the task of voting is made more difficult. Moreover, candidates in primaries often deliberately state their positions ambiguously, not wishing to alienate voters with opposing views or to unnecessarily constrain their messages later in the campaign. Instead of highlighting issues, they often campaign on the basis of background and personality, seeking to present themselves as likable, competent leaders and the best bet to win in November.

As we noted in Chapter 6, press coverage of the early primaries can play a key role in determining candidate trajectories. Candidates who win the "expectations game" (who do better than expected in Iowa and New Hampshire) are labeled serious contenders, while the rest of the field is left to gradually wither away. In recent years, the importance of early primary successes has been amplified because the Iowa and New Hampshire contests are no longer isolated events. Instead, a host of states have moved up their primaries to follow closely on the heels of New Hampshire. Thus the primary process has become "front-loaded." In 2004, a candidate could accumulate the number of delegates required to win the Democratic nomination as early as March 2.

The major consequence of front-loading is a serious reduction in the flow of information between candidates and voters. In 2004, thirteen different primaries were held between January 27 (New Hampshire) and February 17 (the last primary before Super Tuesday)—on average, one primary every other day! Further compressing the process, eleven states scheduled their primaries for March 2. In a context of rapid-fire primary elections occurring in far-flung locations, it is virtually impossible for the candidates—no matter how well financed they might be—to reach a majority of primary voters. There is simply not enough time to mount an adequate advertising campaign or to schedule multiple visits to primary states. Time and resource constraints make it inevitable that voters in early primaries will lack information when they go to the polls.

When they don't have much information, voters must fall back on available cues. Given the media's penchant for horse race coverage of primaries, voters are likely to know which candidates are doing well and which ones are fairing poorly. As primaries occur and the media seize upon the latest results to handicap the race further, voters encounter an abundance of information that they can use to assess the relative viability of the candidates. As Brady and Johnston (1987) put it:

> Citizens . . . learn too slowly about every aspect of the candidates except their viability. And, one of the major reasons that citizens learn quickly about viability is the enormous emphasis placed on the horse race by the media, especially right after the Iowa caucuses and the New Hampshire primary. (p. 184)

Because viability is all that most voters have to go on, a candidate who comes to dominate the early races benefits from momentum, standing to reap a whirlwind of public support in the upcoming primaries. Thus, early results and media coverage of these results reward candidates who perform especially well.

In primaries, voting on the basis of viability is far from irrational. After all, it is in the voters' interest to select a candidate who can unify the party and defeat the opposition in November. In fact, some primary voters consciously vote for the candidate who may be only their second or third choice in terms of personal attributes and the issues, but who they view as the candidate with the best prospects of winning the White House. In 2004, nearly 30 percent of those who voted in the 2004 Iowa caucuses rated "can beat Bush" as the most important attribute they were looking for in the candidates.

The 2004 Democratic primary campaign provides a textbook example of electoral momentum, both positive and negative. Over the space of a few weeks, beginning with the Iowa caucuses, Senator John Kerry rose from a self-financed, underachieving candidate to the presumptive nominee, while Howard Dean fell from front-runner to underdog to certain loser.

Figure 9.10 traces the emergence of the Kerry candidacy in nationwide opinion polls between December 2003 and February 2004. For comparative purposes we also show the level of support for Dean, Edwards, and Clark.

In mid-December, Kerry was at the bottom of the group, with less than 5 percent backing from Democrats and independents. Fearing elimination, the Kerry campaign decided to go all out in Iowa. They closed their field offices in other states and devoted all their resources to Iowa. Senator Kerry campaigned continuously in the state during the ten days before the caucuses.

The Kerry campaign's investment in Iowa clearly paid rich dividends. On January 9, ten days before the caucuses, Kerry's support nationwide was at 10 percent. Two weeks later, after his unexpected victory in Iowa, his poll numbers had climbed to 30 percent. Between the Iowa victory and his win in New Hampshire, Kerry's national support climbed to 45 percent. Following his victories in Missouri, South Carolina, and four other states on February 6, he climbed still further, to 48 percent. Thus, in a matter of just four weeks (January 9 to February 6), Kerry had registered a meteoric rise in the national polls.

While Kerry's candidacy was booming, Howard Dean's support was collapsing. Dean went into Iowa with a double-digit lead over his closest competitor (at that time, General Wesley Clark). Two weeks later, after his loss

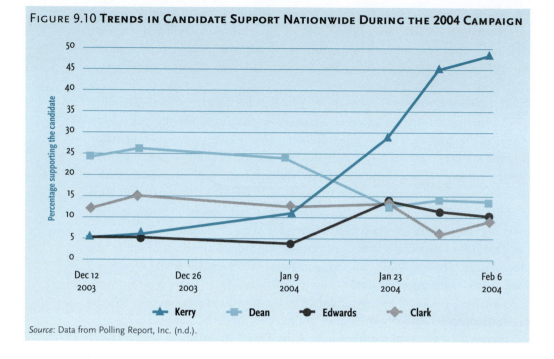

FIGURE 9.10 TRENDS IN CANDIDATE SUPPORT NATIONWIDE DURING THE 2004 CAMPAIGN

Source: Data from Polling Report, Inc. (n.d.).

in Iowa and the "scream heard around the country," his support was cut in half (from 25 to 12 percent). Dean was unable to halt this reverse momentum; for all practical purposes the loss in Iowa was the death knell of his campaign.

Events in Iowa had no less of a dramatic impact on New Hampshire voters (see Figure 9.11). At the beginning of the year, Dean was the choice of almost 40 percent of New Hampshire Democrats. Two days after the Iowa caucuses, his support had fallen to 15 percent. For Senator Kerry, whose low point in New Hampshire was 10 percent (in mid January), the Iowa victory produced a huge increase of more than 24 points. Kerry had established himself as the clear front-runner with a substantial lead over the rest of the field.

Such dramatic fluctuations in candidate support are unusual. Since the large-scale adoption of primaries, initial front-runners have typically maintained their advantage and eventually secured the nomination. Vice President Gore, for example, had relatively little difficulty overtaking Senator Bradley in 2000. On the Republican side that year, even though Senator McCain scored a major upset win over the front-running George Bush in New Hampshire, McCain's momentum was short-lived. He was defeated in the next primary (South Carolina) and was out of the race soon after.

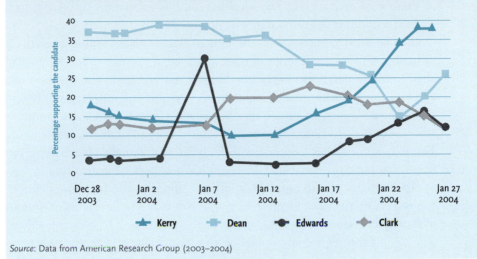

FIGURE 9.11 TRENDS IN NEW HAMPSHIRE POLLS DURING THE 2004 CAMPAIGN

Source: Data from American Research Group (2003–2004)

Apart from 2004, other cases of "dark horse" candidates emerging from their early primary successes include Jimmy Carter, who was catapulted from relative obscurity to win the 1976 Iowa caucuses and New Hampshire primary and, eventually, the presidency. Eight years later, in a particularly dramatic case of momentum, the little-known Senator Gary Hart finished third in the Iowa caucuses behind the odds-on favorite Walter Mondale and 1972 nominee George McGovern. His third-place showing was surprise enough to provide a surge in media attention. Hart went on to score a remarkable upset in New Hampshire, where he defeated former Vice President Mondale by nearly ten thousand votes. At that moment, national polls showed Mondale with only a slight lead over Hart. The Mondale campaign was forced to invest in a major advertising campaign questioning Senator Hart's credentials (including a famous commercial modeled on the McDonald's "where's the beef?" query). Mondale eventually hung on to win the nomination, but as Senator Hart himself acknowledged, "You can get awful famous in this country in seven days." (Four years later he might have added that you can become equally infamous just as fast.)

Campaigns and Turnout

Campaigns have a clear interest in getting out the vote, but only among voters who support them. Among partisans of the other side, or swing voters who are leaning toward voting against them, campaigns would prefer that as few of them vote as possible. The ideal outcome is maximum turnout among supporters, minimum turnout among opponents.

Unlike most other nations, the United States makes voting a relatively difficult task. Despite a series of reforms aimed at increasing the number of eligible voters (such as eliminating literacy requirements and the poll tax, and lowering the voting age to eighteen), Americans still must register before they can cast votes. In most states, voters must register at least a month in advance of the election. Only six states have adopted same-day registration. The two-step process, coupled with high rates of mobility (each time you move, you need to re-register), is a significant impediment to voting.

In comparison with most other affluent, industrialized societies, American voter turnout is low. Figure 9.12 graphs two different indicators of turnout in national elections: the percentages of the population that are eligible to vote and of the registered population that cast ballots.[9] Clearly, registered voters are regular voters; turnout in this group approximates turnout in the

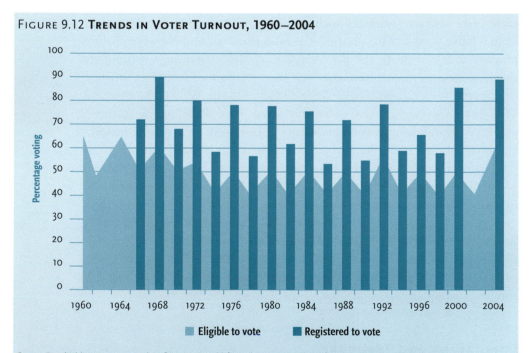

FIGURE 9.12 **TRENDS IN VOTER TURNOUT, 1960–2004**

Source: For eligible-voter turnout, data from McDonald & Popkin, 2001 (updated figures retrieved August 5, 2005, from http://elections.gmu.edu/voter_turnout.htm). For registered-voter turnout, data from the Federal Election Commission (retrieved August 5, 2005, from www.eac.gov/election_resources.asp?format=none).

European democracies. Among the *eligible* population, however, turnout is much lower—in most off-year elections, less than a majority.

The sawtooth pattern of eligible-voter turnout suggests that the decibel level of the campaign stimulates people to vote. When the candidates and their activities are more visible, more people vote. In presidential elections, the media buzz and the level of advertising (at least in the battleground states) generate a sufficient level of interest and information; turnout increases to two-thirds of registered voters and a slight majority of all voting-eligible adults. In off-year elections, as media coverage drops off the campaigns generate less excitement, voters find it too burdensome to acquire information, and turnout drops considerably. Thus, turnout depends on the level of voter *stimulation*.

The most effective form of stimulation is personal contact. Campaigns often send volunteers door to door, make reminder telephone calls (often with recorded voice messages from VIPs about the importance of voting), provide absentee ballots for those unable to make it to the polls, and generally urge their supporters to vote. These get-out-the-vote efforts are likely to be concentrated in areas where the election is hotly contested. In the case of the 2000 presidential election in Florida, an increased turnout of only five hundred voters on the Democratic side would have swung the election to Al Gore.

Voter canvassing is effective. Yale researchers Alan Gerber and Donald Green (2002) found that, when civic groups contacted adult registered voters face to face, the rate of turnout increased by nearly 10 percent. Contacting voters by direct mail also stimulated higher turnout, but only by a slight margin. Somewhat surprisingly, telephone calls were found to have no effect at all.

Two groups that are the most likely to require campaign outreach if they are to vote at all are the young and members of ethnic minorities. Eighteen-year-olds are busy with their personal affairs—transitioning to college or getting a job. They are less likely to be connected to a network of politically attentive friends or acquaintances. Youth culture includes a healthy dose of cynicism, which makes young people view the act of voting with disdain. For these reasons and more, the turnout rate of eighteen- to twenty-one-year-olds has never exceeded 30 percent. In the 1998 congressional elections, youth voters numbered 13 percent of the voting-age population, and a mere 5 percent of those who voted. When we look at actual (as opposed to self-reported) turnout, the level of abstention among younger voters is remarkable. In the 2002 gubernatorial election in California, for instance, a mere 11 percent of eighteen-year-olds voted.[10]

The consequences of age-related imbalances in political participation for the policy process are obvious. Elected officials respond to the preferences of voters, not to nonvoters. As rational actors, candidates and parties tend to ignore the young, thereby contributing to the disillusionment of young voters and perpetuating a vicious cycle that discourages young voters from participating in the electoral process.

The second group of voters who suffer from electoral underrepresentation are racial and ethnic minorities. In the case of African-Americans, the gap can be attributed to lower socioeconomic status. In the case of Hispanics, language and unfamiliarity with voting procedures may be key barriers. Whatever the explanation, the underrepresentation of minorities in the electorate has significant policy consequences. The wedge appeals discussed in Chapter 6 are successful only because whites remain the dominant voting bloc. Consider the case of California, where the influx of Latino immigrants has altered the ethnic composition of the state population quite dramatically. Whereas whites accounted for 60 percent of the adult population of the state in 1992, they numbered only 47 percent in 2003. The Latino share of the population, on the other hand, increased from 24 to 33 percent. But even though Latinos make up a third of the population, they are a much smaller group within the electorate. Whites remain the largest group within the electorate, accounting for some 70 percent of voters in 2002. Despite the inflow of immigrants over the last decade, the California electorate today is a virtual mirror image of the California population in 1980—70 percent white and only 14 percent Latino. Whites have retained their dominant political status, primarily because of low voter turnout among Latinos.

Voter mobilization drives can be especially effective when targeted at groups that lack the motivation to vote. The Yale studies demonstrate that canvassing young people significantly increased their probability of turning out to vote. In a different study, Stanford researchers attempted to raise youth turnout by providing a free interactive election CD featuring youth-oriented diversions such as politically oriented arcade games and interactive quizzes. Although the great majority of the eighteen- to twenty-five-year-olds who were mailed the CD ignored it, those who chose to use it voted at a higher rate in the 2002 California election than did a control group that did not receive the CD (Iyengar & Jackman, 2003). The Stanford study suggests that new media may be an effective means of reaching young voters.

Campaigns are interested not only in boosting turnout; at times they may also attempt to achieve the opposite result by discouraging would-be opponents from voting. The incentives to demobilize are considerable. In the first place, as virtually every study of campaign effects demonstrates, very few partisans can be converted. Running ads that attempt to persuade Democrats to vote Republican is not a good use of scarce resources. Persuading Democrats that the Democratic candidate may have undesirable attributes, however, may be easier to accomplish. If some Democrats become sufficiently unenthusiastic about their candidate, they may decide not to bother with the election. Rather than casting a vote for the other party, these Democrats may prefer not to vote.

Thus, negative campaigning can have a negative impact on turnout. In the experiments conducted by Ansolabehere and Iyengar (1995), exposure to negative rather than positive campaign ads reduced participants' interest in voting by nearly 5 percent. Among viewers who considered themselves independents (who tend to find political campaigns far from interesting to begin with), the demobilizing effects of negative advertising were doubled: independents who watched negative rather than positive ads were nearly 10 percent less likely to say that they intended to vote. For nonpartisans, negative campaigning not only diminishes their opinion of the candidates, but also engenders cynicism about the process.[11]

Campaign managers and candidates are well aware of the effects of negative campaigning on turnout. Why else would negative campaigning prove so popular? They are more diplomatic, however, in their public accounts of the strategy. Fearing the controversy that accompanies discussion of intentional "vote suppression," practitioners are not inclined to acknowledge their efforts publicly. In the immediate aftermath of the New Jersey gubernatorial election of 1993, Republican consultant Ed Rollins openly admitted (in a C-SPAN broadcast) that the winning Republican strategy included systematic efforts to reduce African-American turnout. Once Rollins's comments had made the news, civic groups threatened litigation to overturn the election result on the grounds that minority voters had been disenfranchised. Rollins immediately recanted, claiming that he had exaggerated the role of campaign tactics. In an op-ed piece for the *Washington Post*, Rollins explained, "I spun myself out of control."

Conclusion

Campaigns do not occur in a vacuum. Candidates design their messages to fit the political environment. During times of international tension, candidates run as advocates of a strong military; during times of recession, they

propose policies that stimulate economic expansion. Individually and cumulatively, the effect of campaign messages is either to activate or to reinforce
viewers' long-term political predispositions (their party identification), as
well as their assessments of the performance of the incumbent administration. The most frequent instance of the reinforcement effect is the shepherding of wayward partisans back into the fold. Thus, the contradiction
between the ability to forecast elections on the basis of structural indicators
that have little to do with day-to-day campaign activities and the candidates'
substantial investments in media campaigning is more apparent than real.

A common criticism of modern campaigns is that they are light on substance (issues). Sound bites and thirty-second commercials, the critics suggest, are inherently superficial forms of political discourse. The news media
are equally responsible, given their unwillingness to elevate issues to the
same level of newsworthiness as campaign strategy and the horse race. Voters have to look harder to become informed about the issues, and in most
cases they don't. At the level of the candidates' personal qualities, however,
campaigns do prove informative. By election day, most voters can compare
the candidates on questions of competence, experience, or integrity.

A second criticism of media-based campaigns is that they intend to
deceive and manipulate. Advertisements that deal in symbols and slogans
rather than careful and well-documented analysis are thought to deflect voters from the "real" issues of the day. Here the evidence suggests that the critics have underestimated the intelligence of the electorate. When voters
change their minds during campaigns (something they don't do often), it is
invariably in the direction of the "correct" partisan or retrospective vote.
Thus, the cumulative effect of the campaign is at least as likely to "enlighten"
as to manipulate.

CHAPTER 9 SUMMARY

1. There are two competing perspectives on the question of how much
campaigns influence voter behavior:

- In the minimalist view, the general political and economic context in
which elections occur is just as important as anything the candidates
themselves might do or say during the campaign. Evidence shows that,
at least in the case of presidential elections, the results can be predicted

with a high degree of accuracy from indicators of economic growth and public approval of the incumbent administration.

- The booming campaign industry suggests a different conclusion. Campaign consultants claim that well-executed campaigns can produce a significant increase in the candidate's level of support. Growing evidence supports the existence of campaign effects.

2. Between these two positions is a more realistic middle ground: Every election occurs within a distinct political context to which the candidates adapt their messages. Campaign professionals are aware of the political context and design their messages accordingly, positioning their clients to capitalize on what voters deem important.

3. Political scientists have devised a variety of statistical models—most of which combine the incumbent's popularity with the state of the economy—for forecasting the results of presidential elections. Voters are expected to reelect the incumbent during times of economic growth but to opt for change during times of economic distress.

4. One of the primary effects of campaigns is reinforcement, bringing voters' candidate preferences in line with their party identification. As a campaign progresses and more voters encounter the candidates' messages, they are increasingly inclined to vote for their party's candidate.

5. Another task of campaigns is to attract swing (undecided) voters, who lack strong attachment to a party and thus are susceptible to image- and issue-oriented appeals. The behavior of independent voters is most clearly linked to their impressions of the candidates' personalities. Swing voters may also base their choice on candidates' policy platforms, siding with the candidate whose positions most closely match their own.

6. Campaigns also have an educational impact. This is especially important for independent or swing voters, who must figure out how to decide between candidates during the campaign. Campaigns deliver information about their candidate's personal background and positions on major issues.

7. Primaries represent a special case of campaign effects because the principal determinant of vote choice—party identification—is no longer applicable. With a relatively large field of sometimes unfamiliar candidates, voters must fall back on cues such as the relative viability of the candidates.

8. Campaigns can also significantly affect the level of voter turnout. While striving to increase turnout among their supporters, campaigns may simultaneously take steps to discourage would-be opponents from voting.

FURTHER READINGS

Ansolabehere, S., & Iyengar, S. (1995). *Going negative: How attack ads shrink and polarize the electorate*. New York: Free Press.

Bartels, L. M., & Zaller, J. (2001). Presidential vote models: A recount. *PS, 33*, 9–20.

Brady, H. E., & Johnston, R. (1987). What's the primary message: Horse race or issue journalism? In G. R. Orren & N. W. Polsby (Eds.), *Media and momentum: The New Hampshire primary and nomination politics* (pp. 127–186). Chatham, NJ: Chatham House.

Campbell, A. (1960). Surge and decline: A study of electoral change. *Public Opinion Quarterly, 24*, 397–418.

Campbell, J. E. (2004). Introduction—The 2004 presidential election forecasts. *PS: Political Science and Politics, 37*, 733–735.

Fiorina, M. P. (1981). *Retrospective voting in American national elections*. New Haven, CT: Yale University Press.

Gelman, A., & King, G. (1993). Why are American presidential election polls so variable when votes are so predictable? *British Journal of Political Science, 23*, 409–451.

Gerber, A. S., & Green, D. P. (2000). The effects of canvassing, telephone calls, and direct mail on voter turnout: A field experiment. *American Political Science Review, 94*, 653–663.

Green, D., Palmquist, B., & Schickler, E. (2002). *Partisan hearts and minds: Political parties and the social identities of voters*. New Haven, CT: Yale University Press.

Iyengar, S., & Petrocik, J. R. (2000). Basic rule voting: The impact of campaigns on party- and approval-based voting. In J. Thurber, C. J. Nelson, & D. A. Dulio (Eds.), *Crowded airwaves: Campaign advertising in elections* (pp. 113–148). Washington, DC: Brookings Institution Press.

Johnston, R., Hagen, M. G., & Jamieson, K. H. (2004). *The 2000 presidential election and the foundations of party politics*. New York: Cambridge University Press.

Lazarsfeld, P. F., Berelson, B. R., & Gaudet, H. (1948). *The people's choice*. New York: Columbia University Press.

Mayer, W. G. (2003). The basic dynamics of the contemporary nomination process: An expanded view. In W. G. Mayer (Ed.), *The making of the presidential candidates 2004* (pp. 83–132). Lanham, MD: Rowman & Littlefield.

McDonald, M. P., & Popkin, S. L. (2001). The myth of the vanishing voter. *American Political Science Review, 95,* 963–974.

Shaw, D. R. (2005). *The race to 270: The Electoral College campaign strategies of 2000 and 2004.* Chicago: University of Chicago Press.

NOTES

1. Although partisan attachments are considered stable dispositions, there is evidence that some voters change their identification to make it consistent with their opinions on the issues and the candidates.

2. Since the label *independent* speaks well of the respondent's civic virtue, the designation is likely to include many "closet partisans."

3. In the case of the 2004 campaign, the level of partisan polarization was considerable, leaving little room for campaigns to achieve further reinforcement. Even before Labor Day, the number of undecided voters was just above 5 percent, suggesting an unusually entrenched electorate.

4. Much later, after he had retired from public life, former president Ford joked that he had merely been fifteen years ahead of his time!

5. Vice President Gore subsequently issued a press release noting that he had accompanied Witt on numerous tours, including one in neighboring New Mexico.

6. A young woman, Mary Jo Kopechne, had accompanied Senator Kennedy to a party. She drowned after the senator lost control of his car while driving across a bridge. Senator Kennedy did not report the accident until the following day.

7. It is difficult to make strong causal claims about these media differences because television viewers and radio listeners at the time differed in several ways, including their pre-debate feelings about Kennedy and Nixon.

8. In fact, Governor Reagan had borrowed his line from Spencer Tracy in the 1948 movie *State of the Union.* Popkin (1994) suggests that Reagan may have been influenced by the movie script because the moderator's name was Breen—very similar to "Green."

9. The voting-eligible population is a more appropriate definition of the electorate than the voting-age population because it excludes two groups that are deprived of voting rights: noncitizens and convicted felons.

10. We computed this result from the California secretary of state's turnout database (available on CD from the California secretary of state).

11. It is important to note that evidence of demobilization is limited to a handful of experimental studies in which the tone of the ad campaign was manipulated while all other factors were held constant. Survey-based studies, which lack any semblance of control over the content of the advertising message, have found no connection between advertising tone and turnout. Some survey-based studies even suggest that negative campaigning boosts turnout. A compilation of all published studies on the subject (both experimental and survey-based) thus concluded that there was no relationship between negative campaigning and turnout (Lau, Sigelman, Heldman, & Babbitt, 1999).

THE CONSEQUENCES OF GOING PUBLIC

ONCE ELECTED, public officials face a conundrum. To succeed in office they must remain well liked by the public. Elected officials are usually in a better position than ordinary voters to analyze the merits of policy proposals. But because the public is generally uninformed about the intricacies of policy debates, decisions that result in good policy are not necessarily popular.

How do incumbents reconcile the need to maintain their popularity with doing what's best for the nation? This chapter focuses on the implications of going public for the exercise of leadership. We begin by tracing the ups and downs of presidential popularity over the past four decades in an attempt to assess whether the public responds more to real-world events or to news media coverage of these events. The evidence shows that voters are sensitive to events; they reward or penalize presidents running for reelection depending on the state of the economy. Our analysis also indicates that in the national security arena, where news is powerfully shaped by government officials, the president's popularity depends more on news coverage than on events; the greater the coverage of terrorism, the more popular the president. Media management matters.

In Chapter 7 we discussed the ability of presidents to leverage their popularity into enhanced standing with rival elites. Here we will address the implications of going public for the exercise of political leadership. On the surface at least, the use of popularity as a bargaining chip to influence rival elites means that presidents and the policies they pursue will be responsive to public opinion. At the same time, though, a system predicated on personal popularity creates strong disincentives for officials to lead; the expression and pursuit of clearly defined policy initiatives may jeopardize popularity.

Theories of Presidential Popularity

In October 1983, a suicide bomber rammed a truck filled with explosives into the barracks used by American marines on peacekeeping duty in Lebanon. Nearly three hundred marines died. By any measure, the event represented a military disaster. That evening, President Reagan addressed the nation on prime-time television. Surprisingly, his popularity actually increased in the immediate aftermath, leading some to label Reagan the "Teflon president." The Beirut tragedy suggests that presidents can use symbolic appeals or staged rhetoric to maintain high approval ratings even in the face of events that signify obvious policy or performance failures.

Research suggests that three principal factors influence presidential popularity: length of time in office, the course of events, and public relations.[1] Let's look at each of these.

INEVITABLE DECLINE?

Some theorists have suggested that a president's support inevitably declines over time. Given sufficient time, even the most popular president will eventually decline in popularity. This systematic erosion in public approval is attributed to presidential decision making: over the course of the term, as presidents make decisions and take positions, they accumulate opponents. According to this view, there is nothing the president can do to forestall the effects of time. The downward trend in popularity has led some scholars to propose the idea of the "throwaway presidency," which suggests that "the probability of failure is always tending toward 100 percent" (Lowi, 1981, p. 11).

However, several presidencies have not conformed to the general theory of inevitable decline. As Figure 10.1 indicates, President Reagan experienced two major drops in popularity, and on both occasions he recovered. During the prolonged 1981–82 recession, his approval dropped 20 points, but by the summer of 1984, his approval rating had rebounded, and he was reelected in a landslide. During his second term, Reagan's standing fell in early 1985 following allegations of corruption in the Department of Labor. A more serious scandal erupted in November 1986, when it was revealed that the administration had secretly sold arms to Iran and illegally channeled the proceeds to the Nicaraguan Contras. The observations immediately before and after the news of the Iran–Contra scandal show that Reagan's approval rating fell from 63 to 47 percent. Once again, however, Reagan proved buoyant. By the end of his second term, his popularity stood at 63 percent, higher than when he first entered office.

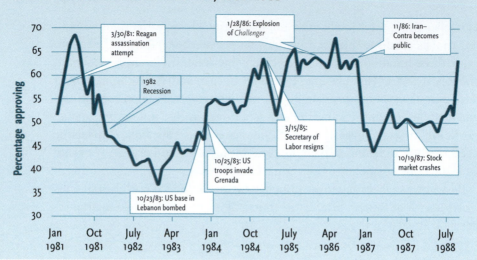

FIGURE 10.1 REAGAN APPROVAL RATINGS, 1981–1988

The case of Bill Clinton provides an even more convincing rebuttal of the theory of inevitable decline (see Figure 10.2). President Clinton's popularity suffered a series of early setbacks associated with controversies surrounding some of his cabinet nominees, his position on gays in the military, and somewhat later, the resounding congressional defeat of health care reform. In between, Clinton's ratings got a boost when he sent American troops into Somalia to oversee relief operations. By 1996, Clinton was well positioned in the polls and went on to defeat Senator Dole easily in the 1996 election.

The Lewinsky scandal erupted early in President Clinton's second term, creating a firestorm of controversy that eventually developed into a full-scale effort to remove him from office. Yet in the immediate aftermath of the allegations, Clinton's job approval actually increased! When the president appeared on television to deny the affair, with the First Lady at his side, one poll showed an 8-point increase in popularity from the previous day. The rebound in his popularity continued during the period leading up to the House vote on impeachment. Ultimately, Clinton's approval ratings stabilized in the 60 to 65 percent range. Maintaining this level of public approval in the midst of extreme political adversity was an important signal to moderate Senate Republicans. When it came time to vote on Clinton's impeachment, a sufficient number of them deserted their party to acquit him.[2]

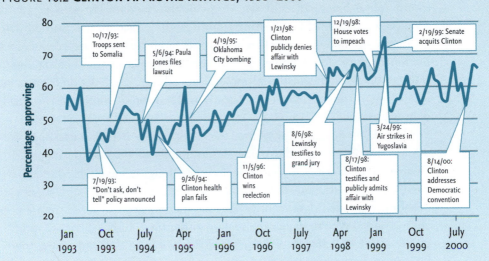

FIGURE 10.2 **CLINTON APPROVAL RATINGS, 1993–2000**

REAL-WORLD CUES

As the cases of Presidents Reagan and Clinton illustrate, presidents are not necessarily doomed to end their terms with low approval ratings from the public. A more plausible explanation attributes changes in presidential popularity to the unfolding of events and issues. Peace and prosperity generally produce high ratings and assured reelection; recessions, military defeats, and policy debacles do the opposite. According to this "environmental connection" account, the American public holds the president responsible for the

In Focus: Theories of Presidential Popularity

Research suggests that three principal factors influence presidential popularity:

- **Length of time in office.** Over the course of the term, as presidents make decisions and take positions, they accumulate opponents and thus lose popularity.

- **The course of real-world events.** The American public holds the president responsible for the state of the nation. When events suggest that the United States is doing well, the president's popularity increases, but it drops when events imply less satisfactory outcomes for the country.

- **Public relations efforts.** By influencing the way in which events are defined and framed in news accounts, the president is able to exert substantial influence over his standing with the public.

state of the nation. When events signify that the country is doing well (for example, the unemployment rate drops or the Saddam Hussein regime is toppled with minimal loss of American life), the president is rewarded with an approval bonus. Conversely, when events imply less satisfactory outcomes for the country (for example, the number of American troop casualties in Iraq continues to increase, with no end in sight, or the federal government leaves the victims of Hurricane Katrina to fend for themselves), the president is punished.

The frequency and duration of these approval-enhancing and approval-diminishing events are the major determinants of presidential popularity. During the Lewinsky scandal—which, other things being equal, should have been an approval-diminishing event for President Clinton—the American economy expanded significantly; personal income grew by more than 2 percent, a rate of growth higher than at any other time during Clinton's term in office. The net change in Clinton's popularity during this period was therefore positive: the booming state of the economy more than neutralized the Lewinsky revelations.

The impact of events on popularity raises important questions about the real significance of vocal leadership and going public. Is it simply that popular presidents are those who happen to be lucky enough to hold office during prolonged periods of peace and prosperity? Or do the president's prowess as a communicator, his ability to capitalize on the symbolism and trappings of high office, and his skill in cultivating and framing news coverage produce varying images of effective leadership? Is "merchandising no match for history" (Neustadt, 1960, p. 73)? Or is the interpretation of history sometimes subject to shrewd management by a president? Perhaps President Clinton would not have survived the Lewinsky scandal had he remained silent and simply counted on the state of the economy to protect him from his opponents.

THE ROLE OF PRESIDENTIAL RHETORIC

Scholars have tried to trace the connection between presidential rhetoric and shifts in popularity, but with inconsistent results. Some studies show that major presidential speeches boost public approval and that the effects of speechmaking on popularity are stronger than the corresponding effects of events. Other studies show precisely the opposite—namely, that once the effects of events and the state of the economy are taken into account, the frequency of presidential speechmaking and international travel add little to approval ratings. This view implies that President Clinton owed his surprising buoyancy during the Lewinsky scandal not to any media tour de force, but to the public's satisfaction with the state of the nation. Collectively, the studies suggest that practitioners' beliefs about the importance of spin and public relations may be exaggerated. Perhaps presidential rhetoric falls on deaf ears. Had Ronald Reagan—the "great communicator"—held office during the energy crisis or prolonged periods of inflation, he, too, probably would have suffered significant declines in popularity.

We concede that real-world events are important cues for the public. It is well known that people overattribute responsibility for national events to the chief executive. As we'll discuss, however, we remain skeptical about the claim that events themselves count for more than media representations of these events.

WHY MEDIA MANAGEMENT MATTERS

There are several reasons to believe that media management has an impact on presidential popularity. In the first place, the real-world events of greatest importance today concern national security and international affairs, not the state of the American economy. These are classic mediated events, and ones over which the president exercises especially strong leverage. (Except for residents of New York City, Washington DC, and rural Pennsylvania, the 9/11 attacks were encountered only through news coverage and not through direct experience.) Indeed, our analysis of presidential popularity reveals that changes in the level of television news coverage that is accorded terrorism are a more powerful predictor of presidential popularity than are changes in the actual incidence of terrorism.

Moreover, although it is true that the national audience for presidential speeches has shrunk (fewer people watch the State of the Union address today than did in 1995), presidents still exercise opinion leadership over more narrowly defined audiences. A presidential speech on tax cuts in Cleveland, for example, will likely elicit prime local news coverage on Ohio television stations. At bottom, the key difficulty with the argument that "history trumps media management" is that events do not speak for themselves but require interpretation and explanation. Thus, the distinction between an approval-enhancing and an approval-diminishing event is typically blurred, and contingent on media treatment.

The case of the American invasion of Grenada, which proved to be a significant approval-enhancing event for the Reagan administration, is revealing.

As we noted in Chapter 4, the administration prevented the press from directly covering the invasion and then fed reporters a steady stream of stories and images that portrayed the invasion in the most favorable light possible. Thus, the public's understanding of the invasion reflected the administration's framing of the event rather than any independent reading of conditions in Grenada. Had the media treated the invasion of Grenada as a "public relations" exercise or another case of US domination in the Americas, public reaction might have been less than enthusiastic.

Unlike the invasion of Grenada and all subsequent US military actions, the media were granted relatively free rein to cover events in the case of "Operation Restore Hope"—the use of American troops to oversee humanitarian relief efforts in Somalia in December 1992. The very fact that media access was granted suggests that the Bush administration saw the operation as an approval-enhancing event. After all, American troops were on a mission of mercy. Media coverage of the operation, however, turned out to be less than charitable. In fact, as Zaller and Chiu (2000) demonstrated, news coverage of the Somalia operation was the most negative of any major foreign policy event of the 1990s.

The coverage was more critical because American reporters, no longer confined to Washington and solely reliant on official sources, could turn to field representatives of international relief organizations or foreign diplomats stationed in Somalia for competing and equally authoritative accounts of the situation. Zaller and Chiu concluded their examination of the Somalia episode by noting,

> There is little evidence that reporters are indexing their Somalia coverage to the views of the American government or, still less, to the views of Congress or the president. The views of the president are certainly reported . . . but they do not frame or dominate the account. Rather, the bulk of coverage seems to reflect the opinions of a range of expert sources, many of them non-Americans. (p. 78)

In a final case illustrating the importance of the media's interpretation of events, consider a more recent example. Had President George W. Bush gone before Congress in 2003 and justified the invasion of Iraq as an exercise in "spreading freedom around the world," he would most likely have been ridiculed. But by invoking the threat of weapons of mass destruction and Iraqi collusion with terrorists, he was able to elicit near unanimous congressional support for going to war.

In short, events do not speak for themselves. By influencing the way in which events are defined and framed in news accounts, the president is able to exert substantial influence over his standing with the public.

THE RALLY EFFECT

The importance of media management to presidential popularity comes into sharp relief in the case of the so-called rally phenomenon. In the aftermath of major foreign policy actions undertaken by the US government, people rally behind the president. George H. W. Bush achieved a new high in the history of the Gallup poll when his approval rate soared to 85 percent in the immediate aftermath of Operation Desert Storm. Following the 9/11 attacks, his son's popularity increased even further, to 87 percent (see Figure 10.3). In both instances, Americans were nearly unanimous in evaluating their president favorably. Generally, whenever the president acts as commander in chief, Americans bury their partisan differences and rally to the side of their leader.

What is intriguing about rally effects is that they frequently occur when the triggering event represents a failure of American policy and leadership. President Kennedy's popularity increased following the attempted invasion of Cuba, even though it proved to be a spectacular failure.[3] President Carter actually benefited when Iranian militants stormed the American embassy in Tehran, taking the occupants hostage. Reagan's popularity improved in the immediate aftermath of the *Challenger* disaster, and (as documented in Figure 10.3) George H. W. Bush gained significantly in the polls when Iraq annexed Kuwait, a major US ally (and oil supplier) in the Middle East.

The importance of rally events to presidential popularity is obvious when we examine the ten largest month-to-month changes in presidential popularity (see Figure 10.4). In six of the ten cases, the change in approval was positive, and five of the six rallies were stimulated by foreign policy or national security events. Three of the four instances of widespread withdrawal of public approval occurred in the aftermath of domestic political controversy: the Iran–Contra scandal under Reagan, the so-called Travelgate affair early in President Clinton's first term, and the resignation of Eisenhower's secretary of labor over the administration's lax enforcement of the Taft–Hartley Act of 1947.

The most plausible explanation of rally events is the indexing process described in Chapter 4. Foreign policy and national security events are easier to frame in a manner that supports administration policy. During times of international tension, the president's spin is less subject to challenge, and

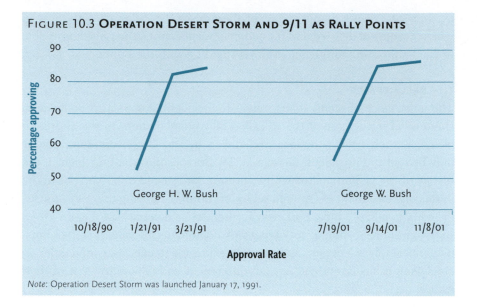

FIGURE 10.3 OPERATION DESERT STORM AND 9/11 AS RALLY POINTS

Note: Operation Desert Storm was launched January 17, 1991.

the public responds accordingly. But when opposition leaders openly contest the president's interpretation of events (as is typical during a political scandal), the media messages become one-sided in the opposite direction, and the public turns against the president.

The 1990 Iraqi invasion of Kuwait provides a clear example of the ebb and flow of elite discourse. Initially the event was a significant rally point because of the silence of congressional Democrats. Congress happened not to be in session during the first month of the Iraqi occupation, and the administration's accounts of its various "successes" (such as the creation of a worldwide coalition in opposition to Saddam Hussein) went unchallenged. After Congress reconvened in September, some prominent Democrats expressed skepticism about the timetable proposed by President Bush, suggesting that economic sanctions against Iraq should be given more time. On September 20, 1990, the *New York Times* noted, "Congressional criticism of the Bush Administration's position on the Persian Gulf, nonexistent in the first days after Iraq's invasion of Kuwait, then muted, is growing louder on both sides of the aisle as lawmakers openly attack the President on several major points" (Apple, 1990). As Americans began to encounter more critical news reports, President Bush's popularity fell from 71 percent in August to 55 percent in November. In general, then, the public's evaluations of the incumbent president rise and fall in accordance with elite cues provided by

FIGURE 10.4 **TOP TEN MONTH-TO-MONTH CHANGES IN PRESIDENTIAL POPULARITY**

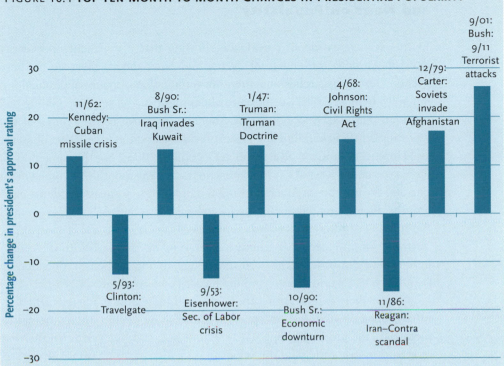

the media: the louder the criticism of the president's actions, the lower the probability that the public will rally around the president.

In sum, the sensitivity of presidential popularity to ongoing issues and events depends on the ability of the White House to portray events as either good news or bad news and its ability to silence would-be critics. The president's level of influence over the news is thus the critical mediator between the onset of events and the ensuing changes in the public's evaluations of the president.

In Focus: The Rally Effect

The term *rally effect* describes how, in the aftermath of major foreign policy actions undertaken by the US government, people rally behind the president. Generally, whenever the president acts as commander in chief, Americans bury their partisan differences and throw their support behind their leader.

Assessing the Impact of Events and News on Popularity

In this section we present evidence showing that a president's popularity depends on both the course of events and news media coverage of these events. Our analysis relies on a monthly compilation of national public opinion polls. In most cases, the measure of popularity is the standard Gallup poll question that asks respondents whether they approve or disapprove of the way President X is handling the job as president, and the time frame of analysis is limited to January 1968 through December 2003.[4] For the same period, we also compiled a set of key indicators, including the monthly unemployment rate and the number of Americans injured or killed in terrorist incidents each month.[5] Finally, to incorporate media coverage into the analysis, we counted the number of references to "unemployment" or "layoffs" and "terrorism" or "terrorists" in the three major networks' evening newscasts.[6] With these data in hand, we can observe the correspondence among changes in presidential popularity, real-world events, and broadcast news coverage.

Our prediction concerning the real-world indicators is obvious. By definition, unemployment is an approval-diminishing event; when unemployment falls, the president's popularity should rise, and vice versa.[7] In the case of terrorism, we anticipate the opposite: terrorist attacks with resulting loss of American life cast the president in the nonpartisan role of commander in chief and should rally the public to his side.

Our expectation concerning the effects of news coverage also varies across issue arenas. Given the president's dominance in the national security arena, news coverage of terrorism is more likely to reflect the administration's perspective on events than are news reports on unemployment. Thus, media coverage of terrorism should prove beneficial to the president, and coverage of unemployment (which focuses on rising rather than falling unemployment) should have the opposite effect.

We begin by plotting the simple trends in popularity, events, and news coverage. Figure 10.5 shows the monthly approval ratings of the president, unemployment levels, and the levels of unemployment-related news coverage. Figure 10.6 repeats the exercise, this time substituting terrorism for unemployment.

For more precise statistical estimates of the relative effects of events and news coverage on popularity, we resorted to time-series analysis. The relevant technical details of the analysis are given in the appendix to this chapter; in what follows we provide only an overview of the findings.

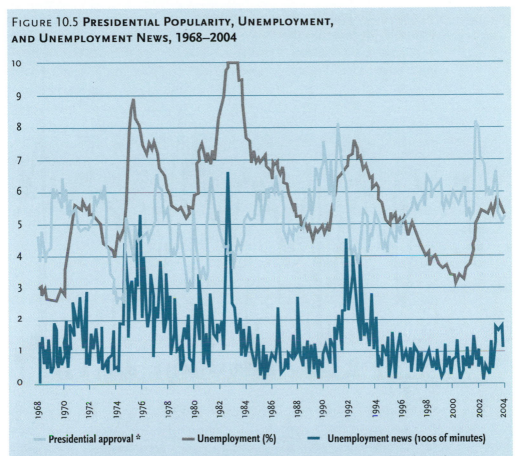

FIGURE 10.5 **PRESIDENTIAL POPULARITY, UNEMPLOYMENT, AND UNEMPLOYMENT NEWS, 1968–2004**

— Presidential approval *   — Unemployment (%)   — Unemployment news (100s of minutes)

Analysis: Changes in the rate of unemployment corresponded negatively with changes in presidential popularity. Television newscoverage of unemployment was also inversely related to popularity. The level of television coverage of unemployment was generally responsive to the rate of unemployment: when unemployment increased, so, too, did the volume of news. *Note:* The y-axis is capped at 10. Presidential approval is expressed on a scale of 1–10. Unemployment rates over 10 percent are not displayed on the chart (unemployment reached a peak of 10.8 percent in November and December 1982).

Overall, the time-series analysis revealed that presidential popularity was more responsive to economic events than to news coverage of these events. Increases in the unemployment rate created a significant "drag" on public approval, no matter how much coverage the issue elicited. In the case of terrorism, however, popularity was boosted by both events and media coverage. Both the number of American victims and the amount of news coverage exerted significant and positive effects on the level of public approval of the

FIGURE 10.6 PRESIDENTIAL POPULARITY, TERRORIST EVENTS, AND TERRORISM NEWS, 1968–2004

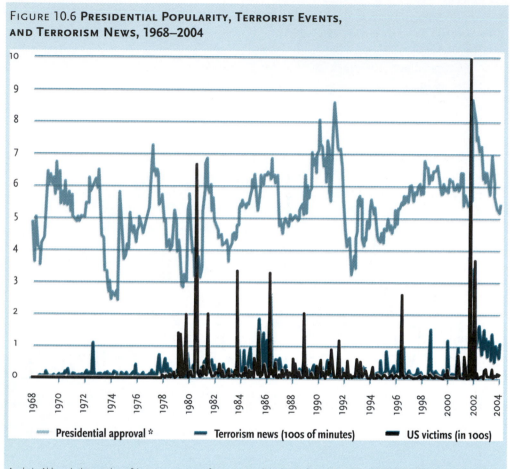

Analysis: Although the number of American victims of terrorism and the level of presidential popularity were essentially unrelated, popularity ratings did respond to the level of terrorism news. Interestingly, the level of terrorism news was uncorrelated with the number of American victims; other attributes of terrorist events, such as the location of the incident or the mode of violence are more important ingredients of newsworthiness than the sheer number of Americans injured or killed.

*Note: The y-axis is capped at 10. Presidential approval is expressed on a scale of 1–10. The number of US victims over a thousand is not displayed on the chart (US victims reached a peak of 2,973 in September 2001).

president. Our findings thus confirm that economic events have a life of their own that is independent of news media offerings.

During periods of rising unemployment, people hear about layoffs either through word of mouth or by observing activity in the workplace. For economic issues, accordingly, news coverage is redundant; people hold the president responsible because of their own experiences. For issues of national security, however, the president's ability to influence interpretations of events proves to be a significant political asset. Television news coverage, which typically features government officials promoting their efforts to combat terrorism, has the effect of making people significantly more inclined to support their president.

When we limited our analysis to President George W. Bush, it was clear that he owed his popularity largely to the 9/11 attacks, the subsequent military campaigns, and the unusually heavy amount of terrorism-related news generated by these events. For Bush, news coverage of terrorism was the only significant predictor of changes in his popularity.

On balance, where does the analysis leave us with respect to the debate on merchandising versus history? History trumped merchandising in the case of the economy, but both factors were important when the president turned his attention to matters of national security. In the post-9/11 era, however, events proved no match for news. The amount of news coverage devoted to terrorism was the paramount influence on presidential popularity. In fact, the persistence of terrorism as a major issue on the governmental and media agendas since 9/11 produced an unusually prolonged rally effect. Unlike the Gulf War, which disappeared from the television screen almost immediately after the cessation of hostilities (to President George H. W. Bush's disadvantage), the legacy of the 9/11 attacks included two major US military interventions (and occupations). The steady drumbeat of terrorism-related news helped make the 9/11 rally the longest on record. On September 1, 2001, President Bush's approval stood at 54 percent. The immediate impact of the terrorist attacks was to raise his approval level to 87 percent. It was nearly two years later (August 2003) before Bush's popularity returned to the pre-9/11 baseline.

In summary, popularity is not driven entirely by media management or by history, but by a combination of the two. In the case of unemployment, an issue with several "observables" (such as friends and neighbors who have lost their jobs), the state of the economy is a key determinant of the president's popularity. As unemployment rises, the president's approval level falls. In the case of national security issues, however, the tables are turned. Events have less significance than media representations of the events. Since presidents exercise considerable influence over the content of national security news, presidents can more easily maintain their popularity independent of the course of events.

Going Public and Public Policy: Power to the People?

Presidents use their leverage over the news to score points with the public. Popularity increases the president's influence in Washington. Some have suggested that the popularity game not only strengthens the president's ability to get things done, but also makes the policy process more responsive to public opinion. Because elected officials seek to remain popular, they are also motivated to enact policies supported by the public.

Our position concerning the impact of going public on the policy process is less optimistic, primarily because the need to maintain high levels of public approval often deters the president from exercising policy leadership. In addition, as we'll outline, catering to public opinion comes with high opportunity costs and increases the risks of governmental stalemate and gridlock.

At the very least, the widespread belief that popularity translates into power has increased the allocation of staff resources to media management at the expense of policy research and development. As we noted in Chapter 7, managing the press has burgeoned into a major organizational objective within both the executive and legislative branches. In the case of the former, key presidential advisors spend more time crafting media strategies than developing policy initiatives. As early as 1978, the media imperative was clear to Lloyd Cutler, President Carter's special counsel for domestic policy:

> I was surprised by how much the substantive decisions in the White House are affected by press deadlines, and, in particular by the evening television news. So that if something happened, let us say, on a Monday, or somebody strongly criticized the President or one of his programs, everything stopped! Whatever you'd been working on as the great priority of the next morning you had to put aside in order to reach a decision about how the President would respond in time for the evening television news. (Ansolabehere, Behr, & Iyengar, 1993, p. 202)

The more ominous concern about the increasing use of vocal leadership is the strong possibility that elected officials will be compelled to follow public opinion, without having offered any issue leadership along the way. Going public rests on the assumption that public approval is necessary for the president to govern. To remain popular, presidents must aim to deliver popular policies. However, the mere fact that they pursue policies favored by majority opinion tells us little about the substantive or programmatic rationale underlying policy decisions. The decision might be driven by beliefs about the substantive merits of the policy and its effectiveness in meeting the problem at hand or, alternatively, by the desire to maintain public approval and gain reelection. Thus, evaluating the system of going public requires that we decipher some of the programmatic and strategic reasons underlying policy making.

By the usual standards, elected leaders are expected to use their expertise and sense of what is best for the nation to make independent policy
choices. Leaders should not slavishly follow public opinion. Ordinary citizens, who cannot be bothered to keep up with the technical complexities of
policy debates, entrust the responsibility of choosing policies to elected officials. Under media politics, however, officials face strong incentives to cater
to public opinion. Rather than formulating policy on the basis of a coherent
theory or systematic cost–benefit analysis and then attempting to bring voters on board, public officials may be guided primarily by their reading of
polls. When the results of theory, cost–benefit analysis, and public opinion
polling all point in the same direction, elected officials have an easy choice:
they select the optimal and most popular policy. But their task becomes more
difficult when the public prefers a policy that officials believe to be ineffective or even counterproductive. Should they deliberately pander to the views
of the public and risk making the country worse off, or should they support
the less popular but more effective alternative and risk voter incomprehen-
sion or wrath (no doubt to be accompanied by a barrage of negative advertisements in the next campaign)?

There is little hard evidence bearing on how elected officials resolve the
conflict between maintaining public approval on the one hand, and making
sound policy decisions on the other. Canes-Wrone, Herron, and Shotts (2001)
recently developed a formal model that identifies the range of possible outcomes. Assume that policies are either popular or unpopular with the public and judged as either effective or ineffective from the perspective of the
policy maker. The pairing of "popular" and "effective" is of little interest
because in this case public opinion is enlightened and the decision maker
enjoys the luxury of doing good while simultaneously scoring points with voters. The remaining combinations, however, are more revealing.

"True leadership" occurs when the decision maker proposes an unpopular but effective policy. In such instances, elected officials are prepared to
sacrifice their own political interests for the public good. A recent example
(working on the assumption that NAFTA was an effective policy) was Bill
Clinton's support for NAFTA (the North American Free Trade Agreement)
during the 1992 presidential campaign, despite only lukewarm support from
the public and intense opposition from labor unions and environmentalists—
both of which were key Democratic constituencies (to say nothing of the
criticism voiced by third-party candidate Ross Perot).

Over the years, the issue of taxes has provided a litmus test of true leadership in Washington. The public instinctively opposes higher taxes but insists
that government continue to deliver benefits and services. Efforts to persuade

voters that it's impossible to have their cake and eat it too are risky. At the outset of the 1984 presidential campaign, Democratic nominee Walter Mondale announced on national television that the size of the federal budget deficit left him no choice but to raise taxes if elected. In November, Mondale carried only his home state. His resounding defeat is still cited by campaign consultants as a textbook example of how not to campaign.

Six years later, President George H. W. Bush faced a similar dilemma. When accepting his party's nomination in 1988, he had offered the slogan "Read my lips: No new taxes" as a means of cementing the Republican conservative base to his generally moderate candidacy. When Bush took office, the budget deficit amounted to about 3 percent of the gross domestic product. As the economy slowed, however, the deficit mushroomed. By the summer of 1990 it was clear that unless Congress and the president took action, red ink could reach $160 billion.

In June 1990, after weeks of negotiations with the Democratic-controlled Congress, the president announced that he would support "tax revenue increases." The compromise budget package increased the marginal tax rate and phased out exemptions for high-income taxpayers. Bush was also forced to renege on his pledge to reduce the capital gains tax. The budget deal had severe consequences for Bush's political fortunes. Conservatives bashed him for breaking his promise on taxes and encouraged Patrick Buchanan to challenge Bush in the 1992 primaries. Bush's popularity never fully recovered; in November he was defeated by the relatively unknown Bill Clinton.

As the Mondale and Bush cases suggest, politicians who advocate or preside over the raising of taxes suffer at the polls. More generally, the successful exercise of leadership requires a highly restricted set of circumstances. First, the policy debate must occur some time before the election, giving voters enough time to observe the beneficial consequences of the unpopular policy and the elected official time to persuade voters of the merits of the decision. Second, the policy maker must enjoy a high level of popularity to begin with, thus providing a measure of protection from candidates who might strategically seek to run in opposition. In effect, leadership is more likely when there is a longer time horizon and the incumbent is not subject to a serious reelection threat. Canes-Wrone and Shotts (2004) show that incumbents with unusually high or low levels of public approval are more likely to lead on the merits—the former because of their security blanket, the latter because they have nothing to lose and everything to gain. But when the election is likely to be close, as it is in most recent presidential races, candidates refuse to lead.

A revealing instance of the pressures against true leadership occurred in 1996 during the campaign to pass Proposition 209 in California. This measure, which won handily, sought to end affirmative action in all state programs. Opponents of Proposition 209, who were drawn disproportionately from California Democrats, appealed to President Clinton for help. At the time, Clinton's national popularity stood at nearly 60 percent, and Clinton led his Republican opponent by more than 20 points in California polls. Thus, conditions were ripe for Clinton to go public with his opposition to the measure. Despite repeated requests to campaign against Proposition 209, however, the president maintained a "deafening silence" until the closing days of the campaign.

The campaign over Proposition 209 demonstrates that high levels of popularity and weak electoral opposition are insufficient conditions for overcoming the fear of offending voters. When given the opportunity to lead, elected officials either pander or remain silent. In the words of conservative critic Arianna Huffington (2000), "As we march into the next century, the motto of every politician seems to be: 'I am their leader; I shall follow them'" (p. 77).

An especially dangerous form of pandering is making decisions solely on the basis of image building. In some situations, presidents need to appear tough and willing to take decisive action. After several months of failed diplomatic efforts to secure the release of the American hostages in Iran, President Carter came under intense political pressure. His ratings were falling, and he faced a serious challenger for the 1980 presidential nomination (Senator Ted Kennedy). Even though intelligence reports indicated that the American hostages had been scattered throughout Tehran, Carter authorized a helicopter rescue mission. The mission was aborted when two of the helicopters developed engine trouble en route and a third crashed into an accompanying transport plane. Why did the president approve such a high-risk mission? In Lowi's (1985) words, "A peace-loving, religious man like Jimmy Carter did not take the risk of the Iranian rescue mission merely to give himself a convenient level to move American public opinion. The leverage worked the other way: public opinion had forced upon the president an act of the sheerest adventurism" (p. 173).

In practice, the distinction between policy making on the merits and pandering to maintain popularity is never clear. For one thing, public opinion is not uniform and simple; elected officials face multiple layers of opinion. Responding to each layer comes with different benefits and costs. Most voters pay little attention to day-to-day government actions, but small groups of voters (the "issue publics" identified in Chapter 5) have strong preferences and carefully monitor the actions of their leaders. These activists are the lifeblood of campaigns. For elected officials to alienate their key supporters would be tantamount to political suicide. In some cases, therefore, leaders pursue policies that, although unpopular with the general public, have intense support among activists.

Politicians resolve the dilemma of responding to vocal minorities without alienating the silent majority in a variety of ways. First, they increasingly resort to what Shapiro and Jacobs (2000) term "crafted rhetoric." On controversial issues, they explain their decisions in ways that allow them to maintain support in both camps. In the face of ardent support from their Evangelical base but majority opposition to a ban on same-sex marriage, Republican senators explained their proposed constitutional amendment as an effort to "save traditional marriage." Second, incumbents adjust their priorities to the electoral timetable. The period immediately following the election is devoted to satisfying their activists. As the next election draws near, policy makers shift their emphasis to satisfying the ideological center. In 2004, for example, President George W. Bush persuaded Congress to add a prescription drug coverage plan to Medicare. The program, which would benefit millions of seniors, was estimated to cost approximately five hundred billion dollars. Shortly after the election, the cost estimate ballooned to 1.3 trillion dollars.

Another liability of going public is that it raises the level of conflict between the executive and legislative branches, making compromise and accommodation more difficult. As the president increasingly turns to rhetorical leadership, opponents in Congress and their backers have every reason to respond in kind. The current battle over the introduction of private retirement accounts is typical. President Bush made several public appearances across the country to promote his Social Security reform package. Soon, Republican-leaning interest groups joined the fray by running advertisements attacking the AARP (formerly called the American Association of Retired Persons) for opposing private accounts. Not to be outdone, the AARP fought back with advertisements describing the Bush proposals as an effort to reduce Social Security benefits (see, for example, Video Feature 7.3). Here's how the *New York Times* described the ongoing battle for public opinion (Justice, 2005):

> Taking its cues from the success of last year's Swift boat veterans' campaign in the presidential race, a conservative lobbying organization has hired some of the same consultants to orchestrate attacks on one of President Bush's toughest opponents in the battle to overhaul Social Security.

The lobbying group, USA Next, which has poured millions of dollars into Republican policy battles, now says it plans to spend as much as $10 million on commercials and other tactics assailing AARP, the powerhouse lobby opposing the private investment accounts at the center of Mr. Bush's plan.

"They are the boulder in the middle of the highway to personal savings accounts," said Charlie Jarvis, president of USA Next. "We will be the dynamite that removes them . . . We are going to take them on in hand-to-hand combat."

It is difficult to see any differences between the tactics used to influence the passage of Social Security legislation in 2005 and those used to reelect President Bush in 2004. As the use of campaign techniques escalates, the opposing sides only become more entrenched in their respective positions. In the words of Jeffrey Tulis (1987), "We face the very real prospect of our two political branches talking past each other to a vast amorphous constituency" (p. 178). Under these circumstances, the prospects for cooperation and compromise are slim.

Conclusion

In the final analysis, going public represents a catch-22 of sorts. Presidents need to maintain their popularity to be effective in office. Their inherent newsworthiness and influence over the content of news provides them with considerable "Teflon." Nonetheless, the pressure to remain popular makes them averse to taking on difficult problems unless "quick-fix" solutions are available. Proposing tough answers to tough problems costs popular support; without support, the president has insufficient capital with which to address these problems. The less-than-satisfactory result is that popularity becomes an end in itself.

CHAPTER 10 SUMMARY

1. Research suggests that three principal factors influence presidential popularity:

   - *Length of time in office.* Some theorists have suggested that over the course of the term, as presidents make decisions and take positions, they accumulate opponents and lose support. But some presidencies have not conformed to this theory.

- *The course of events.* The American public holds the president responsible for the state of the nation. When events signify that the United States is doing well, the president's popularity increases, but it drops when events imply less satisfactory outcomes for the country.

- *Public relations.* By influencing how events are defined and framed in news accounts, presidents can significantly affect their personal standing with the public.

2. In the rally effect, the public supports the president in the aftermath of major foreign policy actions—even when those actions may represent a failure of American policy and leadership. During times of international tension, opponents are afraid to speak out against the president—making the president's spin less subject to challenge—and the public responds accordingly.

3. In the case of policy arenas (such as foreign policy) that people cannot really experience directly, presidents can more easily maintain popularity independent of the course of events. In the case of issues that the public can experience firsthand (such as the state of the economy), real-world events are key determinants of the president's popularity.

4. An optimistic perspective on the impact of going public sees it as a strategy that not only strengthens the president's ability to get things done, but also makes the policy process more responsive to public opinion. In this view, because elected officials seek to remain popular, they are motivated to enact policies supported by the public.

5. An alternative perspective, however, suggests that the need to maintain high levels of public approval often deters the president from exercising policy leadership. Instead of using their expertise at making sense of what's best for the nation to make independent policy choices, leaders may defer to public opinion, which is generally uninformed.

FURTHER READINGS

Brody, R. A. (1991). *Assessing the president: The media, elite opinion and public support.* Stanford, CA: Stanford University Press.

Canes-Wrone, B., Herron, M. C., & Shotts, K. W. (2001). Leadership and pandering: A theory of executive policymaking. *American Journal of Political Science, 45,* 532–550.

Hetherington, M. J., & Nelson, M. (2003). Anatomy of a rally effect: George W. Bush and the war on terrorism. *PS: Political Science and Politics, 36,* 37–42.

Kernell, S. (1986). *Going public: New strategies of presidential leadership.* Washington, DC: Congressional Quarterly Press.

Lowi, T. J. (1985). *The personal president: Power invested, promise unfulfilled.* Ithaca, NY: Cornell University Press.

Neustadt, R. (1960). *Presidential power: The politics of leadership.* New York: Wiley.

Shapiro, R. Y., & Jacobs, L. R. (2000). Who leads and who follows? U.S. presidents, public opinion, and foreign policy. In B. L. Nacos, R. Y. Shapiro, & P. Isernia (Eds.), *Decisionmaking in a glass house: Mass media, public opinion, and American and European foreign policy in the 21st century* (pp. 223–245). Lanham, MD: Rowman & Littlefield.

Tulis, J. K. (1987). *The rhetorical presidency.* Chatham, NJ: Chatham House.

Zaller, J. R. (1998). Monica Lewinsky's contribution to political science. *PS: Political Science and Politics, 31,* 182–189.

NOTES

1. At any given moment in time, the president's popularity can be explained by basic partisan predispositions. That is, when the incumbent is Republican, Republicans approve and Democrats disapprove. We are more interested here in explaining short-term or cyclical changes in popularity.

2. On the first count (perjury before the grand jury), ten Republican senators voted "not guilty." On the second count (obstruction of justice), five Republicans defected.

3. The invasion "force" consisted of a loosely organized group of Cuban exiles who were captured with minimal effort by the Cubans and later returned to the United States in exchange for shipments of food and medical supplies.

4. For the months in which there were multiple surveys, we computed the average popularity rating. We did not extend the analysis further back in history because our key indicator of real-world events in the area of terrorism is available only from 1968.

5. We took the terrorism victim count from the ITERATE—International Terrorism: Attributes of Terrorist Events—database (see Mickolus, Sandler, Murdock, & Flemming, 2003).

6. We obtained this information by searching Vanderbilt University's Television News Archive (http://tvnews.vanderbilt.edu), which contains brief text-based summaries of each news report aired on the networks' national newscasts.

7. Initially we had also included the consumer price index (CPI) in the analysis as a measure of inflation. However, we found no evidence that changes in the CPI influenced popularity.

APPENDIX TO CHAPTER 10
TIME-SERIES ANALYSIS

To obtain more precise statistical estimates of the relative effects of events and news coverage on presidential popularity—the topic of this chapter—we resorted to time-series analysis. We specified the time-series model as a *first-order autoregressive process*, by which we mean that the level of popularity depends on the level of the previous month. (This specification was found to fit the data better than any other lag function.) We then analyzed the popularity data against lagged values (once again using a lag of one month) of both event indicators. Thus, the unemployment rate and number of American casualties due to terrorism in January 2004 were matched with the president's approval level in February 2004. The measures of news coverage, on the other hand, were not lagged, because we expected the effects of news to be more immediate (on the assumption that people have poor memories for the content of newscasts aired in the previous month).

In addition to the indicators of real-world events and news coverage, we controlled for several factors known to be important determinants of the presidential popularity series. These included a dichotomous (two-category) variable corresponding to the period of the Watergate scandal and the first lag in the number of American military deaths in Vietnam and Iraq. Prolonged scandals and increasing numbers of military dead are known to reduce presidential standing. Thus the equation for predicting popularity at time 2 (t) included the level of popularity at time 1 ($t - 1$), the unemployment rate and number of American casualties of terrorism at time 1, the level of news coverage for unemployment and terrorism at time 2, the Watergate scandal variable, and the number of military casualties in Vietnam and Iraq.

In order to take into account variations in the policies pursued by different administrations, we estimated the effects of events and news coverage separately for Democratic and Republican presidents. Previous research suggests that unemployment is more costly for Democratic presidents. Given their reputation as advocates of increased military strength (as well as the chain of events surrounding the presidency of George W. Bush), we further anticipated that Republican presidents would be the principal beneficiaries of terrorist events and news coverage. Because of the dramatic increase in the measures of terrorist events and terrorism news after September 2001, we reran the analysis of Republican presidential popularity both with and without the time period from September 2001 to December 2003.

The "impact" coefficients associated with the event and news coverage measures are presented in Table A10.1. For the entire time period and all

TABLE A10.1 **IMPACT OF EVENTS AND NEWS COVERAGE ON**
PRESIDENTIAL POPULARITY, 1968–2003

	All Presidents, 1968–2003	Democrats, 1968–2003	Republicans, 1968–2003	Republicans, 1968–Aug 2001	G. W. Bush, Sep 2001–Dec 2003
Unemployment rate	−2.060**	−1.960$^+$	−1.881$^+$	−2.258*	
	(0.970)	(1.430)	(1.278)	(1.298)	
Unemployment news coverage					
US casualties in terrorist attacks	0.006**	0.008**	0.005$^+$		
	(0.003)	(0.004)	(0.004)		
Terrorism news coverage	0.043***		0.056***	0.029$^+$	0.093***
	(0.006)		(0.006)	(0.018)	(0.014)
Popularity ($t-1$)	(0.020)	(0.028)	(0.029)	(0.029)	(0.159)
	0.902***	0.928***	0.888***	0.889***	0.848***
Number of cases	410	155	255	219	37

***<0.001, ** <0.01, * <0.05, $^+$ <0.10
Note: A positive coefficient shows a greater-than-expected boost to popularity (given the state of popularity in the previous month); a negative coefficient signifies an impetus in the opposite direction. Blank cells indicate the absence of any detectable effect. Coefficients marked by asterisks are statistically significant. Numbers in parentheses are standard errors.

presidents, the unemployment rate was the most powerful predictor of popularity (not counting the lagged value of popularity). Contrary to expectations, rising unemployment was equally damaging to both Democratic and Republican presidents; every increase in the unemployment rate lowered presidential approval by some 2 points.

American casualties in terrorist incidents proved significant as rally events. The magnitude of the effect was considerably smaller than the effect of unemployment, however. For all presidents, an additional 165 American casualties per month increased popularity by 1 point. Contrary to expectations, the effect of American casualties was similar for Democratic and Republican presidents.

Turning to the effects of broadcast news, after we adjusted for the effects of events and the previous level of popularity, news coverage of unemployment had no impact whatsoever. News about terrorism, however, provided presidents with a significant boost. Across the entire period, twenty-three minutes of television coverage per month increased the president's popularity by 1 point. As expected, this effect was limited to Republican incumbents; for Democrats, the sign of the news coefficient was basically zero, but for Republicans every eighteen minutes of additional news coverage per month produced an increase of 1 point in their popularity.

When we compared the results with and without the post-9/11 period, there were some striking differences in the importance of events and news coverage. For one thing, the impact of terrorism news was multiplied by a factor of three in the post-9/11 period.[1] After the September 11 attacks, an increase of eleven minutes in monthly terrorism news was sufficient to increase popularity by 1 point. The impact of terrorism *events*, however, proved no different before and after 9/11. For the latter period, the only relevant predictor of Bush's popularity was media coverage of terrorism.

NOTE

1. Even though they were not statistically significant, the effects of unemployment on Bush's post-9/11 ratings were of similar magnitude to the effects for all other Republican presidents. It is difficult to compare the significance of the coefficients before and after 9/11, however, since the post-9/11 series is limited to only thirty-seven observations.

CHAPTER 11

EVALUATING MEDIA POLITICS

From Jon Stewart's appearance on CNN's Crossfire, October 15, 2004
(in discussion with Paul Begala and Tucker Carlson):

STEWART: I made a special effort to come on the show today, because I have privately, amongst my friends and also in occasional newspapers and television shows, mentioned this show as being bad.

BEGALA: We have noticed.

STEWART: And I wanted to—I felt that that wasn't fair and I should come here and tell you that I don't—it's not so much that it's bad, as it's hurting America. But I wanted to come here today and say . . . Stop, stop, stop, stop hurting America. And come work for us, because we, as the people . . .

CARLSON: How do you pay?

STEWART: The people? Not well.

* * * * *

David Bartlett, President, Radio-Television News Directors Association
(as cited in Barta, 1996):

The job of a journalist is not to simply stand back and let the candidates say their piece. If I'm the public, what I'm buying is the experience, the analysis, the skepticism of a competent journalist. That's what journalism is. The rest is either publicity or reprinting.

UNDER IDEAL CONDITIONS, the news media would invigorate the democratic process by providing a widely accessible forum, supplying "quality" news about the issues of the day, and keeping public officials constantly under the microscope. Present-day practice, however, is quite different. David Bartlett's comments and the Stewart–Begala–Carlson exchange on *Crossfire* illustrate the core problem of modern political journalism. Journalists aspire to deliver more than mere descriptions of the candidates' words and deeds on the campaign trail. But by turning to analysis and interpretation, journalists not only leave their audience uninformed, but also risk turning them off. In this concluding chapter, we suggest some approaches for addressing what we take to be the two most glaring failures of American media: (1) the absence of a substantive or policy-oriented electoral forum and (2) the substitution of journalists and analysts for the candidates as the principal voices in the news.

To deal with the problem of inadequate "substance," we suggest that broadcast outlets be required to provide candidates with free time in the closing days of the campaign. We also propose a system of grading news organizations based on the substantive content of their programming, with the goal of generating greater awareness of the problem and improving the quality and content of the news delivered. In the case of print media, we advocate a more expansive form of candidate endorsements; instead of limiting endorsements to a single editorial column published a few days before the election, we suggest that newspapers publish a series of articles explaining in detail the rationale for preferring one candidate over the other (or offering detailed comparisons of the candidates' positions). Because American newspapers are evenly divided in the partisan direction of their candidate endorsements, collectively these more substantial endorsements would better inform the reading public.

On the subject of giving candidates greater voice, we offer a more radical treatment for the trivialization of American politics through sound bites and ads. A technology-driven system of direct, or "unmediated," political communication now has the potential to alter the electoral dialogue in a manner as sweeping as the advent of television. Once information technology becomes as ubiquitous as television, candidates will be able to bypass the news media and communicate directly with voters, and voters should be better able to make decisions based on the candidates' issue positions. Preliminary research suggests that direct candidate-to-voter communication does, in fact, increase voter interest and participation in the process.

Let's discuss each of these recommendations in greater detail.

Redirecting the Focus to Issues

Perhaps the most glaring weakness of modern media-based campaigns is the invisibility of policy issues. Above all else, a meaningful electoral contest should present a clash of ideas, allowing voters to select between candidates or parties on the basis of policy proposals and performance. The present circuslike atmosphere in which campaigns are conducted all but precludes serious attention to policy issues. Questions of program impacts, trade-offs, costs, and benefits cannot be discussed in full, or even at all, within the confines of sound bites and paid advertisements.

To illustrate this point in the context of one social problem, consider crime. The overarching issue is prevention. One approach is to beef up enforcement (focusing on retribution); the opposite approach is to deal with the perceived underlying problems of educational access and employment opportunities (focusing on economic mobility). Which model (or combination of models) will work best in practice? Should voters opt for three-strikes laws or similar policies of deterrence, or would they benefit more from supporting public education and job-training programs?

Meaningful evidence on these questions is available. However, the subject is complex, and candidates who argue for nuanced positions risk appearing sympathetic to criminals. Accordingly, most candidates rely on slogans and symbolism in lieu of serious analysis. The news media, preoccupied with the horse race and strategy, do little to encourage informed debate. Under these circumstances, voters have little choice but to align themselves with proposals that they find intuitively plausible or resonant with basic cultural values—no matter how shortsighted or counterproductive these proposals might be in actuality.

The history of the three-strikes legislation in California provides ample evidence of the triumph of imagery and symbolism over objective analysis. In 1994, prompted by the abduction and brutal murder of twelve-year-old Polly Klaas, California became the second state (following Washington) to adopt three-strikes legislation. Fanned by media coverage and red-hot public outrage, the California legislature rushed to enact the most stringent of the three-strikes bills that had been introduced. No scheduled public hearings were held; no policy experts were called to testify. As Willie Brown, the long-time speaker of the California Assembly advised his Democratic colleagues, "Better get the hell out of the way" (Domanick, 2004, p. 141).

California's three-strikes law made the number of felony convictions ("strikes") rather than the severity of the crime the basis for sentencing.

Hundreds of people were sentenced to a minimum of twenty-five years in prison for petty theft or drug use because the offense represented their third conviction. In one of the most glaring cases of strikes-based sentencing, Leandro Andrade was sentenced to two consecutive twenty-five-year terms for stealing $150 worth of videotapes from two stores.[1]

The Andrade case was hardly atypical. As of September 2004, the California prison population included 40,232 inmates who had been sentenced for either second- or third-strike crimes. Of these, fewer than 40 percent had committed violent crimes such as murder, manslaughter, rape, or child molestation. The rest were serving sentences for property or drug-related crimes.

The severity of the sentences imposed on nonviolent offenders has emerged as the focal point of a debate about criminal justice policy. Reform-minded groups have attempted, unsuccessfully, to persuade the California legislature to amend the law to limit the definition of *strikes* to violent offenses. In 2004, with the financial support of a wealthy corporate executive,[2] these groups placed Proposition 66 on the California ballot. The measure would have restricted the definition of the third strike to violent felonies.

Proposition 66 was endorsed by virtually every major newspaper in California and backed by the Democratic, Green, and Libertarian party organizations. Advocates argued that the measure was a long-overdue reform of an irrational, unfair, and cruel policy that equated petty thieves with violent criminals. They pointed out that, of the twenty-three states with three-strikes programs, California is a startling exception: the only state that fails to distinguish between violent and nonviolent crimes. They also pointed out that the resulting cost to the California taxpayer is substantial—a minimum of $750,000 to house an inmate in prison for twenty-five years. The policy trade-offs were underscored on the editorial page of the *Sacramento Bee* ("Prop. 66 Reform," 2004): "California's prison-industrial complex is strangling the state's future. It's soaking up dollars that could go to education, housing, transportation and other basic infrastructure that enhances the state's prosperity and quality of life."

Despite these striking statistics, the overwhelming majority of the state's elected officials declared their opposition to Proposition 66. In addition to Governor Schwarzenegger and Attorney General Bill Lockyer, former governors Pete Wilson (who had signed the original bill into law), George Deukmejian, Gray Davis, and Jerry Brown all spoke out against weakening the three-strikes law. The list of official supporters also included the district attorney of every county, virtually all law enforcement agencies, fourteen state senators, and twenty-nine members of the state assembly. In contrast to this campaign of opposition led by all-stars who apparently feared negative public reaction, the most prominent proponent of the measure was Irvine mayor Larry Agran.

Armed with an infusion of funds from billionaire Henry Nicholas III, the opponents of Proposition 66 subjected the electorate to a last-minute barrage of television advertising. In one of the ads, Schwarzenegger warned that "child molesters, rapists and killers" would be roaming the streets if the measure passed. In another ad, a rape victim tearfully pleaded with voters not to release her assailant (see Video Feature 11.1).

The impact of the "No on Proposition 66" campaign was pivotal. Nearly three-fourths of the California public had expressed support for the measure during the early stages of the campaign. As late as October 13 (a mere two weeks before the election), 65 percent of the Field Poll sample stated that they intended to vote for Proposition 66. (The same poll showed that a substantial majority correctly identified the policy intent of the proposition.) Then, in response to the advertisements and the campaign appearances of the governor, public sentiment shifted dramatically. In the final Field Poll, taken a few days before the election, the level of support had plummeted 10 points (from 65 to 55 percent), while the ranks of the opposition had swelled by 15 points (from 18 to 33 percent). This trajectory continued: on election day the measure was defeated by 53 to 47 percent.

What was missing from the debate over Proposition 66? Voters were not told that California practice deviates from the rest of the nation or that California has imprisoned nearly four times as many people under its three-strikes law as all the other states combined![3] Even the most attentive voters would have been hard-pressed to encounter information about the actual impact of the three-strikes law on the crime rate. In fact, the available evidence suggests that the massive effort to incarcerate has had no impact on crime rates.

Not only were voters deprived of evidence concerning the effectiveness of three-strikes laws as a deterrent, but the debate over Proposition 66 also ignored questions of cost effectiveness. In 2004 the California Department of Corrections budget amounted to six billion dollars, and the department employed more personnel than any other state government agency. In 2003 the budget for the department of corrections in New York State (which lacks a three-strikes law) was less than two billion dollars. California has the unique distinction of ranking first in the nation in the amount spent on prisons, but thirty-eighth on expenditures per pupil.

None of these arguments against Proposition 66 were publicized during the 2004 campaign because the supporters of Proposition 66 were not as

VIDEO FEATURE 11.1
Ads Attacking Proposition 66

well financed as their opponents. News coverage of the proposition was extensive by the standards of local races: during the entire month of October, some ninety articles appeared in major daily newspapers. But, as Figure 11.1 shows, the coverage provided readers with much more information about polling and endorsements than about the substantive arguments pro and con. For most voters, therefore, the only source of information was television advertising that attacked Proposition 66 as "soft on crime."

What might the election result have been if the California news media had provided a wide range of perspectives both for and against three strikes and the alternative "equality of opportunity" model of crime prevention? And how would people have voted if the coverage had been loud enough and at a time of general interest in the election so that it might have caught the eye of even less attentive citizens?

There are conflicting views on the differences (or lack thereof) between informed and uninformed opinion. According to one stream of research, informed and uninformed voters are more apt to agree than disagree. Proponents of this view suggest that most people can approximate their "full-information" opinions by combining simple cues with widely available psychological heuristics or shortcuts. Opponents, on the other hand, cite evidence that informed and uninformed opinions are frequently at odds. In a recent analysis, for instance, Bartels (2005) shows that there was a significant difference between more- and less-informed Americans in their position on

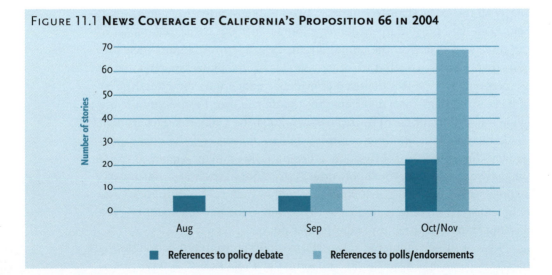

FIGURE 11.1 **NEWS COVERAGE OF CALIFORNIA'S PROPOSITION 66 IN 2004**

President Bush's tax cuts: support for the cuts came disproportionately from the less informed.

The most convincing evidence of the distinctiveness of informed opinion comes from studies showing that, when people are given the arguments on both sides of an issue, they often change their positions, even when the issue represents a matter of pressing national importance. James Fishkin and his collaborators have devised a technique known as *deliberative polling* for assessing the state of informed opinion (see Fishkin, 1995). The method works as follows. A representative sample of voters is first surveyed and then provided with briefing documents that lay out the arguments for and against particular policy alternatives. The participants in the deliberative poll read the briefing materials and discuss the issues in small groups (either face to face or online). Following the final group discussion, participants complete a second survey, thus permitting observation of changes in their attitudes before and after deliberation. Typically, a control group that does not deliberate answers the same questions at the end of the process. Thus, deliberative polling is a form of quasi experimentation for shedding light on the effects of substantive information and debate on political attitudes and policy preferences.

The results of more than twenty deliberative polls covering a variety of issues in several countries demonstrate that delivery of information often changes the participants' policy preferences (both individually and in the aggregate). In one deliberative poll conducted in 2002, a year before the US invasion of Iraq, the discussions focused on the general use of military intervention as an instrument of foreign policy. The results showed that deliberation made people significantly more likely to prefer multilateral over unilateral intervention. The same study also showed that the foreign policy priorities of informed citizens were quite different from the priorities of the uninformed; the former were much more likely to support increased American foreign aid, as well as efforts to raise the standard of living in underdeveloped nations. In short, informed opinion favored economic assistance rather than military force as the major instrument of American foreign policy.

Extrapolating from these results, it seems plausible to infer that Proposition 66 would likely have passed in a full-information environment. Voters who had been exposed to more than scare tactics might have responded more favorably to the measure (as indicated by the large majorities favoring the measure before the media campaign). More generally, a system of reporting that is more hospitable to policy debate can change the behavior of both candidates and voters. If candidates realize that the details of their positions on crime are newsworthy, they will adapt and spend more time developing them; for their part, voters given a steady stream of reports that focus on the candidates' issue positions rather than on the strategy or horse race are likely to become more informed on the issues and, as documented in deliberative polls, may also change their preferences.

To recap, media-based campaigns systematically underproduce information about the issues. Politicians have little incentive to address issues because they know that the media is not inclined to reprint their "white papers" (detailed reports on issues). For their part, the media, hoping to increase their audience share, seek out alternative topics for discussion. The only way out of this vicious circle is for society to develop institutions and standards that encourage (or mandate) news organizations to take their civic obligations more seriously and to make available space or broadcast time for explicit policy debates.

Giving Candidates Free Media Time

For decades, campaign reformers have urged Congress and the FCC to strengthen the public interest responsibilities of broadcasters. As we noted in Chapter 2, the United States is the only democracy that does not require broadcasters to provide at least specified minimal levels of public affairs coverage in exchange for their use of the public airwaves. During the 2004 election year, a typical political ad aired nearly two million times in the top one hundred media markets. If stations were required to provide just as much free time to candidates as the advertising time that they sell, the total amount of free time in 2004 would have exceeded 150 hours (for all campaigns) in each media market!

In recent years, a coalition of reform groups has pressured Congress to enact legislation that would require television networks and local stations to provide free time for candidates and ballot questions during the last month of the campaign. Their intent is not just to increase the sheer amount of election-related programming, but also to improve the quality of programming. Requiring candidates to make their free-time presentations in person increases accountability and makes it more likely that the discussion will focus on policy. As Kathleen Jamieson noted in her testimony before the FCC in 1996:

> My reading of history suggests that when candidates speak in their own
> voice, rather than in the voice-overs of ads, or in the editing form of sound

bites in news, their discourse is more likely to be constructive. And that means to argue rather than assert, to advocate rather than attack, and to be accountable. Their discourse is also, in that form, more likely to be civil. Those are all characteristics I think we ought to be trying to increase in political discourse. (FCC, 1996)

As is true with most policy innovations, the details of implementation often work against the intent of the policy makers. One such practical road-block concerns the equal-time requirement. Would the networks be required to grant the same amount of free time to the dozens of minor-party presidential candidates? In 1996 the problem was sidestepped when the FCC ruled that free television time for major candidates was exempt from the equal-time provisions under the "bona fide news event" doctrine. A more difficult problem is scheduling the candidate appearances. In the 1996 experiment, all the networks (with the exception of ABC) adopted a proposal promoted by Rupert Murdoch (who owns the Fox network) to allocate brief blocks of time to Democrat Bill Clinton and Republican Bob Dole. The participating networks made available short segments of time ranging from a low of five ninety-second segments (NBC) to a high of twelve two-and-a-half-minute segments (PBS, CNN, UPN). In most cases, the two candidates appeared on alternate nights during the same week and spoke on topics of their own choosing.[4]

As predicted by the proponents, the content of the free-time presentations tended to be substantive. The candidates focused on policy advocacy and their records, rather than on slogans or personal attacks. In comparison with broadcast news, the free appearances were three times more likely to focus on issues (Jamieson, 1997, p. 8). In effect, the free airtime produced "quality" substantive content.

Unfortunately, the candidate presentations reached relatively few voters. For one thing, the 1996 contest was unusually one-sided; Clinton maintained a massive lead in the polls throughout, and public interest in the race was low. Moreover, apolitical viewers could simply switch channels to avoid watching Clinton or Dole.[5] Proponents of the experiment had requested that the networks "roadblock" the appearances (air the appearances at the same time) so as to maximize the viewing audience. However, the networks chose to run the candidate appearances at different times. CBS, for example, aired the segments during the evening network newscast, and NBC aired them during *Dateline*. Surveys conducted after the election showed that the lack of simultaneous programming was a serious liability; less than 25 percent of the public reported that they had watched any of the candidates' presentations. Given the typically inflated nature of self-reports, the true level of exposure is probably closer to 10 percent.

Undaunted, proponents of free time introduced a more ambitious measure in the US Senate. Co-sponsored by Senators McCain, Feingold, and Durbin, the bill would have required broadcasters to air at least two hours a week of candidate and ballot measure programming for at least six weeks during the campaign. Stations would have to broadcast the free segments between 5:00 PM and 11:30 PM. Moreover, television stations would be required to subsidize federal candidates' television time through a system of vouchers financed by a tax on broadcasters. For the entire cycle, the proposal made available $650 million of free airtime for individual candidates and $100 million for each party.[6]

It goes without saying that the broadcasting industry strenuously opposed the McCain–Feingold–Durbin bill. Broadcast companies claimed that the law amounted to an arbitrary "taking" of private property (prohibited by the Fifth Amendment) and that the free-time requirement would infringe upon their First Amendment free speech rights. As a result of their intense lobbying, the bill died in committee. The 2004 campaign returned to business as usual: television news coverage of the campaign was minuscule and broadcasters took in $1.6 billion from political advertisers.

The unwillingness of broadcasters to accept their public service obligations and provide free time to candidates suggests an alternative remedy to the problem of nonsubstantive campaigns; the strategy would be to bypass broadcasters and deliver substantive information concerning the candidates' positions on the issues directly to every voter. In one scenario, nonpartisan civic groups would pose the questions, and the candidates would produce videos of their answers, which would then be assembled on a CD or DVD and mailed to every registered voter. The cost of such an effort would be less than a hundred million dollars, a small fraction of the total amount spent on campaign advertising in the 2004 campaign. We'll return to the theme of bypassing the media shortly.

Unlike broadcast media, newspapers and magazines cannot be required to provide minimal levels of campaign coverage. Instead, a media watchdog group or ombudsman could be established to monitor the level of substantive content in election news in print media. The results, if published each week during September and October, might attract considerable publicity and work as a necessary disincentive for editors preoccupied with the horse race. An institutionalized system for monitoring issue-oriented coverage among the major print outlets would also foster competition to be rated as the most "civic" news source (and to avoid last place in the "substance" ratings), thus increasing editors' willingness to run issue-oriented stories in place of the horse race. If afforded coverage of their policy proposals, elected officials have a significant incentive to talk about the issues at some length. The end result would be some semblance of a genuine debate.

Encouraging a More Partisan Press

Journalists are hardly appropriate intermediaries between voters and candidates. As paid professionals, they are more interested in getting the story "right" (avoiding any semblance of partisan bias) and less interested in helping voters identify the candidate who has the better ideas, programs, or track record. It is this arm's-length treatment of candidates and parties that is partly responsible for the low level of coverage accorded to issues. Evaluating the strengths and weaknesses of the competing candidates' positions on global climate change would leave journalists open to charges of bias. The supply of substantive, issue-oriented coverage could be increased if news organizations were more explicit about their political preferences.

The tradition of a partisan press is hardly contrary to democracy (as witnessed by several European democracies), and it is not foreign to the United States. In fact, American political campaigns originated in the early eighteenth century when activist newspaper editors allied themselves with the Jeffersonian Republicans. The Federalists countered in 1798 by passing the Alien and Sedition Acts, but their attempts at censorship only accelerated politicization of the press. By the middle of the nineteenth century, most American newspapers were openly affiliated with a party:

> Partisan newspapers and loosely organized parties (aided by government subsidies) combined to create a hitherto unrecognized institution, the newspaper-based party, which dominated the American political scene in the antebellum years, remained strong in the late nineteenth century, and did not disappear completely until the twentieth century. (Pasley, 2001, p. 17)

The presence of a vigorous partisan press helped create a sense of common identity among party supporters. Urgent notices in the party newspaper, as well as the availability of manpower provided by the urban machines, were especially useful when it was time to get voters to the polls. The heyday of the partisan press and strong party organizations generated the highest levels of voter turnout in American history. In the presidential campaign of 1896, Democrat William Jennings Bryan traveled the entire length of the country delivering hundreds of speeches to enthusiastic supporters. Bryan's appeal was based entirely on issues, most notably his opposition to free trade and the gold standard. The Republican campaign, masterminded by Marc Hanna (the first paid political consultant) brought in thousands of supporters to Washington, where they would listen to McKinley rebut Bryan's populist positions on the issues. Both parties mobilized their supporters with brass-band parades and torch-lit marches; on election day, nearly 80 percent of the electorate voted.

As the urban population grew and printing costs fell, newspaper publishers began to realize that they could more easily expand their circulation by shedding their partisan ties and appealing to readers on the basis of the everyday utility of their product rather than the correctness of their politics. Once mass-circulation media and professional journalism came of age, the die was cast for the current system of media politics. All it took was the advent of the direct primary and the weakening of the political party organizations for journalists to replace party leaders as the central players in the campaign.

The practice of professional journalism does not preclude the expression of partisan preferences. In fact, as we noted in Chapter 3, the public is already widely skeptical about the objectivity of reporters. No matter how scrupulously objective or balanced the coverage of events and issues is, partisans inevitably see the news as slanted in favor of their opponents. Bias is very much in the eyes of the beholder.

One occasion when the press reveals a more explicit bias is the endorsement of candidates at the end of a campaign. American newspapers have always endorsed candidates, although, as a recent study by Ansolabehere, Lessem, and Snyder (in press) notes, the manner of their endorsement has become less articulated and more candidate-oriented than party-oriented. Candidate endorsements can be seen either as an attempt at transparency (revealing the editors' preferences to the reader) or as an attempt at persuasion. By endorsing candidates, the press is casting a partisan vote. Empirical research into the effects of endorsements on reader preferences typically finds a nontrivial effect: endorsed candidates tend to do better at the polls.

The frequency with which newspapers endorse candidates suggests that the practice has no adverse impact on circulation. Newspapers do not make endorsements strategically; that is, they do not favor candidates from the majority party. Publishers do not seem to fear that readers supporting the nonendorsed candidate will cancel their subscriptions.

Endorsements may not hurt circulation, but is there a market for partisan or biased journalism? The gradual emergence of Fox News as the cable ratings leader suggests that, in a highly competitive market environment, a clear political slant allows a new organization to grow by creating a niche for itself. Recent theoretical work by economists corroborates this observation by showing that, under competition and diversity of opinion among readers, newspapers will provide content that is more biased: "Competition forces newspapers to cater to the prejudices of their readers, and greater competition typically results in more aggressive catering to such prejudices as competitors strive to divide the market" (Mullainathan & Schleifer, 2005, p. 18). Thus, rational newspaper owners stand to gain by injecting more rather than less political slant or bias into their news. Perhaps newspapers that are more explicitly pro-Republican or pro-Democratic in their editorial pages can use their ideological transparency as a means of attracting readers.

No matter what the implications for circulation and revenue, a more rather than less partisan press will have the effect of increasing the supply of issue-oriented news. At the very least, we recommend that newspapers increase the amount of editorial space devoted to their endorsements. Supporting a candidate requires a rationale; newspapers can use the occasion of their endorsement to run a series of editorials explaining why the endorsed candidate's positions are preferable to the opponent's. On the whole, the availability of newspapers balanced between Democratic and Republican bias will enable motivated readers who monitor multiple news sources to encounter both sides of the debate.

Fostering Direct Communication Between Candidates and Voters

Today's information technology offers a promising avenue for a renewal of *direct* communications between candidates and voters. Three-fourths of all American households have a personal computer, and the great majority are connected to the Internet. About ninety-four million Americans go online on a typical day, according to a recent Pew Internet and American Life Project survey (Rainie & Shermak, 2005).

Given the rapid proliferation of technology, it is not surprising that candidates and political groups have made their presence known online. From the president down to city council members, elected officials offer a wealth of information on their Web sites. Visitors may browse through speeches, view television commercials, complete surveys, and even contribute money. To date, however, campaign Web sites have not attracted much traffic. Political junkies may make regular visits to rnc.org or clinton.senate.gov, but for most Americans, seeking information about candidates or issues takes a backseat to shopping or catching up on the latest baseball scores as Web pastimes. Adding to the lack of online exposure, the more entertaining campaign content appears typically in the form of television advertisements, and most Web surfers do not have the bandwidth necessary for accessing multimedia presentations.

Given the opportunity costs of acquiring political information online, a potentially more attention-getting form of direct interaction between candidates and voters is the portable "handbook"—now cast in the form of a data storage device. A campaign handbook—which is a more substantive counterpart to the traditional direct-mail campaign—delivers the same multimedia content and richness of coverage as a political Web site but can reach a wider audience. To put a CD or DVD into one's home or office computer requires neither sophisticated hardware nor a fast Internet connection—and certainly CD usage does not demand a level of interest or commitment comparable to that of the political news "junkie" who is willing to spend time finding and comparing various political Web sites. As Americans become more sophisticated in their use of computers, multitasking will be effortless; in between working on a spreadsheet or e-mail message, one might browse the CD. Since the cost of mass-producing CDs is trivial, electronic voter guides are an especially inexpensive form of voter outreach.

The 2000 presidential election provided the first opportunity to test the potential impact of direct campaign communication. As described in Chapter 5, the Political Communication Lab at Stanford University produced an extensive and easily accessible election database, which was distributed free of cost to any voter who requested it. Compiled in both text and multimedia format, the database included Vice President Gore's and Governor Bush's campaign speeches, a full collection of the televised ads aired by the candidates and their respective parties, and the complete text of the two party platforms. In total, the CD amounted to over six hundred pages of text and three hours of multimedia presentation.

The availability of the CD was advertised through banner ads on popular election-related Web sites.[7] The CD was also featured on several popular "freebie" shopping Web sites, where users are directed to sites that offer giveaways. Over thirty thousand voters (representing all fifty states) requested a copy of the CD.

In order to assess the impact of the CD on citizens' attitudes, the CD was distributed to a representative sample of registered voters a few weeks before the 2000 election. The recipients were contacted in advance, informed that the CD was a nonpartisan compilation of the candidates' positions on the issues, and told that they were free to use the CD at their convenience.[8] Of those who received the CD, 35 percent actually used it. Participants were surveyed shortly after the election. Respondents who had, in fact, used the CD were more likely to state that they voted, expressed greater interest in the campaign, and felt that their opinions mattered (indicating political efficacy, a feeling of political power).[9] The simple differences between the CD user group and a baseline control group showed clearly that exposure to the CD significantly increased measures of political involvement.

Can we be confident that these differences are genuine treatment effects and not merely an indication of greater motivation among CD users? As might be expected, users and nonusers differed systematically—the former being drawn disproportionately from people with histories of voting, and higher socioeconomic status. To isolate the effects of CD use from the built-in differences in the composition of CD user and nonuser groups, the researchers reestimated the treatment effects after matching CD users with individuals in the control group on the relevant factors that discriminated between users and nonusers.[10] Even after the greater political motivation of CD users was taken into account, the results showed that use of an election CD, in and of itself, stimulated a sense of involvement in the campaign.

REACHING THE TECHNOLOGY GENERATION

Direct candidate-to-voter communication is likely to have the greatest impact on younger Americans. Youth make up the vanguard of computer-based media users. School-age children and young adults are considerably overrepresented among all computer and Internet users. Three out of four Americans under the age of eighteen have access to a computer; on average, they use it for more than thirty minutes every day. Not only are the young especially adept with new technologies, but they have also integrated technology into their personal lives as never before.

From doing homework, chatting with friends, playing games, and listening to or creating music, to downloading and watching the latest movies, the personal computer is a core element of contemporary youth culture. In the words of a seventeen-year-old respondent in a recent Pew Internet & American Life Project survey, "I multi-task every single second I am online. At this very moment I am watching TV, checking my email every two minutes, reading a newsgroup about who shot JFK, burning some music to a CD, and writing this message" (Lenhart, Rainie, & Lewis, 2001, p. 10). Thus, in stark contrast to their underrepresentation in any form of political action, youth are dominant in their daily use of information technology. From our perspective, the important question is whether their attraction to technology can be harnessed to stimulate a greater sense of involvement in political campaigns.

Of course, young people are attracted to technology not because they seek political enlightenment, but rather for social interaction and personal stimulation. If technologically enhanced political material is to catch their eye, the presentation must necessarily include popular elements of youth culture, most notably video games and contemporary music. Stanford researchers tested this assumption by producing a youth-oriented election CD for the 2002 gubernatorial campaign in California. The CD presented an exhaustive, easily searchable database about Democrat Gray Davis and his Republican opponent, Bill Simon, supplemented with a variety of interactive games, contests, and quizzes that were all designed to make the presentation especially appealing to youth. For instance, the CD featured two different "Whack-a-Pol" games (see Video Feature 11.2) in which users had to hit as many rapidly moving political targets (politicians or interest groups) with a hammer, a music quiz asking users to identify popular songs and associate the artists with candidates or causes, a similar celebrity quiz, and a self-administered "rate your campaign IQ" test.

VIDEO FEATURE 11.2 Whack-a-Pol

What were the effects of using the CD? Even after adjusting for the overrepresentation of especially "participant" subjects among the ranks of CD users, the CD group's actual turnout rate exceeded turnout among the control group by a significant margin. CD users were also more likely to express interest in the campaign.

The campaign CD studies suggest that high-tech campaigns have the potential to mobilize youth. Moreover, unlike ordinary get-out-the-vote methods, a CD campaign instills internal rather than external political motivation and is thus more likely to have a long-lasting effect on youth attitudes. Conventional mobilization campaigns, by providing the target recipient with a salient external rationale for voting, may actually impede the development of participant attitudes. At the very least, these campaigns have no effects whatsoever on the dispositions known to encourage political participation.[11] Elec-

tion handbooks place the recipient in a more active posture, at least as compared with potential voters who are targeted by telephone or door-to-door
campaigns. The fact that members of the targeted audience are free to use
the CD on their own has important psychological implications.

Social psychologists have long known that behavior affects self-percep-
tion. Typically, individuals attribute their own actions to either dispositional
(internal) or situational (external) causes. Someone who votes, for instance,
may believe that she decided to vote on her own or, alternatively, that she
was influenced to vote by a phone call or campaign worker. Attributing the
act to internal factors contributes to "intrinsic motivation," which is known
to encourage long-term learning of the act in question. In one classic study,
preschoolers who were promised a reward for drawing were later found to
approach drawing materials less frequently than those who were not led to
expect any reward.

The implications of the findings on intrinsic motivation for youth political participation are clear: young people who encounter campaign information of their own accord and spend time interacting with political material
may come to see themselves as interested in politics. The relatively inexpensive "act" of using a campaign CD or visiting a political Web site may then
open the door to more significant acts, including registering to vote and discussing the campaign with parents or friends. Thus a relatively trivial and
unobtrusive addition to one's "technology space" promises greater long-term
payoffs than do conventional efforts at mobilization. The reason for this effect
of technology use is simple: an eighteen-year-old who, in the course of playing a computer game, learns that certain groups or causes he dislikes are on
a particular candidate's "team" has a compelling basis (his actual behavior) for
claiming an interest in politics. An eighteen-year-old who receives a phone
call urging him to vote has some basis for claiming precisely the opposite.

To sum up, the proliferation of information technology makes possible
alternative forms of campaigning that cast voters in a more independent role.
Consider the contrast between voters with access to election CDs and those
who rely on network television. The former, with minimal effort, could sample from an extensive compilation of information featuring the candidates in
their own words; the latter would have access to a daily sound bite and
accounts of the horse race. Rather than waiting passively, and most likely in
vain, for the media to provide coverage of relevant issues, CD users could
seek out information that was personally meaningful. The studies of CD use
suggest that this newfound independence fosters a general sense of political
involvement.

Electronic voter handbooks are also attractive on more mundane economic grounds. When mass-produced, the cost of producing and mailing each CD is less than seventy cents. Not only are CDs cost-effective, but they also represent more than mere pleas to vote. They deliver relevant information, as well as the opportunity to encounter the candidates in their own words—all with minimal effort. In short, either in terms of cost or in terms of the breadth of treatment outcomes, digital technology represents a potentially effective form of delivering information that is not provided by the news media, but that is essential to the exercise of informed choice.

The principal disadvantage of technology-based campaigns is a relatively low "contact rate." Slightly more than one-third of the registered voters who were mailed the 2000 election CD actually used it, even though the recipients were drawn from a panel of people who had agreed to participate in a certain number of research studies.[12] When a CD was mailed to a sample of young voters during the 2004 election, fewer than 10 percent actually used it. Thus, exposure to campaign CDs is lower than that achieved by more traditional forms of voter canvassing. As technology spreads, however, the proportion of voters with the skills to use election CDs will grow. Sponsorship by credible, nonpartisan civic groups can only further increase the likelihood of CD use. In the case of youth CDs, distribution in high schools and incorporation into the social studies curricula could further enhance their visibility. A systematic CD campaign, carried out in collaboration with educators and civic groups could easily reach a majority of young voters.

The benefits of election handbooks for voters are clear, but bypassing the media is just as advantageous for the candidates. They can distribute their messages widely, devoid of criticism and media analysis. At seventy cents per household, a CD-based campaign is affordable even for minor-party candidates. As strategic actors, candidates can be expected to take advantage of this new mode of direct campaigning by addressing a more complete range of policy positions than can be conveyed in sound bites. The fact that the CD is just as transparent a forum as televised advertising or candidate debates makes it unlikely that CD content will be any more misleading or deceptive than standard campaign presentations are. On the contrary, as the evidence on free-time appearances indicates, candidates are far more inclined to provide arguments and advocacy rather than slogans and personal attacks when they deliver messages in person. In the end, the use of campaign handbooks better realizes voter independence, the breadth and depth of the policy debate, and candidates' control over their messages. These gains, significant in themselves, may ultimately be significantly augmented by the collective benefit of having a more enthusiastic and engaged citizenry.

Conclusion

As we enter the twenty-first century, American politics stands at a critical crossroads. For decades, candidates and elected officials depended on the news media to get their messages out—with predictable consequences. The media used their newfound influence to develop new forms of reporting that reduced candidates' control over their messages but enhanced the voice of the journalist. In the process, journalists were sidetracked from their public service obligations, and voters were left uninformed, confused, and cynical.

The development of new technologies affords society an opportunity to escape the sideshow of combat between the candidates and the press. Voters can gain access to information that is more substantive than that provided by mainstream news organizations' coverage of the campaign. Technology also makes possible more-personalized forms of candidate-to-voter and voter-to-voter communication. Although there is good reason to hope that new forms of campaign communication will provide a better way to inform and engage voters, the fundamental dynamic of media politics will remain unchanged: instead of television advertising, politicians will turn to voter handbooks, e-mail announcements of their most recent accomplishments, and online town hall meetings to score points with voters. What will be different, however, is the substantive content of their messages and the reduced cost of communicating with voters.

Given access to voters, candidates are unlikely to campaign on the basis of their strategies or the state of the horse race; instead, they will talk about their accomplishments and positions on the issues. Reaching voters via information technology is far less expensive than mounting a full-scale advertising campaign. The lower entry costs will make for a larger pool of candidates, a more multisided flow of information, and eventually, more-competitive elections. As we enter the postmedia era, the electoral process could well be rejuvenated.

CHAPTER 11 SUMMARY

1. The system of media politics in the United States today may be seen as having two main shortcomings: (a) the absence of a substantive or policy-oriented electoral forum, and (b) the substitution of journalists and analysts for the candidates as the principal voices in the news.

2. Some scholars argue that the electorate's lack of policy information is inconsequential. According to one stream of research, most people can

approximate their "full-information" opinions by combining simple cues with widely available psychological heuristics or shortcuts. Other scholars cite evidence that informed and uninformed opinions are frequently at odds. A significant body of research has demonstrated that when people are given the arguments on both sides of an issue, they often change their positions.

3. Suggestions for addressing the lack of a policy-oriented electoral forum include the following:

   • Require broadcast outlets to provide candidates with free airtime in the closing days of the campaign.

   • Grade news organizations on the substantive content of their programming, with the goal of generating greater awareness of the problem and improving the quality and content of the news delivered.

   • Return to a more partisan press, in which the print media would adopt a more expansive form of candidate endorsements. Since American newspapers are evenly divided in the partisan direction of their candidate endorsements, collectively these more substantial endorsements would better inform the reading public.

4. One suggestion for addressing the marginalization of candidate voices is to have candidates adopt a technology-driven system of direct or "unmediated" political communication to bypass the news media and communicate directly with voters, improving voters' ability to make decisions on the basis of the candidates' issue positions. Preliminary research suggests that direct candidate-to-voter communication does, in fact, increase voter interest and participation in the process.

FURTHER READINGS

Althaus, S. (1998). Information effects in collective preferences. *American Political Science Review, 92,* 545–558.

Ansolabehere, S., Lessem, R., & Snyder, J. M. (in press). *The orientation of newspaper endorsements in US elections, 1940–2002. Quarterly Journal of Political Science.*

Bartels, L. M. (2005). Homer gets a tax cut: Inequality and public policy in the American mind. *Perspectives on Politics, 3*(1), 15–31.

Fishkin, J. (1995). *The voice of the people.* New Haven, CT: Yale University Press.

Hamilton, J. T. (2003). *All the news that's fit to sell: How the market transforms information into news*. Princeton, NJ: Princeton University Press.

Lupia, A. (1994). Shortcuts versus encyclopedias: Information and voting behavior in California insurance reform elections. *American Political Science Review, 88*, 63–76.

Pasley, J. L. (2001). *The tyranny of printers: Newspaper politics in the early American republic*. Charlottesville: University of Virginia Press.

NOTES

1. The Andrade case was the basis for a prolonged legal challenge to the California three-strikes law on the grounds that the sentence constituted "cruel and unusual punishment." The US Court of Appeals for the Ninth Circuit upheld the challenge, but the California attorney general appealed the decision to the US Supreme Court. In a five-to-four vote, the Supreme Court overturned the appellate decision and reinstated the sentence.

2. The major donor was Jerry Keenan, whose contribution amounted to two million dollars. Opponents of the measure were quick to point out that Mr. Keenan's motives were less than pure, his son having been convicted of drunken driving. The "Yes on 66" campaign was also the beneficiary of a five-hundred-thousand-dollar contribution from financier George Soros (whose impartiality was not questioned).

3. Making the imbalance even more striking is the fact that the population of California is roughly one-third of the total population of the remaining three-strikes states.

4. The A. H. Belo Corporation, owner of several television stations across the country, extended the free-time program to gubernatorial and congressional candidates.

5. CBS and CNN both provided ratings data for the days that they aired the candidate appearances. Surprisingly, in neither case was there any evidence of significant channel switching.

6. The voucher system was based on a matching formula. Candidates who were able to raise a minimum amount of money in private contributions would receive three dollars in vouchers for one dollar of cash contributions.

7. Buyers could order the candidate CD either on the Internet (via an online order form) or by calling a toll-free telephone number.

8. Participants were recruited from the national research panel maintained by Knowledge Networks (www.knowledgenetworks.com).

9. The index of efficacy consisted of three items to which respondents could agree or disagree: (1) "Sometimes politics and government seem so complicated that a person like me can't really understand what's going on." (2) "Public officials don't care much what people like me think." (3) "People like me have no say about what the government does."

10. In technical terms, the matching-based treatment effect is defined as the difference in the outcome variable between subgroups of treated and control subjects with identical covariate values, averaged over the matching covariate classes (for details on the matching methodology and estimator, see Iyengar & Jackman, 2003a).

11. In fact, Green and Gerber (2001) report that telephone calls encouraging young people to vote have no effects at all on standard participant predispositions.

12. Participants in the Knowledge Networks panel are required to complete surveys on a regular basis in exchange for free Internet access.

Bibliography

Chapter 1

Correctional Association of New York. (2004). *Trends in New York State prison commitments*. Retrieved from www.correctionalassociation.org/publications/TRENDSFebruary
20041.pdf.

US Department of Justice. (2004, June). Office of Justice Programs, Bureau of Justice Statistics. *State prison expenditures, 2001* (NCJ 202949). Retrieved from www.ojp.usdoj.gov/
bjs/pub/pdf/spe01.pdf.

Chapter 2

Amy, D. J. (n.d.). *Proportional representation voting systems*. Retrieved October 11, 2004, from
the Proportional Representation Library Web site: www.mtholyoke.edu/acad/polit/damy/
BeginnningReading/PRsystems.htm.

Aslama, M., Hellman, H., & Sauri, T. (2004). Does market entry regulation matter? Competition in television broadcasting and program diversity in Finland, 1993–2002. *The International Journal for Communication Studies, 66*, 113–132. Retrieved from http://web
.lexis-nexis.com.

Bagdikian, B. H. (2000). *The media monopoly* (6th ed.). Boston: Beacon.

Bennett, W. L. (2003). The burglar alarm that just keeps ringing: A response to Zaller. *Political Communication, 20*, 131–138.

Benton Foundation. (1999, January). *The public interest standard in television broadcasting*.
Washington, DC: Advisory Committee on Public Interest Obligations of Digital Television Broadcasters. Retrieved March 15, 2005, from www.benton.org/publibrary/piac/
sec2.html.

Bishop, R., & Hakanen, E. A. (2002). In the public interest? The state of local television
programming fifteen years after deregulation. *Journal of Communication Inquiry, 26*,
261–276.

Blais, A., & Massicotte, L. (2002). Electoral systems. In L. LeDuc, R. G. Niemi, & P. Norris (Eds.), *Comparing democracies 2: New challenges in the study of elections and voting* (pp. 40–69). London: Sage.

Blumler, J. G., & Kavanagh, D. (1999). The third age of political communication: Influences and features. *Political Communication, 16,* 209–230.

Brants, K. (1998). Who's afraid of infotainment? *European Journal of Communication, 13,* 315–335.

California Secretary of State (n.d.). *Presidential candidate qualification procedures (American Independent, Green, Libertarian, Natural Law, Peace and Freedom, and Republican Parties).* Retrieved March 17, 2005, from California Secretary of State Web site: www .ss.ca.gov/elections/cand_qual_pres_other.pdf.

Columbia Journalism Review. (2004). *Who owns what: News Corporation.* New York: Author. Retrieved March 17, 2005, from the Columbia Journalism Review Web site: www .cjr.org/tools/owners/newscorp.asp.

Craig, D. B. (2000). *Fireside politics: Radio and political culture in the United States, 1920–1940.* Baltimore: Johns Hopkins University Press.

Dalton, R. J., & Wattenberg, M. P. (2001). *Parties without partisans: Political change in advanced industrial democracies.* New York: Oxford University Press.

Denver, D., Hands, G., Fisher, J., & MacAllister, I. (2003). Constituency campaigning in Britain, 1992–2001: Centralization and modernization. *Party Politics, 9,* 541–559.

Djankov, S., McLiesh, C., Nenova, T., & Shleifer, A. (2001, June). *Who owns the media?* (Working Paper No. 2620). Washington, DC: World Bank, Office of the Senior Vice President, Development Economics. Retrieved March 14, 2005, from the World Bank Web site: econ.worldbank.org/files/2225_wps2620.pdf.

Ely, B. (2002). Savings and loan crisis. In D. R. Henderson (Ed.), *Concise encyclopedia of economics.* Retrieved March 11, 2005, from the Library of Economics and Liberty Web site: www.econlib.org/library/Enc/SavingsandLoanCrisis.html.

Gilliam, F. D., Jr., & Iyengar, S. (2000). Prime suspects: The influence of local television news on the viewing public. *American Journal of Political Science, 44,* 560–573.

Goldmark, P. C., Jr. (2001). *Old values, new world: Harnessing the legacy of independent journalism for the future* (with a report of the Fourth Annual Aspen Institute Conference on Journalism and Society, "The evolution of journalism in a changing market economy," by D. Bollier). Washington, DC: Aspen Institute.

Graber, D. (2003). The media and democracy: Beyond myths and stereotypes. *Annual Review of Political Science, 6,* 139–160.

Gunther, R., & Mughan, A. (Eds.). (2000). *Democracy and the media: A comparative perspective.* Cambridge, England: Cambridge University Press.

Hallin, D. C., & Mancini, P. (2004). *Comparing media systems: Three models of media and politics.* Cambridge, England: Cambridge University Press.

Hart, J. A. (2004). *Technology, television, and competition: The politics of digital television.* New York: Cambridge University Press.

Hazan, R. Y. (2002). Candidate selection. In L. LeDuc, R. G. Niemi, & P. Norris, *Comparing democracies 2: New challenges in the study of elections and voting* (pp. 108–126). London: Sage.

Heinderyckx, F. (1993). Television news programmes in Western Europe: A comparative study. *European Journal of Communication, 8,* 425–450.

Hodess, R., Tedesco, J. C., and L. L. Kaid. 2000. British party election broadcasts: A comparison of 1992 with 1997. *Harvard International Journal of Press/Politics, 5,* 55–70.

Holtz-Bacha, C., & Norris, P. (2001). To entertain, inform and educate: Still the role of public television? *Political Communication, 18,* 123–140.

Iyengar, S. (1997). Overview of media-based political campaigns. In S. Iyengar & R. Reeves (Eds.), *Do the media govern?* (pp. 143–148). Thousand Oaks, CA: Sage.

Kaid, L. L., & Jones, C. A. (2004). United States of America. In B. Lange & D. Ward, *The media and elections: A handbook and comparative study* (pp. 25–59). Mahwah, NJ: Erlbaum.

Katz, R. S. (1990). Party as linkage? A vestigial function? *European Journal of Political Research, 18,* 143–161.

Kelly, M., Mazzoleni, G., & McQuail, D. (2004). *The media in Europe: The Euromedia handbook.* London: Sage.

Krasnow, E. G. (1997). *The "public interest" standard: The elusive search for the Holy Grail.* Briefing paper prepared for the Advisory Committee on Public Interest Obligations of Digital Television Broadcasters. Retrieved April 2, 2005, from www.mediainstitute .org/gore/STUDIES/krasnow.html.

Krüger, U. M. (1996). Boulevardisierung der Information im Privatfernsehen. *Media Perspektiven, 7,* 362–375.

Krüger, U. M. (1997). Politikberichterstattung in den Fernsehnachrichten: Nachrichtenangebote öffentlich-rechtlicher und privater Fernsehsender 1996 im Vergleich. *Media Perspektiven, 5,* 256–268.

Lacy, S., & Simon, T. F. (1993). *The economics and regulation of United States newspapers.* Norwood, NJ: Ablex.

Mair, P., & van Biezen, I. (2001). Party membership in twenty European democracies. *Party Politics, 7,* 5–21.

Mancini, P. (1999). New frontiers in political professionalism. *Political Communication, 16,* 231–245.

Mauboussin, E. (2004). France. In B. Lange & D. Ward, *The media and elections: A handbook and comparative study* (pp. 101–122). Mahwah, NJ: Erlbaum.

Mazzoleni, G., & Schulz, W. (1999). "Mediatization" of politics: A challenge for democracy? *Political Communication, 16,* 247–261.

McNicholas, A., & Ward, D. (2004). United Kingdom. In B. Lange & D. Ward, *The media and elections: A handbook and comparative study* (pp. 145–164). Mahwah, NJ: Erlbaum.

Meier, H. E. (2003). Beyond convergence: Understanding programming strategies of public broadcasters in competitive environments. *European Journal of Communication, 18,* 337–365.

Nelson, H. L., & Teeter, D. L., Jr. (1978). *Law of mass communications.* Mineola, NY: Foundation Press.

Noam, E. (1991). *Television in Europe.* New York: Oxford University Press.

Norris, P. (2002). Campaign communications. In L. LeDuc, R. G. Niemi, & P. Norris (Eds.), *Comparing democracies 2: New challenges in the study of elections and voting* (pp. 127–147). Thousand Oaks, CA: Sage.

Number of TV Households in America [1950–1978]. (2005). Retrieved March 10, 2005, from the TV History Web site: www.tvhistory.tv/Annual_TV_Households_50-78.JPG.

Ofcom. (2004). *Ofcom review of public service television broadcasting: Phase 1—Is television special?* London: Ofcom. Retrieved March 7, 2005, from the Ofcom Web site: www.ofcom.org.uk/consult/condocs/psb/psb/psb.pdf.

O'Hagan, J., & Jennings, M. (2003). Public broadcasting in Europe: Rationale, licence fee, and other issues. *Journal of Cultural Economics, 27,* 31–56.

Patterson, T. E. (1993). *Out of order.* New York: Knopf.

Patterson, T. E. (2002). *The vanishing voter: Public involvement in an age of uncertainty.* New York: Knopf.

Picard, R. G. (2001, August). *Audience economics of European Union public service broadcasters: Assessing performance in competitive markets.* Paper presented at the annual meeting of the Association for Education in Journalism and Mass Communication, Washington, DC.

Plasser, F. (2000). American campaign techniques worldwide. *Harvard International Journal of Press/Politics, 5,* 33–54.

Polsby, N. W. (1983). *Consequences of party reform.* New York: Oxford University Press.

Price, D. (2001). *Ownership of cultural businesses: An international comparative profile.* Quebec, Canada: Department of Canadian Heritage, Cultural Development Sector, Publishing and Policy Programs. Retrieved March 13, 2005, from www.pch.gc.ca/progs/ac-ca/progs/esm-ms/dprice0_e.cfm.

Project for Excellence in Journalism. (2003, April 29). *Does ownership matter in local television news: A Five-Year Study of Ownership and Quality.* Retrieved March 19, 2005, from the Project for Excellence in Journalism Web site: www.journalism.org/resources/research/reports/ownership/Ownership2.pdf.

Project for Excellence in Journalism. (2004a). *The state of the news media, 2004: Local TV—Ownership.* Retrieved March 7, 2005, from the State of the News Media Web site: www.stateofthenewsmedia.org/2004/narrative_localtv_ownership.asp?cat=5&media=6.

Project for Excellence in Journalism. (2004b). *The state of the news media, 2004: Newspapers—Ownership.* Retrieved March 7, 2005, from the State of the News Media Web site: www.stateofthenewsmedia.org/2004/narrative_newspapers_ownership.asp?cat=5&media=2.

Project for Excellence in Journalism. (2004c). *The state of the news media, 2004: Overview—Ownership.* Retrieved March 7, 2005, from the State of the News Media Web site: www.stateofthenewsmedia.org/2004/narrative_overview_ownership.asp?media=1.

Rahat, G., & Hazan, R. Y. (2001). Candidate selection methods: An analytical framework. *Party Politics, 7,* 297–322.

Reporters Without Borders. (2004). *Third annual worldwide press freedom index.* Retrieved May 1, 2005, from www.rsf.org/article.php3?id_article=11715.

Roppen, J. (1997, August). *The problem of no effects of media concentration.* Paper presented at the 13th Nordic Conference of Media Research, Jyväskylä, Finland.

Sanders, D., & Norris, P. (2002). *Advocacy versus attack: The impact of political advertising in the 2001 UK general election.* Unpublished manuscript. Retrieved March 9, 2005, from ksghome.harvard.edu/~pnorris/ACROBAT/peb.pdf.

Schudson, M. (1998). *The good citizen: A history of American civic life.* New York: Free Press.

Schulz, W., Zeh, R., & Quiring, O. (2005). Voters in a changing media environment: A data-based retrospective on consequences of media change in Germany. *European Journal of Communication, 20*, 55–88.

Seyd, P., & Whitely, P. (2004). British party members: An overview. *Party Politics, 10*, 355–366.

Silbey, J. H. (2002). The rise and fall of American political parties, 1790–1993. In L. S. Maisel (Ed.), *The parties respond: Changes in American parties and campaigns* (4th ed., pp. 3–18). Boulder, CO: Westview.

Sinclair Broadcast Group. (2004, October 19). Sinclair to air "A POW Story." *Sinclair Broadcast Group press release*. Retrieved March 9, 2005, from www.sbgi.net/press/release_20041019_87.shtml.

Sniderman, P., Brody, R., & Tetlock, P. E. (1991). The role of heuristics in political reasoning: A theory sketch. In P. Sniderman, R. Brody, & P. E. Tetlock (Eds.), *Reasoning and choice: Explorations in political psychology* (pp. 14–30). Cambridge, England: Cambridge University Press.

Steinberg, C. (1980). *TV facts*. New York: Facts on File.

Vermont Secretary of State. (n.d.). *Vermont presidential primary and general election: Calendar and procedures for 2004*. Retrieved March 9, 2005, from the Vermont Secretary of State Web site: http://vermont-elections.org/elections1/presidential_info_2004.html.

Wattenberg, M. (1996). *The decline of American political parties, 1952–1994*. Cambridge, MA: Harvard University Press.

Wayne, S. J. (2004). *Presidential nominations and American democracy*. Retrieved March 10, 2005, from the US Department of State Web site: usinfo.state.gov/products/pubs/election04/nominate.htm.

Wieten, J., Murdock, G., & Dahlgren, P. (Eds.). (2000). *Television across Europe: A comparative introduction*. London: Sage.

Williams, Granville. (2003). *European media ownership: Threats on the landscape. A survey of who owns what in Europe* (Upd. ed.). Brussels, Belgium: European Federation of Journalists. Retrieved September 18, 2004, from the International Federation of Journalists Web site: www.ifj.org/pdfs/europeownershipupdate2003.pdf.

The World Factbook. (2005). Retrieved May 17, 2005, from the CIA Web site: www.cia.gov/cia/publications/factbook.

Zaller, J. R. (2003). A new standard of news quality: Burglar alarms for the monitorial citizen. *Political Communication, 20*, 109–130.

Zechowski, S. (n.d.). Public interest, convenience, and necessity. In H. Newcomb (Ed.), *The encyclopedia of television*. Retrieved March 10, 2005, from the Museum of Broadcast Communications Web site: www.museum.tv/archives/etv/P/htmlP/publicintere/publicintere.htm.

Zuckerman, E. (2003, August). *Global attention profiles—A working paper: First steps towards a quantitative approach to the study of media attention*. Cambridge, MA: Harvard Law School, Berkman Center for Internet and Society. Retrieved March 10, 2005, from the Global Attention Profiles Web site: http://h2odev.law.harvard.edu/ezuckerman/paper.pdf.

Chapter 3

Allen, C. (2001). *News is people: The rise of local TV news and the fall of news from New York*. Ames, IA: Blackwell.

Alliance for Better Campaigns. (2003, November). Broadcasters black out public affairs pro-
        gramming. *The Political Standard,* 6(4), Story 299. Retrieved March 9, 2005, from
        www.bettercampaigns.org/standard/display.php?StoryID=299.

Alliance for Better Campaigns. (2004, May). Network news coverage of '04 primaries falls
        short, study finds. *The Political Standard,* 7(2), Story 314. Retrieved March 9, 2005,
        from www.bettercampaigns.org/standard/display.php?StoryID=314.

Bagdikian, B. H. (2000). *The media monopoly* (6th ed.). Boston: Beacon.

Baker, C. E. (2002). *Media, markets, and democracy.* New York: Cambridge University Press.

Barringer, F. (2001, April 9). Minority staff members in journalism are fewer. *The New York
        Times,* p. C12.

Baum, M. A. (2005). Talking the vote: Why presidential candidates hit the talk show circuit.
        American Journal of Political Science, 49, 213–234.

Bode, K. (1992, March). Pull the plug: We have the power to say no, to abandon our photo-
        op addiction. *The Quill, 80,* 10–13.

Broder, D. (1992, March). It's time to replace sloganeering with simple shoe-leather reporting.
        The Quill, 80, 8–9.

Capella, J. N., & Jamieson, K. H. (1997). *Spiral of cynicism: The press and the public good.* New
        York: Oxford University Press.

Carter, Bill. (2005, December 24). Microsoft quits MSNBC TV, but Web partnership remains.
        The New York Times, p. C1.

Center for Media and Public Affairs. (2000). Campaign 2000 final: How TV news covered the
        general election campaign. *Media Monitor, 16*(6), 1–9.

Crouse, T. (1972). *The boys on the bus.* New York: Random House.

Dalton, R. J., Beck, P. A., & Huckfeldt, R. (1998). Partisan cues and the media: Information
        flows in the 1992 presidential election. *American Political Science Review, 92,* 111–126.

Editor and Publisher Yearbook. (2003). New York: Editor & Publisher Co.

Gilliam, F. D., Jr., & Iyengar, S. (2000). Prime suspects: The influence of local television news
        on the viewing public. *American Journal of Political Science, 44,* 560–573.

Gilliam, F. D., Jr., Iyengar, S., Simon, A., & Wright, O. (1996). Crime in black and white: The
        violent, scary world of local news. In S. Iyengar & R. Reeves (Eds.), *Do the media govern?
        Politicians, voters, and reporters in America* (pp. 287–295). Thousand Oaks, CA: Sage.

Hallin, D. C. (1986). *The uncensored war: The media and Vietnam.* Berkeley: University of Cal-
        ifornia Press.

Hamilton, J. T. (2003). *All the news that's fit to sell: How the market transforms information into
        news.* Princeton, NJ: Princeton University Press.

Hamlin, J. (2003, March 22). NBC declares victory in TV ratings battle. *San Francisco Chron-
        icle,* p. W2.

Hess, S. J. (2000, November 7). Dwindling TV coverage fell to new low. *USA Today,* p. 8A.

Hofstetter, C. R. (1976). *Bias in the news.* Columbus: Ohio State University Press.

Iyengar, S. (1991). *Is anyone responsible?* Chicago: University of Chicago Press.

Iyengar, S., Norpoth, H., & Hahn, K. (2004). Consumer demand for election news: The
        horserace sells. *Journal of Politics, 66,* 157–175.

Kalb, M. (2001). *One scandalous story: Clinton, Lewinsky, and thirteen days that tarnished
        American journalism.* New York: Free Press.

Kaplan, M., Goldstein, K., & Hale, M. (2005). *Local news coverage of the 2004 campaigns: An
        analysis of nightly broadcasts in 11 markets.* University of Southern California, Annenberg

School for Communication, Lear Center Local News Archive. Retrieved March 19, 2005, from www.localnewsarchive.org/pdf/LCLNAFinal2004.pdf.

Klite, P. K., Bardwell, R. A., & Salzman, J. (1997). Local TV news: Getting away with murder. *Harvard International Journal of Press/Politics, 2*, 102–112.

Kurtz, H. (1999). *Media meltdown.* Annual Carlos McClatchy Lecture, Stanford University.

Lichter, S. R. (2001). A plague on both parties: Substance and fairness in TV election news. *Harvard International Journal of Press/Politics, 6*, 8–30.

Lichter, S. R., Rothman, S., & Lichter, L. S. (1986). *The media elite: America's new powerbrokers.* Bethesda, MD: Adler & Adler.

McChesney, R. W. (1999). *Rich media, poor democracy: Communication politics in dubious times.* Urbana: University of Illinois Press.

Moisy, C. (1996). *The foreign news flow in the information age* (Discussion Paper D-23). Cambridge, MA: Joan Shorenstein Center on the Press, Politics, and Public Policy, Kennedy School of Government, Harvard University.

Niven, D. (2001). Bias in the news: Partisanship and negativity in coverage of presidents George Bush and Bill Clinton. *Harvard International Journal of Press/Politics, 6*, 31–46.

Norris, P. (1996). The restless searchlight: Network news framing of the post Cold-War world. *Political Communication, 12*, 357–370.

Noyes, R. (2004). *The liberal media: Every poll shows journalists are more liberal than the American public—and the public knows it.* Alexandria, VA: Media Research Center. Retrieved March 22, 2005, from the Media Research Center Web site: www.mrc.org/special reports/2004/pdf/liberal_media.pdf.

Patterson, T. E. (2000). *How soft news and critical journalism are shrinking the news audience and weakening democracy.* Cambridge, MA: Joan Shorenstein Center on the Press, Politics, and Public Policy, Kennedy School of Government, Harvard University.

Pew Research Center for the People and the Press. (2004, June 8). *News audiences increasingly politicized: Online news audiences larger, more diverse.* Retrieved July 26, 2005, from http://people-press.org/reports/display.php3?PageID=833.

Pew Research Center for the People and the Press. (2005, January 25). *The media: More voices, less credibility.* Retrieved July 26, 2005, from http://people-press.org/commentary/display.php3?AnalysisID=105.

Project for Excellence in Journalism. (2004). *The state of the news media, 2004: Network TV—Audience.* Retrieved March 17, 2005, from the State of the News Media Web site: www.stateofthenewsmedia.org/2004/narrative_networktv_audience.asp?cat=3&media=4.

Robinson, M. J., & Sheehan, M. A. (1983). *Over the wire and on TV.* New York: Russell Sage Foundation.

Rosen, J., & Taylor, P. (1992). *The new news v. the old news: The press and politics in the 1990s.* New York: Twentieth Century Fund Press.

Scarry, E. (1993). Watching and authorizing the Gulf War. In M. Gerber, J. Matlock, & R. L. Walkowitz (Eds.), *Media spectacles* (pp. 57–73). New York: Routledge.

Sigal, L. (1973). *Reporters and officials.* Lexington, MA: Heath.

Simon, A. F. (1997). Television news and international earthquake relief. *Journal of Communication, 47*(3), 82 93.

Slattery, K. L., & Hakanen, E. A. (1994). Sensationalism versus public affairs content of local TV news: Pennsylvania revisited. *Journal of Broadcasting and Electronic Media, 38*, 205–216.

Stevens, M. (n.d.). "History of newspapers," Colliers Encyclopedia. Retrieved August 17, 2004, from www.nyu.edu/classes/stephens/Collier's%20page.htm.

Vallone, R. P., Ross, L., & Lepper, M. R. (1985). The hostile media phenomenon: Biased perception and perceptions of media bias in coverage of the "Beirut Massacre." *Journal of Personality and Social Psychology, 49*, 577–585.

Weaver, D., & Wilhoit, G. C. (1986). *The American journalist: A portrait of US newspeople and their work*. Bloomington: Indiana University Press.

Wolinsky, L. C., Sparks, J., Funk, J., Rooney, E., Lyon, G., & Sweet, L. (1991). Refereeing the TV campaign. *Washington Journalism Review, 13*, 22–29.

Zaller, J. R. (2004, September). *The relationship between news quality and market share in network TV news*. Paper presented at the annual meeting of the American Political Science Association, Chicago.

Chapter 4

Althaus, S. (2003). When news norms collide, follow the lead: New evidence for press independence. *Political Communication, 20*, 381–414.

Althaus, S., Edy, J., Entman, R., & Phalen, P. (1996). Revising the indexing hypothesis: Officials, media and the Libya crisis. *Political Communication, 13*, 407–421.

Ansolabehere, S., Behr, R., & Iyengar, S. (1993). *The media game: American politics in the television age*. New York: Macmillan.

Arlen, M. J. (1969). *Living-room war: Writings about television*. New York: Viking.

Bennett, W. L. (1990). Toward a theory of press-state relations. *Journal of Communication, 40*, 103–125.

Braestrup, P. (1977). *Big story: How the American press and television reported and interpreted the crisis of Tet 1968 in Vietnam and Washington*. Boulder, CO: Westview.

CNN. (2004, April 29). *Worldwide terrorist attacks down in 2003*. Retrieved July 26, 2005, from www.cnn.com/2004/US/04/29/terror.report.

Conetta, C. (2003, October 20). *The wages of war: Iraqi combatant and noncombatant fatalities in the 2003 conflict* (Project on Defense Alternatives Research Monograph No. 8). Retrieved July 26, 2005, from the Project on Defense Alternatives Web site: www.comw.org/pda/0310rm8.html.

Conetta, C. (2004, February 18). *Disappearing the dead: Iraq, Afghanistan, and the idea of a "new warfare"* (Project on Defense Alternatives Research Monograph No. 9). Retrieved March 19, 2005, from the Project on Defense Alternatives Web site: www.comw.org/pda/0402rm9.html.

Cook, T. E. (1994). Domesticating a crisis: Washington newsbeats and the network news after the Iraq invasion of Kuwait. In W. L. Bennett and D. L. Paletz (Eds.), *Taken by storm: The media, public opinion, and U.S. foreign policy in the Gulf War* (pp. 105–130). Chicago: University of Chicago Press.

Cook, T. E. (1998). *Governing with the news: The news media as a political institution*. Chicago: University of Chicago Press.

Dorman, W. A. (1997). Press theory and journalistic practice: The case of the Gulf War. In S. Iyengar & R. Reeves (Eds.), *Do the media govern? Politicians, voters and reporters in America* (pp. 118–125). Thousand Oaks, CA: Sage.

Entman, R. M. (2004). *Projections of power: Framing news, public opinion, and U.S. foreign policy.* Chicago: University of Chicago Press.

Frenznick, D. A. (1992). The First Amendment on the battlefield: A constitutional analysis of press access to military operations in Grenada, Panama and the Persian Gulf. *Pacific Law Journal, 23,* 315–359.

"From the editors: The Times and Iraq." (2004, May 26). *The New York Times,* p. A10.

Gans, H. J. (1980). *Deciding what's news* (1st Vintage Books ed.). New York: Vintage Books/ Random House.

Hallin, D., Manoff, R., & Weddle, J. (1993). Sourcing patterns of national security reporters. *Journalism Quarterly, 70,* 753–766.

Karnow, S. (1997). *Vietnam: A history* (2nd ed.). New York: Penguin.

Krueger, A. B., & Laitin, D. (2004, May 17). Are we winning the war on terror? [Editorial]. *The Washington Post,* p. A21.

Lewis, G. N., & Postol, T. A. (1993). Video evidence on the effectiveness of Patriot during the 1991 Gulf War. *Science and Global Security, 4,* 1–63.

Lichty, L. W. (1982). Video versus print. *The Wilson Quarterly, 6,* 48–57.

Livingston, S., & Bennett, W. L. (2003). Gatekeeping, indexing, and live-event news: Is technology altering the construction of news? *Political Communication, 20,* 363–380.

Manheim, J. B. (1995). Managing images to influence US foreign policy. In S. Iyengar & R. Reeves (Eds.), *Do the media govern?* (pp. 379–390). Thousand Oaks, CA: Sage.

Mermin, J. (1999). *Debating war and peace: Media coverage of U.S. intervention in the post-Vietnam era.* Princeton, NJ: Princeton University Press.

Mueller, J. (1973). *War, presidents and public opinion.* New York: Wiley.

Rendall, S., & Broughel, T. (2003, May/June). Amplifying officials, squelching dissent: FAIR study finds democracy poorly served by war coverage. *Extra! The Magazine of FAIR.* Retrieved March 19, 2005, from the Fairness in Accuracy and Reporting Web site: www.fair.org/index.php?page=1145.

Sigal, L. (1973). *Reporters and officials.* Lexington, MA: Heath.

US Department of State. (2004, June 22). *Remarks on the release of the revised Patterns of Global Terrorism 2003 annual report.* Retrieved July 26, 2005, from www.state.gov/s/ct/ rls/rm/2004/33801.htm.

Zaller, J. R. (1994). Elite leadership of mass opinion: New evidence from the Gulf War. In W. L. Bennett and D. L. Paletz (Eds.), *Taken by storm: The media, public opinion, and U.S. foreign policy in the Gulf War* (pp. 186–209). Chicago: University of Chicago Press.

Zaller, J. R., & Chiu, D. (2000). Government's little helper: U.S. press coverage of foreign policy crises, 1946–1999. In B. L. Nacos, R. Y. Shapiro, & P. Isernia (Eds.), *Decisionmaking in a glass house: Mass media, public opinion, and American foreign policy in the 21st century* (pp. 61–84). Lanham, MD: Rowman & Littlefield.

Chapter 5

Bimber, B. (2003). *Information and American democracy: Technology in the evolution of political power.* New York: Cambridge University Press.

Bimber, B., & Davis, R. (2003). *Campaigning online: The Internet in U.S. elections.* New York: Oxford University Press.

Burns, N., Schlozman, K. L., & Verba, S. (2000). *What if politics weren't a man's game? Gender, citizen participation, and the lessons of politics.* Unpublished manuscript, Princeton University.

CyberJournalist.net. (2005, August 22). *Top news sites for June 2005.* Retrieved March 22, 2006, from the CyberJournalist.net Web site: www.cyberjournalist.net/news/002975.php.

Festinger, L. (1957). *A theory of cognitive dissonance.* Stanford, CA: Stanford University Press.

Iyengar, S. (1990). Shortcuts to political knowledge: Selective attention and the accessibility bias. In J. A. Ferejohn & J. H. Kuklinski (Eds.), *Information and the democratic process* (pp. 161–185). Champaign: University of Illinois Press.

Iyengar, S., Hahn, K. S., Krosnick, J. A., & Walker, J. (2005). *Selective exposure to campaign communication: The role of anticipated agreement, interest in politics, and issue salience.* Unpublished manuscript, Department of Communication, Stanford University.

Jost, J. T., Glaser, J., Sulloway, F., & Kruglanski, A. W. (2003). Exceptions that prove the rule: Using a theory of motivated social cognition to account for ideological incongruities and political anomalies (reply to Greenberg & Jonas). *Psychological Bulletin, 129,* 383–393.

Kraut, R., Lundmark, V., Patterson, M., Kiesler, S., Mukopadhyay, T., & Scherlis, W. (1998). The Internet paradox: A social technology that reduces social involvement and psychological well-being. *American Psychologist, 53,* 1017–1031.

Krosnick, J. A. (1990). Government policy and citizen passion: A study of issue publics in contemporary America. *Political Behavior, 12,* 59–92.

Lazarsfeld, P. F., Berelson, B. R., & Gaudet, H. (1948). *The people's choice.* New York: Columbia University Press.

McCloskey, H., & Chong, D. (1985). Similarities and differences between left-wing and right-wing radicals. *British Journal of Political Science, 15,* 329–363.

Nie, N. H., & Erbring, L. (2000). *Internet and society: A preliminary report.* Stanford, CA: Stanford Institute for the Quantitative Study of Society.

Nie, N. H., & Hillygus, D. S. (2002a). The impact of Internet use on sociability: Time-diary findings. *IT & Society, 1*(1), 1–20.

Nie, N. H., & Hillygus, D. S. (2002b). Where does Internet time come from?: A reconnaissance. *IT & Society, 1*(2), 1–20.

Pew Research Center for the People and the Press. (2005, June 26). *Public more critical of press, but goodwill persists.* Retrieved October 7, 2005, from http://people-press.org/reports/print.php3?PageID=972.

Price, V., & Zaller, J. (1993). Who gets the news? Alternative measures of news reception and their implications for research. *Public Opinion Quarterly, 57,* 133–164.

Rheingold, H. (2002). *Smart mobs: The next social revolution.* Cambridge, MA: Basic Books.

Robinson, J. P., Kestnbaum, M., Neustadtl, A., & Alvarez, A. (2002). Information technology and functional time displacement. *IT & Society, 1,* 21–36.

Samuel, A. (2004, October 18). Web plays U.S. election wild card. *The Toronto Star,* p. D1.

Schramm, W., & Carter, R. F. (1959). Effectiveness of a political telethon. *Public Opinion Quarterly, 23,* 121–126.

Sears, D. O., & Freedman, J. L. (1967). Selective exposure to information: A critical review. *Public Opinion Quarterly, 31,* 194–213.

Sunstein, C. (2001). *Republic.com.* Princeton, NJ: Princeton University Press.

Chapter 6

Allen, M., & Balz, D. (2004, May 5). Bush, in Ohio, paints Kerry as unreliable. *The Washington Post*, p. A8.

Ansolabehere, S., & Iyengar, S. (1995). *Going negative: How attack ads shrink and polarize the electorate*. New York: Free Press.

Ansolabehere, S., Snyder, J. M., & Ueda, M. (2004). Did firms profit from soft money? *Election Law Journal, 3*, 193–198.

Bartels, L. M. (1988). *Presidential primaries and the dynamics of public choice*. Princeton, NJ: Princeton University Press.

Buckley v. Valeo, 424 U.S. 1 (1976).

Farhi, P. (2004, June 16). Voters are harder to reach as media outlets multiply. *The Washington Post*, p. A1.

Hertzel, M. G., Martin, J. S., & Meschke, J. F. (2003, June). *Corporate soft money donations and firm performance*. Paper presented at the Financial Management Association International European Conference, Dublin, Ireland.

Iyengar, S., Lowenstein, D. H., & Masket, S. (2001). The stealth campaign: Experimental studies of slate mail in California. *Journal of Law and Politics, 17*, 295–332.

Iyengar, S., Valentino, N. A., Ansolabehere, S., & Simon, A. F. (1997). Running as a woman: Gender stereotyping in political campaigns. In P. Norris (Ed.), *Women, media, and politics* (pp. 77–98). Oxford, England: Oxford University Press.

Jacobson, G. C. (1997). *The politics of congressional elections* (4th ed.). New York: Longman.

Kaplan, M. (2003, August 13). Getting out the vote: The media and the circus. *San Francisco Chronicle*. Retrieved April 3, 2005, from www.learcenter.org/pdf/SFoped.pdf.

Kraus, S. (1962). *The great debates*. Bloomington: Indiana University Press.

Lau, R. R., Sigelman, L., Heldman, C., & Babbitt, P. (1999). The effects of negative political advertisements: A meta-analytic assessment. *American Political Science Review, 93*, 851–875.

Mayer, W. G. (2003). The basic dynamics of the contemporary nomination process: An expanded view. In W. G. Mayer (Ed.), *The making of the presidential candidates 2004* (pp. 83–132). Lanham, MD: Rowman & Littlefield.

Mutz, D. C. (1995). Effects of horse-race coverage on campaign coffers: Strategic contributing in presidential primaries. *Journal of Politics, 57*, 1015–1042.

Petrocik, J. R. (1996). Issue ownership in presidential elections, with a 1980 case study. *American Journal of Political Science, 40*, 825–850.

Pew Research Center for the People and the Press. (2004, November 11). *Voters liked campaign 2004, but too much "mud-slinging"—Moral values: How important?* Retrieved March 23, 2005, from the Pew Research Center for the People and the Press Web site: http://people-press.org/reports/display.php3?ReportID=233.

Popkin, S. L. (1994). *The reasoning voter: Communication and persuasion in presidential campaigns* (2nd ed.). Chicago: University of Chicago Press.

Rutenberg, J. (2004, July 18). Campaigns use TV preferences to find voters. *The New York Times*, p. A1.

Shaw, D. R. (2005). *The race to 270: The Electoral College and the campaign strategies of 2000 and 2004*. Chicago: University of Chicago Press.

Simon, A. F. (2002). *The winning message: Candidate behavior, campaign discourse, and democ-racy*. Cambridge, England: Cambridge University Press.

Wisconsin Public Television. (1998–2001). *Historical timeline*. Retrieved July 20, 2005, from PBS Online: www.pbs.org/30secondcandidate/timeline/years/1968.html.

Chapter 7

Ansolabehere, S., Behr, R., & Iyengar, S. (1991). Mass media and elections: An overview. *American Politics Quarterly, 19*, 109–139.

Ansolabehere, S., Behr, R., & Iyengar, S. (1993). *The media game: American politics in the tel-evision age*. New York: Macmillan.

Arnold, R. D. (2004). *Congress, the press, and political accountability*. Princeton, NJ: Princeton University Press.

Auletta, K. (2004, January 19). Fortress Bush: How the White House keeps the press under control. *The New Yorker*. Retrieved March 28, 2006, from the *New Yorker* web site: www.newyorker.com/fact/content/?040119fa_fact2.

Baum, M. A., & Kernell, S. (1999). Has cable ended the golden age of presidential television? *American Political Science Review, 93*, 99–114.

Behr, R. L., & Iyengar, S. (1985). Television news, real-world cues, and changes in the public agenda. *Public Opinion Quarterly, 49*, 38–57.

Billings, E. (2004, June 2). Democrats eye fall "contract." *Roll Call.*

Brace, P., & Hinckley, B. (1991). The structure of presidential approval: Constraints within and across presidencies. *Journal of Politics, 53*, 993–1017.

Brody, R. A. (1991). *Assessing the president: The media, elite opinion and public support*. Stan-ford, CA: Stanford University Press.

Bush expounds on theme of freedom: President says, "I firmly planted the flag of liberty." (2005, January 27). Transcript of the January 26, 2005, presidential press conference; retrieved July 20, 2005, from CNN's Web site: www.cnn.com/2005/ALLPOLITICS/01/26/bush.

Canes-Wrone, B. (2001). The president's legislative influence from public appeals. *American Journal of Political Science, 45*, 313–329.

Canes-Wrone, B., & de Marchi, S. (2002). Presidential approval and legislative success. *Jour-nal of Politics, 64*, 491–509.

Cohen, J. E. (2004). If the news is so bad, why are presidential polls so high? Presidents, the news media, and the mass public in an era of new media. *Presidential Studies Quar-terly, 34*, 493–515.

Cook, T. E. (1986). House members as newsmakers: The effects of televising Congress. *Leg-islative Studies Quarterly, 11*, 203–226.

Cook, T. E. (1989). *Making laws and making news: Media strategies in the US House of Repre-sentatives*. Washington, DC: Brookings Institution Press.

Cook, T. E. (1998). *Governing with the news: The news media as a political institution*. Chicago: University of Chicago Press.

Evans, D. (2004). *Greasing the wheels: Using pork barrel politics to build majority coalitions in Congress*. Cambridge, England: Cambridge University Press.

Fleisher, R., & Bond, J. (1988). Are there two presidencies? Yes, but only for Republicans. *The Journal of Politics, 50*, 747–767.

Grossman, M. B., & Kumar, M. J. (1981). *Portraying the president*. Baltimore: Johns Hopkins University Press.

Hart, R. P. (1987). *The sound of leadership: Presidential communication in the modern age*. Chicago: University of Chicago Press.

Hertsgaard, M. (1988). *On bended knee: The press and the Reagan presidency*. New York: Farrar, Straus, and Giroux.

Hess, S. J. (1991). *Live from Capitol Hill!* Washington, DC: Brookings Institution Press.

Hutchings, V. L. (1998). Issue salience and support for civil rights legislation among Southern Democrats. *Legislative Studies Quarterly, 23*, 521–544.

Kernell, S. (1986). *Going public: New strategies of presidential leadership*. Washington, DC: Congressional Quarterly Press.

Kornblut, A. (2005, February 19). Administration is warned about its publicity videos. *The New York Times*, p. A11.

Kumar, M. J. (2003a). The contemporary presidency: Communications operations in the White House of President George W. Bush: Making news on his terms. *Presidential Studies Quarterly, 33*, 366–393.

Kumar, M. J. (2003b). The White House and the press: News organizations as a presidential resource and as a source of pressure. *Presidential Studies Quarterly, 33*, 669–683.

Kumar, M. J. (2005). Presidential press conferences: The importance and evolution of an enduring forum. *Presidential Studies Quarterly, 35*, 166–192.

Maltese, J. A. (1994). *Spin control: The White House Office of Communications and the management of presidential news* (2nd ed.). Chapel Hill: University of North Carolina Press.

Mayhew, D. W. (1974). *Congress: The electoral connection*. New Haven, CT: Yale University Press.

Meinke, S. R., & Anderson, W. D. (2001). Influencing from impaired administrations: Presidents, White House scandal, and legislative leadership. *Legislative Studies Quarterly, 26*, 639–659.

Pertschuk, M. (2001). *Smoke in their eyes: Lessons in movement leadership from the tobacco wars*. Nashville, TN: Vanderbilt University Press.

Policy Agendas Project. (2004, September 8). *The New York Times index* [Electronic data set]. University of Washington, Center for American Politics and Public Policy. Retrieved October 1, 2004, from www.policyagendas.org/datasets/index.html.

Polsby, N. W. 1983. *Consequences of party reform*. New York: Oxford University Press.

Project for Excellence in Journalism. (2001, April 30). *The first 100 days: How Bush versus Clinton fared in the press*. Retrieved March 21, 2005, from the Project for Excellence in Journalism Web site: www.journalism.org/resources/research/reports/100days/default.asp.

Rivers, D., & Rose, N. L. (1985). Passing the president's program: Public opinion and presidential influence in Congress. *American Journal of Political Science, 29*, 183–196.

Rohde, D. W., & Simon, D. M. (1985). Presidential vetoes and congressional response: A study of institutional conflict. *American Journal of Political Science, 29*, 397–427.

Speakes, L. (with Pack, R.). (1988). *Speaking out: The Reagan presidency from inside the White House*. New York: Scribner.

Tenpas, K. D. (2004, June 29). *President Bush's 2004 campaign travel*. Washington, DC: Brookings Institution. Retrieved March 22, 2005, from the Brookings Institution Web site: www.brookings.edu/dybdocroot/views/papers/tenpas/20040629.pdf.

The Thomas nomination: Hearing captures big TV audience. (1991, October 13). *The New York Times*, p. A28.

Tulis, J. K. (1987). *The rhetorical presidency*. Chatham, NJ: Chatham House.

Vinson, D. C. (2003). *Through local eyes: Local media coverage of congress and its members*. Cresskill, NJ: Hampton.

Wildavsky, A. (1991). The two presidencies. In S. Shull (Ed.), *The two presidencies: A quarter century assessment* (pp. 11–25). Chicago: Nelson-Hall.

Wood, B. D. (2004). Presidential rhetoric and economic leadership. *Presidential Studies Quarterly, 34,* 573–606.

Chapter 8

Abadie, A., & Imbens, G. (2002). *Simple and bias-corrected matching estimators* (NBER Technical Working Paper No. 283). Cambridge, MA: National Bureau of Economic Research.

Ansolabehere, S., Behr, R., & Iyengar, S. (1993). *The media game: American politics in the television age*. New York: Macmillan.

Ansolabehere, S., & Iyengar, S. (1995). *Going negative: How attack ads shrink and polarize the electorate*. New York: Free Press.

Ansolabehere, S., & Iyengar, S. (1998). *Message forgotten: Misreporting in surveys and the bias towards minimal effects*. Unpublished manuscript, Department of Political Science, Massachusetts Institute of Technology.

Ansolabehere, S., Iyengar, S., & Simon, A. (1999). Replicating experiments using aggregate and survey data: The case of negative advertising and turnout. *American Political Science Review, 93,* 901–910.

Bartels, L. M. (1988). *Presidential primaries and the dynamics of public choice*. Princeton, NJ: Princeton University Press.

Bartels, L. M. (1993). Messages delivered: The political impact of media exposure. *American Political Science Review, 87,* 267–285.

Bartels, L. M. (1997). *How campaigns matter*. Unpublished manuscript, Princeton University.

Baum, M. A. (2002). Sex, lies and war: How soft news brings foreign policy to the inattentive public. *American Political Science Review, 96,* 91–109.

Baumgartner, F. R., & Jones, B. D. (1993). *Agendas and instability in American politics*. Chicago: University of Chicago Press.

Behr, R. L., & Iyengar, S. (1985). Television news, real-world cues, and changes in the public agenda. *Public Opinion Quarterly, 49,* 38–57.

Berelson, B., Lazarsfeld, P. F., & McPhee, W. (1954). *Voting*. Chicago: University of Chicago Press.

Boyer, P. (1986). Famine in Africa: The TV accident that exploded. In M. Emery & T. Smythe (Eds.), *Readings in mass communications*. Dubuque, IA: William C. Brown.

Bradburn, N., Rips, L. J., & and Shevell, S. K. (1987). Answering autobiographical questions: The impact of memory and inference on surveys. *Science, 236,* 157–161.

Cappella, J., & Jamieson, K. H. (1997). *Spiral of cynicism: The press and the public good*. New York: Oxford University Press.

Cohen, B. E. (1963). *The press and foreign policy*. Princeton, NJ: Princeton University Press.

Converse, P. (1962). Information flow and the stability of partisan attitudes. *Public Opinion Quarterly, 26*, 578–599.

Dearing, J. W., & Rogers, E. M. (1996). *Agenda-setting*. Thousand Oaks, CA: Sage.

Delli Carpini, M. X., & Keeter, S. (1996). *What Americans know about politics and why it matters*. New Haven, CT: Yale University Press.

Dimock, M. A., & Popkin, S. L. (1997). Political knowledge in comparative perspective. In S. Iyengar & R. Reeves (Eds.), *Do the media govern? Politicians, voters and reporters in America* (pp. 217–224). Thousand Oaks, CA: Sage.

Druckman, J. N. (2001a). The implications of framing effects for citizen competence. *Political Behavior, 23*, 225–256.

Druckman, J. N. (2001b). On the limits of framing effects: Who can frame? *The Journal of Politics, 63*, 1041–1066.

Druckman, J. N. (2004). Priming the vote: Campaign effects in a U.S. Senate election. *Political Psychology, 25*, 577–594.

Druckman, J. N., & Holmes, J. W. (2004). Does presidential rhetoric matter? Priming and presidential approval. *Presidential Studies Quarterly, 34*, 755–778.

Druckman, J. N., & Nelson, K R. (2003). Framing and deliberation: How citizens' conversations limit elite influence. *American Journal of Political Science, 47*, 729–745.

Entman, R. M., & Rojecki, A. (2000). *The black image in the white mind: Media and race in America*. Chicago: University of Chicago Press.

Erbring, L., Goldenberg, E. N., & Miller, A. H. (1980). Front-page news and real-world cues: A new look at agenda-setting by the media. *American Journal of Political Science, 24*, 16–49.

Fiorina, M. P. (1976). The voting decision: Instrumental and expressive aspects. *Journal of Politics, 38*, 390–413.

Gilliam, F. D., Jr., & Iyengar, S. (2000). Prime suspects: The influence of local television news on the viewing public. *American Journal of Political Science, 44*, 560–573.

Haider-Markel, D. P., & Joslyn, M. R. (2001). Gun policy, opinion, tragedy, and blame attribution: The conditional influence of issue frames. *The Journal of Politics, 63*, 520–543.

Hearold, S. (1986). A synthesis of 1043 effects of television on social behavior. In G. Comstock (Ed.), *Public communication and behavior* (Vol. 1, pp. 65–133). New York: Academic Press.

Hovland, C. L. (1959). Reconciling conflicting results derived from experimental and survey studies of attitude change. *The American Psychologist, 14*, 8–17.

Hovland, C. I., Janis, I. L., & Kelley, H. H. (1953). *Communications and persuasion: Psychological studies in opinion change*. New Haven, CT: Yale University Press.

Hovland, C. I., Lumsdaine, A. A., & Sheffield, F. D. (1949). A baseline for measurement of percentage change. In C. I. Hovland, A. A. Lumsdaine, & F. D. Sheffield (Eds.), *Experiments on Mass Communication* (pp. 284–289). Princeton, NJ: Princeton University Press.

Imbens, G. W. (2003). *Non-parametric estimation of average treatment effects under exogeneity: A review* (NBER Technical Working Paper No. 0294). Cambridge, MA: National Bureau of Economic Research.

Iyengar, S. (1991). *Is anyone responsible?* Chicago: University of Chicago Press.

Iyengar, S., & Jackman, S. (2003, August). *Can information technology energize voters? Experimental evidence from the 2000 and 2002 campaigns*. Paper presented at the annual meeting of the American Political Science Association, Philadelphia.

Iyengar, S., & Kinder, D. R. (1987). *News that matters: Television and American opinion*. Chicago: University of Chicago Press.

Iyengar, S., Luskin, R., & Fishkin, J. (2003, August). *Facilitating informed public opinion: Evidence from face-to-face and online Deliberative Polls*. Paper presented at the annual meeting of the American Political Science Association, Philadelphia.

Iyengar, S., & Simon, A. F. (1993). News coverage of the Gulf War and public opinion: A study of agenda-setting, priming, and framing. *Communication Research, 20*, 365–383.

Iyengar, S., & Simon, A. F. (2000). New perspectives and evidence on political communication and campaign effects. *Annual Review of Psychology, 51*, 149–169.

Iyengar, S., & Valentino, N. A. (2000). Who says what? Source credibility as a mediator of campaign advertising. In A. Lupia, M. D. McCubbins, & S. L. Popkin (Eds.), *Elements of reason: Cognition, choice and the bounds of rationality* (pp. 108–129). Cambridge, England: Cambridge University Press.

Iyengar, S., Valentino, N. A., Ansolabehere, S., & Simon, A. F. (1997). Running as a woman: Gender stereotyping in political campaigns. In P. Norris (Ed.), *Women, media, and politics* (pp. 77–98). Oxford, England: Oxford University Press.

Johnston, R., Blais, A., Brady, H. E., & Crete, J. (1992). *Letting the people decide: Dynamics of a Canadian election*. Stanford, CA: Stanford University Press

Johnston, R., Hagen, M. G., & Jamieson, K. H. (2004). *The 2000 presidential election and the foundations of party politics*. New York: Cambridge University Press.

Kahn, K. F. (1994). The distorted mirror: Press coverage of women candidates for statewide office. *Journal of Politics, 56*, 154–174.

Kahn, K. F., & Gordon, A. (1997). How women campaign for the U.S. Senate. In P. Norris (Ed..), *Women, media, and politics* (pp. 59–76). New York: Oxford University Press.

Klapper, J. T. (1960). *The effects of mass communications*. New York: Free Press.

Krosnick, J. A., & Brannon, L. A. (1993). The impact of the Gulf War on the ingredients of presidential evaluations: Multidimensional effects of political involvement. *American Political Science Review, 87*, 963–978.

Krosnick, J. A., & Kinder, D. R. (1990). Altering the foundations of support for the president through priming. *American Political Science Review, 84*, 497–512.

Krosnick, J. A., Lacy, D., & Lowe, L. (1998, July). *When is environmental damage Americans' most important problem? A test of agenda-setting vs. the issue-attention cycle*. Paper presented at the annual meeting of the International Society of Political Psychology, Montreal, Canada.

Kull, S., Ramsay, C., & Lewis, E. (2003). Misperceptions, the media, and the Iraq war. *Political Science Quarterly, 118*, 569–598.

Kull, S., Ramsay, C., Subias, S., Lewis, E., & Warf, P. (2003, October 2). *Misperceptions, the media and the Iraq war*. Washington, DC: Program on International Policy Attitudes (PIPA). Retrieved March 21, 2005, from the PIPA Web site: www.pipa.org/Online Reports/Iraq/Media_10_02_03_Report.pdf.

Kull, S., Ramsay, C., Subias, S., Weber, S., & Lewis, E. (2004, October 21). *The separate realities of Bush and Kerry supporters*. Washington, DC: Program on International Policy Attitudes (PIPA). Retrieved March 21, 2005, from the PIPA Web site: www.pipa.org/OnlineReports/Iraq/IraqRealities_Oct04/IraqRealities%20Oct04%20rpt.pdf.

Lazarsfeld, P. F., Berelson, B. R., & Gaudet, H. (1948). *The people's choice*. New York: Columbia University Press.

Lippmann, W. (1922). *Public opinion*. New York: Harcourt Brace.

Lippmann, W. (1925). *The phantom public*. New York: Macmillan.

Lodge, M., McGraw, K., & Stroh, P. (1989). An impression-driven model of candidate evaluation. *American Political Science Review, 83*, 399–419.

Lupia, A., & McCubbins, M. D. (1998). *The democratic dilemma: Can citizens learn what they need to know?* New York: Cambridge University Press.

Luskin, R. L., Iyengar S., & Fishkin, J. (2005, August). *The deliberative citizen*. Paper presented at the annual meeting of the American Political Science Association, Washington, DC.

MacKuen, M. B. (1981). *More than news: Media power in public affairs*. Beverly Hills, CA: Sage.

McCombs, M. C., & Shaw, D. L. (1972). The agenda-setting function of mass media. *Public Opinion Quarterly, 36*, 176–187.

McGuire, W. J. (1999). *Constructing social psychology: Creative and critical processes*. New York: Cambridge University Press.

Mendelberg, T. (1997). Executing Hortons: Racial crime in the 1988 presidential campaign. *Public Opinion Quarterly, 61*, 134–157.

Mendelsohn, N. (1996). The media and interpersonal communications: The priming of issues, leaders, and party identification. *The Journal of Politics, 58*, 112–125.

Miller, J. M., & Krosnick, J. A. (2000). News media impact on the ingredients of presidential evaluations: Politically knowledgeable citizens are guided by a trusted source. *American Journal of Political Science, 44*, 295–309.

Mondak, J. J. (1995). Newspapers and political awareness. *American Journal of Political Science, 39*, 513–527.

Mutz, D. C. (1997). Mechanisms of momentum: Does thinking make it so? *Journal of Politics, 59*, 104–125.

Nelson, T. E., & Kinder, D. R. (1996). Issue frames and group-centrism in American public opinion. *Journal of Politics, 58*, 1055–1078.

Nelson, T. E., Oxley, Z. M., & Clawson, R. A. (1997). Toward a psychology of framing effects. *Political Behavior, 19*, 221–246.

Patterson, T. E., & McClure, R. D. (1976). *The unseeing eye: The myth of television power in national politics*. New York: Putnam.

Pew Research Center for the People and the Press. (2004, January 11). *Cable and Internet loom large in fragmented political news universe*. Retrieved March 23, 2005, from the Pew Research Center for the People and the Press Web site: http://people-press.org/reports/display.php3?ReportID=200.

Pierce, J. C., & Lovrich, N. P. (1982). Survey measurement of political participation: Selective effects of recall in petition signing. *Social Science Quarterly, 63*, 164–171.

Policy Agendas Project. (2004). *The New York Times index and congressional hearings* [Electronic data sets]. University of Washington, Center for American Politics and Public Policy. Retrieved from www.policyagendas.org/datasets/index.html#congressHear.

Popkin, S. L. (1994). *The reasoning voter: Communication and persuasion in presidential campaigns* (2nd ed.). Chicago: University of Chicago Press.

Price, V., & Na, E. (2000, May). *Citizen deliberation and resistance to framing effects*. Paper presented at the annual meeting of the American Association for Public Opinion Research, Portland, OR.

Price, V., & Zaller, J. (1993). Who gets the news? Alternative measures of news reception and their implications for research. *Public Opinion Quarterly, 57*, 133–164.

Priest, D., & Pincus, W. (2004, October 7). U.S. "almost all wrong" on weapons: Report on Iraq contradicts Bush administration claims. *The Washington Post*, p. A1.

Prior, M. (2003). Any good news in soft news? The impact of soft news preference on political knowledge. *Political Communication, 20*, 149–171.

Program on International Policy Attitudes. (2004). Online reports on Iraq. Available from www.pipa.org/online_reports.html.

Rendall, S., & Broughel, T. (2003, May/June). Amplifying officials, squelching dissent: FAIR study finds democracy poorly served by war coverage. *Extra! The Magazine of FAIR.* Retrieved March 19, 2005, from the Fairness in Accuracy and Reporting Web site: www.fair.org/index.php?page=1145.

Rosenbaum, P. R., & Rubin, B. D. (1983). The central role of the propensity score in observational studies for causal effects. *Biometrika, 70*, 41–55.

Sears, D. O. (1986). College sophomores in the laboratory: Influences of a narrow data base on the social psychology of human nature. *Journal of Personality and Social Psychology, 51*, 515–530.

Shea, C. (1999, November 22). Is voter ignorance killing democracy? *Salon.* Retrieved December 2, 2004, from www.salon.com/books/it/1999/11/22/voter/print.html.

Smith, T. W. (1987). That which we call welfare by any other name would smell sweeter: An analysis of the impact of question wording on response patterns. *Public Opinion Quarterly, 51*, 75–83.

Sniderman, P., Brody, R., & Tetlock, P. E. (1991). The role of heuristics in political reasoning: A theory sketch. In P. Sniderman, R. Brody, & P. E. Tetlock (Eds.), *Reasoning and choice: Explorations in political psychology* (pp. 14–30). Cambridge, England: Cambridge University Press.

Tversky, A., & Kahneman, D. (1981). The framing of decisions and the psychology of choice. *Science, 211*, 453–458.

Vavreck, L. (2004). *The dangers of self-reports of political behaviour.* Unpublished manuscript, University of California, Los Angeles.

Wattenberg, M. P., & Brians, C. L. (1999). Negative campaign advertising: Mobilizer or demobilizer? *American Political Science Review, 93*, 891–899.

Wittman, D. A. (1989). Why democracies produce efficient results. *Journal of Political Economy, 97*, 1395–1424.

Wood, D. B. (1999). Who influences whom? The president, congress, and the media. *American Political Science Review, 93*, 327–344.

Zaller, J. R. (1992). *The nature and origins of mass opinion.* New York: Cambridge University Press.

Chapter 9

Aldrich, J. H. (1980). *Before the convention.* Chicago: University of Chicago Press.

Althaus, S., Nardulli, P., & Shaw, D. (2002). Candidate appearances in presidential elections, 1972–2000. *Political Communication, 19*, 49–72.

American Research Group. (2003–2004). *The New Hampshire poll.* Retrieved August 5, 2005, from the American Research Group Web site: www.americanresearchgroup.com/nhpoll/demtrack.

Ansolabehere, S., & Iyengar, S. (1995). *Going negative: How attack ads shrink and polarize the electorate*. New York: Free Press.

Bartels, L. M. (2004). Lots of opinion, not much action: The study of mass politics from Key to Kinder. In E. D. Mansfield & R. Sisson (Eds.), *The evolution of political knowledge: Theory and inquiry in American politics* (pp. 153–157). Columbus: Ohio State University Press.

Bartels, L. M., & Zaller, J. (2001). Presidential vote models: A recount. *PS, 33*, 9–20.

Berelson, B., Lazarsfeld, P. F., & McPhee, W. (1954). *Voting*. Chicago: University of Chicago Press.

Best, S. J., & Hubbard, C. (1999). Maximizing minimal effects: The impact of early primary season debates on voter preferences. *American Politics Quarterly, 27*, 450–467.

Brady, H. E., & Johnston, R. (1987). What's the primary message: Horse race or issue journalism? In G. R. Orren & N. W. Polsby (Eds.), *Media and momentum: The New Hampshire primary and nomination politics* (pp. 127–186). Chatham, NJ: Chatham House.

Buchanan, B. (1991). *Electing a president: The Markle Commission research on Campaign '88*. Austin: University of Texas Press.

Campbell, A. (1960). Surge and decline: A study of electoral change. *Public Opinion Quarterly, 24*, 397–418.

Campbell, J. E. (1987). A revised theory of surge and decline. *American Journal of Political Science, 31*, 965–979.

Campbell, J. E. (2004). Introduction—The 2004 presidential election forecasts. *PS: Political Science and Politics, 37*, 733–735.

Druckman, J. (2003). The power of television images: The first Kennedy-Nixon debate revisited. *Journal of Politics, 65*, 559–571.

Erikson, R. S., MacKuen, M. B., & Stimson, J. A. (2002). *The macro polity*. New York: Cambridge University Press.

Fair, R. (1978). The effect of economic events on votes for the president. *The Review of Economic and Statistics, 60*, 159–173.

Fair, R. (2002). *Predicting presidential elections and other things*. Stanford, CA: Stanford University Press.

Fiorina, M. P. (1981). *Retrospective voting in American national elections*. New Haven, CT: Yale University Press.

Garand, J. C., & Campbell, J. E. (Eds.). (1996). Forecasting the 1996 elections [Special issue]. *American Politics Quarterly, 24*(4).

Geer, J. G. (2004, September). *The rise of negativity in presidential campaigns: Causes and consequences*. Paper presented at the annual meeting of the American Political Science Association, Chicago.

Gelman, A., & King, G. (1993). Why are American presidential election polls so variable when votes are so predictable? *British Journal of Political Science, 23*, 409–451.

Gerber, A. S., & Green, D. P. (2000). The effects of canvassing, telephone calls, and direct mail on voter turnout: A field experiment. *American Political Science Review, 94*, 653–663.

Gerber, A. S., Green, D. P., & Nickerson, D. W. (2002, May 7). *Getting out the youth vote in local elections: Results from six door-to-door canvassing experiments*. Unpublished report, Center for Information and Research on Civic Learning and Engagement, University of Maryland, College Park.

Green, D., Palmquist, B., & Schickler, E. (2002). *Partisan hearts and minds: Political parties and the social identities of voters*. New Haven, CT: Yale University Press.

Hauck, R. J.-P. (Ed.). (2001). Election 2000 special—Al Gore and George Bush's not-so-excellent adventure [Special issue]. *PS: Political Science and Politics, 34*(1).

Houston, D. A., Doan, K. A., & Roskos-Ewoldsen, D. R. (1999). Negative political advertising and choice conflict. *Journal of Experimental Psychology: Applied, 5,* 3–16.

Iyengar, S., & Jackman, S. (2003, November). *Technology and politics: Incentives for youth participation*. Paper presented at the International Conference on Civic Education Research, New Orleans, LA.

Iyengar, S., Luskin, R., & Fishkin, J. (2004, April). *Deliberative public opinion in presidential primaries: Evidence from the online Deliberative Poll*. Paper presented at the Voice and Citizenship: Rethinking Theory and Practice in Political Communication Conference, University of Washington, Department of Communication, Seattle.

Iyengar, S., & Petrocik, J. R. (2000). Basic rule voting: The impact of campaigns on party- and approval-based voting. In J. Thurber, C. J. Nelson, & D. A. Dulio (Eds.), *Crowded airwaves: Campaign advertising in elections* (pp. 113–148). Washington, DC: Brookings Institution Press.

Johnston, R., Hagen, M. G., & Jamieson, K. H. (2004). *The 2000 presidential election and the foundations of party politics*. New York: Cambridge University Press.

Keith, B. E., Magleby, D. B., Nelson, C. J., Orr, E., Westlye, M. C., & Wolfinger, R. E. (1992). *The myth of the independent voter*. Berkeley: University of California Press.

Kinder, D. R. (1998). Opinion and action in the realm of politics. In D. T. Gilbert, S. T. Fiske, & G. Lindzay (Eds.), *Handbook of social psychology* (Vol. 2, pp. 778–867). Boston: McGraw-Hill.

Klapper, J. T. (1960). *The effects of mass communications*. New York: Free Press.

Lau, R. R., Sigelman, L., Heldman, C., & Babbitt, P. (1999). The effects of negative political advertisements: A meta-analytic assessment. *American Political Science Review, 93,* 851–875.

Lazarsfeld, P. F., Berelson, B. R., & Gaudet, H. (1948). *The people's choice*. New York: Columbia University Press.

Mayer, W. G. (2003). The basic dynamics of the contemporary nomination process: An expanded view. In W. G. Mayer (Ed.), *The making of the presidential candidates 2004* (pp. 83–132). Lanham, MD: Rowman & Littlefield.

Mayer, W. G., & Busch, A. E. (2003). *The front-loading problem in presidential nominations*. Washington, DC: Brookings Institution Press.

McDonald, M. P., & Popkin, S. L. (2001). The myth of the vanishing voter. *American Political Science Review, 95,* 963–974.

The National Election Studies (www.electionstudies.org). (2000). The 2000 National Election Study [Data set]. Ann Arbor, MI: University of Michigan, Center for Political Studies [producer and distributor].

Niemi, R. G., & Jennings, M. K. (1991). Issues and inheritance in the study of party identification. *American Journal of Political Science, 35,* 970–988.

Perloff, R. M. (1998). *Political communication: Politics, press, and public in America*. Mahwah, NJ: Erlbaum.

Petrocik, J. R. (1996). Issue ownership in presidential elections, with a 1980 case study. *American Journal of Political Science, 40,* 825–850.

Polling Report, Inc. (n.d.) *White House 2004: Democratic nomination*. Retrieved August 5, 2005, from the Polling Report Web site: www.pollingreport.com/wh04dem.htm.

Popkin, S. L. (1994). *The reasoning voter: Communication and persuasion in presidential campaigns* (2nd ed.). Chicago: University of Chicago Press.

Robinson, M. J., & Sheehan, M. A. (1983). *Over the wire and on TV*. New York: Russell Sage Foundation.

Sears, D. O., & Chaffee, S. (1979). Uses and effects of the 1976 debates: An overview of empirical studies. In Sidney Kraus (Ed.), *The great debates: Carter vs. Ford, 1976* (pp. 223–261). Bloomington: Indiana University Press.

Shaw, D. R. (1999). The effect of TV ads and candidate appearances on statewide presidential votes, 1988–1996. *American Political Science Review, 93*, 345–361.

Shaw, D. R. (2004). Door-to-door with the GOP. *Hoover's Digest, 4*. Retrieved March 1, 2005, from www.hooverdigest.org/044/shaw.html.

Shaw, D. R. (2005). *A simple game: Uncovering campaign strategies and effects in the 2000 and 2004 presidential elections*. Chicago: University of Chicago Press.

Tufte, E. R. (1978). *Political control of the economy*. Princeton, NJ: Princeton University Press.

Wattenberg, M. P., & Brians, C. L. (1999). Negative campaign advertising: Mobilizer or demobilizer? *American Political Science Review, 93*, 891–899.

Chapter 10

Ansolabehere, S., Behr, R., & Iyengar, S. (1993). *The media game: American politics in the television age*. New York: Macmillan.

Apple, R. W. (1990, September 20). Confrontation in the Gulf: Criticism of US Gulf policy growing louder in Congress. *The New York Times*, p. A10.

Beck, N., & Katz, J. N. (1995). What to do (and not to do) with time-series and cross-section data. *American Political Science Review, 89*, 634–647.

Brace, P., & Hinckley, B. (1991). The structure of presidential approval: Constraints within and across presidencies. *Journal of Politics, 53*, 993–1017.

Brody, R. A. (1991). *Assessing the president: The media, elite opinion and public support*. Stanford, CA: Stanford University Press.

Canes-Wrone, B., Herron, M. C., & Shotts, K. W. (2001). Leadership and pandering: A theory of executive policymaking. *American Journal of Political Science, 45*, 532–550.

Canes-Wrone, B., & Shotts, K. W. (2004). The conditional nature of presidential responsiveness to public opinion. *American Journal of Political Science, 48*, 690–706.

Edwards, G. C., III. (2003). *On deaf ears: The limits of the bully pulpit*. New Haven, CT: Yale University Press.

Entman, R. M. (2004). *Projections of power: Framing news, public opinion, and U.S. foreign policy*. Chicago: University of Chicago Press.

Entman, R. M., & Page, B. I. (1994). The news before the storm: The Iraq war debate and the limits to media independence. In W. L. Bennett & D. L. Paletz (Eds.), *Taken by storm: The media, public opinion, and U.S. foreign policy in the Gulf War* (pp. 82–101). Chicago: University of Chicago Press.

Gronke, P., & Brehm, J. (2002). History, heterogeneity, and presidential approval: A modified ARCH approach. *Electoral Studies, 21*, 425–452.

Gubala, S. M., & Dietz, N. (2002, April). *The presidential-economic dance: Are "new" economic variables "in rhythm" with traditional economic indicators and presidential approval?* Paper presented at the annual meeting of the Midwest Political Science Association, Chicago.

Hetherington, M. J., & Nelson, M. (2003). Anatomy of a rally effect: George W. Bush and the war on terrorism. *PS: Political Science and Politics, 36,* 37–42.

Hibbs, D. A., Rivers, D., & Vasilatos, N. (1982). On the demand for economic outcomes: Macroeconomic performance and mass political support in the United States, Great Britain, and Germany. *Journal of Politics, 43,* 426–462.

Huffington, A. (2000). *How to overthrow the government.* New York: ReganBooks.

Iyengar, S., & Kinder, D. R. (1987). *News that matters: Television and American opinion.* Chicago: University of Chicago Press.

Justice, G. (2005, February 21). A new battle for advisors to Swift Vets. *The New York Times,* p. A1.

Kernell, S. (1978). Explaining presidential popularity. *American Political Science Review, 72,* 506–522.

Kernell, S. (1986). *Going public: New strategies of presidential leadership.* Washington, DC: Congressional Quarterly Press.

Lemann, N. (1996, October 7). California here we come . . . Will the Golden State's ugly rumble over affirmative action spread to the rest of the nation? *Time, 148,* 44.

Lowi, T. J. (1981). *Incomplete conquest: Governing America.* New York: Holt, Rinehart, & Winston.

Lowi, T. J. (1985). *The personal president: Power invested, promise unfulfilled.* Ithaca, NY: Cornell University Press.

McCleary, R., & Hay, R. A., Jr. (1980). *Applied time series analysis for the social sciences.* Beverly Hills, CA: Sage.

Mickolus, E. F., Sandler, T., Murdock, J. M., & P. A. Flemming. (2003, July 27). *International terrorism: Attributes of terrorist events 1968–2002.* Unpublished data codebook, available at www.columbia.edu/cgi-bin/eds/pre.pl?C1385-3+doc+iterate3.cbk.

Mueller, J. (1973). *War, presidents and public opinion.* New York: Wiley.

Neustadt, R. (1960). *Presidential power: The politics of leadership.* New York: Wiley.

Ostrom, C. W., & Simon, D. M. (1985). Promise and performance: A dynamic model of presidential popularity. *American Political Science Review, 79,* 334–358.

Ostrom, C. W., & Simon, D. M. (1989). The man in the Teflon suit? The environmental connection, political drama, and popular support in the Reagan presidency. *Public Opinion Quarterly, 53,* 353–387.

Ragsdale, L. (1984). The politics of presidential speechmaking, 1949–1980. *American Political Science Review, 78,* 971–984.

Shapiro, R. Y., & Jacobs, L. R. (2000). Who leads and who follows? U.S. presidents, public opinion, and foreign policy. In B. L. Nacos, R. Y. Shapiro, & P. Isernia (Eds.), *Decisionmaking in a glass house: Mass media, public opinion, and American and European foreign policy in the 21st century* (pp. 223–245). Lanham, MD: Rowman & Littlefield.

Stimson, J. A. (1976). Public support for the American president: A cyclical model. *Public Opinion Quarterly, 40,* 1–21.

Tulis, J. K. (1987). *The rhetorical presidency.* Chatham, NJ: Chatham House.

Zaller, J. R. (1991). Information, values, and opinions. *American Political Science Review, 85,* 1215–1237.

Zaller, J. R. (1998). Monica Lewinsky's contribution to political science. *PS: Political Science and Politics, 31,* 182–189.

Zaller, J. R., & Chiu, D. (2000). Government's little helper: U.S. press coverage of foreign policy crises, 1946–1999. In B. L. Nacos, R. Y. Shapiro, & P. Isernia (Eds.), *Decision-making in a glass house: Mass media, public opinion, and American foreign policy in the 21st century* (pp. 61–84). Lanham, MD: Rowman & Littlefield.

Chapter 11

Althaus, S. (1998). Information effects in collective preferences. *American Political Science Review, 92,* 545–558.

Ansolabehere, S., Lessem, R., & Snyder, J. M. (in press). *The orientation of newspaper endorsements in US elections, 1940–2002. Quarterly Journal of Political Science.*

Barta, C. (1996). How fair is election coverage? *Issues of Democracy (Free and Fair Elections issue), 1*(13), 12–16. Retrieved March 25, 2005, from http://usinfo.state.gov/journals/itdhr/0996/ijde/ijde0996.pdf.

Bartels, L. M. (1996). Uninformed voters: Information effects in presidential elections. *American Journal of Political Science, 40,* 194–230.

Bartels, L. M. (2005). Homer gets a tax cut: Inequality and public policy in the American mind. *Perspectives on Politics, 3*(1), 15–31.

Burnham, W. D. (1982). *The current crisis in American politics.* Oxford, England: Oxford University Press.

Chambers, W. N., & Burnham, W. D. (Eds.). (1967). *The American party systems: Stages of political development.* New York: Oxford University Press.

Delli Carpini, M. X., & Keeter, S. (1996). *What Americans know about politics and why it matters.* New Haven, CT: Yale University Press.

Domanick, J. (2004). *Cruel justice.* Berkeley: University of California Press.

Federal Communications Commission. (1996, June 25). *En banc hearing of the commissioners on network proposals to provide time to presidential candidates.* Retrieved September 10, 2005, from www.fcc.gov/Reports/eb062596.txt.

Fishkin, J. (1995). *The voice of the people.* New Haven, CT: Yale University Press.

Green, D. P., & Gerber, A. S. (2001). *Getting out the youth vote: Results from randomized field experiments.* Unpublished report to the Pew Charitable Trusts, Institution for Social and Policy Studies.

Hamilton, J. T. (2003). *All the news that's fit to sell: How the market transforms information into news.* Princeton, NJ: Princeton University Press.

Iyengar, S., & Jackman, S. (2003a, August). *Can information technology energize voters? Experimental evidence from the 2000 and 2002 campaigns.* Paper presented at the annual meeting of the American Political Science Association, Philadelphia.

Iyengar, S., & Jackman, S. (2003b, November). *Technology and politics: Incentives for youth participation.* Paper presented at the International Conference on Civic Education Research, New Orleans, LA.

Iyengar, S., Luskin, R., & Fishkin, J. (2003, August). *Facilitating informed public opinion: Evidence from face-to-face and online Deliberative Polls.* Paper presented at the annual meeting of the American Political Science Association, Philadelphia.

Jamieson, K. H. (1997, March 11). Presentation of research. In *Free air time and campaign reform: A report of the conference held by the Annenberg Public Policy Center at the University of Pennsylvania and the Free TV for Straight Talk Coalition* (pp. 6–8). Retrieved March 25, 2005, from the Annenberg Public Policy Center Web site: www.annenberg-publicpolicycenter.org/03_political_communication/freetime/REP15.PDF.

Lenhart, A., Rainie, L., & Lewis, L. (2001, June 20). *Teenage life online: The rise of the instant-message generation and the Internet's impact on friendships and family relationships.* Washington, DC: Pew Internet & American Life Project.

Lepper, M. R., Greene, D., & Nisbett, R. E. (1973). Undermining children's intrinsic interest with extrinsic reward: A test of the "over-justification" hypothesis. *Journal of Personality and Social Psychology, 28,* 129–137.

Lepper, M. R., & Henderlong, J. (2000). Turning "play" into "work" and "work" into "play": 25 years of research on intrinsic versus extrinsic motivation. In C. Sansone & J. Harackiewicz (Eds.), *Intrinsic motivation: Controversies and new directions* (pp. 257–307). San Diego, CA: Academic Press.

Levine, P., & Lopez, M. (2002, September). *Youth voter turnout has declined, by any measure.* College Park, MD: Center for Information and Research on Civic Learning and Engagement, University of Maryland. Retrieved March 25, 2005, from www.civicyouth.org/research/products/Measuring_Youth_Voter_Turnout.pdf.

Lupia, A. (1994). Shortcuts versus encyclopedias: Information and voting behavior in California insurance reform elections. *American Political Science Review, 88,* 63–76.

Luskin, R. C. (2002). From denial to extenuation (and finally beyond): Political sophistication and citizen competence. In J. H. Kuklinski (Ed.), *Political psychology and political behaviour* (pp. 217–250). New York: Cambridge University Press.

Luskin, R. C., Fishkin, J. S., & Jowell, R. (2002). Considered opinions: Deliberative polling in Britain. *British Journal of Political Science, 32,* 455–487.

Macallair, D., & Males, M. (1999). *Striking out: The failure of California's "three strikes and you're out" law.* San Francisco: Justice Policy Institute.

Mullainathan, S., & Shleifer, A. (2005). The market for news. *American Economic Review, 95,* 1031–1053.

Pasley, J. L. (2001). *The tyranny of printers: Newspaper politics in the early American republic.* Charlottesville: University of Virginia Press.

Popkin, S. L. (1994). *The reasoning voter: Communication and persuasion in presidential campaigns* (2nd ed.). Chicago: University of Chicago Press.

Prop. 66 reform: Defeated but not deterred [Editorial]. (2004, November 6). *Sacramento Bee.* Retrieved September 15, 2005, from www.sacbee.com/content/opinion/story/11332538p-12247209c.html.

Rainie, L., & J. Shermak. (n.d.). *Search engine use November 2005* [Data memo]. Retrieved April 7, 2006, from the Pew/Internet Web site: www.pewinternet.org/pdfs/PIP_Search Data_1105.pdf.

Ross, L., & Nisbett, R. (1991). *The person and the situation: Perspectives of social psychology.* New York: McGraw-Hill.

Schiraldi, V., Colburn, J., & Lotke, E. (2004, September 23). *3 strikes and you're out: An examination of 3-strike laws 10 years after their enactment.* Washington, DC: Justice Policy Institute. Retrieved March 25, 2005, from www.justicepolicy.org/article.php?list=type&type=102.

Schneider, D. J., Hastorf, A. H., & Ellsworth, P. C. (1979). *Person perception* (2nd ed.). Reading, MA: Addison-Wesley.

Stolzenberg, L., & d'Alessio, S. J. (1997). Three strikes and you're out: The impact of California's new mandatory sentencing law on serious crime rates. *Crime and Delinquency, 43,* 457–469.

US Department of Commerce. (2002, February). *A nation online: How Americans are expanding their use of the Internet.* Retrieved September 10, 2005, from www.ntia.doc.gov/ntiahome/dn/anationonline2.pdf.

Waldman, P. (1998, February). *Free time and advertising: The 1997 New Jersey governor's race* (Report 18). Philadelphia: Annenberg Public Policy Center, University of Pennsylvania. Retrieved March 25, 2005, from www.annenbergpublicpolicycenter.org/03_political_communication/freetime/REP18.PDF.

Weaver, D., & Wilhoit, G. C. (1986). *The American journalist: A portrait of US newspeople and their work.* Bloomington: Indiana University Press.

Index